France at War

France at War

Vichy and the Historians

Edited by
Sarah Fishman
Laura Lee Downs
Ioannis Sinanoglou
Leonard V. Smith
Robert Zaretsky

Translator
David Lake

Oxford • New York

First published in 2000 by
Berg
Editorial offices:
150 Cowley Road, Oxford OX4 1JJ, UK
838 Broadway, Third Floor, New York, NY 10003-4812, USA

Berg is the imprint of Oxford International Publishers Ltd.

Library of Congress Cataloging-in-Publication Data

A catalogue record for this book is available from the Library of Congress.

British Library Cataloguing-in-Publication Data

A catalogue record for this book is available from the British Library.

ISBN 1 85973 299 2 (Cloth)

Typeset by JS Typesetting, Wellingborough, Northants.
Printed in the United Kingdom by WBC Book Manufacturers, Bridgend,
Mid Glamorgan.

Contents

Acknowledgements ix

Introduction 1
Sarah Fishman and *Leonard V. Smith*

Part I Vichy France and *l'ère paxtonienne*

1 The Paxtonian Revolution 13
Jean-Pierre Azéma

2 *Chaque livre un évenement:* Robert Paxton and the French, from '*briseur de glace*' to '*iconoclaste tranquille*' 21
John Sweets

3 *Vichy et les juifs:* After Fifteen Years 35
Michael Marrus

4 Vichy Studies in France: Before and After Paxton 49
Stanley Hoffmann

Part II The Vichy Regime, Collaboration and Resistance: A Reshuffling of Categories

5 Collaboration French-style: A European Perspective 61
Yves Durand

6 Writing the History of Military Occupations 77
Philippe Burrin

7 Communitarians, Non-conformists and the Search for a 'New Man' in Vichy France 91
John Hellman

8 Vichy Singular and Plural 107
Denis Peschanski

9 Rural France and Resistance 125
H.R. Kedward

10 The Countryside and the City: Some Notes on the Collaboration Model during the Vichy Period 145
Bertram M. Gordon

11 The Resistance and Vichy 161
Dominique Veillon

Part III Everyday Life: Culture, Institutions, Public Opinion under the Occupation

12 1940–1944: Double-Think in France 181
Pierre Laborie

13 Vichy and Abortion: Policing the Body and the New Moral Order in Everyday Life 191
Miranda Pollard

14 Youth in Vichy France: The Juvenile Crime Wave and its Implications 205
Sarah Fishman

15 Everyday Culture in Occupied France 221
Jean-Pierre Rioux

16 Catholics, the Vichy Interlude, and After 231
W. D. Halls

Part IV Myth, Memory and Representation

17 Out of the Picture: Foreign Labor in Wartime France 249
Sarah Farmer

18 *Tragedies bulgares et françaises:* Tzvetan Todorov and the Writing of History 261
Robert Zaretsky

19 Why Be So Cruel? Some Modest Proposals to Cure the Vichy Syndrome 275
Pascal Ory

20 The Historian, a Site of Memory 285
Henry Rousso

Appendix 303

Contributors and Editors 309

Select Bibliography 313

Index 323

Acknowledgements

We wish to thank the Sterling Currier Fund, an endowment of Reid Hall, Columbia University's study center in Paris, Pearl Spiro, Office of the Provost at Columbia, and Columbia's Maison Française for generously supporting the Symposium in honor of Robert Paxton at Columbia in September of 1997 and the publication of this book. The burden of putting together a symposium never falls equally among the organizers. Here, Ioannis Sinanoglou performed service nothing short of heroic, cheerfully coordinating local arrangements for twenty scholars from six countries. We should also like to thank Maike Bohn at Berg Publishers for her interest, encouragement and indulgence! Thanks also to Dean Ted Estess and the Honors College at the University of Houston for providing funds for a work study student, and thanks especially to that student, Mindi Morris, for helping us pull together the volume. We also gratefully acknowledge the help of Paula Schwartz and Kara Hagen and the meticulous editing of David Phelps. Simon Kitson most generously allowed us to adapt a bibliography he had assembled for our bibliography. Finally, all five editors express their deepest gratitude to Robert O. Paxton for, in a variety of ways, providing intellectual inspiration to us all. Her co-editors wish to thank Sarah Fishman for the critical role she has played in the life of this book – from its first inception as the conference at Columbia to the coordination of editing and translation to the often maddening details of final editorial work.

Introduction

Sarah Fishman and *Leonard V. Smith*

It would be difficult to overstate just how deeply the years of the Vichy regime and the German Occupation scarred the history of France. The armistice following the crushing German military victory of June 1940 left France divided – militarily, politically, socially and geographically. A new group of political figures came to power, led by First World War hero Marshal Philippe Pétain. Breaking with the dishonored and defeated Third Republic, they created a new regime that they called simply the French State (*l'État français*), to govern the country from the spa town of Vichy. Germany directly occupied the northern two-thirds of France, including the entire Atlantic coast. Following the successful Allied invasion of North Africa in November 1942, the German army occupied the entire country until France's liberation in August and September of 1944.

Politically, the Vichy regime exacerbated a series of long-standing divisions in France. Conflict between Collaborators and the Resistance built on previous battles between Left and Right, Republicans and old or new authoritarians, Catholics and Anticlericals. The period surrounding the Liberation in 1944, according to some scholars, brought France to the brink of civil war. Beginning in the 1970s, internal strife also came to characterize an intense and sometimes agonized search for the meaning of the Occupation years. This struggle has been part and parcel of the evolution of the French nation ever since 1945, and has been described by Henry Rousso as the 'Vichy syndrome'. In the title of a later book, Rousso provocatively borrowed a phrase from German historian Ernst Nolte, *Vergangenheit, die nicht vergehen will*, to characterize the Vichy years as an 'ever-present past'.[1]

The most recent manifestation of the Vichy syndrome took place late in 1997 in Bordeaux. Maurice Papon, general secretary of the Gironde prefecture from 1942 to the end of the war, was finally brought to trial after nearly two decades of delay and doubt. Papon had held a number of important positions after the war, among them prefect of the Paris police and minister of the budget. He was charged with being an accomplice in crimes against humanity – a charge based on the role he played in the deportation of Jews from Bordeaux to Drancy, and eventually to Auschwitz, from 1942 to 1944. The prosecution called a number of historians as expert witnesses, among them one American, Professor Robert O. Paxton of Columbia University. That a foreigner should be asked to comment in a judicial proceeding concerning some of the most painful years of French history illustrated the profound impact of Paxton's work. Some historians (including at least one of our contributors), expressed unease at what they saw as the intervention by historians in the historical process itself.[2] The trial was a media event, in France and to some extent overseas. But the ambiguous verdict both illustrated and perpetuated the lingering inability or unwillingness on the part of the French to agree on a single interpretation of what happened during the Occupation years. On 2 April 1998, the court sentenced Papon to ten years in prison after a jury found him guilty of complicity in crimes against humanity. However, the judges decided to free Papon, who had served only nine nights in jail and one night in a hospital, while he awaited his appeal. Given his age and infirmity, his case may never be definitively resolved. Clearly, whatever the outcome of the Papon case or the fate of Papon personally, the Vichy syndrome is not yet in remission. Vichy continues to have an uncertain and contested legacy.

This book proposes to examine the ways in which scholars have analyzed the historical legacy of Vichy. Our starting-point, Paxton's pathbreaking book, *Vichy France: Old Guard and New Order,* inspired a conference held at Columbia University in September 1997. The conference marked the twenty-fifth anniversary of the publication that book, as well as the occasion of Paxton's retirement. But we did not see the conference simply as an act of commemoration, nor do we see this volume as a *festschrift*. Rather, the conference and the volume both sample and evaluate a quarter-century of scholarship on Vichy, and point to new directions for future research.

The Liberation of France in 1944 brought with it a relatively benign interpretation of the Occupation supported by popular and scholarly opinion until the 1970s. The French adopted a historical narrative that divided them least, one that portrayed the Vichy years as little more than a 'parenthesis' resulting from a temporary rupture between the French state and the French nation. According to this narrative, Marshal Pétain, a venerable military leader who had intervened in 1917 to protect the French army from the worst excesses of a war of attrition, did his best as head of the French state to shield his country from Germany's cruel vengeance. But in the end a small but powerful cabal of active collaborators, key among them Prime Minister Pierre Laval, manipulated Pétain into accepting increasingly harsh German demands, such as the adoption of antisemitic policies and the repression of the French Resistance. Yet all the while, and beneath the machinations of the traitorous cabal, lay a nation of '40 million resisters' who detested the Vichy regime and anxiously awaited liberation and a return to democracy. This narrative satisfied people across the political spectrum. Gaullists and other conservatives, as well as Communists and Socialists, could all present themselves as triumphant heroes, resisters who reconciled state and nation at the Liberation.

To be sure, even before the publication of Paxton's book in 1972, cracks had begun to appear in the edifice of accepted wisdom about Vichy. Most significantly, Marcel Ophuls's searingly personal 260-minute documentary, *Le Chagrin et la pitié* (*The Sorrow and The Pity*), produced for French television in 1970 but barred from television broadcasting in France until the 1980s, portrayed anything but a French nation unified in obdurate resistance to the invader. Pétainists, collaborators, and a great many fence-sitters took their place alongside resisters in the documentary's interviews, which presented a nation consumed by indecision and self-doubt. Also by the early 1970s, a number of scholars had begun questioning the accepted interpretation, disclosing more active collaboration with the Germans and more cooperation between state and nation within France than had previously been suspected.

Yet in both its tone and its content *Vichy France: Old Guard and New Order* broke new ground. With the French archival record inaccessible, Paxton made his case by supplementing published French materials like post-war trial transcripts with unpublished French government documents he found, not in the French archives, but in German and American archival collections. He meticulously, pitilessly and dispassionately pulled apart the myths underpinning the historiographical consensus about France's experience during the Vichy years. Paxton clearly stated his position in the first sentence of his first chapter: 'Collaboration was not a German demand to which some Frenchmen acceded, through sympathy or guile. Collaboration was a French proposal that Hitler ultimately rejected.'[3] For Germany considered France not a potential ally, but rather a source of war booty and conscript labor, and a staging area for attacking Britain. Yet from 1940 to 1944 all the major figures at Vichy, including Pétain, sought real collaboration in hopes of carving out a role for France in Hitler's New Europe. Vichy consistently offered *more* than the Germans asked for, notably in the areas of antisemitic and labor policies. Paxton argued that Marshal Pétain was neither senile nor politically detached from his ministers. He documented the widespread relief that greeted Pétain's arrival in power, as well as the substantial popular support enjoyed by the regime at the outset. The regime gradually lost this support, as the war dragged on, as repression increased, as the labor draft of men to work in Germany hit home, and as people witnessed round-ups of Jews. Most of all, Vichy lost support as it became clear that Germany would lose the war. Yet the regime stubbornly clung to collaboration to the bitter end. In short, Vichy did not play a 'double game' of endeavoring to protect the nation from the worst cruelties of the invaders until the Allies could liberate France – quite the reverse.

A firestorm of controversy greeted the publication of the French edition of Paxton's book in 1973, as the book reopened painful divisions papered over by the myth of '40 million resisters.' The Left generally praised the book, conveniently overlooking Paxton's conclusions about the slow growth of the Resistance even among Communists. Some centrists were made uneasy by Paxton's dismantling of the 'double game' thesis and by the variety of connections he drew in personnel and policies between Vichy and the republics that preceded and succeeded it. But the most hostile critics came from the political Right, for whom the book plainly struck a raw nerve. Commentators such as Dominque Jamet and Paul Auphan, former Vichy naval minister, questioned Paxton's credentials, accused him of anti-French prejudice, and suggested that the history of Vichy was a matter most appropriately dealt with by the French themselves.[4]

Yet, when the dust settled, Paxton's book had played a key role in transforming the model for understanding the Vichy years. As Stanley Hoffmann once noted, a picture painted in stark black and white had been replaced by one painted in dirty grays. In the twenty-five years since the publication of *Vichy France,* historians have have added yet other colors to the palette. Historians on both sides of the Atlantic have advanced a much more nuanced understanding of the almost infinite fragmentation of opinion in France under the Occupation. Formerly straightforward categories of 'Resistance' and 'Collaboration' have been pulled apart and reconstructed. Historians have also expanded their study of the Vichy years into a variety of areas in social and cultural history. Chapters in this collection recount the vicissitudes of the reception of Paxton's work in France, assess his achievement in the context of changing attitudes toward Vichy, develop and refine his insights into that era, and explore new topics.

Part I focuses on Paxton and the paradigm his work established. Jean-Pierre Azéma shows how Paxton drew upon the work of precursors like Stanley Hoffmann, Eberhard Jäckel, Alan Milward and Henri Michel, pulling their threads together into a whole that dramatically departed from existing conclusions. John Sweets points out that the vast majority of serious scholars in France reacted very favorably to Paxton's book. Historical memory of Paxton's book as an 'event' was based less on the number of unfavorable reviews, which was small, than on their strident tone and their refusal to accept the evidence behind Paxton's case. Michael Marrus examines French antisemitic policies in the context of the broader Nazi program to eliminate Europe's Jews. He points out that Holocaust scholars unwittingly tended to accept what Vichy officials claimed in self-defense after the war – that they had struggled to limit German demands. *Vichy France and the Jews* (1981), a book he co-authored with Paxton, finally linked the European enterprise of genocide to the petty back-room politics at Vichy. Stanley Hoffmann analyzes the periodization of Vichy historiography, contesting the more recent myth that the French have refused to confront their past. This myth, he concludes, has become as distorting as the original myth of '40 million resisters' that Paxton demolished.

Part II considers how the last twenty-five years of scholarship have rendered problematic our understanding of the Vichy regime and such formerly clear categories as collaboration and resistance. Yves Durand advocates placing the collaboration of Vichy France into a European context. The obsession with proving Vichy's sinister role in collaboration has led to something of a negative hubris, the elevation of French collaboration into something singular. Historians keen on indicting France have overlooked the similar behavior adopted by other collaborationist regimes such as that in Norway, and by administrations in countries with governments in exile, such as Belgium. Philippe Burrin argues that there is much we still do not understand about the forced cohabitation of Germans and French during the Second World War. He urges a comparison with other occupations, such as the German occupations of northern France after the Franco-Prussian War of 1870–71 and during the First World War, as well as with the French occupations of parts of Germany after 1918 and after 1945.

As a prelude to the Vichy regime, John Hellman discusses 'communitarian non-conformism' as it developed in Europe in the 1930s. He outlines characteristic attitudes such as anti-individualism, alienation from liberal democracy, elitism, europeanism and personalism, and demonstrates the impact non-conformist movements had on many people who became prominent players at Vichy. Denis Peschanski considers two key aspects of Paxton's argument about the nature of the Vichy regime. Paxton strongly argued on the one hand that Vichy was 'singular', meaning that a single logic unified the choice to collaborate with Germany and Vichy's domestic program, the National Revolution. But Paxton also acknowledged the competing visions, the 'plurality' of Vichy, its ability to incorporate ideas not just from traditionalists, corporatists and fascists, but also from technocrats, syndicalists and even the political Left. Peschanski explores Vichy in the singular and in the plural, and introduces recent research inspired by both aspects of the regime. Dominique Veillon challenges us to reject the notion that people chose '*either* Vichy, *or* the resistance'. Some people, perhaps most notably François Mitterrand, were simultaneously pro-Vichy and pro-Resistance. Although they considered themselves part of the Vichy consensus in 1940, they gradually broke with the regime, often in accordance with the very principles that led them to support Vichy in the first place.

Two other chapters in Part II explore how writing the history of rural France during the war breaks down neat behavioral categories. Bertram Gordon emphasizes the diversity of rural communities, and warns against assuming that because Vichy loved an essentialist image of the peasant, the peasants necessarily loved Vichy in return. Roderick Kedward advocates an anthropological analysis that places rural resistance into a wider history of peasant culture in France and elsewhere. Careful, locally researched case studies of the Resistance have overturned a model that privileges urban over rural resistance, and have deepened our understanding of rural populations as historical actors in their own right.

Part III deals with everyday life, culture, institutions and public opinion under the German occupation. How the French people reacted to defeat, occupation and Vichy has been a particularly contentious issue; the question of public support for Pétain and the Vichy regime, if and when opinion 'turned', in turn validates judgments about whether the French behaved well or badly during the war. Pierre Laborie hopes to encourage historians to move beyond such simplistic interpretations. He contends that fluctuations of public opinion in wartime France, from near-universal support of Pétain in 1940 to near-universal support of de Gaulle in 1944, can best be explained by the 'sensibility of double-thinking'. Daily life in Vichy strongly lent itself to doublethink. For example, during the war many people believed, contrary to his public pro-collaboration pronouncements, that Pétain was playing a 'double game'. Even people in the Resistance, who fully rejected collaboration, were forced to lead a complex, dual, public/clandestine life.

Miranda Pollard notes that while Vichy intensified anti-abortion rhetoric and made abortion a form of treason, it devoted few resources to repressing it. Still, Pollard argues that the ideology underpinning Vichy family policies was far more reactionary than the popular attitudes about the family and abortion inherited from the Third Republic. Sarah Fishman argues that the tripling of juvenile crime by 1942 indicates the limits of the National Revolution's ability to reshape the youth of France. She concludes that adolescent petty crime represented only one of the many wartime coping strategies people adopted that blurred distinctions between legal and illegal.

Jean-Pierre Rioux urges a new approach to studying the cultural history of the Vichy years. He argues that despite the Occupation and Vichy's attempts at a National Revolution, cultural life retained a surprising degree of autonomy. The war years nurtured a rich and dynamic cultural life, best considered through integrating cultural history with the history of daily life, re-examining cultural dissidence, and comparing France's cultural history during the war with that of other nations at war. W. D. Halls considers the impact of the war years on the Catholic Church in France. He argues that the Vichy years did not disrupt the basic pattern of Catholic history in twentieth-century France, in that the Catholic hierarchy generally remained consistently anti-totalitarian but pro-authoritarian. Despite Vichy's official support of the Catholic Church, the wartime experience did not result in the rechristianization of France.

Part IV considers the ongoing reconstruction of the memory of the Vichy years. In a variety of ways, the chapters explore the interplay among the Vichy regime, French national identity in the twentieth century, and the crimes against humanity perpetrated during the war. Two chapters by American scholars show Paxton's influence in their attention to rectifying the historical record and to determining some sort of moral balance sheet. Sarah Farmer argues that the carefully constructed narrative of the 'martyred village' of Oradour-sur-Glane pointedly excluded foreigners among the victims, conscript laborers from the Foreign Workers Group (*Groupement de Travail Étranger*). The pure martyr had to be purely 'French'. Robert Zaretsky analyzes how an intellectual of Bulgarian origin, Tzvetan Todorov, tackled the moral issues of the Vichy years. Todorov's analysis of the tragedy of Saint-Amand was driven no less by his own experience in totalitarian Bulgaria than by his theoretical explorations of the moral foundations of history writing. His life and his thought recall the universal implications of the Vichy experience.

Chapters by two French historians show perhaps a less obvious aspect of Paxton's influence, in their reflection on the relationship between then and now. If *Vichy France*, by Paxton's own admission, was informed by American hubris in Vietnam (the backdrop against which the book was written), the essays by Pascal Ory and Henry Rousso are informed by what both see as a *fin-de-siècle* crisis in French identity. Ory sees in this crisis both the origins of the Vichy syndrome and the possibility of its resolution. The breakdown of a certain idea of national continuity after 1970 fed internal struggles over the meaning of the Vichy years. Yet the demise of 'eternal France' as construed by de Gaulle and his republic also, perhaps, made it possible for the French to reflect on their past in more generous terms. For the same France that assured national continuity from 1939 through 1945 also assured the continuity thereafter of retrospection, self-analysis, and reconsideration of France's political and moral responsibility. Henry Rousso argues that Robert Paxton himself became a 'site of memory' in the processes through which the French continue to construct their past. Yet in making Paxton something of an icon, the French have selectively, and at times mistakenly, read his analysis in ways that have prevented them unnecessarily from reaching closure on the Vichy years. They have drawn lessons from Vichy that Rousso sees as dubiously relevant to France at the dawn of the next century.

This collection develops several broad themes. First, the essays explore how Paxton came to be not just the historian who 'broke the mirror', but one who, as Rousso put it, himself became a 'site of memory'. His work set the paradigm for a generation of researchers. In the tradition of Paxton himself, up to the time of his appearance at the Papon trial, the chapters here straddle and frequently challenge the boundaries between scholarship and moral judgment. Complexity represents the volume's second theme. Nearly every author calls for taking into account variety and nuance. Their work complicates what had often been considered simple categories, such as the peasantry or even the Resistance. These chapters call on readers to refine further our understanding of the behavior, ideologies and policies of groups at Vichy, and to listen more closely to the varied and sometimes contradictory voices of everyday people.

Finally, many scholars promote what the political sociologist Theda Skocpol might label 'putting the Germans back in'. Most historians and the vast majority of the French public now acknowledge that Vichy chose to collaborate, and used the defeat to impose a new moral order in France. Yet the pendulum should not swing so far as to obscure the fact that none of what happened in France would have come to pass had Germany not defeated France in 1940. Germany did after all impose certain constraints on France similar to those imposed on other occupied or satellite countries. To lose sight of that basic reality is, in a way, to repeat the pattern that led politicians at Vichy toward Germany in the first place, being unaware, unconcerned and uninformed about the war beyond France's borders.

Notes

1. Eric Conan and Henry Rousso, *Vichy: An Ever-Present Past*, Nathan Bracher, trans. (Hanover, 1998; originally published in 1994 as *Vichy: un passé qui ne passe pas*). The expression came from the title of a controversial article by Nolte published in 1986 in the *Frankfurter Allgemeine Zeitung.*
2. Henry Rousso, *La hantise du passé* (Paris, 1998): 86–138.
3. Robert Paxton, *Vichy France: Old Guard and New Order, 1940–1944* (New York, 1972): 52.
4. Dominique Jamet, *L'Aurore*, 9 February 1973; Paul Auphan, *Le Monde,* 'Correspondance', 17 May 1973. For a detailed discussion of the variety of reactions to Paxton's book in France, see John Sweets, '*Chaque livre un évenément*: Robert Paxton and the French, from *briseur de glace* to *iconoclaste tranquille*' (Chapter 2 below).

Part I
Vichy and *l'ère paxtonienne*

–1–

The Paxtonian Revolution

Jean-Pierre Azéma

Let me backtrack twenty-five years. I was at the time a young scholar who, one fine day in 1972, received an evaluation copy of an English-language manuscript entitled *Vichy France: Old Guard and New Order, 1940–1944*,[1] accompanied by a single, but highly intimidating annotation: 'the manuscript has just been turned down by Gallimard' (rumor had it that it was Pierre Nora personally who had finally said no). I was being asked to evaluate the book of a Mr Robert Paxton, whose name meant nothing to me at the time (in my defense, I should point out that his dissertation on the Armistice Army, published in 1966,[2] had gone virtually unnoticed; Paxton devotees will confirm that the work has yet to be translated into French). I consequently read the manuscript with considerable circumspection, but soon noted that it contained no major error, and that in fact it completed the thesis of Eberhard Jaeckel,[3] which I had read. My conclusion was that this approach to Vichy was not only new, but very convincing and solidly based on documentary evidence; I recommended to Seuil that they take the risk of publishing it. I even suggested that they might want to have it translated by my mother, Claude Bertrand, a professional translator. It turned out to be the last translation she was to produce. All this to say that the book that was to be published in France as *La France de Vichy* has always held a special place for me, for reasons personal as well as professional.

I have given this piece the somewhat pompous title of 'The Paxtonian Revolution'. Yet, like many revolutions, it was preceded by signs of what was to come, in this particular case, books that I shall briefly discuss.

I imagine that Paxton, as an avid reader, might have been inspired by four works. First, Eberhard Jaeckel's doctoral dissertation, published in Stuttgart in 1966, and translated into French in 1968 as *La France dans l'Europe de Hitler*, is a very solid, detailed work that makes excellent use of German sources, sources that had been almost entirely neglected by French historians at that time. Jaeckel challenges the historian Robert Aron's view[4] by showing – with plentiful evidence – that Vichy very much followed behind Hitler, who, always in the driver's seat, was unwilling to collaborate seriously with France and refused to make any concessions of a political nature. The German trap thus became more comprehensible, the machinations of a state collaboration that was increasingly difficult to bear after the decisive events of November 1942. Jaeckel's book had little impact in France, in part because the events of May '68 brought about an entirely different line of questioning. Jaeckel's theses were further developed by Alan Milward in *The New Order and the French Economy*,[5] which notably put forward the idea that France was the most thoroughly exploited nation in all of occupied Europe.

The third book to consider is Henri Michel's *Vichy année 40*, published by Laffont in 1966.[6] Michel moved beyond the exclusive use of the High Court trial transcripts and took into account the five volumes of documents generated by the *Délégation française auprès de la Commission française d'armistice*, as well as two volumes from the archives of the Wilhelmstrasse; Michel's sources allowed him to reverse Aron's perspective and ultimately produce a more satisfactory interpretation of the October 1940 meeting of Pétain and Hitler in Montoire. He added – and this point was important – that 'to a certain extent, the National Revolution was inspired by collaboration'; he was unable, however, to escape the rather prevalent bias of the time that portrayed Vichy as a chaotic enterprise, a regime of failures. (For example, Henri Michel seemed to adopt as his own view a statement made by Robert Trochu (former Vichy propagandist) at Pétain's trial: 'things happened in the kingdom of Vichy pretty much as in those Negro kingdoms where it isn't the king who rules, especially when he's old'.) This led Michel to underestimate the specificity of the new regime and consequently the potential repercussions of the measures of exclusion and repression.

The last item is the conference René Remond organized in 1970 at the Fondation Nationale de Sciences Politiques.[7] It is notable – as well as perfectly typical of the difficulties one could encounter by bringing up Vichy at a conference – that a certain Henri Michel refused to participate, arguing that Vichy figures were to be heard, which would tend to make their views more acceptable and thus rehabilitate Vichy. Remond felt obliged to justify his project at some length in the introduction he wrote when the proceedings of the conference were published. Henri Michel would have been more astute to point out that only the 'good' Vichy was being considered, as the studies only went up to April 1942, and that virtually nothing was said about the repression and exclusion of Jews. I should add that Pierre Renouvin had essentially forbidden René Remond from pursuing the prosopographic research on the members of the ministerial staffs that we had begun in his seminar. In short, the conference was of some interest, though it remained unnecessarily timid.

Then came the French publication of Paxton's *La France de Vichy 1940–1944*. In the clan of historians as well as among the somewhat more educated readers of *Le Monde* and *Le Figaro*, the book's publication had the effect of a minor bombshell. Why? Because the book was the first to propose an overall interpretation of Vichy France, and an unconventional one, and because putting together the various pieces of the puzzle created an explosive mixture. In fact, this is what caused the irritation, even unleashed the fury of those who, after reading André Siegfried and Robert Aron, were seeking more soothing, comforting explanations for the trauma of 1940–44.

What Paxton wanted to prove, by enlarging his perspective and by the strength of his arguments, was that Vichy was a coherent whole that followed from the choices made by signing the Armistice of June 1940. I quote from p. 137:

> The French quest for a settlement with Germany was only one side of collaboration. Collaboration is not seen as a whole without its domestic dimension. Externally, the armistice position rested upon a certainty of German victory and a preference for peace and stability over a last-ditch resistance to the finish. Internally, the armistice position offered a historic opportunity for change such as France had not seen since 1870 – indeed, perhaps not since 1789.

In other words, there was an inextricable link – whatever variations might have been adopted – between, on the one hand, a strategy of betting on a victory by the Reich in order to position France as well as possible in a peace settlement, which led to the political choice of state collaboration, and, on the other hand, an indispensable cultural revolution labeled the National Revolution. This is what gave the Vichy regime its relative coherence. Paxton made it clear that the relative weight of these two imperatives obviously changed over time: initially Pétain accepted state collaboration so as to be able to launch his National Revolution, his grand plan; with Laval, however, relations with the Reich were of prime importance, to the degree that there was an active effort to orchestrate domestic policy, especially in the area of repression.

Following in Jaeckel's footsteps, Paxton used his superb knowledge of German sources to map out the main lines of state collaboration (naturally adopting Stanley Hoffmann's distinction between state collaboration, or the relations between French officials and the German Reich, and collaborationism, motivated by pro-fascist ideological conviction). But while Jaeckel's starting-point was the policies various Nazi officials advocated toward France, Paxton emphasized what he considered to be primordial, that is, 'Vichy initiatives' attempting to implement the collaboration the French State sought (at least through to the end of 1943), despite being rebuffed by Hitler. Paxton's second chapter, entitled 'The French Quest for Collaboration', is all the more appropriate given that France was the only country of occupied Europe to enjoy some freedom of action, at least until total war became a reality. Need I point out that Paxton, well-armed with evidence, definitively swept away the myth, obligingly kept alive by those in Pétain's camp, of Pétain as a sly fox who managed to pull the wool over the eyes of that poor fool Hitler, who had asked for the collaboration in the first place, as well as the myth of the double game, best symbolized by the famous secret telegrams of Algiers?[8] Paxton also emphasizes the Vichy government's desperate 1944 attempts to extricate itself from the situation by proposing itself as a mediator for a compromise peace settlement aimed at the Soviet Union.

In that period, as we know, an authoritarian regime, unlike any other twentieth-century French government, had taken hold. Paxton did not make the mistake of considering the Vichy regime to be the same thing as fascism pure and simple, as did some studies at the time that were rushed into print by historians affiliated with the French Communist Party. Rather, he explored, in considerable detail for the time, the corridors of power of that authoritarian regime. In contrast to Henri Michel, he stressed the peculiarities and perversities of this regime, whose way of operating proved to be of scant interest to the Reich. And unlike the conference sponsored by the Fondation Nationale de Sciences Politiques, he insisted on themes of exclusion and repression, especially as they applied to Jews. While he was surely aware of the continuities that existed between this France of the forties and the post-war period, especially those relating to the increasing power of political technocrats, he did not lose sight of the particularities of Vichy. And Paxton was right to assert that the various changes of the guard in no way obliterated the essential solidarity of Vichy, which must be considered as a whole (as used to be said of the French revolution), with Pétain acting as a unifying element for that authoritarian regime with charismatic tendencies. If the idea of a military state was not necessarily written into Vichy in the summer of 1940, the military was a perfect fit for the structure of the regime.

Let us pause a moment to consider the sources used by Paxton. If we look at the bibliography of the 1973 French edition, we notice quite simply that – contrary to what some have claimed – he received no special treatment from the French National Archives. He used every means at his disposal to supplement the published or unpublished accounts of the High Court trials, but also compared this fragmentary information with German sources from that period. The result was successful and continues to be valid, as we can see from the two following examples.

First example: he put to excellent use what had already been pointed out by Stanley Hoffmann in a prescient article:[9] Vichy was a pluralist dictatorship, in that all the different parties of the Right joined in. The traditionalist reactionaries, largely belonging to the Action Française camp, were flanked by 'enlightened liberals' such as Pierre-Etienne Flandin or Joseph Barthélemy, and relieved by 'technicians' who, laboring out of the limelight, were responsible for – as François Darlan would say – 'keeping the pot boiling and getting along with the krauts'.

Second example: Paxton, inspired by historian Joseph Billig,[10] whose work was largely neglected at the time, took note of the very specific and fearsome ethnocentrism expressed by virtually all the officials of the Vichy state, and foresaw the magnitude of the regime's complicity in the persecution and deportation of French Jews.

How does this hold up almost thirty years later? Has the Paxton of our youth aged well? The answer is a resounding yes.

There is no doubt in our mind that the combined efforts of Jaeckel and Paxton are still authoritative. Of course we know more today about French–Italian, French–Spanish, and French–British relations; but the main course, French–German relations, is still served à la Paxton. Jean-Baptiste Duroselle's *L'Abîme*, considered by many to be Duroselle's finest work,[11] provided the necessary confirmation of Paxton's theses using the archives of the French Foreign Ministry. (Parenthetically, one can legitimately wonder how François-Georges Dreyfus and several others can continue writing in a neo-Aronian vein.) We should further note that the works of Claude Huan and Hervé Couteau-Begarie (in particular their biography of Darlan)[12] also confirm Paxton's view by stressing the Admiral's importance to the proconsulate.

Let us now move to analyses of the regime itself, which have obviously been further refined. The opening of the French National Archives in the late 1970s, the questions posed by France's Jewish community, and the changes in the kinds of questions being asked have all led to a broadening of this field of inquiry. Significant contributions have been made in all areas. Let me cite a few at random, without any attempt to be exhaustive: youth (see especially the works of W. D. Halls);[13] Churches (as evidenced by the Lyon and Grenoble conferences,[14] and more recently by the conference devoted to Protestant Churches); economic policies (investigated notably by Henry Rousso);[15] civil servants (see the excellent doctoral thesis of Marc-Olivier Baruch);[16] cultural policies (well-covered by Jean-Pierre Rioux and Henry Rousso);[17] the difficulties of everyday life (see Dominique Veillon);[18] the uprooted (see Yves Durand's work on prisoners of war);[19] the outcast, specifically Jews (covered especially in the works of Serge Klarsfeld, André Kaspi, René Poznanski, and of course the book co-authored by Michael Marrus and Paxton);[20] and finally, the history of the memory of the Vichy syndrome, pioneered by Henry Rousso.[21]

Looking at this rapidly drawn up list, it becomes apparent that the focus has shifted away from Vichy's corridors of power and toward the dark years seen from the street level, away from Vichy France and toward the French under Vichy. It was hard for Robert Paxton, without sufficiently reliable documentation, to get an accurate reading of the average Frenchman's heart and soul. And it seems significant to me that the most fragile aspect of Paxton's book remains the section on public opinion, underestimating (probably as a result of biases introduced into the Prefects' reports) the fact that, from the end of 1941 on, the majority of French people were ambivalent in their attitude toward the regime. Only with Pierre Laborie's work on public opinion have we been able fully to appreciate the complexity of the attitudes adopted by the average French person from start to finish.[22] Aside from that, what was written about the actual corridors of power continues to be amazingly accurate.

Our investigation of Vichy France has thus broadened considerably since 1973. Nevertheless, it must be noted that we have not yet been able to resolve one of the questions posed at the end of *Vichy France*. Robert Paxton claimed not only that Vichy had been unable to save France from the worst, that its supposed function as a shield was a myth, and that the regime had made the most basic of political mistakes by decreeing a 'National Revolution' under the gaze and even the control of an occupier, but also that France, of all the occupied countries of Western Europe, was the least well protected. We do not yet have a comparative study that might help resolve this question.

Notes

1. Robert O. Paxton, *Vichy France: Old Guard and New Order, 1940–1944* (New York, 1972). Paxton, *La France de Vichy, 1940–1944* (Paris, 1973).

2. Robert O. Paxton, *Parades and Politics at Vichy: The French Officer Corps Under Marshal Pétain* (Princeton, NJ, 1966).
3. Eberhard Jaeckel, *Frankreich in Hitlers Europa* (Stuttgart, 1966); *La France dans l'Europe de Hitler* (Paris, 1968).
4. Robert Aron, *Histoire de Vichy, 1940–1944* (Paris, 1954).
5. Alan S. Milward, *The New Order and the French Economy* (Oxford, 1970).
6. Henri Michel, *Vichy année 40* (Paris, 1966).
7. *Le gouvernement de Vichy: 1940–1942* (Paris, 1972).
8. This is a reference to the allegation that Pétain had authorized Darlan to negotiate with the Allies after their landing in Algiers in November 1942. While the existence of 'secret telegrams' authorizing such negotiations was one of the lines of defense used by Pétainists after the war, there is no proof of Pétain's support for Darlan's contacts with the Americans in North Africa.
9. Stanley Hoffmann, *Revue française de science politique*, 6, No. 1 (1956): 44–69.
10. Joseph Billig, *La Commisariat général aux questions juives, 1941–1944* (Paris, 1955–60).
11. Jean-Baptiste Duroselle, *L'Abîme: 1939–1945* (Paris, 1982).
12. Claude Huan and Hervé Couteau-Begarie, *Darlan* (Paris, 1989)
13. W. D. Halls, *The Youth of Vichy France* (Oxford, 1981).
14. Xavier de Montclos (ed.), *Eglises et Chrétiens dans la deuxième guerre mondiale* (Lyons, 1978–1982); Pierre Bolle and Jean Goded (eds.), *Spiritualité, théologie, et résistance* (Grenoble, 1987); W. D. Halls, *Politics, Society and Christianity in Vichy France* (Oxford, 1995).
15. Henry Rousso, 'L'Organisation industrielle de Vichy', *Revue d'histoire de la deuxième Guerre mondiale,* 116 (1979): 27–44.
16. Marc Olivier Baruch, *Servir l'Etat français: l'administration en France de 1940 à 1944* (Paris, 1997).
17. Jean-Pierre Rioux (ed.), *Politique et pratiques culturelles dans la France de Vichy* (Brussels, 1990).
18. Dominique Veillon, *Vivre et survivre en France: 1939–1947* (Paris, 1995).
19. Yves Durand, *La Vie quotidienne des prisonniers de guerre dans les stalags, les oflags et les kommandos: 1939–1945* (Paris, 1987).
20. Serge Klarsfeld, *Vichy–Auschwitz: le rôle de Vichy dans la solution finale de la question juive en France, 1942* (Paris, 1983); Klarsfeld, *The Children of Izieu: A Human Tragedy* (New York, 1985); Klarsfeld, *Le Calendrier de la Persecution des juifs en France, 1940–1944*

(Paris, 1993); André Kaspi, *Les Juifs pendant l'Occupation* (Paris, 1991); Michael Marrus and Robert O. Paxton, *Vichy France and the Jews* (New York, 1981).

21. Henry Rousso, *The Vichy Syndrome: History and Memory in France Since 1944* (Cambridge, MA, 1991).
22. Pierre Laborie, *L'Opinion française sous Vichy* (Paris, 1990).

–2–

Chaque livre un événement: Robert Paxton and the French, from *briseur de glace* to *iconoclaste tranquille*[1]

John F. Sweets

Over the years, Robert Paxton has grown on the French. Viewed at first as the radical Young Turk whose uncompromising indictment of the Vichy regime shattered the Pétainist myth of a 'double game' and challenged the Gaullist myth of 'a nation of resisters', by the 1980s he was accepted as the dean of the Vichy specialists. Each of his new publications was greeted in France as a major event, *un événement*, 'a happening', as we might have said in the late sixties and early seventies when Paxton was drafting his now classic *Vichy France: Old Guard and New Order, 1940–1944*. In reading the laudatory reviews of his most recent book on French fascism, one finds it hard to imagine that this 'tranquil iconoclast'[2] once seemed so threatening to a part of the French reading public and scholarly community.

French reaction to Paxton's first book, *Parades and Politics at Vichy*, gave no forewarning of the storm of controversy that was to surround his second major publication on Vichy. Jean-Pierre Azéma claimed some years later that French specialists knew the book 'very well';[3] but it is difficult to imagine how that could be true. Although review copies were sent to many of the major newspapers and scholarly journals in France, only the *Revue française de science politique* took notice of *Parades and Politics* in a brief, eight-line commentary, which devoted over one-half of the notice simply to listing sources Paxton had consulted.[4] The *Revue d'histoire de la deuxième guerre mondiale* included the book under its '*Bibliographie*' of books received in April 1967, but did not review the book, and to my knowledge, no other written acknowledgment of the publication of *Parades and Politics* appeared in the French press or scholarly journals. Paxton personally donated a copy of the book to the Bibliothèque Nationale, explaining its availability to potential readers there.

Consequently, Paxton was not so much astonished by the tumultuous reception that greeted his classic study, *La France de Vichy*, as he was relieved and delighted by the mere fact that notice had been taken of it. By contrast with its reception in the United States, where *Vichy France* was hailed immediately by Gordon Wright, Philip Bankwitz, and Henry Ehrmann as a definitive study that was unlikely to be fundamentally altered by subsequent research,[5] in France, to put it mildly, the book met with a greater variety of opinion. 'What has come over him, this American who is pulling our skeletons out of the closet?' asked Paul Gillet, whose February 1973 review in *Le Monde* launched several weeks of polemical exchanges in that newspaper's columns.[6] Actually, most French reviews of the book were favorable, some strongly so;[7] but the stridently negative tone and lack of civility of some of the first reactions is striking. By emphasizing the initiative of Pétain and his associates in the policy of collaboration, minimizing the role of German pressure for policies such as Vichy's antisemitic laws, and arguing that, through their passivity, the mass of the French population had been functional collaborators, Paxton touched a raw nerve in French perceptions of themselves and their behavior during the Second World War. It was fitting that Henry Rousso included the publication of *La France de Vichy* in 'The Broken Mirror' phase of his 'Vichy Syndrome'.[8]

The historical context of the publication of *La France de Vichy* may explain why, as one commentator predicted, quite a few 'French berets would be knocked askew'[9] by Paxton's work. Appearing in the wake of two films, *Le Chagrin et la Pitié* and *Français, si vous saviez*, which had already stirred up bitter memories, the arrival of Paxton's book also coincided with the comic opera attempt by Pétainists to 'kidnap' the remains of the Maréchal's body from the Ile de Yeu, and to transfer his coffin to Verdun, the site of his greatest unsullied glory. As Stanley Hoffmann wrote, in those years the debate about Vichy in France invariably turned to 'psychodrama'.[10] A laudatory reviewer for *Défense Nationale* questioned whether or not the French public could appreciate the book dispassionately. They were, he wrote:

> . . . not ready, we believe, to judge this work with the serenity and detachment which presided over its creation. Vichy remains terribly close and present in our memory, in the conscience and almost in the flesh of most French people. The passage of time is not far enough advanced to wipe away their impressions, to salve their wounds, to calm their enthusiasm or their disgust. Above all the passage of time is far from having given all French people the courage to be honest with themselves, to admit what they really thought, said or did at the time.[11]

Strong emotions certainly colored some responses to Paxton's work. This was particularly evident among Pétain loyalists such as Admiral Paul Auphan and Vichy apologists like Alfred Fabre-Luce. For Auphan, who was to be one of his most persistent public critics, Paxton's book was 'not only laced with gaps and errors': it was 'an emotional exposé which tries to twist history in order to arouse American opinion against traditional France'. The book, he asserted, was nothing more than 'a pamphlet to justify an opinion'.[12] Vichy, he argued, was 'a matter better kept between Frenchmen'[13] and, under the title 'The Truth about a Bad Book'[14] he wrote a detailed critique for the Association to Defend the Memory of Marshal Pétain.

Auphan accused Paxton, to whom he attributed an unconscious 'scorn for the French', of using German documents to execute the French before a 'moral firing squad'. Paxton was, after all, only eight years old at the time of the fall of France, a boy playing a carefree game of ball on the other side of the Atlantic, 'while his country's leaders had helped throw us [France] into war'. How could this American, now a professor at the 'far-distant Columbia University' dare to suggest that 'the only choice for bloodied and unfortunate France in 1940 was revolution and subversive warfare'?[15]

If Admiral Auphan may be taken to represent an extreme, and to be honest, not a very sophisticated position, he was not the only critic to express himself or herself in sharply negative tones. Michel Denis described Paxton disapprovingly as a 'pseudo-marxist' who looked at Vichy through 'distorted lenses'. Only a professor in his ivory tower on the other side of the Atlantic could suggest, argued Denis, that France should have tried a gigantic 'Mediterranean Dunkirk' in June 1940. He added that Paxton rejected testimony of Vichy origin, while 'swallowing whole and even with jubilation' whatever he found in the German documents about Vichy official opinion.[16]

In *Contrepoint* Alain-Gérard Slama accused Paxton of purposely deciding to write 'a sensational work' on Vichy. Thinking that the 'winds of history had sufficiently turned back in the Marshal's favor, that the wounds were healing too quickly, that it was time to demolish the fable of the sword and the shield', Paxton had decided 'to twist the knife in the wound again'. 'Having studied collaboration, Paxton knew enough about French masochism', wrote Slama, 'to be sure to find, from *Le Nouvel Observateur* to *Mademoiselle Age Tendre*, commentators who would rejoice to see their country dragged through the mud, even if by an American.'[17] Elsewhere, Slama claimed that Paxton's book 'reads like a novel. Unfortunately, it is fiction,' and regretted that 'an American historian had tried to insert his analysis in a quarrel which is, for the French,' he argued with incredible myopia, '*in the past*.'[18]

In *L'Aurore* Dominique Jamet questioned both Paxton's scholarship and his qualification to teach. He expressed fears that Paxton would 'indelibly imprint on young minds flagrant counter-verities, whatever the reason, be it incompetence or bad faith'. Jamet did not begrudge Paxton his recourse to German documents, even noting that French researchers too often ignored them; but he claimed that Paxton did not know how to interpret them properly, because he had 'quite simply ignored their historical context'. 'The point is to know whether,' he wrote, 'when confronted by a sadist armed with a machine gun who asks you to say "I love you", one is entirely sincere in telling him "I love you." Mr. Paxton is persuaded that this is the case.'[19]

There seemed to be no shortage of readers eager to give this 'questionable professor'[20] lessons in the practice of his profession. One reader wrote to Paxton to ask whether it was simply political naïveté, 'found so often in Americans', or 'deliberate willfulness' that could explain 'Why you would have said the opposite of the truth unless you had been ordered to do so.' And 'who are you really working for?' he asked.[21] Another French reader, striking a 'Yankee Go Home' pose, wrote to Paxton to share his 'astonishment and indignation'. 'I am very shocked,' he wrote, 'that a foreigner dares to criticize the policies of France and what is more of its head of government . . . If Marshal Pétain committed a few errors (due to his advanced age or to his entourage) only the French have the right to make judgments about that.' This writer closed his letter with some pointed advice about Professor Paxton's future research: 'I think that you have enough to do, if you wish to occupy yourself with your own country.'[22] According to a review published in the *Revue de la Politique Française*:

> One might have hoped that twenty-eight years after the war an American historian would display a certain impartiality – and above all, a greater caution – in approaching the problem of Vichy and the occupation. Unfortunately, such is not the case: . . . Paxton wrote his book in 1972 exactly as others wrote about the same subject just after the war. The passing of time has not made him more lucid than his predecessors. That is too bad, because apparently Mister Paxton went to a lot of trouble and shuffled a lot of paper. It is just that he retained only those parts highlighted by the victors and has neglected all other testimonies. Thus, the blunders, confusion, and errors that discredit the whole work.[23]

Given the vehemence of some of these reactions, it is not surprising that Paxton found consolation in the fact that the majority of the published reviews of his work were more supportive. Still, he was puzzled by the mixed reception he received from the scholarly community in contrast to the favorable treatment evident in most of the popular magazines and newspapers. As he wrote to his colleague, Ezra Suleiman, in late June 1973: 'I do confess to disappointment at not being well-received at Sciences Po. It is curious that the critical reception has been the inverse of what I expected: journalists have discussed the major issues I raise, while the scholars so far have listed errors of detail, real or presumed. Odd.'[24] At the origin of the exchange of letters between Paxton and Suleiman was a review in which Janine Bourdin confessed to a 'certain malaise' in approaching Paxton's book, fearing that her scientific detachment and objectivity might have been shaken by the aggressive advertising campaign that had preceded the book's publication, proclaiming: 'Just Wait for Paxton!' Although 'often seduced by the liveliness and perspicacity of numerous passages,' ultimately, Bourdin was 'not really convinced' by Paxton's arguments. She was troubled by his 'imprecise use of terms and mistakes about details of fact', noting, in a major triumph of nit-picking, that René Belin should have been called the 'Secretary of the *Fédération nationale des PTT*' rather than 'one of the directors of the union of telephone employees'.[25]

Curiously, at a moment when two of its three directors, René Rémond and Pierre Renouvin, were prominent contemporary history specialists, the *Revue Historique* chose not to review the original English edition of Paxton's work. When a review of the French version finally appeared in that journal, almost three years after its publication in France, the reviewer was not particularly enthusiastic about it. Georges Soutou acknowledged that Paxton provided 'precious and abundant information about the internal politics of Vichy', but felt that the author had failed to recognize the significance of the leaders' 'Byzantine' quarrels and had devoted inadequate attention to developments in the French Empire. Soutou claimed that Eberhard Jaeckel had been more discriminating than Paxton in his use of the crucial German documents. Like Bourdin, Soutou also pointed to minor errors of fact; and he shared her opinion that Paxton's judgment about Vichy's antisemitism was over-harsh. He concluded that the book was 'more an essay than a definitive work'.[26]

Beneath the surface of the scholarly criticism of Paxton's classic work, one may detect traces of a 'turf war', as grudging admiration for his work perhaps mingled with regret that it had been an American rather than a French scholar who had written the book. When the book appeared in

France, the leading French authority on the Vichy period was Henri Michel, patron of the *Revue d'histoire de la deuxième guerre mondiale.* In his largely positive published review of Paxton's book, Michel began by stating that 'without reservation this is the best general study to have appeared to date on *l'Etat français*, its leaders, and their policies'. Although he pointed to minor errors of fact, noted that some useful sources had been overlooked, and argued that Paxton failed to appreciate adequately the role of the French Resistance, Michel concluded his review by restating that the book was a 'masterpiece'. Still, he wondered whether he might not have detected 'a slight whiff of hostility to France . . . from a book whose documentation and interpretations deserve so much praise'.[27] Even if puzzled by this parting shot, readers of Michel's review would have been hard pressed to imagine the angry tone that pervaded the personal letters he had sent to Stanley Hoffmann and Paxton a year before the publication of his review.

In January 1973 Michel wrote to Hoffmann to say that he had been astonished by Hoffmann's preface to Paxton's book. 'In six pages', he wrote, 'you manage to talk about a mediocre film with no historical merit and you say not a word about the works of the Committee for the History of the Second World War and the review that it publishes.' This, to Michel's mind was a deliberate insult on Hoffmann's part, something he had not expected from 'a man whom I have welcomed in my office, had over to my house . . . That's what I would call "a very short memory".' Michel concluded the letter with a pointed indication that he had no friendly salutations whatsoever to extend to Professor Hoffmann.[28] Hoffmann's reply to Michel began with an expression of incredulity that a man whose work he admired so much would stoop to such a level of pettiness. But after explaining why the preface to Paxton's book was not the appropriate forum to talk about Michel's journal and other publications, Hoffmann wrote: 'I hope that I am wrong to suspect that your agitation comes, rather than from my omission, from the fact that a young American professor has so audaciously and so learnedly treated a subject which until now was considered by French university protectionism a little like their private turf.'[29]

Michel's correspondence with Paxton was less vehement in tone. Three days after his letter to Hoffmann, Michel wrote Paxton to congratulate him on his 'excellent work', but also to lament the absence of contact and cooperation between American and French scholars. Michel regretted in particular, that Paxton had not worked with the French Committee for the History of the Second World War while doing research for his book. Because he had been 'poorly counseled' before coming to Paris, his book contained several gaps and mistakes that might have been 'easily avoided'. Michel hoped that in the future they might establish contact and 'a cooperation that would be profitable for both parties'.[30] In response, Paxton thanked Michel for the compliments about his book, but reminded him that he had come to the French Committee earlier when he was working on *Parades and Politics at Vichy*. Perhaps Michel had forgotten, he suggested, because Paxton was then a 'young researcher with a bad accent', and his approaches had produced no results. Later Paxton had sent a copy of the published work to Michel, but it had not been reviewed; so, he added, he was all the more happy that Michel had decided to review *La France de Vichy*, and he trusted that the review would focus on the main arguments rather than the possible errors of detail.[31]

If the Michel–Hoffmann–Paxton correspondence represented one rather peculiar aspect of the French reaction to Paxton's work, it should be re-emphasized that the majority of French scholars, and most writers in the popular press, welcomed the book and acknowledged its historiographical importance. For Jean-Pierre Rioux, *La France de Vichy* was a 'great work' which offered a dose of 'public health' to the French people. Even if her looking-glass might be shattered in the process, 'France must look at herself', he wrote, 'in this mirror held up with neither ostentation nor weakness.'[32] Marc Ferro remarked that Paxton had written a 'strong, refreshing, book' in a 'magisterial' fashion that would shake up both Pétainists and Gaullists.[33] *Témoignage Chrétien* proclaimed: 'Finally the great book on "Vichy" that we have been waiting for,'[34] and Jean Charles added: 'finally a true "History of Vichy" that puts Robert Aron's book in its proper place'.[35] The *Revue Générale* called it a 'magisterial work that is very likely to be definitive on the subject'.[36] *Education* proclaimed: 'Paxton's work will, without any doubt, advance the de-mythification of a period that has great need of it';[37] and organs as diverse as the conservative *Le Figaro* and the Communist *Cahiers d'Histoire de l'Institut Maurice Thorez* applauded the author's 'devastating indictment' of the Vichy regime.[38]

A full recording of the eulogistic citations about *La France de Vichy* would require more space than this article permits. One measure of the book's impact in France is the fact that at least sixty-five reviews or commentaries appeared in the French media. How many other scholarly works written by an American have received that much attention in France? Twenty-five years after the publication in France of *La France de Vichy*, some of the original criticism the book received in France seems petty and even ludicrous, while those French writers who hailed the book as pathbreaking and authoritative must find satisfaction in the book's staying power as a standard work. Significantly, the most recent general survey of the Vichy era published in France, Philippe Burrin's *La France à l'heure allemande*,[39] confirms in all respects the main lines of Paxton's interpretation of the behavior of the Vichy government. Like other authors who have followed in his wake, rather than replacing Paxton's classic study, Burrin complements it with a detailed examination of responses to the occupation by various social categories. In only two areas, interpretation of the evolution of public opinion under Vichy and of the French Resistance, have criticisms expressed at the time of the book's appearance been echoed or confirmed by subsequent research. In 1973 Jean Charles noted that Paxton had underestimated 'the evolution over time of public opinion under Vichy',[40] and a review in the *Journal de Genève* stated: 'Too focused on the personnel of the regime and its official policies, Paxton has forgotten that in the end it is the masses who make history, even by their inertia.'[41] The view that public opinion turned away from Vichy more massively and more precociously than Paxton had suggested was shared by scholars in Paris for the 1990 colloquium on 'Vichy and the French people', and articulated convincingly that same year in Pierre Laborie's excellent book.[42] That the role of the French Resistance might have been insufficiently appreciated by Paxton has been suggested by a number of local and regional studies, including those by Jacqueline Sainclivier, François Marcot, Jean-Marie Guillon, Pierre Laborie, and and Yves Durand, and in my own work on the Auvergne.

When *La France de Vichy* was published, Marc Ferro claimed that one of the most interesting points of the book was that, 'like *The Sorrow and the Pity*', Paxton had demonstrated 'to what point the majority of public opinion supported [Vichy's] Moral Order'.[43] Years later, Jean-Pierre Azéma noted 'the greatest irritation and controversy' about the book: the French 'suspected Robert Paxton not only of going after Vichy France, but also of being very critical of the French people under Vichy'.[44] Similarly, a letter I received in 1987 from a retired French schoolteacher stated that she had been so 'bruised' by Paxton's book that she was almost ashamed to be French. She thanked me for *Choices in Vichy France*, because it demonstrated that perhaps not all the French had behaved so ignominiously during the occupation as she had believed from reading Paxton.[45] More recent scholarship has modified Paxton's conclusions in the direction of a clearer delineation of popular attitudes and behavior during the Vichy era, and an insistence on greater distinctions between the French political regime and the French people. This later scholarship has enriched our understanding of the Vichy era, without fundamentally challenging Paxton's findings as to the nature and behavior of the Vichy regime.

After the initial controversy about his book subsided, Robert Paxton's work rapidly came to be recognized as authoritative. Although Henry Rousso has described sales in France of *La France de Vichy* as 'fairly modest', the more than 58,000 copies sold in the decade after its appearance were certainly impressive for a scholarly study, particularly during a time in which Karen Offen has shown that the typical monograph on French history sold less than one thousand copies in the United States.[46] Rousso also noted that the textbooks concerning Vichy used by French teachers in the 1980s clearly indicated that Paxton had 'dethroned Aron'.[47] Robert Paxton recalled that the large crowd and warm reception that greeted him for a public lecture at the *Ecole de Sciences Politiques* in the late 1970s, shortly before the publication in 1981 of *Vichy et les Juifs*, marked for him the realization that he had come to be fully accepted by the scholarly community in France.[48] From that time forward his general framework for the study of Vichy was rarely challenged.

Still, Paxton was surprised that the book he and Michael Marrus devoted to Vichy's treatment of the Jews arrived in France to the virtually unanimous praise of French commentators. Despite the fact that the subject treated was one of the most sensitive issues of the occupation era, and that the book reinforced Paxton's original criticism of Vichy policies, he received no negative letters from French readers, and reviewers expressed few reservations in print about the book's arguments or conclusions. The widespread acceptance by 1981 of Paxton's general interpretation of the Vichy experience was apparent in the large number of reviewers who prefaced their remarks about *Vichy et les Juifs* with complimentary references to his 'indispensable', 'famous', and 'now classic', 'standard work' in the field, *La France de Vichy*.[49] For Pierre Enckell, Robert Paxton was quite simply the American 'who had made the French see the reality of Vichy', and he predicted that *Vichy et les Juifs*, like its predecessor, would also be 'a standard work'.[50] One has only to glance at citations from the flood of scholarly work in the past fifteen years on the situation of the Jews in France during the occupation to recognize the importance of this book as a launching pad for later research. As Renée Poznanski remarked: 'The Paxtonian Revolution – completed and detailed in *Vichy et les Juifs* . . . – brought about a total revision of the analysis of the doctrines and the consequences of the antisemitic policies of the French regime under the Occupation.'[51]

'Ah, what a beautiful, wonderful book,' wrote Claude Lévy of Marrus and Paxton's study, 'solid, serious, well documented, critical and sad, devastating! But justice has finally been served . . .'.[52] Gilles Lambert, described the book as 'the work of historians without a partisan position, written without any sentimentality,' and noted that it was 'based on a careful, lucid analysis of French and German archives'.[53] Jean-Pierre Azéma praised the rich documentation of 'this remarkably well-informed book', demonstrating 'once and for all, that Vichy's state antisemitism arose and functioned – at first – independently of any pressure from the Reich'.[54] Although acknowledging that reading the book 'leaves a bitter taste in one's mouth', Annette Wieviorka suggested that being separated by an ocean from the history they were writing probably helped Marrus and Paxton to produce 'an analysis that is as objective and dispassionate as possible'.[55]

With the exception of one former government official who accused Marrus and Paxton of a 'tender disdain'[56] for France, virtually all reviewers shared Wieviorka's positive assessment of both the quality and tone of *Vichy et les Juifs*. Most often highlighted in the reviews was the central theme that French policy had its origin in a native French antisemitism and that the original antisemitic policies had been undertaken by Vichy without German pressure. French readers were particularly struck by the evidence that Jews had been safer in the southeastern part of France under Italian occupation than they had been in the territories controlled directly by Vichy. Frequently, reviewers described the book as instructive for contemporary France, which was experiencing an unfortunate revival of racism and sporadic antisemitic actions. As Jacques Madaule wrote in *Sens*, 'Here is an indispensable book, not only for those interested in the sad history of yesterday, but also for those who are troubled to see returning today the same perils we faced forty years ago.'[57] Jean-Pierre Rioux hoped that Marrus and Paxton's 'fine book' would have a salutary effect on the French. 'Let it be read reverently by all of us,' he wrote, 'discussed and dissected in the public square. It will be good for the moral health and historical memory of a country which, all things considered, has never collectively absorbed the shock of the dark years.'[58]

As with *Vichy France*, subsequent research has done little to alter the compelling findings of Marrus and Paxton with regard to the actions of the Vichy government. The only reservations confirmed or elaborated upon by later research concerned the authors' interpretation of public opinion, and their possible minimization of resistance to the application of Vichy's antisemitic policies. Some reviewers accepted the idea that 'at least a silent consensus'[59] of public opinion underlay the success of Vichy's antisemitic policies. As Daniel Lindberg remarked, the book was '. . . not only devastating for the Vichy regime itself, which has hardly any reputation left to preserve, but also for a very representative part, unfortunately, of all of civil society'.[60] But others, including Jean-Pierre Azéma, Georges Weller, and Nicole Racine-Furland, agreed with Roger Berg, who argued that occasionally Marrus and Paxton had taken the prefects' reports too literally as a reflection of popular opinion, and that their account did not explain satisfactorily how 75 per cent of the Jews in France had escaped deportation.[61] The authors had admitted in their book that assessing public opinion towards the Jews during the Occupation was very difficult, and a decade after the appearance of *Vichy et les Juifs*, Paxton acknowledged: 'I regret that in our book we did not adequately emphasize the actions of French citizens who helped the Jews.'[62]

Having authored three major studies concerning wartime France, Robert Paxton has come to be accepted in France as the scholar whose works, perhaps more than those of any other writer, have shaped scholarly understanding of the Vichy Regime. As suggested by this paper's title, his publications have been greeted in France as 'major events' – *événements*. French reviewers of his recent book on rural fascism in France during the inter-war years state prosaically that he is the American who 'in the 1970s introduced the French to the Vichy regime', and predict confidently that his next book will once again be a pathbreaking study taking his readers 'beyond the realm of myth'.[63] Taking the liberty of concluding with a personal anecdote, I might add that Paxton's reputation is even operative in France in the world of advertising and promotion.

When my book, *Choices in Vichy France*, was translated into French in 1996, my publisher, obviously thinking that this would help sales, distributed it to bookstores around the country with a flyer stating that I was a 'disciple of the historian Paxton'. For the television program, *Le Cercle de Minuit*, the hostess, Laure Adler, introduced me as 'a disciple of the great American historian Robert Paxton', and in several newspaper articles and radio broadcasts, I was repeatedly labeled either as a student or disciple of Professor Paxton. Of all the French commentators, only Jean-Pierre Rioux, in a review of my book, entitled 'Clérmont with neither sorrow nor pity', noted that I was 'the anti-Ophuls and even, in passing, the anti-Paxton'.[64] Discussing these developments over supper one fall evening with my French colleague, François Marcot, I pondered whether or not to take advantage of an upcoming appearance to clarify that I had studied with Joel Colton rather than Professor Paxton, and that, as Rioux had detected, I was not entirely 'a disciple' of the latter. To which François responded, 'You know, my friend, all of us, French or Americans, who have done research since the 1970s on the Vichy period, even those of us who have differed with his interpretation on certain issues, are still disciples of Robert Paxton.' Certainly this sentiment, no doubt shared by all scholars in the field, bespeaks an achievement rarely attained in our profession, and much to be admired.

Notes

1. My thanks to Marie-Claire Ruet, *documentaliste* at the *Musée de la Résistance et de la Déportation*, Besançon, for her help with my research, and to Robert Paxton, who graciously consented to an interview and shared his personal files concerning the publications discussed here. The Appendix lists reviews of Paxton's *Vichy France* and *Vichy et les juifs* that appeared in France.
2. Ruth Zylberman, 'Robert Paxton: un américain tranquille à Vichy', *L'Histoire*, No. 203, October 1996.
3. *Esprit*, No. 427, September 1973.
4. *Revue française de science politique*, February 1967.
5. *Political Science Quarterly*, Vol. 88, #4, December 1973; *American Historical Review*, Vol. 69, October 1975; *The American Political Science Review*, Vol. 69, October 1975.
6. *Le Monde des Livres*, 1 February 1973.
7. Of sixty-five reviews or notices of the book, thirty-four were positive or contained neutral description; eighteen were negative; nine included both praise and criticism; and two were simple description without evaluation.
8. Henry Rousso, *The Vichy Syndrome, History and Memory in France since 1944* (Cambridge, MA, 1991).
9. Frantz-André Burguet, *Magazine Littéraire*, April 1973.
10. Stanley Hoffmann, in Robert O. Paxton, *La France de Vichy* (Paris, 1973), Préface,
11. A.N., *Défense Nationale*, July 1973.
12. *Le Monde des Livres*, 22 March 1973.
13. *La Monde*, 'Correspondence', 17 May 1973.
14. *Le Maréchal*, No. 90, April–May 1973.
15. Ibid.
16. Michel Denis, *La France Catholique – Ecclesia*, 18 May 1973.
17. Alain-Gérard Slama, 'Les yeux d'Abetz, *Contrepoint*, Vol. 10, April 1973.

18. A.-G. S., *Les Informations*, 26 February 1973 (emphasis mine).
19. Dominique Jamet, *L'Aurore*, 9 February 1973.
20. Pierre van Altena, *Aspects de la France*, 17 May 1973.
21. Jean Paillard to Paxton, 26 March 1973.
22. Loyer(?) to Paxton, 7 March 1973.
23. *Revue de la Politique Française*, March 1973.
24. Paxton to Suleiman, 29 June 1973.
25. Janine Bourdin, *Revue française de science politique*, Vol. 23, no. 3, June 1973. Later, the *Revue* failed to review *Vichy France and the Jews* in either English or French version.
26. Georges Soutou, *Revue Historique*, no. 516, October–December, 1975.
27. Henri Michel, *Revue d'histoire de la deuxiéme guerre mondiale*, no. 93, January 1974.
28. Michel to Hoffmann, 27 January 1973.
29. Hoffmann to Michel, 7 February 1973.
30. Michel to Paxton, 30 January 1973.
31. Paxton to Michel, 10 February 1973.
32. Jean-Pierre Rioux, 'Vichy, notre vieux démon,' *Biblio, hebdo,* no. 68, 1 March 1973.
33. Marc Ferro, 'maréchal, nous sommes toujours là,' *La Quinzaine Littéraire*, 16–28 February 1973.
34. F. Fonvieille Alquier, *Témoignage Chrétien*, 22 February 1973.
35. Jean Charles, *La Nouvelle Critique*, no. 63, April 1973.
36. *Revue Générale*, May 1973.
37. Gérard Fournier, *L'Education*, 22 March 1973.
38. Jean-François Kahn, *Le Figaro*, 10 February 1973, and Roger Martelli, *Cahiers d'Histoire de l'Institut Maurice Thorez*, no. 3, Nouvelle série (31), April–May–June 1973.
39. Phillippe Burrin, *La France à l'heure allemande* (Paris, 1995).
40. Jean Charles, *La Nouvelle Critique*, No. 63, April 1973.
41. *Journal de Genève*, 28 April 1973.
42. Pierre Laborie, *L'Opinion française sous Vichy* (Paris, 1990); Jean-Pierre Azéma and François Bédarida (eds), *Vichy et les Français* (Paris, 1992).
43. Marc Ferro, *La Quinzaine Littéraire*, 16–28 February 1973.
44. Azéma, *Vichy et les Français*, 29.
45. Marie Louise Blum to John Sweets, 26 June 1987.
46. Karen Offen, 'Reflections on the Publishing Crisis in French History', *French Historical Studies*, Vol 14, no. 4, Fall 1986, 592–3.
47. Rousso, *The Vichy Syndrome*, 269.

48. Paxton to Sweets, 21 May 1997.
49. M. C. Kok-Escalle, *Centre Protestant d'Etudes et de Documentation*, No. 265; Paul Dupont, *L'Humanité*, May(?) 1981; J. Ch., *Les Echos*, 2 June 1982; Emile Malet, *Le Quotidien de Paris*, 14 May 1981; Jean-François Vilar, *Rouge*, No. 970, 22–28 May 1981; Daniel Lindberg, *Le Matin*, 7 May 1981; and Guy Morel, *Le Patriote résistant; journal des déportés, internés, et familles*, No. 501, July 1981.
50. Pierre Enckell, *Les Nouvelles Littéraires*, 11 June 1981.
51. Renée Poznanski, *Etre Juif en France pendant la Second Guerre Mondiale* (Paris, 1994), 686.
52. Claude Lévy, *Information Juive*, 1–6 June 1981.
53. Gilles Lambert, *Le Figaro*, 22 May 1981.
54. Jean-Pierre Azéma, *La Quinzaine Littéraire*, 16 September 1981.
55. Annette Wieviorka, 'La France à toujours mal à Vichy,' *Témoignage Chrétien*, 6 July 1981.
56. 'Une mise au point de Phillipe Serre', *Le Matin*, 8 July 1981.
57. Jacques Madaule, *Sens*, 1982–3, 74–5.
58. Jean-Pierre Rioux, *La Croix*, 17–18 May 1981.
59. Arnold Mandel, 'Vichy, c'était bien la France . . . ,' *L'Arche*, 18 June 1981.
60. Daniel Lindberg, *Le Matin*, 7 May 1981.
61. Roger Berg, *Tribune Juive*, 30 October–5 November 1981; Jean Pierre Azéma, *La Quinzaine Littéraire*, 16 September 1981; Georges Wellers, *Le Monde Juif*, No. 103, July-September 1981 and *Revue d'histoire de la deuxième guerre mondiale et des conflits contemporains*, No. 133, January 1984; Nicole Racine-Furlaud, *Revue française de science politique*, Vol. 33, #4, August 1983; Serge Klarsfeld, *Vichy–Auschwitz*, 2 vols (Paris, 1983 and 1985); and Asher Cohen, *Persécutions et sauvetages, Juifs et Français sous l'Occupation et sous Vichy* (Paris, 1993), are among those who emphasize French aid to the Jews.
62. Annette Lévy-Willard, 'Vichy did the work of the Nazis: An interview with Robert Paxton', in Richard J. Golsan (ed.), *Memory, the Holocaust, and French Justice* (Hanover, NH, 1996): 58.
63. Nicolas Weill, *Le Monde*, 25 October 1996, and Ruth Zylberman, 'Robert Paxton, un Américain tranquille à Vichy', *L'Histoire*, No. 203, October 1996.
64. Jean-Pierre Rioux, 'Clérmont sans chagrin ni pitié', *Le Monde*, 25 October 1996. Robert Paxton very thoughtfully sent me a copy of the review with the quip: 'I just hope this "anti-Paxton" thing doesn't get out of hand!'

–3–

Vichy France and the Jews: After Fifteen Years

Michael R. Marrus

Those familiar with some of the documentation of the wartime deportation of Jews from France will remember the withering telephone call made by *SS-Obersturmbannführer* Adolf Eichmann in Berlin to *Obersturmführer* Heinz Röthke, the recently appointed *Judenreferat*, or SS man in Paris in charge of Jewish matters, on 15 July 1942. Eichmann was furious. One of the railway transports carrying Jews 'to the East' had been canceled, disrupting the elaborately organized schedule then in place. 'This was a matter of prestige,' the *Obersturmbannführer* insisted. 'Difficult negotiations had been successfully conducted with the Reich Transport Ministry for these convoys, and now Paris was canceling a train. Such a thing had never happened before. The whole affair was "disgraceful".' Drastic consequences might follow from such an outrage, Eichmann intimated. He was even 'wondering whether he shouldn't drop France entirely as a country to be evacuated'. Chastised, Röthke begged his superior not to take such action, and promised to make amends.[1] And thereafter the trains, with their complete cargo of Jews, left on time.

This exchange reminds us of how France fitted into a much wider Nazi program for European Jews. To the Germans, the Final Solution in France was part of a Europe-wide enterprise, with a sometimes-intricate interrelationship of many parts. Railway timetables were a crucial element, and they had to be strictly followed. Transports had to be full, and had to meet schedules worked out elsewhere, or else scarce resources would be wasted. And the matter was urgent, not subject to procrastination or delay. How different were the perspectives of Vichy, where narrow horizons went hand in hand with an inflated sense of the place of France in the New Order of Europe. Particularly when it came to unpleasant subjects, such as the Jews, French decision-makers seldom lifted their sights to consider long-term objectives or developments in other countries. Indeed, when the trains rolled eastwards to Auschwitz, with cattle cars jammed with Jewish men, women and children, French authorities preferred not to think about the Jews at all. As we hear Eichmann's threat to Röthke, the exchange prompts reflection on how France fitted into the larger picture. That was Eichmann's problem, and it is also the issue I want to examine in this brief study.

Discussing this issue in the final chapter of *Vichy France and the Jews*, Robert Paxton and I addressed French interpretations of Vichy, part of a debate that was then quite fresh. Had our optic been different, however, we might have engaged conventional treatments of the Holocaust, in which some of the same issues were raised. For at least as much as with the French memory of Vichy, specialists in the wartime murder of European Jews for a long time ignored the responsibility of the French regime for anti-Jewish policies during the occupation era and the French contribution to the murderous outcome during the second half of the war. Notably, even before Robert Aron's 1955 *Histoire de Vichy*, both Léon Poliakov and Gerald Reitlinger suggested that Vichy blunted the impact of the final solution, ultimately saving Jews from deportation and murder. Poliakov's *Bréviaire de haine*, published in 1951, was the pioneering work on the Nazis' wartime assault on European Jews. Himself a victim of Vichy and German persecution, Poliakov was nevertheless remarkably indulgent in the pages he devoted to the deportation of Jews from France. The toll of the Final Solution in that country – which he estimated at 30 per cent – was significantly smaller than neighboring Belgium and the Netherlands, estimated at 55 per cent and 79 per cent respectively. In explanation, Poliakov concluded, 'Vichy was the predominant factor.'[2] Through the very existence of an autonomous zone, Jewish refugees by the thousands were able to find shelter from the Germans. Vichy's role in the Final Solution, Poliakov went on, was determined by Pierre Laval, whose policy it was to get rid of foreign Jews and, to the extent it was possible, to protect French Jews in both zones. Crucially, Vichy's opposition to the Germans on Jewish policy stiffened in 1943 as knowledge spread about what was happening to Jews in Poland. Laval refused to denaturalize masses of French Jews, preventing a massive round-up planned for June and July of that year. The Germans were thus thrown on their own resources, with results that were thereby limited.[3]

In a book first published in 1953, the Englishman Gerald Reitlinger offered an even more positive evaluation. Like Poliakov, Reitlinger emphasized Vichy's distinction between French and foreign Jews. 'The most collaborationist French officials persisted in regarding a French-born Jew and even a naturalized Jew as a Frenchman,' he claimed.[4] The *Commissariat général aux questions juives* never had much support from the French government, he went on. Its commissioner, Xavier Vallat, stoutly resisted the imposition of the Jewish badge. The French persistently obstructed German policies, with the result that, as his final section was titled, the final solution was 'not achieved'. 'No Jewish community in Occupied Europe came off so lightly, except in Italy and Denmark,' Reitlinger concluded, 'and this was due in large measure to the tactics of Laval, a man who was shot by his compatriots for treason.'[5]

Finally, Raul Hilberg's 1961 *The Destruction of the European Jews*, a masterful overview, and still the most authoritative treatment of what its author called 'the machinery of destruction', adopted more or less the same line. Like Poliakov and Reitlinger, Hilberg took as his point of departure Vichy's efforts to limit German demands when it came to the Jews. Most of his lengthy section dealing with France was devoted to explaining this determination, and hence the 'success' of Vichy's strategy. 'To no small extent that strategy met with success,' Hilberg asserted. 'By giving up a part, most of the whole was saved.'[6] Drawing extensively on the German documents, Hilberg did examine the period prior to the deportations, when Vichy issued laws and ordinances against the Jews, applicable in both the occupied and unoccupied zones. But he offered no assessment of the independent Vichy drive against the Jews and made no evaluation of its impact on the final solution. Remarkably, he found a 'French reluctance to acquire Jewish property' through a process of Aryanization.[7] Vichy's approach to the Germans' demands, he indicated, was basically defensive. 'Almost from the beginning of the occupation, the Vichy regime sensed that under increasing German pressure it would have to shift to a second line of defense. If the destruction process could not be halted at a certain point, efforts would have to be made to deflect the full force of the attack from the old-established, assimilated Jews to the newly arrived immigrants and refugees.'[8] Like Reitlinger, Hilberg seems to have responded sympathetically to Pierre Laval's contention on the eve of his execution, which he quoted sympathetically: 'I did all I could, considering the fact that my first duty was to my fellow-countrymen of Jewish extraction, whose interests I could not sacrifice. The right of asylum was not respected in this case. How could it have been otherwise in a country which was occupied by the German army? How could the Jews have been better protected in a country where the Gestapo ran riot?'[9]

Reference to these early treatments of what we have come to term the Holocaust adds a useful perspective on the alleged particular susceptibility of the French for evading responsibility for the wartime persecution of the Jews and for complicity in their destruction. We are repeatedly told that the French have special difficulty 'confronting their Vichy past', that they fear 'skeletons in the national closet', and that they are particularly disposed to mythmaking about the wartime period.[10] To be sure, a similar story can be told about other countries. Switzerland comes immediately to mind because of recent discussions of its wartime role; but in Belgium, the Netherlands, Sweden and even Denmark such charges have for a long time been leveled by local commentators. It is equally remarkable that these three writers I have mentioned, men who were centrally concerned with the Europe-wide process of mass murder and who had no reason to be over-generous toward the French, seem to have come independently to interpretations highly indulgent towards Vichy. Why should this be?

One explanation may have to do with the slow process by which the horrors of the Holocaust were formulated as a coherent Europe-wide program and assimilated into the general consciousness.[11] As historians have repeatedly stressed, it took time to put wartime genocide into perspective. The dominant view in the post-war era, accented by the International Military Tribunal at Nuremberg, was of a criminal enterprise planned and directed by the Nazi leadership, whose fortunes were promoted on a continental scale by German militarism. Understandably enough, Germany and Nazism were at the center of attention, and sometimes crowded out analysis of bystanders and collaborators. Certainly, in this perception, the hotels and offices and small-scale intrigues of Vichy – to non-French, the very image of parochialism – were hard to link with genocide, assembly-line killing, gas chambers and the slaughter of millions. One did not have to be a partisan of Laval, Pétain, or the National Revolution to see Auschwitz, Treblinka, and even Buchenwald and Bergen-Belsen as another planet – *l'univers concentrationnaire*, to take the title of a well-known book published in France in 1946.[12]

Second, as people began to grasp the chronology of the final solution, attention focused principally on the period of deportations and mass murder, in the second half of the war, rather than the period 1940–42, during which the Vichy regime, operating largely on its own, and without direction from the Germans, defined its anti-Jewish program. The result was that the link between the two was not fully understood. Of our three authors, Reitlinger had the least to say about Vichy's early initiatives, while both Poliakov and Hilberg said more. But in all three cases, the relative inattention to this first period tended to diminish the importance of this persecution in the round-ups and deportations to come. This was the connection that Robert Paxton and I took pains to underscore:

> The measures of those first two years had catastrophic effects upon the Jews of France. Snapping the material links that bound Jews to French society, Vichy confiscated their property through aryanization, dismissed them from government service, excluded them from professions and higher education. Thousands of productive French Jews were thus turned into refugees, who swelled the ranks of those already uprooted by other states, and who offered self-fulfilling validation of the popular animus against 'parasites.' Vichy also snapped the legal links that normally offered protection to citizens and visitors. Officials entrusted with upholding constitutional guarantees deprived a segment of French citizenry of them, owing to circumstances of ancestry rather than for anything individuals had done. The way was open for legal disabilities without limit in the name of administrative convenience or the rulers' taste. Finally, Vichy snapped the links of moral solidarity among peoples. Even though he never pronounced the word 'Jew' in a public statement, Marshal Pétain lent his immense prestige implicitly to a systematic propaganda of collective denigration. Two years of government measures that linked national revival to anti-Semitism dulled the consciences of many French people toward a group officially blamed for everything from high prices to the defeat. The first two years of Vichy made it hard to see the Jews as victims rather than as problems.[13]

A third reason for indulgence toward Vichy was an insufficient appreciation of the authentic French roots of the anti-Jewish drive of these first two years. Early analysts, aware of Vichy's independent animus against Jews, understood correctly that the Germans were the far more radical of the two. 'Two horses awkwardly in harness,' was how Poliakov put it, 'in which the wild Hitlerian mare forced the pace for the slower Vichy animal that had its own rhythm.'[14] For these pioneers, the demonic character of Nazism was understandably at the center of attention. Overlooked or downplayed, as a rule, was the alacrity with which Vichy plunged into anti-Jewish legislation in the early months of the regime, the energy that Vichy poured into its anti-Jewish project, the way in which antisemitic laws were closely integrated into the wider project of the *Révolution nationale*, the meticulous attention to detail, the keen sense of competition with the Germans to take the upper hand in the business of persecuting the Jews. And so it was common to see the Germans as regularly having the upper hand, with the French as the ones who were constantly making distinctions, posing limits, and eventually dragging their feet.

To be sure, there was a real difference in ideology. To the Nazi leadership, whose tone was set by a Jewish-obsessed Führer, the Jews were an all-powerful force lurking behind every national issue, a malignant, manipulative, menacing threat to the health of the German people.

Dealing with this challenge, in a policy informed by what Saul Friedländer has recently referred to as a 'redemptive anti-Semitism,' was essential for the future of the Nazi regime.[15] At Vichy, on the other hand, while antisemitism was certainly pervasive, there was much less ideological cohesion on the matter than in the Nazi state, and much less salience to the issue as a critical underpinning of the regime. At Vichy, few seem to have been concerned about a *final* solution to the Jewish problem, European or otherwise; while pervasive, antisemitism was also secondary. The main preoccupation, which underlay virtually every aspect of the *Révolution nationale*, was to extend French jurisdiction on Jewish and other issues, and eventually to reunify the country.

Despite these differences, it should be emphasized, the anti-Jewish program of the *Révolution nationale* was fully consonant with the officially proclaimed goals of Nazism concerning the Jews as they applied to western Europe for more than a year after the defeat of France in 1940. While in the newly conquered east the Germans' imaginations roamed freely over the territories designated as part of the *Lebensraum*, or living space of the newly enlarged Reich, and while the first of the anticipated vast transfers of population entailed by German expansion were being undertaken, in the west the Germans operated far more cautiously. Although the goal there too was to eliminate the Jews, the Germans realized that for the time being this was impossible. With channels of emigration blocked, and the support of the local populations uncertain, Nazi officials set more limited goals for the Jews: to enumerate them, reduce their presence everywhere in Europe, control their movements, strip them of their property, and sometimes concentrate them in particular locations. Ultimately, the Germans identified a 'final goal', a comprehensive, urgently required solution, as yet unspecified and undetermined, that would probably involve some process of mass migration. Vichy shared these objectives, although French policy-makers sought to maximize the benefits and minimize the burdens of carrying out an anti-Jewish program. Far from representing a different orientation, then, Vichy's legalistic approach to the Jewish question fitted nicely with the Germans' realization that priorities were elsewhere, and that only so much could be done while the war continued.

Worth noting in this context is that Vichy's persecution of Jews in France was launched and continued during a time of massive upheaval and terrible suffering for Jewish populations elsewhere. Our preoccupation with the catastrophic impact of the Final Solution should not obscure the fact that information about murderous policies in central and eastern Europe during the earlier period was widely available in France, as it was in other countries. Pre-war outrages, of course, notably *Kristallnacht*, had received ample exposure in the French press. Hitler's blood-curdling declarations about the Jews were reported as well. During 1941, Radio Moscow and other propaganda organs reported on the slaughter of Jews in the east.[16] To be sure, such information was not always believed, and ordinary people often responded with indifference. But one can hardly label indifferent those at Vichy who were in charge of Jewish policy, who believed they had difficult Jewish problems to solve, and who put their minds to such issues on a regular, continuing basis. Throughout this period, let us recall, the propaganda organs of the regime poured forth antisemitic propaganda, inciting opinion against Jews, and calling for even more drastic action against them. Energetically, Vichy officials struggled to close loopholes and open up new fronts against the Jews. It is possible that somewhere, some of those involved in such persecution were somehow unaware that they were part of a much wider anti-Jewish enterprise, led by the Nazis. But they could not have been many.

What we now identify as the 'Final Solution', and what many German officials themselves understood by that term, resulted from a deliberate shift of Nazi policy to a coordinated, Europe-wide program of mass murder, involving east and west, and operating according to an urgent new timetable. Historians continue to differ on the timing of that shift, with some seeing it as part of the planning process for Operation Barbarossa, the German invasion of the Soviet Union in 1941, but most understanding it as springing from the campaign against the Soviets itself, part of the more widespread radicalization of the regime that attended upon what was referred to as a *Vernichtungskrieg*, a war of destruction. But of the change itself there is little doubt. This was the source of the urgency that underlies Eichmann's telegram to Heinz Röthke. 'The Jewish Question must be resolved in the course of the war,' said Franz Rademacher of the German Foreign Office in early 1942, 'for only so can it be solved without a worldwide outcry.'[17] Across Europe, Nazi Jewish experts struggled to bring localities into line.

Let us shift attention for a moment back to Eichmann, who as we saw at the beginning of this article had many things on his mind besides France. To what degree did Vichy or its policies influence decisions in Berlin? Seen in wider perspective, we should understand the relatively minor place France had in the Nazis' mobilization against the Jews, and why this – together with geographic factors and the growing support Jews received from the French population – rather than any deliberately undertaken 'sabotage' accounts for so many Jews escaping the Final Solution. At the beginning of 1942, when there were around 300,000

Jews in France, SS Jewish specialists were mainly concerned with parts of Poland and the newly conquered territory of the Soviet Union, where the Jewish population was more than ten times as great – over 2,250,000 alone in the 'General Government', German-occupied Poland not absorbed into the Reich, and 400,000 in the region of Bialystok. The Warsaw ghetto contained about 350,000 Jews, and that of Lodz, just over 100,000.

In March 1942, when the first train of Jewish deportees left France, the Germans began the killing process of what came to be called Aktion Reinhard, named after the assassinated Reinhard Heydrich, an ambitious program intended to finish off the Jews of the General Government. Under the direction of Odilo Globocnik, the SS police boss for the Lublin district, this massive project involved the deportation of hundreds of thousands of Jews to Belzec, Sobibor, and Treblinka, to be killed with poison gas. Aktion Reinhard lasted twenty-one months, and finished in November 1943. The toll was an estimated 1.7 million murdered.[18] While not directly in charge, Eichmann certainly had to worry about the trains, and his calculations for western Europe always had to take into account what was going on in the east. Activity there was intense. A meeting he attended at the Ministry of Transport in Berlin in September 1942, for example, specified eight trains daily heading for the death camps from the districts of Warsaw, Radom, Cracow, Lvov and Lublin. Additional plans, never realized, included 200,000 Jews from Romania. Not to mention, at the end, the transport necessary to ship the personal effects of the Jews to Germany – an estimated 1,500 freight cars in all, including about 450 cars of household goods and other belongings, 260 cars of bedding, 248 cars of clothing, 100 cars of shoes, and hundreds more with rags of various kinds.[19]

As Eichmann explained in stultifying detail at his trial in Jerusalem, deporting Jews was a complex process involving extensive planning, negotiation, organization and communication.[20] Himmler himself set priorities. Eichmann's Gestapo superior Müller was in the picture, as the Jerusalem court was reminded again and again. With all Europe to worry about, Eichmann was a busy man. Invariably, local conditions involved both positive and negative factors. On the positive side, as Paxton and I argued in 1981, the Germans' work was greatly facilitated by two years of Vichy persecution, in both the Occupied and Unoccupied zones – offering the Germans more substantial help than they received anywhere else in western Europe.[21] To be sure, Eichmann's deputies in France – Dannecker, then Röthke, and later Brunner – did run into difficulties with the French from time to time, and also with the Italians, whose opposition to the persecution and deportation of the Jews was much more forthright. But such difficulties were hardly extraordinary. Contrary to widespread belief, the Final Solution never functioned smoothly, problems constantly arose, and German officials simply put their minds to maneuvering around obstacles placed in their path. Goal-driven, Eichmann rose to assume a key position in the apparatus of the Final Solution precisely because he was able to deal with the opposition raised by Vichy. 'A pathfinder and a supreme practitioner of destruction,' as Hilberg calls him, Eichmann was more than a match for Pétain, Laval and their colleagues.[22]

Strikingly absent from the works of Poliakov, Reitlinger and Hilberg, was an assessment of how much was known about the murders in eastern Europe – a line of inquiry now taken up in practically every overview of the subject. Assessments differ, of course, but I think it fair to say that the more we have learned about the flow of information, the more abundant appears the evidence of what was happening. Read in the light of what we know, statements gleaned from many kinds of sources tell a similar, chilling story. 'Preparations are now under way for a final settling of accounts,' Hitler was quoted as saying about European Jewry in a headline in Marcel Déat's newspaper *L'Oeuvre* in February 1942.[23] In March, in Bratislava, even before regular convoys left France for the east, the Papal nuncio Giuseppe Burzio wrote to the Vatican: 'The deportation of 80,000 persons to Poland at the mercy of the Germans means to condemn a greater part of them to certain death.'[24] In July, as the convoys began to leave Drancy on a regular basis, the collaborationist *Au Pilori* declared that 'the reign of the Jews was coming to an end'. 'Worldwide events now under way – the importance of which goes beyond us, and which can only be judged much later – have decided the fate of the Jewish race in Europe, in Asia and in Africa.'[25] In September, when the round-ups of Jews from France caused a flurry of attention in London, Winston Churchill referred to the French deportations as 'the most bestial, the most squalid and the most senseless of all [the Germans'] offenses,' which were occurring 'in every land into which their armies have broken'.[26] And on 17 December 1942, eleven Allied governments and the French National Committee declared: 'From all the occupied countries Jews are being transported in conditions of appalling horror and brutality to Eastern Europe. In Poland, which has been made the principal Nazi slaughter-house, the ghettos established by the German invader are being systematically emptied of all Jews except for a few highly skilled workers required for war industries. None of those taken away are ever heard from again.'[27]

Did Vichy 'know'? Paxton and I attempted to answer this question, and many others have treated it as well, extending the analysis to the victims, the general population, and to the world outside. But while important, I would venture to suggest that in this context knowledge is far less important than interest. Most of the evidence we have suggests that Vichy policy-makers had only the vaguest interest in the Europe-wide impact of Germany's new mobilization against the Jews. Indeed, throughout the occupation years French officials left no trace of an inquiry into the extent of Jewish losses in the other countries with which comparisons are often made, and there is no indication that Vichy personalities paid any attention to them. So far as can be seen, no models for alternative strategies occurred to French decision-makers, no other courses were tried, no hints of regret at the time were recorded, and indeed the entire question of Jewish persecution was considered of secondary importance. As to the more particular question of knowledge about the death camps in the east, this is our inquiry, not that of Vichy. No one at Vichy seems to have looked into the evidence that was accumulating. No one seems to have written about it, so far as we know, or talked about it. As Renée Poznanski observes, 'The real question has nothing really to do with what the directors of the French state knew – or did not know – for they didn't want to know.'[28]

In the wake of the war, historians such as Poliakov, Reitlinger and Hilberg were right to speculate as they did about the relatively high proportion of Jews who escaped the Final Solution in France. Vichy's distinction between French and foreign Jews seemed to provide the key, quite possibly because this kind of discrimination, quite commonly applied elsewhere in western Europe, was so energetically insisted upon by French authorities. But looking from the French, as opposed to the European standpoint, and with an eye to the challenges Eichmann and his henchmen had to face, we asked rather how it had been possible to round up and deport so many, before the end in 1944.[29]

That last reference calls to mind a point that I think is often overlooked in comparing the death tolls in various European countries. Any such comparison must always take into account the way in which the war ended. For the most decisive influence on the extent of the killing was the course of the fighting in Europe, something over which the men of Vichy had no influence at all. In France, the deportations came to an end in mid-August 1944 because of the Liberation; elsewhere, where the Germans remained in control, convoys carrying Jews to their deaths continued until the winter of 1944–5. We must always remember that if the war had lasted another year or so there would probably have been no Jews left in France – or anywhere else in Europe for that matter. And so what is really measured in various comparative assessments is the *pace* of victimization in various places, something determined at least as much by the Germans' own priorities, the force they applied and the fortunes of war, as by local conditions.

The more we know about Vichy, I conclude, the more distasteful it seems. Nothing was more characteristic of the regime, in its narrowness, its vanity, its legalism, and also its cruelty, than its posture on the Jewish question. While it is true that Vichy had no murderous intent, that it made some distinctions, sometimes, between French and foreign Jews, and also that the regime was increasingly less enthusiastic about its anti-Jewish drive in the latter part of the war, its policies nevertheless victimized Jews mightily, and made the Germans' task easier when it came to the Final Solution. Driven by a handful of ideologues who truly cared about the Jewish issue, the political leadership sought to use the issue for wider advantage. Armies of bureaucrats went along. Their spirit was admirably summed up by Vichy's Minister of the Interior of 1940, later governor-general of Algeria, who at the trial of Philippe Pétain declared his credo: 'Je ne suis pas républicain, je ne suis pas antirépublicain, je suis un fonctionnaire.'[30]

Vichy's last priority was to maintain the state apparatus, which included the entire anti-Jewish enterprise. Through May, June, and July 1944, the edifice remained intact, laws continued to be enforced, stolen property was administered, and Jews were harassed. Vichy struggled to remain in charge.[31] Why did these structures not collapse? At the end of his *Vichy France* Robert Paxton suggested the reason was that so many refused to contemplate the abyss that would open with the end of state authority:

> Those who cling to the social order above all may do so by self-interest or merely by inertia. In either case, they know more clearly what they are against than what they are for. So blinded, they perform jobs that may be admirable in themselves but are tinctured with evil by the overall effects of the system. Even Frenchmen of the best intentions, faced with the harsh alternative of doing one's job, whose risks were moral and abstract, or practicing civil disobedience, whose risks were material and immediate, went on doing the job. The same may be said of the German occupiers. Many of them were 'good Germans,' men of cultivation, confident that their country's success outweighed a few moral blemishes, dutifully fulfilling some minor blameless function in a regime whose cumulative effect was brutish. . . . The deeds of occupier and occupied alike suggest that there come cruel times when to save a nation's deepest values one must disobey the state. France after 1940 was one those times.[32]

Notes

1. Henri Monneray (ed.), *La Persécution des Juifs en France et dans les autres pays de l'Ouest presentée par la France à Nuremberg* (Paris, 1947): 131–2.
2. Léon Poliakov, *Bréviaire de haine: le IIIe Reich et les Juifs* (Paris, 1951): 268.
3. Ibid.: 269–73.
4. Gerald Reitlinger, *The Final Solution: the Attempt to Exterminate the Jews of Europe, 1939–1945* (New York, 1961): 305.
5. Ibid.: 306, 313, 326, 328.
6. Raul Hilberg, *The Destruction of the European Jews* (Chicago, 1961) p. 389. Hilberg modified his position slightly in the revised edition of his work that appeared in 1985: 'To some extent, that strategy met with success. By giving up a part, most of the whole was saved,' *The Destruction of the European Jews* (New York, 1985), II: 609. Except where indicated, other references in these notes to this work refer to the earlier edition.
7. Hilberg, *Destruction of the European Jews:* 396. This sentence remains intact in the 1985 edition, *Destruction of the European Jews*, II: 626.
8. Ibid.: 400.
9. Ibid.: 407.
10. For a critical view, see Michael R. Marrus, 'Coming to Terms with Vichy', *Holocaust and Genocide Studies*, 9 (1995): 23–41.
11. For the early history of this process see Annette Wieviorka, *Déportation et génocide: entre la mémoire et l'oubli* (Paris, 1992); Pieter Lagrou, 'Victims of Genocide and National Memory: Belgium, France and the Netherlands, 1945–1965', *Past and Present*, No. 154 (February, 1997): 181–222.
12. David Rousset, *L'univers concentrationnaire* (Paris, 1946).
13. Michael R. Marrus and Robert O. Paxton, *Vichy France and the Jews* (New York, 1981): 369.
14. Poliakov, *Bréviaire de haine*: 85.
15. Saul Friedländer, *Nazi Germany and the Jews*, Vol. I, *The Years of Persecution, 1933–1939* (New York, 1997), *passim.*
16. Renée Poznanski, 'Qui savait quoi dans le monde?', in Stéphane Courtois and Adam Rayski (eds), *Qui savait quoi? L'extermination des Juifs 1941–1945* (Paris, 1987): 32.
17. Christopher R. Browning, *The Final Solution and the German Foreign Office: A Study of Referat D III of Abteilung Deutschland, 1940–1943* (New York, 1978): 83, March 1942.

18. See Yitzhak Arad, *Belzec, Sobibor, Treblinka: The Operation Reinhard Death Camps* (Bloomington, Indiana, 1987).
19. Ibid.: 158.
20. State of Israel, Ministry of Justice, *The Trial of Adolf Eichmann: Record of Proceedings in the District Court of Jerusalem* (9 vols, Jerusalem, 1993–5), IV, 1473.
21. Marrus and Paxton, *Vichy France and the Jews:* 369.
22. Raul Hilberg, *Perpetrators Victims Bystanders: The Jewish Catastrophe 1933–1945* (New York, 1992): 41.
23. Philippe Burrin, 'Que savait les collaborationnnistes?', in Courtois and Rayski, *Qui savait quoi:* 75.
24. Walter Laqueur, *The Terrible Secret: An Investigation into the Suppression of Information about Hitler's 'Final Solution'* (London: Weidenfeld & Nicolson, 1980): 56.
25. Burrin, 'Que savait les collaborationnnistes?': 76.
26. Martin Gilbert, *Auschwitz and the Allies* (New York, 1981): 68.
27. Bernard Wasserstein, *Britain and the Jews of Europe 1939–1945* (Oxford, 1979): 173.
28. Renée Poznanski, *Etre Juif en France pendant la Seconde Guerre Mondiale* (Paris, 1994): 422.
29. For a very different view see John P. Fox, 'How far did Vichy France "sabotage" the imperatives of Wannsee?', in David Cesarani (ed.), *The Final Solution: Origins and Implementation* (London, 1994): 194–214. His answer is: 'quite far'.
30. Fred Kupferman, *Le Procès de Vichy: Pucheu, Pétain, Laval* (Brussels, 1980): 112.
31. See especially Poznanski, *Etre Juif en France pendant la Seconde Guerre Mondiale*: 635–50.
32. Robert O. Paxton, *Vichy France: Old Guard and New Order, 1940–1944* (New York, 1972): 382–3.

–4–

Vichy Studies in France: Before and After Paxton

Stanley Hoffmann

There is a specifically French problem of national memory. France is a nation steeped in history – not because, as in the United States, the beginning is revered as a fundamental golden age whose promises have to be kept, but because of the sense that France was the first true nation-state, yet remains a permanent *chantier*, a continuing construction to which each generation contributes. Hence a paradoxical contrast: in the United States, history is seen as open-ended, and as a story of progress, yet all the developments grow out of the original seeds; in France, history is felt to be much less open, it is shaped or straitjacketed by the double heritage of the Old Regime and the Jacobin state, it can bring progress or regression; yet still, as in the United States, the construction is never finished. As in the case of most other European countries, the past is present because the French live among its legacies, material, like cathedrals, war memorials, museums, castles; and spiritual, in the form of secular and religious rites and celebrations (as David Bell has remarked, the religious and the secular ones are closely related: revolutionary rituals borrowed a lot from Jesuit ceremonies). What makes the French case distinctive even within Europe is the importance of history and of the literary heritage in the school curriculum: the French past and French culture play, as cements of French citizenship and national identity, the role played by the Constitution in the US.

What is also distinctive is the depth, often indeed the ferociousness, of rival traditions: Right and Left, Catholic and *laic* – so that the past is not only the glue of citizenship, it is also a divider. What is good and right for one clan is evil for another. France is One, but the French are split; see the first paragraph of Charles de Gaulle's *War Memoirs*,[1] or the titles of Pierre Nora's monumental *Lieux de Memoire: l'Etat* and *la Nation* are followed by *Les Frances*.[2] Each school of thought has its own reading of the past, each one denounces its own *ancien regime*, each one, under stress, looks for support abroad. But there is one thing of which the French all used to be proud: their ability to overcome their divisions when the Nation was threatened, and to subordinate them to *grandes entreprises* in which crimes and atrocities might occur, but not for petty reasons or mean goals.

With such an attitude to the past, Vichy poses a formidable problem. *This* time, the French did not transcend their quarrels. How to cope with this, whom to blame for it: these are issues that oblige the French to come to grips with what the great historian Jean-Baptiste Duroselle has called *La Décadence* and *L'Abîme*.[3] Moreover, there is the peculiar moral baggage carried by collaboration with the Nazis and accommodation to the Nazi 'order' – phenomena of collective guilt and shame, such as choosing hostages, rounding up foreigners and children, hounding resisters, acquiescing to Nazism. Was this in any way excusable, either by reference to intentions (i.e. was Vichy's main concern to alleviate the sufferings of the French?) or by reference to results (such as the survival of the great majority of French Jews)? And even if one looks for extenuating circumstances, is not there something intractable about the situation of defeated and occupied France? Did anyone have the right to make the kinds of choices a Pierre Pucheu and a Pierre Laval made? But does anyone have the right to keep his hands clean by leaving these decisions to others?

II

The answers to these agonizing questions have, so far, come, as I see it, in four phases. Each 'Vichy expert' has his own chronology, and I am aware of it. Anyhow, here is, in brief, my own reading of the 'Vichy Syndrome'.

The first phase is that of the Liberation and after – 1945 to the early 1950s. The archives were closed, the tribunals were open, the Resistance – external and internal – was in power. The prevailing view was that the Vichy years, as the most prominent prosecutor of Vichy leaders put it, were 'four years to be deleted from our history'. Both the Gaullist pedagogical mythology, which I have analyzed elsewhere,[4] and the equally instrumental Communist one, agreed on a reading of those years that was not encumbered by nuances. The purges were going on, and, especially in the beginning, they amounted to a symbolic (and often quite real) excision of cancer. The French, so went the official story, had been, in their great majority, heroes, patriots, and victims. Vichy and collaboration represented a small collection of evil men – evil either (in de Gaulle's version) because of the original sin of the Armistice, which deprived Pétain and his regime of legitimacy even if constitutional lawyers could assert the legality of the Third Republic's *hara-kiri*, or else, in the version favored by the new political class, because Vichy, however legal its coming to power, had betrayed French confidence by its acceptance of a Nazi Europe and by its attempt to reshape France in a reactionary mold. De Gaulle worried about French self-esteem and about the image of France in the world of Yalta; the Communists had a double interest in making people forget about their behavior from the Nazi–Soviet pact to the German invasion of the Soviet Union, and in purging the French elites that had been compromised, so as to make room for new ones the Communist Party could manipulate. And so, the first reflex – present in the temporarily abundant press of Liberated France – was an easy search for scapegoats, which the trials kept feeding. It is remarkable, in retrospect, to note how little they contributed to the actual history of the period. Laval's trial was, to put it mildly, something of a disgrace. Philippe Pétain's was above all an opportunity for the *tenors* of the Third Republic to exonerate themselves of responsibility for the disaster of 1940.

In this first period, a very small minority of former Vichyites and collaborationists fought back. *Aspects de la France*, the Maurassians' last stand, and Maurice Bardèche, brother-in-law of the 'martyred' Robert Brasillach, denounced their judges by pleading either the best intentions or the least bad results. It was a small defensive operation, which was barely audible in the din of these troubled years.

A second period began in the mid-1950s, and lasted until the late 1960s. Especially after de Gaulle's return to power, the basic script remained the same, but there were some revisions. The prevailing view, of the responsibility and guilt of small cliques, of Vichy as a historical aberration, and collaboration as a tiny disgrace, was partly challenged and softened by the first book that was not just a philippic or a *plaidoyer pro domo*, the *Histoire de Vichy* of Robert Aron.[5] It is not as bad a book as has sometimes been suggested. To be sure, the former intellectual companion of Arnaud Dandieu was an amateur historian, and he relied almost exclusively on *témoignages* – the archives were still closed. But it was a comprehensive effort, and its originality lies in he fact that it was neither an all-out assault nor a whitewash. It does not gloss over Vichy's crimes and stupidities. But the tone is far less vengeful or vituperative than in past years, and two important nuances appear. First, the men of Vichy are seen as being themselves the victims of their own miscalculations, illusions and contradictions; the last words are about *amértume infinie* and sadness. Aron's desire is to still the passions and instill compassion.

Secondly, he spends a great deal of space on the infighting in Vichy, and thus implicitly attacks the prevailing view of Vichy as a *bloc*. In particular, he spotlights the contrast between Pétain and his clan, and Laval and his clients.

These nuances reflect the impact – at a time when the Communists are *les séparatistes* and the Gaullists are both in opposition and in trouble – of a revivified attempt by former Vichyites to defend their record. There are, in fact, two such lines of defense. There are the *Pétainistes*, led by Maître Jacques Isorni and several former ministers, such as Admiral Gabriel Auphan, eager to propagate the notion that Pétain had been France's shield, and that the sword of de Gaulle and the Resistance was little more than a small and a blunt kitchen knife. And then, there was the attempt by those close to Laval to present their man as the genuine defender of French interests against German demands and of the Republican heritage against Vichy reactionaries. The three volumes on *La France sous l'occupation*[6] published by the Hoover Institute and put together by René de Chambrun, Laval's indefatigable son-in-law, constituted a monumental enterprise of rehabilitation. Thus, much more energy was being shown in attacking the vindictiveness and partisanship of the purges (see, for instance, Jean Anouilh's play *Pauvre Bitos*).

Since I am as incapable as false modesty as of genuine modesty, allow me to mention my own fragmented efforts, in this period, to study the France of the war years. In articles collected, later, in *Decline or Renewal?* in English, in *Essais sur la France* in French, and in my contribution to *In Search of France*,[7] I tried to analyze the different ideological currents both in Vichy and in collaboration, to show their roots in pre-Vichy France, to discern their legacy to post-Liberation France, to explain how their tactics led inevitably to the quasi-civil war of 1944, and to distinguish different forms of collaboration. These pieces were completely at odds with all attempts at whitewashing I have referred to; but they also suggested that the official story was oversimplified and that the time for serious research had come.

III

The third period is that of the overhaul of this story, from the late 1960s to the late 1970s. It is a period of turbulence, in which different trends collide. It is, of course, the period in which Robert Paxton publishes *Vichy France* – but not yet in France, the subject of this chapter.

With 1968 begins a phase of debunking and derision, opened by Marcel Ophuls, André Harris and Alain de Sédouy in *The Sorrow and the Pity*, made for but not shown on French television. Elsewhere, I have expressed both my admiration for and my reservations about that indictment of a *bonne conscience* fostered by converging post-war myths, and that attack on the behavior of the French – which had been so little examined until then.[8] There followed a flood of books and movies suggesting that much of France, not merely 'bourgeois elites', had been cowardly or complicitous, that collaboration had been a much wider phenomenon than one had believed before, that the choice between collaboration and resistance was something of a (deeply divided) side-show, and that the 'official' version had been lying, cynical and paternalistic. André Harris and Alain de Sédouy's *Français si vous saviez*, which highlights the French need for an authority figure, who could be either de Gaulle or Pétain, was even blunter than *The Sorrow and the Pity*. Interest in the works of literary collaborationists increased in this period.

The killing of sacred cows was more passionate than scholarly. It had the merit not only of questioning *idées reçues* but also of rudely broadening the scene – from Vichy and collaboration, to France and the French. At the same time, serious research began, based on published sources such as the periodicals of the Vichy regime and its institutions. But it remained handicapped by the continuing unavailability of most of the archives, and by a remarkable lack of curiosity about what might be found in foreign archives. As a result, the first serious scholarly attempt at studying *le gouvernement de Vichy* – the colloquium held in March 1970 at *the Fondation Nationale des Sciences Politiques* and the volume that came out if it[9] – stand in perfect contrast with the wave of non-scholarly debunking that was beginning to rise. By focusing exclusively on non-occupied France, by covering only the years 1940–42, by leaving out not only foreign policy but the repressive aspects of Vichy, the colloquium provoked not only *mouvements divers* from several participants (such as the late Georges Lavau, Annie Kriegel, and myself) but contributed to the notion of Vichy as a 'normal regime'. This presentation of a sanitized Vichy thus broke with the official mythology in a way that was very different from the myth-killers of post-1968; here, the casualty was not the 'myth of the resistance' but the assertion that Vichy had been an aberration in French history. René Rémond in particular wanted to reinsert Vichy into Frances's historical continuity, as an avatar of the Right (or rather of the Rights his justly famous book had distinguished).[10]

A fourth period begins with the publication of Paxton's book in France – or rather with the gradual reconsideration of his book. When it first appeared in French, the least one can say is that the reactions of the reviewers were tepid or hostile, ranging from doubts about the ability of a foreign historian who had not lived through these events to understand the torments of the French in general and Vichy in particular, to doubts about the interpretation he had given to his devastating findings concerning official *collaboration d'Etat* in the German archives: were not all these embarrassing *offres de service* just ploys, aimed at softening rather than at serving the enemy? Some of the organizers of the 1970 colloquium had trouble recognizing in Paxton's criminal, cynical and inept Vichy, the Vichy *de bonne compagnie* so many of the witnesses at the colloquium had presented.

But gradually – and perhaps because Paxton's impeccable scholarship coincides with the wave of debunking – the vision he proposed in his book became accepted. The Paxton and Marrus volume on *Vichy and the Jews* received a far more favorable treatment. What had happened? First, there was the systematic research by the members of the new *Institut d'Histoire du Temps Présent* (IHTP). Their work has gradually covered both the regime and France during the occupation, its accommodations[11] (Phillippe Burrin) as well as its fluctuating public opinion[12] (Pierre Laborie) and its social institutions[13] (Claire Andrieu, and at the *Fondation*, Isabel Boussard).[14] The colloquium that led, a few years ago, to the publication of a comprehensive and comparative volume on Vichy and the French offers a stark contrast with the *Fondation*'s colloquium of 1970.[15] Secondly, a younger generation of scholars with greater distance from the events of 1940–44 was more capable both of doing comparative work, and of escaping from the deadly dialectic of defending the official story (which Henri Michel, at the *Comité d'Etude de la 2e guerre mondiale*, the forerunner of IHTP, had maintained) vs. defense of Vichy's good intentions or achievements.

Thirdly, as a result, there was a change of attitude toward history: from history as emotion to history as a field for investigation (although the new authors recognized that complete detachment was impossible and although not all archives are available even now). Thanks to all this, far greater balance has been achieved. The mass of the French are seen neither as heroes, nor as cowards or *salauds*, but as people concerned above all with survival, and increasingly well-disposed toward the Resistance and de Gaulle. The era of indulgence toward Vichy is over: compare *Au revoir les enfants* with *Lacombe Lucien*. But there are more nuances than in the immediate post-war total rejection.

In this period, four major issues have been debated and partly answered. The first is that of the place of Vichy in French history. It is certainly an avatar of the Right(s), but it has its own Left, and two factors made it exceptional, even for the Right: the circumstances (Nazi occupation and the collapse of the Republic) and the *dérapage* of 1943–4, when the fascist and terrorist factions took over. The second issue is the ideological nature of Vichy: all recent studies have shown its complexity, the differences between the regime itself and the Paris-based forces, the strange alliance between an anti-Communist and pacifist fraction of the Left and conservatives closer to Franco and Salazar than to fascism. The third issue could be called: Vichy, shield or poison? The answer is that even if Vichy's claim to have protected the French better than was the case in the other occupied countries is correct (a very dubious 'if', especially when one looks at French workers in Germany), it was a moral disaster. The fourth issue is that of the responsibility of the French. Another myth needs to be killed: that of the refusal of the French to confront their past. In the past twenty-five years, they have faced it again and again – and the past remains divisive; this has been a recurrent feature in French history, and, in this instance, it also results from the bewildering complexity of individual (rather than group) behaviors. Three recent 'affairs', which I will only mention, have shown this: the Touvier affair, the Mitterrand affair, and the reactions to President Jacques Chirac's final taking of the bull by the horns by recognizing French responsibility (in a complicated way: the state he declared guilty for the first time, the Republic innocent – as before – and the Nation, both). The endless trial of Maurice Papon rubbed salt in many wounds, and provided more agonizing questions than answers.

IV

In a sense, Chirac's rejection of an official history that both de Gaulle and the anti-de Gaulle François Mitterrand had maintained (Vichy was not *La France*, France was the Republic, and *l'Etat français* was not the true French state) is the culmination of the *révolution paxtonienne*. Rarely, especially in France, has a foreign scholar played so crucial a role in changing scholarly minds and public attitudes.

This does not mean that there is now a scholarly consensus. The issues debated, with some passion and even exasperation, by Henry Rousso and Eric Conan in their book about this *passé qui ne passe pas*[16] show that there is still room for disagreement, not so much any more about the facts, or even about the basic ethico-political issues (although the Papon trial displayed again the horrible character and complexity of the choices people had to make), but about how history should be written. For instance, what Robert Paxton and Michael Marrus, as well as Serge Klarsfeld,[17] have written on Vichy and the Jews is now widely accepted.

But a battle is being waged about the historian's perspective. Is it fair to make of Vichy's treatment of the Jews the central perspective on Vichy – a regime for which this was just one issue among dozens, in a nation that remained, at best, profoundly indifferent until the deportations of Jews began in the summer of 1942? On the other hand, must the historian adopt the perspective that was dominant at the time and place he studies? I have my own opinion, but it is that of a political scientist. One has the duty to identify what this perspective was, and how it slanted choices and shaped policies. But one has the right, as a scholar dealing with *sciences morales*, to point out the evils these choices and policies entailed. This is exactly what Paxton did, and I hope he will continue to do so for a very long time. He is a model of responsible scholarship, and an exceptional human being.

Notes

1. Charles de Gaulle, *War Memoirs of Charles de Gaulle* (New York, 1955–60, 5 vols).
2. Pierre Nora (ed.), *Les Lieux de mémoire* (Paris, 1984).
3. Jean-Baptiste Duroselle, *L'Abîme, 1939–1945* (Paris, 1982) and *La Décadence: 1932–1939* (Paris, 1979).
4. Stanley Hoffmann, *Decline or Renewal? France Since the 1930s* (New York, 1974).
5. Robert Aron, *Histoire de Vichy, 1940–1944* (Paris, 1954).
6. René de Chambrun, *France during the German Occupation* (Stanford, CA,1986).
7. Stanley Hoffmann, *Decline or Renewal? France Since the 1930s* (New York, 1974); *In Search of France* (Cambridge, MA, 1963); *Sur la France* (Paris, 1976).
8. Stanley Hoffmann, 'In the Looking Glass', in Marcel Ophuls, *The Sorrow and the Pity: A Film* (New York, 1972).
9. *Le gouvernement de Vichy: 1940–1942* (Paris, 1972).
10. René Rémond, *Les droites en France* (Paris, 1982).
11. Philippe Burrin, *La France à l'heure allemande: 1940–1944* (Paris, 1995), trans. *France under the Germans: Collaboration and Compromise*, trans. Janet Lloyd (New York, 1996).
12. Pierre Laborie, *L'Opinion française sous Vichy* (Paris, 1990).

13. Claire Andrieu, *Le Programme commun de la Résistance: des idées dans la guerre* (Paris, 1984).
14. Isabel Boussard, *Vichy et la Corporation Paysanne* (Paris, 1980).
15. The proceedings of the 1970 colloquium were published under the title *Le gouvernement de Vichy: 1940–1942* (Paris, 1972). For the 1990 colloquium, see Jean-Pierre Azéma and François Bédarida (eds), *Le Régime de Vichy et les Français* (Paris, 1992).
16. Henry Rousso and Eric Conan, *Vichy, un passé qui ne passe pas* (Paris, 1994).
17. Michael Marrus and Robert O. Paxton, *Vichy France and the Jews* (New York, 1981); Serge Klarsfeld, *Vichy–Auschwitz: le rôle de Vichy dans la solution finale de la question juive en France, 1942* (Paris, 1983).

Part II
The Vichy Regime, Collaboration and Resistance: A Reshuffling of Categories

–5–

Collaboration French-style: A European Perspective

Yves Durand

The Vichy regime's collaboration with Nazi Germany is by now well established: Robert Paxton's *Vichy France* was a milestone in establishing the facts. Since then, the examination of Vichy's role in the Holocaust has definitively confirmed the French State's contributions to the Nazi New European Order. Does this mean, however, that Vichy should be presented, as it sometimes is these days, as the sole model, the very paradigm of collaboration in Hitler's Europe? Putting French-style collaboration into a European perspective demonstrates that Philippe Pétain, head of the French State at Vichy, and his circle do not deserve even this honor within the annals of indignity.

Definition of Collaboration: Governmental Choice or Ideological Choice?

We must first specify the meaning and limits of the historical phenomenon we are studying, to avoid an over-broad interpretation that would be unfaithful to the facts. Collaboration must not be confused with cohabitation, the forced contacts imposed during an occupation. Nor is it to be taken as the simple application of contractual agreements between victors and vanquished, similar, for example, to those imposed by the armistice upon the French administration in the occupied territories, where it had to 'collaborate' with the occupying powers.[1]

The lack of governmental authority, leaving only an administration in the wake of invasion and subsequent contact with occupying forces, hardly exempted countries such as Belgium or the Netherlands from attitudes comparable to those found in Vichy-style regimes. All occupied countries faced the problem of administrative collaboration. The 1907 Hague Conventions on the Laws and Customs of War anticipated and accepted this form of collaboration; the occupation of the North of France (and of

Belgium) during the First World War confirmed the Hague Convention's value for the protection of the people in the occupied zones. In 1940 Belgian government administrators were instructed prior to the invasion to continue in the exercise of their functions under the occupier's administrative supervision.[2]

Nevertheless, the holders of mere administrative power have considerable difficulty not going beyond the apolitical roles and functions that are normally theirs, even where no sovereign national political authority exists. Belgium's General Secretaries, leaders of the central administration in Brussels, were neither constant nor unanimous in their resistance to the occupying forces' pressures to make decisions that went beyond their mere administrative role, especially after infiltration of the administration by committed collaborationists like Gérard Romsée. The Belgian case can be seen as that of an administration close to Pétainism, but without a Pétain. There was, however, one fundamental difference: the entire nation was not compromised by a sovereign political representation.

Political collaboration is something quite different. For Pétain and the Vichy regime, it was not a matter of applying the armistice of 25 June 1940; quite the opposite in fact, for it was really Vichy's attempt (if an illusory one) to remove itself from the rules of international law that govern the relationships between warring parties and from the dependency accepted in the armistice, in order to establish with Hitler and Nazi Germany new relations between supposedly 'sovereign' states. This kind of collaboration is clearly a voluntary choice. Certainly the pressures of the situation played a role in this choice; but only a particular interpretation of this situation will lead to collaboration, be it ideological or simply based on a dubious concept of *raison d'état.* Ideology, a dominant factor in the attitude of collaborationists like Vidkun Quisling of Norway, played a less decisive role in the cases of state collaboration of the sort occupying forces adopted. The fact remains, however, that Pétain voluntarily *chose* to collaborate, while other French people (though few, initially) resisted the Occupation, and the majority of the French simply endured it.

This choice of collaboration was already implicit in the signing of the armistice, where France agreed to maintain state-to-state relations with Nazi Germany, seen as the clear victor of the latest Franco-German war. It became explicit after Montoire, an October 1940 meeting with the German occupiers Pétain had requested and voluntarily chose to attend. Afterward, Pétain explained to the French people that he had 'freely' entered into a collaboration that would construct the New European Order advocated by the victor of June. Pétain uttered this key sentence in a speech of 30 October 1940: 'It is with honor and in order to maintain

French unity, a unity that has lasted ten centuries, *within the context of constructing the* New European Order, that I begin today on the road of collaboration.' And Pétain continued to play his role until the liberation of France in August 1944, despite the occasional impulse to stray (notably in the fall of 1943, following the example of the King of Italy and Pétain's European counterparts Admiral Myklos Horthy and General Ion Antonescu).[3]

France Was Not the Only Country Whose Political Regime Collaborated with the Nazi Reich

The Europe of Hitler's New Order included other regimes similar to Vichy, headed by individuals in many ways comparable to Pétain. In Greece, General Tsolakoglou also became head of state following his country's defeat. He signed an armistice with the victors and the German and Italian occupying forces that included a commitment to the New European Order. In Yugoslavia, the Germans in a sense 'invented' and brought to power a 'Serbian Pétain', General Nedic, despite the immediately declared resistance of Colonel Mihailovic's Chetniks and Tito's communists.

Countries that were not occupied but that became satellites, such as Hungary, Romania, and Slovakia, had leaders and regimes that could be considered comparable to the French state and its leader: Admiral Horthy in Hungary, Conducator Antonescu in Romania, and Monsignor Tiso in Slovakia. Like Pétain, they all emerged from the upper echelons of their societies. Politically, they were all traditionalists. Moreover, they all believed that Nazi Germany's domination of the European continent would be long-lasting; hence they accepted it and were willing to adapt to it, for the sake of what they considered the best interests of their countries. Their regimes and policies (domestic policy of so-called 'national revolutions' ; foreign policy of collaboration) rested on traditional socio-political forces representative of their personal backgrounds. These same traditional forces supported policies of the 'lesser evil' in countries like Belgium or the Netherlands, where government bureaucracy remained as the only surviving state apparatus. Denmark, the 'freest' of the occupied countries, kept its king and its legitimate government, but nonetheless collaborated, notably in economic matters and in the fight against bolshevism. On the other hand, we must not forget that Denmark's emphatic refusal to go along with the Nazis' antisemitic policies saved the Danish Jews.

Collaboration in Deed: Participation in the Holocaust

The monstrous project of exterminating the Jews of Europe did, however, strike all the other European nations. The contribution of the police, the bureaucracy and the French State in this project is well known. The Vichy regime's antisemitic laws, arrests and internments, and its handing over of both individuals and their possessions to Nazi control, characterize France's participation – conscious or not – in the Holocaust.

Did Vichy, by accepting and even offering to deport Jewish children as well, allow the Nazis to test the feasibility of massive exterminations in gas chambers, as the Belgian historian Maxime Steinberg and others maintain?[4] However one may choose to answer that question, the fact of the matter is that the extermination of children was indeed always part of the Nazi plan: Heinrich Himmler was explicit on this point. Children were deported from all of Europe: Holland, Belgium, all of Central Europe and the Balkans. In Eastern Europe, well before the opening of the gas chambers, there occurred local exterminations, less 'industrial' in nature perhaps, but no less systematic. In Holland, 100,000 of the 120,000 Jews were deported, starting in 1942. The proportion of Jews deported from Belgium, without any help from the local authorities, exceeded that in France.

Nevertheless, the saving of such a high proportion of French Jews cannot in any way be credited to the Vichy regime. Once again, one must remember the fundamental difference between France and Belgium or Holland; in the latter countries, no formal state power was officially involved in the inhuman enterprise, which only the administrative apparatus carried out under the direct control of the occupying authorities.

Even so, in Holland, a certificate of Aryan status was required of civil servants beginning in October 1940. The large conservative political movement Nederlandse Unie chose of its own accord to exclude Jews from its ranks on 1 November 1941; this was not sufficient, however, to prevent its dissolution by the occupier one month later, on 13 December. The protectorate of Bohemia-Moravia also took antisemitic measures as early as February–June 1939. The Gyula Gömbös government of the mid-thirties put in place a veritable arsenal of antisemitic laws. In Croatia, the double ideological foundations of the Ustashi state – clericalism and racism – were inscribed in 30 April 1941 decrees for 'the protection of Aryan blood and the honor of the Croatian people' against Jews, Serbs . . . and others. And we know the cruelty with which the police and the Ustashi army carried out this full-scale 'ethnic cleansing', with the blessing of the Catholic hierarchy and Vatican approval. In Romania, the early measures of exclusion (from the army) and expropriation were followed by the establishment of a National Center for Romanization on 3 May 1941 (two days after the promulgation of Vichy's second Law on the Jews). The deportation of the Jews in Transnistria took on massive proportions by late 1941.

The French State was by no means alone in having assisted in the deportation of Jews (including children) to the Nazi death camps. Tiso's Slovakia also delivered 'its' Jews; it even agreed to pay a certain amount per person to cover the expenses of their 'settlement' by the Polish government. When the Germans, in August 1941, asked the Slovak government to participate in the 'resettlement' of the country's Jews in the 'General Government,' the nation's leaders eagerly accepted. On 10 September 1941, the Slovakian Diet enacted a Jewish Law legalizing these deportations, which were then organized by the Slovakian government under the supervision of a German representative. The Slovakian government even paid the Reich the sum of 500 RM for each deported Jew to cover the expenses of the 'resettlement'. From March to August 1942, 56,000 Slovak Jews were thus taken to the death camps. The deportation of Slovakian Jews occurred at the same time as the one organized in the neighboring protectorate of Bohemia-Moravia, where the first deportation measures, initiated by Eichmann in October 1939, were interrupted and then revived in August 1941. The Bulgarians protected their 'national' Jews, but handed over to the Nazis Jews residing in territory they annexed from Greece and Yugoslavia (9,000 in the spring of 1943, after King Boris III's third visit with Hitler).

The credit given to General Antonescu for having refused to deliver Romanian Jews to the Germans is based on ignorance of his true motives and amnesia regarding the role of Antonescu's agents in deporting Jews from Bessarabia and Bukovina to Transnistria. Approximately 150,000 Jews from Bessarabia and Bukovina (taken back from the Soviet Union between June and July 1941) were deported to Transnistria, which had been conquered by Romanian troops allied with the Wehrmacht. Some 88,000 Jews perished, either during the transfer (marked by systematic acts of violence, especially at border crossings), or of malnutrition, exhaustion and mistreatment at the deportation sites. There were also massacres of Jews perpetrated locally by Romanian soldiers and police, for example in Jassy, where some 10,000 Jews are thought to have died, victims of an organized pogrom.[5]

Other Principal Areas of State Collaboration: Economic Aid and the Crusade Against Bolshevism

If less terrible in its human effects, Vichy's collaboration was perhaps even more aggressive – in terms of practice and its own initiatives – in economic matters, and specifically in delivering a labor force to the Reich. In that arena, Vichy *publicly* associated itself with the occupying forces: in June 1942, it negotiated the *relève,* an obscene replacement deal that repatriated one French prisoner of war for every three skilled laborers who volunteered to go to Germany; it took legislative action, starting in September 1942, to establish a national basis for mandatory work service. After the *relève* ended, Vichy invented a program called 'transformation', which removed many French POWs from the rules and protections of the Geneva Convention in order to transform them into civilian workers on German territory, subject to the laws of the Reich and under the Gestapo's authority. This 'transformed' status in fact served as a model for the Italian *Internati.*

As early as September 1940, Georges Scapini, Vichy's 'ambassador' responsible for the POWs in Berlin, offered German authorities the replacement of the 1,600,000 French POWs held in Germany by French workers recruited (and paid for) by Vichy. At the time, the Germans refused his offer, just as they refused Scapini's April 1941 offer of transformation.[6]

Laval repeated these offers, which were only put into practice in 1942 and 1943 in response to Gauleiter Fritz Sauckel's labor demands, themselves a reflection of the impact of the exhausting war on the Eastern front on German labor needs. Vichy, this time, accepted the responsibility for providing the labor force requested by the occupier, rather than simply submitting to the occupier's demands. Its propaganda – in the form of lectures and posters – was openly displayed next to that of the Germans. In factories, Vichy's agents, working side by side with those of the occupier, forcibly recruited 'volunteers' for the *relève.* A law enacted on 4 September1942 established what the press at the time called 'mandatory work service' (the *Service du Travail Obligatoire*, or STO). The law's unannounced but very clear goal was 'legally' to force French workers to leave for Germany. The recruitment by age group instituted in February 1943 (a true conscription for work in Germany) only extended a voluntary collaboration by Vichy that aimed to satisfy Nazi needs.[7]

Vichy thus distinguished itself from a country like Belgium, where the occupying forces alone carried out the removal of workers. On the other hand, Vichy's attitude (apart from the originality of 'inventions' like the *relève* cited above) closely resembled other countries under Nazi domination. All of them – whether the Danish government or the Hungarian, Bulgarian, Slovakian, or others – reached official agreements with Germany to provide it with the labor force it required, just as they all linked their commercial and financial relations, and their economies to the Reich's war economy via 'compensation accords' – veritable traps, allowing Hitler's Germany to feed its war machine with various kinds of merchandise, while forcing its partners to pay for the privilege. All these countries also agreed to place their contributions to the Reich's war economy – whether men or merchandise – under the banner of the construction of the 'New Europe' and the 'Crusade against Bolshevism'. We know how Laval defended the *relève* to the French people by explaining that 'without it, bolshevism tomorrow would take hold everywhere'.

In one area, however, Vichy did not go as far as the other governments, including that of Denmark. In France, military engagement alongside Nazi Germany remained the province of the Paris collaborationists. They alone promoted the *Légion des volontaires français contre le bolchévisme* (LVF), notwithstanding the fact that Fernand de Brinon, 'Vichy's ambassador to Paris', associated himself in this endeavor with Jacques Doriot, Marcel Déat, Marcel Bucard and others, and Pétain sent his congratulations to these 'number one Frenchmen!' Not until 1943 did the Vichy government authorize enlistments in the Waffen SS, which the Danish government had allowed as early as 1941. The entry into the Vichy government of two 'honorary officers' of the Waffen SS, Joseph Darnand and Philippe Henriot, marked a step in the evolution of the French collaborator state that paralleled developments in other European states. Denmark's Foreign Minister Eric Scavenius announced on 28 June 1941 the drafting of a corps of Danish volunteers (*Freikorps Danmark*) from the Royal Guard and the army for service on the Eastern Front.[8] On 25 November 1941, Denmark joined the newly 'tripartite' anti-Comintern pact, as had previously Hungary, Bulgaria, Finland, Romania, and Slovakia. Vichy never joined this pact; but then again, the Germans never asked.

Motives for State Collaboration: Ideology vs. 'Reasons of State'

As the Danish example shows, anticommunism provided the most broadly shared motivation for the various collaborating states; the central bond of European collaboration, be it state collaboration or 'collaborationism', anticommunism played a major ideological role.

More difficult to measure was the relative weight of antisemitism, versus the blind following of administrative practices combined with either the cynical or the illusory application of *raison d'état*, in explaining collaboration with Germany's Final Solution. What motivated French officials to urge the Germans to deport children along with their parents in the summer of 1942? This attitude was not the result of native antisemitism, nor of state antisemitism (despite the racist laws of the fall of 1940 and the spring of 1941), nor did it reflect public antisemitic opinion, which was much less widespread than has sometimes been claimed. Similar antisemitic legislation in Hungary, Romania, and Slovakia, often enacted earlier, relied on a far more virulent strain of antisemitism within the population. Vichy's antisemitic laws were mostly greeted with indifference by the population at large.[9] However, the vexations imposed by the occupier, such as the wearing of the yellow star, created widespread disapproval, and Vichy's fear of negative public reactions explains the decision not to extend the policy to the southern zone.

When the persecutions started, denunciations of Jews attempting to escape were largely counterbalanced by the saving of a portion of France's Jews, who certainly owe nothing to Vichy's supposed 'protection'. Rather, France's Jews were saved in part by the indifference, and in part by the spontaneous help, both individual and collective, of numerous French people.[10] George Clare, a young Viennese Jew who fled to London in 1939, the son of one of the directors of the Austrian bank Kreditanstalt, explains in his memoir how his parents, refugees in Paris, made their way to the southern zone, where the local population protected them for a time from a French police sergeant intent upon arresting them, who only succeeded in doing so by operating at night. [11] The narrow-minded obstinacy of this policeman demonstrates two things. First, it clarifies Pétain's fundamental responsibility. Because he believed he had to be faithful to Pétain, the policeman was determined to follow his orders by arresting 'foreign' Jews; he would doubtless have felt less compelled to follow orders had they come directly from the Germans. This episode also reveals the heartless nature of the bureaucratic reflex.

Documents preserved in the archives of the Loiret (the location of two of the principal French internment camps for Jews, Pithiviers and Beaune-la-Rolande) point to analogous reflexes, mixed with more ambiguous motives. Government reports illuminate the terrifying methods used to separate children from their mothers when the Germans demanded that the mothers be deported. Reports also illustrated the difficulties the French authorities encountered in improvising a child-care system as a result of the mothers' deportation. One may wonder if such reports played a role in Laval's request to the Germans that they deport the children as well. But it is impossible to know, fundamentally, if the Loiret's prefectorial authorities were simply acting quickly to rid themselves of the heavy burden of caring for children separated from their mothers, or if, on the other hand (as is implied in the text written by the Prefect, with his 'regrets') they were inspired, unconsciously and perhaps perversely, by a kind of humanitarian reflex.[12]

The Orléans prefectorial authorities, upset at seeing Germans arresting Jews (especially 'French' Jews), asked if this did not constitute a challenge to Vichy's 'sovereignty', which for them – just as for Pétain, Laval, or René Bousquet, Vichy Police Commissioner – implied that French police and security forces should carry out such 'petty' tasks required by the occupier. The illusory search for sovereignty was probably the principal motivation – as well as the one fraught with the most consequences – for state collaboration, not only in Vichy, but in all the countries where a government presented itself as a partner of the Germans.

Were Antonescu's policies, sometimes presented as the very example of what Vichy should not do, really all that different (notwithstanding the direct involvement of the Romanian authorities in the massacre of the Jews in Transnistria)? From the archives, we learn that in November 1941, Romanian Foreign Minister Mihaï Antonescu agreed to have the Jews of Romania deported and 'settled' in the 'ghettos of the East', as had neighboring Slovakia. But the Romanian government subsequently refused the German's repeated requests. A close examination of the sources, however, reveals that hypernationalism, exacerbated by the inextricable dispute with neighboring Hungary, inspired Romania's new attitude of refusal. Only because the Germans had not yet asked Horthy to deport the Jews of Transylvania (assigned to Hungary at the Vienna talks) did Conducator Ion Antonescu refuse to play the sinister game of the Final Solution. We also saw that Bulgaria did not deport 'its' Jews, but did deport those of the Greek and Yugoslavian territories it occupied.

Perhaps Laval was also more willing to sacrifice France's 'foreign' Jews (whose deportation was fictively presented as a settlement in the East to work) at a time when the mass of French people were distressed over the 'deportation' of French workers to Germany. Nevertheless Laval, though often characterized as the French Quisling, was probably, among European collaborators, one of those least inspired by ideology.

In Vichy, as in Bucharest, Sofia and elsewhere in Europe, collaboration resulted less from ideology than from the blind following of reasons of state, attempting an illusory defense of the national interest, sovereignty and unity. Ideology, never completely absent, favored the relationships established with the fascists and the Nazis, who, for the time being, controled Europe. But the secondary role of ideology distinguishes state collaboration from collaborationism.

State Collaboration and Collaborationism Within the States

Ideology directly inspired collaborationist movements that all labeled themselves fascist (sometimes emphasizing the revolutionary qualities of the doctrine, sometimes the ultranationalism that constituted one of fascism's foundations). The distinction between collaborationist movements and state collaboration was not always a clear one, however. Their relationship involved both conflict and agreement.

Everywhere – in countries with no government such as Belgium and the Netherlands, and even in Denmark, which maintained democratic institutions – collaborationists and collaborators found themselves working together on government or administrative teams, which always included, to varying degrees, collaborators out of necessity and collaborationists out of affinity. Even when they remained separate from one another (the case in France until 1944) pragmatic positions or ideological affinities – such as anticommunism or antiparliamentarianism – created links between them in the form of movements combining the two tendencies (as in the *Groupe collaboration* in France).

This cohabitation could manifest itself at the very seat of power. Three kinds of models exist: one – a rare case – characterized by the immediate and constant domination of collaborationism; another – much more common – characterized by a lengthy separation of state collaboration and collaborationism until the end of the regime; and a third one characterized by an alliance in power dominated by the traditionalist state collaborators.

The only country where the local fascists, Ante Pavelic and his Ustashis, immediately came to power was Croatia, detached from the invaded Yugoslavia under the double guardianship of its protectors, Hitler and Mussolini. Even in Norway, where the 'model' collaborationist leader Quisling thought he could take power during the German invasion of April 1940, he was initially kept from power by the efforts of the Reich's ambassador Curt Bräuer. Only in January 1942, a year and a half later, did Quisling become head of state. In Slovakia, the nationalist and religious movement incarnated and led by Monsignor Tiso institutionally associated itself with the fascists, led by Vojtek Tuka. There was only one political party, the H'linka party, led by Tiso, while Tuka controlled the militant wing, the H'linka Guard; within the power structure, Tiso led the state and Tuka the government.

In France, the separation was more clearly distinguished in that it was also geographical: on the one hand, the state collaboration of the Vichy government, on the other, Parisian collaborationism. In Paris, fascists constantly invoked Pétain and Montoire to justify their alliance with the Nazi occupier; in Vichy collaborationism always had its partisans like Jacques Benoist-Méchin, before he officially entered the government in 1944 along with fascists like Joseph Darnand, Philippe Henriot and Marcel Déat. The same model can be seen in Hungary, where the fascist Arrow Cross Movement was consistently kept out of the Horthy regime until 1944. At that point the vagaries of war brought about changes in Nazi alliance policies that had an impact on all collaborating governments and changed the nature of the occupation of Hungary, all of which conspired to bring down Horthy in favor of Ferenc Szalasi, the Arrow Cross leader. The relationship between state collaborators and collaborationists proved especially interesting in Romania. The fascists of the Iron Guard, associated, albeit in a secondary role, with the government of Antonescu when he seized power from King Carol II in the Fall of 1940, then attempted to take over by staging a coup against Antonescu in January 1941. The Iron Guard was defeated, and their leader Horia Sima went into exile, protected by his Nazi friends. The separation was from then on geographical, in some ways similar to that in France, except that Horia Sima never obtained anything beyond the mere shadow of power, and that in Germany, as with de Brinon and the handful of French collaborationists of the Sigmaringen governmental delegation.

State Collaboration in the European 'Fascist Constellation'

The ambiguous relations between collaborators and collaborationists were, in a certain sense, representative of the balance within each country between ideology and the practice of statesmanship. The way in which the two faces of collaboration dealt with Nazi dominance allows us to determine the true place of collaboration in political life and in the relations between states in a Europe subject to German hegemony. Even if they refused, for varying lengths of time, internal alliances with fascist movements within their own countries, all the supporters of state collaboration – Pétain and others – accepted international associations with fascist states. Nazi Germany's military successes from 1939 to 1942 allowed it to extend to all of Europe, not just internally but between states, the system of agreements that Hitler, after Mussolini, established with the traditionalists in his own country, a system that Joachim Fest, the German biographer of Hitler, labels the 'fascist constellation'. Nazi Germany's dominant power allowed a European fascist constellation to develop around it.

In terms of collaboration, the relationship with the Hitlerian master was always essential. His influence was felt even within the internal politics of the fascist constellations, in the relations between collaborators and collaborationists. Another look at the Quisling case proves instructive in this regard. German opposition prevented Quisling from assuming power in April 1940. He took power in the winter of 1941/2, but only after Germany failed to find an alternative solution among Norway's traditionalist political forces, and in response to the German army and economy's changing needs over the course of the war. A closer examination of the attitudes of Berlin's representatives in Oslo clearly reveals the extent to which Quisling's fate depended upon differences of opinion and internal conflicts within the Nazi power structure itself (diplomats, military men, ideologues). In this regard, we know that in France each of the Parisian collaborationist groups depended on the good will, financial aid and influence of its locally-based German supporters (Otto Abetz's embassy backed Déat; the SS supported Doriot, and so on); the same pattern developed in Holland, behind Anton Mussert and Rost Van Tonningen, in Belgium, and in other countries.

The Romanian case demonstrated how the traditionalist Antonescu defeated fascist competitors from the Iron Guard during the winter of 1940/1, thanks to the support of Hitler himself and his representatives in Bucharest. On 14 January 1941, five days before launching the final assault on his fascist allies/competitors, Antonescu met with Hitler as part of the preparation for the German attack on the USSR and got the go-ahead to eliminate the Iron Guard. Having brought his country closely into line with Hitler's grand plan of attack against the hated Soviet neighbor, Antonescu retained Hitler's support until the end, as did Tiso in his struggles with Tuka, and as did Pétain, despite Pétain's occasional tendency to go on a 'power strike' (notably in 1943, after the King of Italy left the 'fascist constellation'), until the Liberation forced him to leave Vichy.

Hitler was intent until the very end upon keeping Pétain – and Pétain alone, far more than Laval – in power at Vichy; just as, to the extent possible, Hitler supported in other countries leaders like Pétain rather than declared fascists, who seemed far less likely to satisfy the German Reich's needs. Those needs included the economic exploitation of the dominated country, as well as the neutralization of the opposition that such exploitation tended to provoke. For this, Hitler required a government in power strong enough to guarantee the passivity of populations subjected to domination and German demands, yet weak enough never effectively to oppose Germany or one day unite the people against Germany in a true defense of national interests, nor even to compete with Germany or speak with it on an equal basis, as might happen, the Germans thought, if a government were to be truly 'renovated' by a national fascism.

In all the traditionally democratic countries, the Germans mistrusted anything that might resemble a single-party system. In the protectorate of Bohemia-Moravia, in the Netherlands with the Nederlandse Unie – whose antisemitism we have pointed out – in France with the *Légion française des combattants*, traditionalist political forces sought to create huge single parties, ill-defined and unitary, to support the work of their representatives in collaborating governments and administrations. The Germans, after brief hesitation, outlawed the first two single parties in the Czech and Dutch territories, and from the outset vetoed the extension of the *Légion française des combattants* to the occupied zone.

In Belgium, following Germany's invasion, Henry de Man initiated a vast alliance of the same sort, political in orientation at first, then trade unionist. He soon gave up, in the light of Germany's determined opposition. De Man's first attempt relied for support on the King's entourage, and focused on the role of the Belgian sovereign. This king, we may recall, considered himself a prisoner, and declared officially that he would abstain from all political activity so long as his country was occupied. This did not however prevent the king from meeting with Hitler. And one may wonder whether he would have been so steadfast in his resistance to reassuming his functions as King of Belgium had Hitler not so consistently opposed it. Why the opposition? Perhaps because, in the case of Belgium, the exploitation, weakening, and partial annexation of the country, divided between Walloons and Flemish, required that the royal function, the sole institutional and spiritual link between the two communities, should not be reactivated.

Nazi Germany's establishment of hegemony over the European continent, the differing modes of domination set up in each country, and Germany's goals together created the conditions for the various forms of collaboration and, to a large extent, determined local attitudes. Whether consciously or not, collaborators and collaborationists were equally manipulated by their powerful Nazi partners. Although Pétain and the Vichy state voluntarily chose to associate with that partner in the international fascist constellation, none of the continent's countries subjected to Nazi domination escaped Nazi partnership. Far better than declared fascists, traditionalists provided the Nazi Reich the services it required.

Conclusion

French-style collaboration had its own set of characteristics, both in terms of state collaboration and in terms of its relations with collaborationism and fascism. Putting French collaboration into a European perspective, however, unveils significant equivalencies with other areas of the continent subjected to Nazi hegemony. A deliberate political choice, collaboration affected many other European countries between 1939 and 1945. By its very nature, the Vichy regime was comparable to those of other collaborating nations of Europe. Each regime, of course, had its distinctive traits linked to the specifics of its national situation. Nonetheless, across Europe collaboration engendered behaviors and acts comparable to those of Vichy. Everywhere, it took on basic common traits.

Analysis reveals the similarity of both the motives for state collaboration, and the very nature of the political authorities who practiced it. Were not all collaborators everywhere subjected (voluntarily and blindly) to hegemony, their fates determined above all by Nazi Germany's initiatives? Everywhere, the Nazi was the master of the game, partner to both the collaborationists and the collaborators, on whom he well knew how to play to further his own ends. On his attitude, above all, depended the position and role of each group within the New European Order Hitler's Germany imposed, with which all chose to align themselves. In the final analysis, the entire history of European collaboration depended on Hitler's Germany. That is certainly why all collaboration presents, in France no more nor less than elsewhere, so many common traits.[13]

Notes

1. Article 3 of the Armistice: 'The French government will immediately invite all officials and all French administrative services in the occupied territory to conform to the rules of the German authorities and to collaborate with them in a proper manner.'
2. The booklet distributed to Belgian civil servants predicted: 'They shall create no resistance for the invader . . . If the occupier requires,

they can make a personal pledge in writing to continue to carry out their duties conscientiously.' On 10 June 1940 Belgium's permanent secretaries signed a draft agreement with Germany recognizing that 'the ordinances decreed by the occupier within the context of The Hague Convention are to be followed as Belgian law'; but also that they themselves might issue 'decrees having the force of law'. Beforehand, on 3 June, the Belgian jurists admitted that 'the permanent secretaries seem to be the best qualified organs of power to entrust in the present circumstances with the exercise of both legislative power and royal power within the limits of the occupied territory'. The quotations are from the remarkable book by José Gotovitch and J. Gérard-Libois, *L'An quarante, la Belgique occupée* (Brussels, 1971).

3. The relationship of the king and the traditionalist Italian forces to fascism is the first example and the model for the 'fascist constellation', which was first internal, then external. In breaking, quite belatedly, with his fascist and German allies in September 1943, Victor Emmanuel III inspired similar attempts on the part of all the traditionalist leaders still in power in all the other satellite countries of the Hitlerian Reich, with the exception of Tiso in Slovakia.
4. Maxime Sternberg has notably published: *L'étoile et le fusil. La traque des juifs 1942–1944* (Brussels, 1987) and *Les yeux du témoin et le regard du borgne: L'histoire face au révisionnisme* (Paris, 1990).
5. Asher Cohen, 'La politique anti-juive en Europe 1938–1945', *Guerres mondiales et conflits contemporains* 150 (April 1988): 45–60.
6. For more on Scapini's 'inventions' and proposals in Pétain's name to the Germans in the fall of 1940 and the spring of 1941, see Yves Durand: *Les prisonniers de guerre dans les stalags, les oflags et les kommandos, 1939–1945,* 2nd edition (Paris, 1994): 197–205.
7. A summary treatment of this topic, entitled 'STO: Vichy au service de l'Allemagne' may be found in *L'Histoire* 167 (June 1993).
8. Scavenius was, within the government, a kind of Danish Laval, first favoring alliance with Germany, but later opposing it. He resigned in 1943 during the great civil unrest when the Danish people opposed new German demands. The head of government in June 1941, the Socialist Thorwald Stauning, supported joining the tripartite coalition, as did Scavenius.
9. See the recent publications of Renée Poznanski: *Etre Juif en France pendant la Seconde Guerre Mondiale* (Paris, 1994); and André Kaspi: *Les Juifs pendant l'occupation* (Paris, 1991).
10. One example: in the department of the Creuse, a prefect (cited by

Marrus and Paxton: *Vichy et les juifs,* Paris: Calmann-Lévy, 1981: 176–7) reported there was considerable latent antisemitism. Yet the Guéret high school sheltered from 1942 to 1944 a sizeable number of young Jewish refugees from the occupied zone, integrated, under their own names, with their boarding classmates without much anxiety (among them, the future television journalist Michel Pollak). Four houses of the *Organisation de secours aux enfants* (OSE) sheltered other Jewish children (including André Kaspi); when the children residing in one of the houses (in Saint-Pierre-de-Fursac, where they interacted with the local children at the public school) were threatened with arrest, they all found refuge during the night with their classmates' parents who lived in the village, and almost all were saved.

11. George Clare, *Dernière valse à Vienne* (Paris, 1986).
12. Prefect Morane's report of 3 August 1941 to Vichy officials states: 'the children will remain in the camps until they are able to rejoin their parents. I shall organize the best I can this enormous child care project, with the help of social workers and public health personnel. I have been given verbal assurances that this separation is only temporary, and that the children should be able to rejoin their parents as soon as the camps they are going to outside of France are fully set up. It must nevertheless be said that this violates a deep instinct . . .'. On the copy of the report in the Loiret archives, Morane initially wrote (then crossed out): an 'eminently respectable' instinct.
13. A more complete and detailed account of the different manifestations of political collaboration in Europe can be consulted in: Yves Durand: *Le nouvel ordre européen nazi* (Brussels, 1990).

–6–

Writing the History of Military Occupations

Philippe Burrin

Andrzej Bobkowski, a Pole who lived in France during the Second World War and left behind a valuable journal of those years, noted on 13 October 1943: 'Today, while discussing current events with a Frenchman, I shyly voiced my concern that this whole period would leave a stain on French history. He then replied very seriously: "This period will never be a part of French history. It will belong to the history of the Occupation."'[1]

For a long time, the most widely accepted interpretation of this period seemed to prove this anonymous Frenchman right. Robert Paxton challenged precisely this notion that the 'dark years' can only be understood within the context of German domination, thus forming only a parenthesis in the history of France, in the research that earned him the prominent position he enjoys today in the historiography of the subject. Paxton's approach has been twofold. On the one hand, he demonstrated the considerable autonomy Vichy enjoyed both in terms of diplomacy and strategy, and the link that existed between its domestic and foreign policies. On the other, he raised the issue of the continuity and/or discontinuity between Vichy and the regimes that came before and after it.[2] And he has done so without denying the Occupation either its place or its weight.

Of course, balancing the 'history of France' and 'history of the Occupation' is hardly an easy task. Clearly, a shift in favor of the first approach has taken place in recent decades. By highlighting the Vichy regime and the French people living under it, historians have significantly extended the boundaries of conventional political and military history. A quick glance at the table of contents from the proceedings of a 1990 conference held in Paris, *Le régime de Vichy et les Français,* highlights the extent of the historiographical renewal that continues to this day.[3] But where does that leave the history of the Occupation? In the past, the

German presence tended to block our view of the horizon. Today, Germany appears as a faint shadow in the background, while Vichy occupies center stage. Yet no historian denies that the major portion of the French population lived under German domination, that the occupation authorities tightly controlled the French administration, that the National Revolution was not taken seriously, and that the Pétain myth carried little weight, at least in the occupied zone. A growing number of French people saw the Vichy regime, to the extent that it could be distinguished from the invaders, as fragile, provisional, and easily dismissed, a kind of makeshift government.

I would argue that this historiographical shift in interest rests on a widespread desire to understand French society of the 'dark years'. The younger generation of historians also feels the need to break new ground in the light of advances in social and cultural history. The result has been the emergence of new areas of investigation – the unity and diversity of the Vichy regime, its support within the population, French society's capacity for autonomy, and so on. The new studies came at a point when the study of the Occupation had become mired in a politico-ideological approach focusing entirely on the collaboration–resistance dichotomy, although this approach was beginning to change owing to the introduction of such notions as accommodation and *attentisme* – the 'wait-and see' attitude.[4] The time has perhaps come for a new approach to the history of the Occupation and, on a larger scale, the history of military occupations in general.[5] I should like to suggest three approaches that researchers might profitably follow within the limits of the European setting.

The first approach would be based not so much on history in the strict sense as on historical sociology, whose comparative nature would allow researchers to break out of the limitations of the national framework that characterizes most of the studies made so far. A look at the various occupations of France since 1815 reveals both how unevenly they have been studied, with the overwhelming emphasis being on the 1940–1944 period, while previous occupations have been largely ignored,[6] and the infrequency of cross-references to earlier and subsequent occupations.[7] Needless to say, this sort of compartmentalization stands in the way of potentially fruitful comparative work. Furthermore, a comparative method, in aiming to establish similarities and differences, requires an effort at conceptualization that may well lead historians to new questions.

Such an approach would also prompt an analysis of the very notion of military occupation and the diverse forms it can take. In this area, international law, which, since the mid-nineteenth century, has been developing the definitions and categories that form the basis of our understanding of the phenomenon, can be most useful. According to theorists of international law, military occupation is a transitional phase between invasion and peace settlement, a period governed by legal rules based upon an exchange of obligations. The occupying forces agree to limit their exercise of sovereignty and respect property and people, while in return the civilian population is expected not to endanger the security of the troops. We all know how twentieth-century total wars upset this fragile balance. The important thing to remember here is that military occupation refers to a phenomenon that is limited in time, as opposed to long-lasting domination of a colonial or imperial nature. In fact, the distinction between the two forms of occupation may not always be so clear to the occupied population. Some people may consider an annexation that is formally legitimate in the eyes of international law to be a prolonged military occupation, a point Maurice Barrès's novel *Colette Baudoche* plainly makes about Alsace–Lorraine after 1871.

International law further distinguishes between two major categories: peacetime occupations and wartime occupations.[8] In the first case, the word 'peacetime' refers to the absence of a legal state of war, and the occupation can take the form of a military intervention to overthrow or restore a political regime (such as the American intervention in Grenada), or can serve as a guarantee. In the latter case, the peace treaty allows for the presence of foreign troops to ensure the treaty's enforcement. The scope of the troops' involvement in the administration and social life of the occupied territory is usually very strictly limited. The occupations of France from 1815 to 1818 and from 1871 to 1875 and that of Germany from 1919 to 1930 fall under this category. In a wartime occupation (we must not forget that an armistice does not end the state of war), the occupying forces replace, to varying degrees, the local authorities; this is what happened to a portion of French territory from 1870 to 1871 and from 1914 to 1918. For easily understandable reasons, historians have primarily been interested in wartime occupations.[9]

Finally, the comparative, sociological approach pushes us to consider factors likely to shape a society's reactions to military subjugation. Such reflection is all the more necessary since occupation policies can vary greatly, as the wide disparity in the occupation policies the Nazis imposed in Europe illustrates, in contrast to the relatively uniform policies of Napoleon and even Stalin. Three important factors must be examined here. First, the occupiers' policies: the extreme harshness of the Nazi occupation of Poland made any voluntary adaptation of the population much less likely than it was in the occupied countries of Western Europe, which the Nazis treated, at least initially, far more gently. A second factor, the occupied society's attitudes towards the occupier, is shaped by memories of previous experiences, by national stereotypes, and also by internal tensions within the occupied society, which can actually neutralize, at least in part, memories and stereotypes, as happened in France between 1940 and 1944. A third factor concerns the available alternatives. The attitude of an occupied people will obviously vary depending on the anticipated length of the occupation, and the identity of potential liberators.

The second approach examines the structural effects of occupation on the occupied society's environment and living conditions. Military occupations usually have a rather short lifespan, ranging from a few weeks to a few years, but their disruptive and transforming effects are nonetheless considerable. These effects have in fact increased significantly over the last few centuries, keeping pace with the dramatic growth in the magnitude of wars. Consequently, wars and occupations present vast similarities whose most significant aspects have inspired numerous studies on topics like daily shortages, economic disruption, and the cultural constraints usually created by wartime censorship and propaganda.[10]

Occupations nevertheless present specific characteristics that derive from their very nature. Essentially, a military occupation involves superimposing over the same territory two sovereignties, or at least two administrations. Such superimposition has much farther-reaching consequences in the modern era than it did in ancient times. While in the past, occupation primarily consisted of ensuring the safety of troops and supplies, something that could impose a considerable burden on the local population, over the past two centuries occupation authorities have become increasingly involved in the occupied country's social life, which has itself become increasingly complex. At the very least, this tendency manifests itself in frequent interference in the occupied territory's administration and in the more or less significant disruption of channels of production and distribution that results from appropriations carried out by the occupying authorities. The tendency toward increasing involvement becomes even stronger when the occupying forces try to lay the groundwork for long-lasting influence or domination. This effort leads occupiers to seek political support by playing on ideological divisions and national weaknesses, to re-route channels of production and distribution toward their country, and to shape public opinion by manipulating education and the media. The Allied occupation of Germany and Japan after the Second World War, with the Allies explicitly attempting to reshape these two societies, probably represents the apex of the trend toward interventionist military occupation.

In general, military occupations in the modern era have rarely had enough time to achieve either deep acculturation or deculturation. One should nevertheless not underestimate their effects. The French revolutionary armies, for example, rapidly brought about durable changes in the judicial systems of the countries they invaded.[11] Even more traditional occupations can have notable effects. Let us consider, for example, the consequences of the division of a country into two or more zones, where a portion of the territory is occupied by one foreign power, or several portions by different powers. Aside from the obvious case of Germany after 1945, it would be worthwhile to look at the divergence of perceptions that emerged in France, on a much smaller scale, between the occupied and unoccupied zones, both in 1914–1918 and in 1940–1942. At least in the first case, the formation of two different collective memories of the war perpetuated for a long time the immediate perceptual divergence.[12]

The third approach tackles the face-to-face interaction between occupiers and occupied people, dealing with both groups on the level of both lived experience and symbolic representation. As far as occupiers are concerned, historians have considered the subject from an administrative and institutional point of view, emphasizing policy. However, there are relatively few studies of the occupying forces as a group – an admittedly artificial grouping of men subjected to rigorous training and rigid discipline, but whose behavior nonetheless reflects their society of origin and the way in which they experience the occupation. On this point, for example, the work of John Horne and Alan Kramer has helped us reach a better understanding of the German atrocities committed in the summer of 1914 in Belgium and northern France.[13] Battle fatigue combined at the time with memories of the snipers of 1870–71, the obsessive fear of mutilation, the soldiers' prejudices – particularly Protestant anticlericalism as revealed by their treatment of priests – and probably also with the anxiety of the German elite, as if the image of snipers stirred up fears of internal social conflict.

Once the invasion phase ends, the occupying forces continue to project their identity and that of their society of origin, in part intentionally – for example through orders regarding the behavior of troops towards the local population – but mostly unintentionally. Consider for instance the way German soldiers treated the inhabitants of occupied northern France between 1914 and 1918: constant house searches; seizures of household items; minutely detailed rules regarding the sweeping of sidewalks and the taking out of garbage; mandatory physicals for women to detect venereal disease; issuance of personal identification cards with pictures and fingerprints; red armbands for all men between the ages of 16 and

60; mandatory saluting of German officers enforced by fines or even imprisonment; and so on.[14] Germany treated northern France as an enormous barracks where the imperial army, a separate world that enjoyed considerable autonomy within the Reich, projected its style and values in the absence of any countervailing force exerted by civilian authorities.

By contrast, and in spite of the mass killings perpetrated during the invasion, the behavior of the German troops in 1940 seemed very 'proper' to many French people, marked by memories of the atrocities of the previous war and by what they had heard about Nazi policies in occupied Poland. In France, the German army's relative 'propriety' stemmed primarily from the army's composition. Having been reduced to 100,000 men by the Treaty of Versailles, the German army rapidly rebuilt itself after 1935 with a rapid influx of civilians. Another factor was the army's unconditional obedience to a political regime that placed a high value on propaganda and manipulation, particularly in the occupied western European countries, as revealed by Nazi hostage-taking tactics in France. Whereas traditionally hostages had always been prominent citizens whose lives were supposed to guarantee that the occupiers' orders would be carried out, the Nazis specifically chose in 1941 to target only Jews and Communists, which enabled them to mollify, if not neutralize, the French elite.

We have only minimal knowledge of how the occupying forces experienced their situation. Better understanding would require studying not only military and civilian administrators – their education, training and knowledge of the country – but also the average occupation soldiers' real-life experiences, their daily routines,[15] their contacts with the local population, their perceptions of the occupied population,[16] and finally, their morale. One extremely revealing statistic, the desertion rate, [17] not only indicates views of how the war was progressing, but also reveals something about the surrounding society and an occupation soldier's chances of disappearing into it.

As for the occupied population, several aspects deserve in-depth study, starting with those phenomena that usually go hand-in-hand with invasions: waves of rumors, generalized suspicions of a 'fifth column' (even before the term, the concept itself was prevalent in 1870[18] as well as in 1914) and, especially, rapes. We know about the heated debates that took place in France during the Great War about the fate of children born as a result of rapes committed by German soldiers,[19] and about the equally strong feelings stirred in Germany after 1919 by rapes attributed to French colonial troops.[20] On the other hand, we know far less about the German population's feelings about the hundreds of thousands of rapes, at the very least, committed starting in 1945 by Soviet troops and continuing for an unusually long period of time. A wall of silence continues to surround this huge trauma.[21] The behavior of Soviet soldiers, tolerated if not encouraged by their officers, clearly grew out of a desire to avenge the humiliation and suffering caused by the German occupation. In the eyes of an invaded people, violated women symbolize the violence to which the nation is being subjected. Each woman's tragedy symbolically re-enacts the invasion of the national territory, and the children born as a result become the unbearable incarnation of this humiliation.

Beyond the invasion phase, at least four aspects of the attitudes of occupied people deserve in-depth study. The first deals with the construction of an image of the occupier and how that image is reinforced or modified. To my knowledge, only one work of this kind has been written. Edouard Koshwitz, a German university professor, wrote at the end of the nineteenth century about the French image of their 1870 invaders, a strange picture composed of 'the German smell', a combination of leather, grease, sweet tobacco, and cheap soap, the guttural sounds of the German language, the gluttony of the troops . . . [22] Koshwitz's work strikingly reveals both the stereotyping that takes place in the minds of the occupied people, and the prominence of those 'markers' long identified in studies on racism: odors, eating habits, sexuality, etc. John Dower's powerful study of the mutual representations of the Americans and the Japanese[23] explains how the Pacific war became a racist war on both sides. The Americans forged their image of the Japanese by blending together the concepts of child, madman, savage, and animal. A similar study of the reciprocal perceptions of the Germans and the French, examining the manner in which these perceptions have changed and partially faded away in recent decades, would be very interesting indeed.

The second aspect has to do with the occupied people's definition of the behavior to be displayed in front of the victors, which could be called a code of conduct. One of the only non-violent weapons available to a defeated population is the passive but determined refusal to give even the merest hint of voluntary acceptance of the *de facto* situation. Of course, the presence and dissemination of a code of conduct does not prevent frequent rule-bending, whether through political contacts or simple compromises.[24] However, the most common attitude occupied peoples display is one of distance. Refusing to acknowledge the occupiers, as when one avoids meeting their gaze, is justified as a form of 'dignity' – in France, the word was used both in 1870 and 1940.[25] It would be interesting to identify the roots of this concept: is it the aristocratic code of honor, popularized by nationalism? The Christian concept of pride in suffering? Or perhaps common social practice, especially among the lower classes – like workers who avert their eyes before the boss or foreman?

The third aspect deals with the emotional reactions of occupied peoples. Two emotions in particular take on enormous importance during an occupation: fear and hatred. Despite awareness of its diffuse and sometimes paralyzing presence, historians cannot easily pinpoint fear, usually inspired by the uncertainties of the present and the future.[26] Hatred, when it does not lead to open hostility, easily transforms itself into morbid thoughts and death wishes projected onto the occupying forces.[27] Hatred can also be directed toward the occupier's friends, those who embrace their cause, help them, or socialize with them. The special stigma attached to socializing derives not only from its visibility and from its perceived crossing of the barrier between 'them' and 'us', but also because it puts into play unspoken prohibitions governing relations between the sexes.[28] Women carry a heavy symbolic weight during an occupation. To men, women's relationships with the victors serve as a bitter reminder of their defeat, and hint at discomfiting changes in established social hierarchies.

The last aspect of occupied people's attitudes goes hand in hand with their emotional reactions: violence, both real and symbolic. Very little has been done to catalogue and analyze the forms, images and targets of violence that emerge within the context of an occupation. In the invasion phase, archaic forms of violence – impulsive, unbridled violence, mutilations inflicted upon the enemy's body, etc. – have become less frequent over time, at least if we compare 1870 with 1940,[29] as if the skills of efficient military killing had finally been learned. During the actual occupation, violence against the occupiers is usually held in check by the seriousness of the consequences; what needs to be investigated is the process that causes it to occur. Between 1940 and 1944, for instance, hatred of the occupiers in France did not translate easily into acts of violence. Certainly, the French Resistance took a long time to go from the 'silence of the sea' to the call to kill the invaders.[30] The tendency to resort to violence çannot, of course, be dissociated from conditions particular to each occupation, and especially from the historical evolution of a given society's relationship to violence and that society's changing thresholds of violence.

On the other hand, it seems to me that the period from 1870 to 1940 has witnessed an increasing tendency to attack one's compatriots. First of all, reprisals against friends of the occupiers are precisely where forms of archaic violence are perpetuated. The attacks on women accused of sleeping with foreign soldiers are rarely deadly;[31] rather, they aim to humiliate and stigmatize the women by means of a popular justice inherited from the past: lashings, forced baths,[32] and headshavings.[33] Second, the greatest violence is often directed against the political allies of the occupiers, as in 1943–4. A serious study remains to be done, but it is very likely that, prior to the June 1944 Allied landing, the French killed more French people than German soldiers. There are even instances where the Resistance executed entire families because one of their members was a collaborationist. But the *Milice* committed by far the worst violence, resorting to torture on a grand scale. Violence against one's compatriots connects occupations to the civil war dimension that probably underlies any situation of occupation in the modern era.

By way of conclusion, let us emphasize that the study of occupations offers a unique perspective on the historicity of political allegiance. Under the *Ancien Régime,* a population's loyalty remained rather superficial, with the exception of the wars of religion. Only fear of punishment upon the legitimate government's return to power kept the inhabitants of an occupied territory from immediately recognizing a new sovereign, especially one that maintained their rights and privileges. The relative absence of collective passion reflected the fact that wars were fought between monarchs, and not yet between peoples.[34]

Things changed in the era of nation-states, when foreign occupations have played an important role for two reasons. On the one hand, an occupation experience frequently plays a central role in the 'national story' constructed by various peoples, in a way that obviously distorts, amplifies or magnifies the actual experience. We know what a formative role Napoleon's occupation played in the awakening of German nationalism, and the Prussian occupation in the awakening of French nationalism.[35] On the other hand, occupations have regularly served as touchstones to determine the depth of a national allegiance that has been subjected to ever-increasing attempts to control bodies and minds, and to a greater sensitivity to deviance. Interestingly, perhaps what changed in France from one occupation to the next, between 1914–1918 and 1940–1944 for instance, was really the threshold of tolerance for deviant behaviors. The percentage of people engaging in such behaviors as working for the occupier or denouncing compatriots may not have been much higher in 1940–1944, but such acts had become more politicized and criminalized, especially given the identity crisis so many French people had experienced.

The study of occupations also shows that political allegiance faces different challenges under different types of occupations. The past two centuries have been, in Europe, the era of national occupations, as exemplified by the occupations of Germany by France and France by

Germany. But at both ends of this period, we find imperial occupations: at one end, Napoleonic Europe, and at the other, American and Soviet Europe. In national occupations, governments usually have no goal beyond weakening their opponent by using such classic methods as taking territory, draining financial resources and limiting the size of the military. National occupations do not normally seek to absorb or assimilate the occupied nation – policies that invariably arouse anger and refusal on the part of the opposing nation.

In imperial occupations, however, not only is the victors' political, administrative, and socio-economic model projected onto the occupied territories, but the defeated countries' elite are also co-opted, often retaining at least a semblance of sovereignty, while the defeated nations are integrated into a global military alliance. The degree of respect and autonomy granted occupied peoples in the process of becoming partners varies greatly, as we know from the simultaneous cases of American and Soviet Europe. At any rate, imperial occupations have the deepest and most lasting impact on an occupied society, which will, in relative terms, more readily accept major changes, especially if the occupiers, for example the United States, exert a certain attraction based on political values or the promise of affluence.

Among imperial occupations Nazi Europe stands alone. Hitler's Germany was unique in projecting onto the continent an imperial domination devoid of any universalist dimension. Its ideology was in fact strictly enclosed within a racial exclusivism that entailed the elimination or expulsion of entire peoples, and the subjugation of all others. By denying both the equality and diversity of these various peoples, it led to policies that make up the darkest chapter of the European book of occupations.

Notes

1. Andrzej Bobkowski, *En guerre et en paix. Journal 1940–1944* (Montricher, 1991): 530.
2. I am mostly thinking of *La France de Vichy, 1940–1944* (Paris, 1973), and of the book written with Michael R. Marrus, *Vichy et les Juifs* (Paris, 1981).
3. Jean-Pierre Azéma and François Bédarida (eds), *Le Régime de Vichy et les Français* (Paris, 1992). For a now somewhat outdated reference,

consult Donna Evleth (ed.), *France under the German Occupation 1940–1944. An Annotated Bibliography* (New York, 1991).

4. See Pierre Laborie, *L'Opinion française sous Vichy* (Paris, 1990), or Philippe Burrin, *France Under the Germans: Collaboration and Compromise,* trans. Janet Lloyd (New York, 1996). On the concept of accommodation, I learned from Chris Lorenz's work, *Konstruktion der Vergangenheit. Eine Einfohrung in der Geschichtstheorie* (Cologne, 1997: 383–4, that the Dutch historian J. C. H. Blom had already called for a *scientifisation* of the history of occupation by going beyond the morally charged categories of resistance and collaboration, in favor of newer categories such as accommodation. This goes to show how much our community of historians remains imperfectly transparent, if only because of language barriers.
5. There exists, to my knowledge, no global historical study of occupations beyond Eric Cariton's unsatisfying work, *Occupation: The Policies and Practices of Military Conquerors* (London, 1991)). On the other hand, numerous international law essays provide historical outlines, in particular Doris A. Graber's *The Development of the Law of Belligerent Occupation 1863–1914. A Historical Survey* (New York, 1949). For a first attempt at a comparative approach on a European scale, see the double issue of *Relations Internationales* (numbers 79 and 80, fall and winter 1994) on 'Les occupations en Europe 1914–1949'.
6. Change is in the air for the 1914–1918 period. See, for example, Annette Becker's *Oubliés de la Grande Guerre. Humanitaire et culture de guerre 1914–1918. Populations occupées, deportés civils, prisonniers de guerre* (Paris, 1998).
7. Works dealing with more than one occupation are rare. Let us nevertheless mention Marc Blancpain's *La vie quotidienne dans la France du Nord sous les occupations (1814–1944)* (Paris, 1983); and Richard Cobb's *French and Germans, Germans and French. A Personal Interpretation of France under Two Occupations 1914–1918/1939–1944*, (Hanover, NH, 1983).
8. See Peter Haggenmacher's excellent summary, 'L'occupation militaire en droit international', *Relations internationales,* 79 (Fall 1994): 285–301.
9. This is striking from a quantitative point of view. The historiography of the Allied occupation of Germany after 1918, as opposed to the post-1945 one, is limited to just a few books. See notably Martin Suss's *Rheinessen unter franzözischer Besatzung. Vom Waffenstillstand im November 1918 bis zum Ende der Separatistenunruben im Februar*

1924 (Stuttgart, 1988) and D. G. Williamson's *The British in Germany, 1918–1930: The Reluctant Occupiers* (New York, 1991).

10. On material life in France during the Second World War, consult issues numbers 32–33 of the *Cahiers de l'Institut d'histoire du temps présent* (1996).
11. Cf. T. C. W. Blanning, *The French Revolution in Germany. Occupation and Resistance in the Rhineland 1792–1802* (Oxford, 1983).
12. On the occupied North, see, for example, Annette Becker's 'Mémoire et commémoration: les "atrocités" allemandes de la Première Guerre mondiale dans le nord de la France', *Revue du Nord,* LXXIV, April–June 1992: 339–54.
13. See in particular their article 'German "Atrocities" and Franco-German Opinion. 1914: The Evidence of German Soldiers' Diaries', *Journal of Modern History*, 66/1 (March 1994): 1–33, as well as their book *German Atrocities in 1914.* Meanings and Memories of War (Cambridge, 2000).
14. See, for example, Blancpain's account in *Quand Guillaume II gouvernait de la Somme aux Vosges* (Paris, 1980) 223 ff.
15. Among rare works on the subject, let us mention Etienne Dejonghe's and Jacques Natali's articles, respectively 'Etre "occupant" dans le Nord (vie militaire, culture, loisirs, propagande)', *Revue du Nord,* LXV, 259 (October–December 1983): 707–45, and 'L'occupant allemand à Lyon de 1942 à 1944, d'après les sources allemandes', *Cahiers d'histoire,* XXII, 4 (1977): 441–64.
16. On the evolution of German soldiers' prejudices towards the occupied people from one world war to the other, see for instance Klaus Latzel's comments in 'Tourismus und Gewalt. Kriegswahrnehmungen in Feldpostbriefen', in Hannes Heer and Klaus Naumann (eds), *Vernichtungskrieg. Verbrechen der Wehrmacht 1941–1945* (Hamburg, 1995).
17. Dieter Knippschild, '"Für mich ist der Krieg aus". Deserteure in der Deutschen Wehrmacht', in Norbert Haase and Gerhard Paul (eds), *Die anderen Soldaten. Wehrkraftzersetzung, Gehorsamsverweigerung und Fahnenflucht im Zweiten Weltkrieg,* (Frankfurt a. M., 1995): 123–38.
18. See Alain Corbin, *Le Village des Cannibales* (Paris, 1990).
19. Cf. Ruth Harris, 'The Child of the Barbarian: Rape, Race and Nationalism in France during the First World War', *Past and Present,* 141 (November 1993): 170–206; Stéphane Audoin-Rouzeau, *L'enfant de l'ennemi 1914–1918* (Paris, 1995).
20. See, in particular, Keith Nelson 'The "Black Horror on the Rhine": Race as a Factor in Post-World War I Diplomacy', *Journal of Modern*

History, 42/4 (December 1970): 606–27; Sally Marks, 'Black Watch on the Rhine: A Study in Propaganda, Prejudice, and Prurience', *European Studies Review*, 13/3 (July 1983): 297–333; Gisela Lebzelter 'Die "Schwartze Schmach". Vorurteile–Propaganda–Mythos', *Geschichte und Gesellschaft*, 1985: 37–58.

21. Cf. Barbara Johr, 'Die Ereignisse in Zahlen', in Helke Sander and Barbara Johr (eds), *Befreier und Befreite. Krieg, Verwaltigungen, Kinder*, Munich, (1992): 46–73, and especially Norman M. Naimark, *The Russians in Germany. A History of the Soviet Zone of Occupation 1945–1949* (Cambridge, 1995), Ch. 2. On the rapes committed by the French troops, see Marc Hillel's journalistic investigation *L'occupation française (1945–1949)* (Paris, 1983).
22. Edouard Koshwitz, *Les Français avant, pendant et après la guerre de 1870–71. Etude psychologique basée sur des documents français* (Paris–Leipzig, H. Welter (first edition Heilbronn, 1884), 1897). See also Marc Blancpain's comments in *Quand Guillaume II gouvernait de la Somme aux Vosges* (Paris, 1980): 206.
23. John W. Dower, *War without Mercy. Race and Power in the Pacific War* (New York, 1986).
24. See Stuart J. Woolf's more generally applicable analysis of collaboration in Napoleon's Europe *(Napoléon et la conquête de l'Europe* (Paris, 1990): 321). See also *Occupants–occupés, 1792–1815* (Brussels, 1969) and, on Nazi Europe, consult Wolfgang Benz, Johannes Houwink ten Catem, Gerhard Otto (eds), *Anpassung – Kollaboration – Widerstand. Kollektive Reaktionen auf die Okkupation* (Berlin, 1996).
25. In 1871, the fountain master at Versailles who agreed to operate the fountains for the king of Prussia was criticized by the town's inhabitants for his 'lack of dignity' (Noelle Sauvée-Dauphin, 'L'occupation prussienne à Versailles', in Philippe Levillain and Rainer Riemenschneider (eds), *La guerre de 1870/1871 et ses conséquences* (Bonn, 1990): 244, Note 44.
26. Fear surfaces in a few diaries, such as the dreams recorded by Michel Leiris, *Journal 1922–1989* (Paris, 1992): 362, 377, 387.
27. Back to Bobkowski, who writes on 1 February 1943: 'All human hatred is concentrated in Stalingrad. It is with very deep satisfaction and extreme pleasure that we talk about the death of thousands of people, and it does not even occur to anyone, including myself, that they, too, are human beings. All of occupied Europe is at the circus and watches in cold blood the atrocities that are taking place in the ring'(*En guerre et en paix*: 405).

28. Such a woman becomes a 'Prussian's woman' (Maupassant, 'Le lit 29', in *Boule de Suif et autres histoires de guerre* (Paris, 1991): 179, or a 'Boche's woman' (in 1914–18 and 1940–44).
29. We again refer the reader to Maupassant's war stories *(Boule de Suif,* cited above).
30. *The Silence of the Sea* is the title of a book published clandestinely during the Occupation by Vercors, a resister. It describes the silence maintained by a French family toward a German officer billeted in their home. Cf. Margaret Atack, *Literature and the French Resistance. Cultural Politics and Narrative Forms, 1940–1950* (Manchester and New York, 1989).
31. According to Marc Blancpain, *Quand Guillaume II gouvernait de la Somme aux Vosges*: 216 ff., 246, some pregnant 'Boches' women' were stoned to death during the 1914–1918 occupation.
32. Werth quotes Alexandre Zévaès *(Histoire de la troisième République,* without page references): 'A few girls who had dared . . . go feast with the German officers [after their entrance in Paris on 1 March 1871] were grabbed by the mocking mob: some of them received lashings on the square, others thrown into the Concorde fountain' *(Déposition. Journal 1940–1944* (Paris, 1992), 17 January 1944: 559).
33. See Alain Brossat, *Les Tondues: un carnaval moche* (Paris, 1994).
34. See Hubert van Houtte, *Les occupations étrangères en Belgique sous l'ancien régime* (Paris, 1930), in particular Vol.1.
35. See Michael Jeismann, *Das Vaterland der Feinde. Studien zum nationalen Feindbegriff und Selbstverständnis in Deustchland und Frankreich 1792–1918,* (Stuttgart, 1992) (translated from the French: Centre National de la Recherche Scientifique, 1977).

–7–

Communitarians, Non-conformists, and the Search for a 'New Man' in Vichy France

John Hellman

I. 1930–1940: 'Young Europe', from the *Sohlbergkreis* to Uriage

The Sohlberg mountain in the Black Forest, from 26 July to 3 August 1930, was the setting for the first large meeting of French and German 'youth revolutionaries' organized by young drawing teacher Otto Abetz. The following October, French alumni organized to meet regularly. In March 1931 one of them, a Russian Jew soon calling himself 'Alexandre Marc', seconded by Gabriel Marcel, another Germanophile excited by the new *Existenzphilosophie* (Existentialist philosophy), circulated the first Manifesto for an *Ordre Nouveau.* They declared themselves to be neither individualists nor anarchists but rather 'personalists',[1] and, like many refusing classification on the classical right–left political spectrum, claimed to be 'non-conformists'. Abetz distributed copies of the manifesto prior to the next Franco-German encounter in August. 'Patriots, . . . not Nationalists, Socialists . . . not Materialists, Personalists not anarchists', these Frenchmen were proudly 'European'. In December Marc, returning from a trip to Germany for Le Corbusier's review *Plans*, was visited by architect Louis-Emile Galey and his comrades Georges Izard and Emmanuel Mounier, wanting to start a non-conforming 'Catholic *Plans*'.[2]

In October 1932 the 'Catholic *Plans*' appeared as *Esprit*, and there, the following March, a fictitious German theologian named 'Otto Neumann' (a *nom de plume* of Alexandre Marc) fused Christianity and revolution into a new 'Catholic' personalism that promised a new sort of human being.[3] Then in Belgium Raymond de Becker's *L'Esprit nouveau* appeared, with its own Catholic communitarian personalism, a sister review to Mounier's *Esprit.*[4] The following May, in Paris, Marc's *Ordre Nouveau* began publishing articles by Nietzscheans, technocrats, and

Catholic activists united in the search for a new politics, a 'new man'.[5] In fall 1933 Marc signaled the remarkable fusing of revolution and Christianity in Belgium, where Raymond de Becker had become a sort of 'Belgian Otto Neumann'.[6]

After the 6 February 1934 anti-Republican riots in Paris, the new Dominican review *Sept* began communicating the non-conforming hopes of Mounier, Jacques Maritain and Marc, as a cohort of young *Ordre Nouveau* 'non-conformists' led by the engineer Robert Loustau joined the *Volontaires nationaux* of Colonel de la Rocque's *Croix de Feu* to steer that large veterans' organization toward the New Order.[7] Otto Abetz then started the review *Sohlbergkreis* to propagate the spirit of his original meetings, signaling the importance of the young French and Belgian 'non-conformists'. A few months later in Paris Emmanuel Mounier presided over a congress of the largely Catholic and Brussels-based *Communauté* movement, with prominent religious thinkers Jacques Maritain and Nicholas Berdyaev in attendance. The Belgians' melding of religion and 'non-conforming' revolutionary politics encouraged the French: from November 1934 *Action Catholique* activist Paul Flamand[8] got *Ordre Nouveau* involved with Catholic communitarian projects like the *Société Saint Louis*, the Le Rotoir commune, the communal Editions du Seuil publishers (and, eventually, under Vichy, Flamand's *Jeune France* cultural organization).

In May 1935 the French non-conformists' delegation to the Italian Fascist Party Congress in Rome, led by *Ordre Nouveau*'s Robert Aron, included Mounier of *Esprit*, L.-E. Galey, now a leader of the renegade Radical Gaston Bergery's new '*Front Social*', Paul Marion, a Moscow-trained propagandist now become proponent of an alternative politics,[9] and the royalist Jean de Fabrègues, a former secretary of Charles Maurras now become leader of the Young Right. Inspired by the new 'personalist' and communitarian language, they now wanted to create a 'new man', and were invited to visit the Duce in his Venetian palace. In June, Bergery's and Galey's *La Flèche* called another general meeting in the dissident Communist Jacques Doriot's Saint-Denis in an effort to transcend the old left versus right divisions.[10] When the Loustau group gave up on the *Croix de Feu*,[11] the *Esprit* co-founder Izard tried to bring them together with Jacques Doriot's communist dissidents, the Paul Marion group and Galey's Bergeryists.[12]

The annual *Esprit* congress in September 1935 reintegrated groups excommunicated under anti-fascist pressure, as Loustau offered to Mounier to set up a *centrale téléphonique* for the coalescing youth movements.[13] In November *Esprit* began publishing a regular chronicle of the 'Third Force' emerging against the nascent Popular Front. Bergeryist leader Galey called an 'anti-fascist fascism' best for France – just as Bergery's so-called 'common front against fascism' was moving in a crypto-fascist direction.

The non-conformists' contempt for the 'game' of democratic politics, their authoritarianism and elitism, were evident on the eve of the 1936 Popular Front elections, when François Perroux, the predominant non-conformist economist, suggested that certain 'personalist' structures of the German national-socialist regime might be imitated by France.[14] In June 1936, Doriot founded *the Parti populaire français,* which attracted 'non-conformists' such as Loustau, who published a book outlining its social doctrine.[15] French and Belgian 'non-conformists' met young Hitlerites on a Belgian seaside estate from 11 to 19 July; Mounier's group there had problems with the general Nazi approach and notion of *Volk*, but admitted '. . . almost complete agreement, real possibilities of collaboration . . . on international affairs'.[16] Mounier's resulting 'Personalist Manifesto'[17] urged Catholics to join non-religious comrades in innovative communitarian experiences.[18] The September congress of thirty-two *Esprit* groups agreed to work with the religiously neutral *Ordre Nouveau* people at creating a new politics to set against the Popular Front coalition.[19]

In November, Raymond de Becker described Belgium's 'new politics' at the University of Berlin,[20] and the Germans were informed about corresponding French initiatives.[21] From January 1937, de Becker was working with Paul-Henri Spaak at creating a movement offering 'enormous possibilities' for producing a 'new Belgian',[22] just as the French Dominican *Sept* popularized a Christianized 'Third Way' communitarianism.[23] *Esprit* founders Galey and Izard joined the French Socialist Party (SFIO) to work for its growing 'non-conformist'/ 'personalist wing'.[24]

During the December 1937 Christmas *Jeune Europe* ski camp in Bavaria, Abetz joined discussions on the future of Belgian youth led by Henri Bauchau of *L'Esprit Nouveau*. The next month de Becker formally announced his and Spaak's Belgian 'non-conformist' communitarian personalism (which had, in fact, become a sort of national-socialism). After an exhilarating visit to a Bavarian *Ordensburg* ('Order Castle'), de Becker left the Catholic Church in December 1938, disparaging his old Catholic comrades.[25]

During the summer of 1939 Abetz, forbidden entry to France, visited Brussels, where the leading daily *Le Soir* denounced his subversive activities.[26] By this time German Foreign Minister Joachim von Ribbentrop's agents in Belgium had already helped undermine that country's will to resist: when war was declared in September, Belgium declared itself neutral, and Raymond de Becker and Spaak published the weekly *Ouest*, subsidized by Max Liebe, Abetz's agent in Brussels,[27] to reinforce neutralist sentiment. While de Becker's profile rose in Belgium, Mounier moved from Brussels to Paris. While de Becker was working with Spaak, Mounier and his people were bringing the circle of non-conformists into coherent working relationships.[28] In July 1938 Alexandre Marc and *Ordre Nouveau* established *Centres fédérateurs* for *Esprit*, *Frontisme* and sister movements to 'network' for the envisioned 'Revolution for Order'.[29] That same month a 'new' *Ordre Nouveau* published articles by right-wing 'non-conformists' from Jean de Fabrègues's *Combat*, 'Frontists' from Bergery's *La Flèche* and anti-Communists from the CGT trade union.[30] After the Munich agreements in October 1938 the militant anti-Nazis in the SFIO prevailed against the anti-war 'personalist non-conformists', who left the party in December, calling for a less truculent approach toward Hitler and 'the radical interior rebuilding of France.'[31]

Despite the mobilization of many of their friends, 'non-conformists' held a secret December 1939 meeting in Paris where Paul Flamand and Georges Pelorson (both to be Vichy youth officials in a matter of months) tried to launch a 'non-conformist' publication. In June 1940, on the eve of the German invasion, a 'new' *Esprit* appeared with contributions from both the new Right and the anti-Communist Left, from the ardently religious and the religiously indifferent. They called for new elites to spark a 'French renaissance'; Mounier wrote an open letter to *Commonweal* announcing the world-wide demise of liberal democracy and the appearance of human persons nurtured by communitarian conditions.[32] The Sohlberg and Belgian seaside bonding heralded the belief that individualism and capitalism, materialism and ethnic rivalries were outdated. German Existentialism was a harbinger of a new European sense of self, a 'new man', rooted in defining community experiences.[33]

II. 1940: Defeat and Occupation in Belgium and France

On 10 June 1940, Otto Abetz invited a group of his Belgian friends,[34] newly liberated from French prisons, to his German ambassador's quarters in Paris. Shortly, confiscated media and new organizations were revitalizing Belgium. Max Liebe, German cultural attaché, found that Spaak had left the country, Henri de Man was self-exiled to France, and Léon Degrelle was fighting for the Third Reich on the eastern front; but he did make Raymond de Becker editor of *Le Soir*, and de Becker's *L'Avant-*

Garde comrade Louis Carette (Félicien Marceau)[35] director of Radio Brussels. The same Henri Bauchau who had advised Abetz a few months earlier began running new youth movements intended to create the 'new Belgian'. On 10 July 1940, as the French National Assembly conferred full powers on Marshal Pétain, Gaston Bergery presented them with a declaration condemning the war as unnecessary, unwise and unconstitutional, and demanding 'collaboration' with Germany and a progressive, authoritarian national and social 'new order' at home. Recognizing a world-wide aspiration toward 'a national form of socialism', urging 'a regime which corresponded with those of continental Europe' for France, the sixty-nine signatories were 'clearly in an indecent hurry to bury the Republic and replace it with an authoritarian alternative'.[36] Several Bergeryists were active in the new Vichy administration (e.g. Galey, Maurice Gait, Jean Maze, Georges Pelorson, Armand Petit-Jean, François Gaucher), although Bergery himself was posted as ambassador to the Soviet Union.

At Vichy, Paul Baudouin, an *Action Française*-style Catholic named Minister of Foreign Affairs, planned the new youth administration with his chief of staff Robert Loustau of *Ordre Nouveau*. Baudouin appointed people who were either Catholics, or non-conformists, or, like Loustau, both. Paul Flamand and Pierre Schaeffer from the *Poitevins* community that had just founded Editions du Seuil created the new regime's umbrella cultural organization, *Jeune France*, as well as *Radio Jeunesse*, with its daily propaganda broadcasts.

The first secretary general for youth, Georges Lamirand, had been involved with the Dominicans. While collaborationists found Lamirand too Catholic, non-conformists saw in him a representative mixture of religious idealism and technical competence. While Pétain mused about founding a *maison de jeunesse* in each French village, Lamirand wanted obligatory *maisons des jeunes* in each canton. Catholics and non-conformists agreed that these youth centers would need new leaders distinguished for ideological commitment and 'spirituality'.

At the same time, Paul Flamand headed the *Jeune France* organization in the occupied zone, aided by the well-known literary critic Maurice Blanchot. They promoted training a pedagogical elite to teach in specialized regional schools spreading communitarian zeal in every corner of France, fostering a new kind of nation, a community of communities.[37]

Radio Jeunesse's co-founder Pierre Schaeffer, who also came from scouting, Editions du Seuil, *X-Crise* and *planistes* circles, discovered Vichy's Youth Ministry being run by a happy mixture of Christian activists and 'non-conformists' charged with 'neither Right nor Left' zeal.[38] So

Jeune France, supposedly founded to produce shows for *Radio Jeunesse*, launched an ambitious cultural movement intended to produce new and better sorts of artists.[39] The new culture promised by the French State would not be pluralistic or fashioned by just anyone: *Jeune France*'s members were to be 'neither foreigners nor Jews', to have been recommended by two sponsors, to have undergone a one month 'trial period', and to have been selected by the administrative council. France's new official culture would be populist but hierarchical, creative but traditionalist, innovative but rooted, Péguyist and communitarian, Catholic and spiritualist.[40]

In December 1941 Schaeffer claimed *Jeune France* had gathered all of France's young artists and writers into a veritable 'community'. Mounier thought that rather than living in ivory towers and being corrupted by rich patrons, artists were experiencing renewed contact with the hard realities of daily life and authentic human emotions, drawing new riches and inspiration from the popular soul. He had already envisoned neighborhood *maisons des arts* transcending 'snobbish [academic] aesthetics' and undertaking 'communitarian projects in which architects, painters, musicians, film-makers, theater directors . . . [would] aspire to a common goal . . . [while accepting] free collective discipline . . .'. His list of comrades to run *Jeune France* included people like the poet Pierre Emmanuel, Jean Grenier, Garrone of the Ecole des Roches, the philosopher Gabriel Marcel, the folk musicologist and historian Henri-Irénée Marrou, the Musée de l'Homme folklore expert François Berge, and Alexandre Marc. A Vichy official described a wholesale *Esprit* takeover of *Jeune France*.[41]

The Pétain government's national leadership school, the Ecole Nationale Supérieure des Cadres, was established in Uriage in late summer of 1940 and staffed by a number of individuals who had been preparing for such a role for years – militant anti-Communists, and anti-liberals, many of them serious Catholics. The new thinking about communities producing 'new men'; the theories of communitarian 'personalism' from the reviews *Esprit* or *Ordre Nouveau* seemed to them a good language for the movement of national renovation,[42] useful for fostering an anti-democratic, authoritarian alternative to the Republic, 'neither Right nor Left' but nurturing the human person. Although many of their friends in Germany[43] had been brutally persecuted by the Nazis by 1936, the French personalists still felt part of a transnational movement with trusted comrades in that country.[44]

In October 1940, on his first official visit outside Vichy, Marshal Philippe Pétain graced the 'Baptism' of the entering class of the leadership school, which the next month moved to the Chateau d'Uriage in the Alps above Grenoble. Uriage, as it became known, began producing instructors for a whole network of new leadership schools forming young people dedicated to the Marshal and to national renewal.[45] Uriage was directed by a charismatic Catholic officer, Pierre Dunoyer de Segonzac; Hubert Beuve-Méry, a recognized authority on Nazi Germany and an admirer of Salazar's Portuguese youth movement,[46] became director of studies.

Beuve-Méry worked out a leadership handbook not unlike that of the Brussels-based *Communauté* group or the new ecumenical community founded by Brother Roger at Taizé near Cluny. In its heyday, from the fall of 1940 to Christmas 1942, Uriage's three dozen or so permanent staff enjoyed government favor, but worried about their lack of peasant and working-class clientele. Impressed visitors, such as Pétain's hagiographers and counselors René Benjamin and René Gillouin, found Uriage, in Benjamin's words, a *Château de l'Ame*; Jesuit Henri de Lubac fused Uriage virility with Christian values, while Paul Claudel read his verse on Joan of Arc to the trainees. The school's publication, *Jeunesse . . . France!,* carried analyses of Italian Fascist youth and of the *Hitlerjugend* by the ethnologist Paul-Henri Chombart de Lauwe. Both *Jeunesse . . . France!* and Uriage's mass-circulation *Marche, le magazine français* condemned the Free French and British military efforts in Syria and at the battle of Suffren, in June and July 1941. Several *Esprit* or *Ordre Nouveau* alumni helped shape its social theory and propaganda organs, and the school had its own men throughout the Vichy apparatus, particularly in administrative positions[47] involving its regional schools: there were eleven in the unoccupied zone of metropolitan France alone, many lodged in *châteaux* and loyal to the 'Mother-School' and its Templar monks.[48]

Segonzac, Beuve-Méry and their men were also much admired in organizations like the scouts and the *Compagnons de France*, or among the young Alpine guides in *Jeunesse et montagne*. The alumni group, the *Equipe Nationale d'Uriage*, under Chombart de Lauwe, helped the school publish training guidelines and doctrinal pronouncements, often texts from the pre-war issues of *Esprit* or *Ordre Nouveau*.[49]

A number of lay figures at Vichy criticized Mounierist personalism, notably youth experts Henri Massis and Jean de Fabrègues. Reappearing as a rival ideologue to Mounier, Fabrègues understandably complained to Robert Loustau that Mounier's fuzzy-minded disciples were over-represented at Vichy. Loustau, too, had an authoritarian Catholic's impatience with 'Mounierism', and sent Fabrègues' views to Pierre

Pucheu, who had become one of most influential of the pre-war non-conformists at Vichy.[50] Certainly Mounier generated enthusiasm among young people; but what was his long-term effect? Fabrègues wanted more state authority and sense of duty. Thanks largely to Fabrègues' initiative, *Esprit* was abruptly silenced, and Mounier was eliminated from his influential positions at Uriage and *Jeune France*. After that, many of the remaining National Revolution non-conformists got involved with Paul Marion's Propaganda Ministry, attempting to make *Idées* (run by René Vincent,[52] director of the regime's censorship services[53]) into a serious and realistic expression of thinking about the nature of the 'new man'. Marion also tried to eclipse Uriage with his own National School for Civilian Leadership Training at Mayet-de-Montagne, 25 kilometers from Vichy.

Although black-listing Mounier, Marion recruited *Esprit* co-founder Galey, director of Propaganda for the *Compagnons de France*, as the regime's Directeur du Cinéma (over Robert Brasillach). Galey became Marion's right-hand man, naming Vichy's propagandists for the occupied zone. Jean Maze, another alumnus of *Esprit* and *Frontisme*, directed the *Compagnons* before he was put in charge of youth matters in Marion's ministry. In general, however, the phalanx of non-conformists around the Propaganda Minister Marion came more from the pre-war royalist/Thomist/*Combat* milieu than the old *Esprit* network.

Jean de Fabrègues' authoritarian non-conformists particularly valued the 'prisoner' communitarianism of Jean Guitton, who wrote *Fondements de la Communauté française* as a basic exposition of Vichy's communitarian aspirations. Fabrègues helped introduce the young right-wing non-conformist François Mitterrand to Vichy, remembering how he had zealously promoted the pre-war *Combat* in the Latin Quarter.[54] Fabrègues and Mitterrand, who spoke together to the important *Chantiers de la Jeunesse* (Vichy quasi-military youth workshops for young men in lieu of military service) meeting in Lyons in September 1942, had both been prisoners of war in Germany, and believed that that defining communitarian experience should be crucial to the National Revolution. Mitterrand recommended creating a new sort of elite in the chivalric spirit of the Service d'Ordre Légionnaire (SOL), or the later Milice, Uriage or la Chaine groups:[55] '. . . militias . . . which would allow us to get beyond our fear of what might come out of the Germano-Russian conflict'.[56]

Right-wing 'non-conformists' like Mitterrand had ties to the secret *Cagoule* organization, several of whose members would become prominent in Vichy's official counter-insurgency force, the Milice. These 'non-conformists' soon began employing brutal methods to enforce conformity to Pétainism.[57]

Ordre Nouveau's Jean Jardin, Pierre Laval's wily chief of staff, maintained some contacts with the French Resistance in London – before he left to manage Vichy interests in Switzerland (where he helped secure a haven for Alexandre Marc). Uriage leader Dunoyer de Segonzac kept in touch with the anti-German (but pro-National Revolution) *Combat* resistance network. There were other secret networks, the La Chaine and Uriage rule-bound orders, and a discreet linking of 'think tanks' whose activities were oriented by an inner circle in touch with a centralized strategy and command posts.[58] Paul Marion's Propaganda Ministry supported the 'white fascism' of Fabrègues as an alternative politics suited to the European New Order. They envisioned France's National Revolution as an imposed, 'top-down' operation geared neither toward raising a mass party nor to a violent seizure of power. A few months were spent establishing institutions that looked good on paper, and that much impressed at least some of their first trainees, but that ran into a host of problems. The French National Revolution was quickly divided by rivalries that led to talk, in the highest government circles, of its 'collapse' as early as August 1941.[59]

The *Grande Fête*, an assembly of as many as 1,500 youth leaders from across France, was held from 31 July to 1 August 1942 on the *plateau d'Uriage*. It was a high point in the life of a school that would be closed down by the Laval government at the end of December 1942. The Milice took over the château, opening its own leadership school, which functioned there until attacked by the Resistance on 5 July 1944. The original Uriage network, organized into a secret Order that excluded masons and Jews,[60] coordinated its activities with Uriage's friend Henri Frenay's Combat Resistance group.[61]

At the liberation Hubert Beuve-Méry and his Order were involved in discussions about what to do with the confiscated facilities of the leading pre-war daily *Le Temps*. Under Beuve-Méry's directorship, the resurrected paper, called *Le Monde*, became 'another Uriage' – with communal asceticism and personalist doctrine. *Le Monde*, Editions du Seuil, and *Esprit* ensured a central place for Uriage people in post-war French life. Veteran non-conformists contributed to the establishment of the Ecole Nationale d'Administration, to François Mitterrand's socialist party,[62] to the new post-war *tiers-mondisme*, and to the European integration movement.[63]

* * *

We have seen how a clandestine pre-war network did much to configure the Vichy National Revolution. The Sohlberg and Belgian seaside experiences transmitted electricity to Paris and Brussels, and inspired hopes of a 'new man' living in a new sort of European community. The initiated discovered a new European sense of self, rooted in defining community experiences.

The early Vichy National Revolution was part of a more general communitarian revolt against individualism and against liberal democracy.[64] It demonstrated the direct continuity between what became the Nazi utopian youth movement and Vichy's aspirations. The Francophone communitarians were convinced that original German national-socialism represented a basically healthy reaction against the modern sense of weightlessness and breakdown of community. They held that national-socialism was not intrinsically perverse: its fusing of ethnic and socialist communitarianism, its 'national form of socialism' was a universal aspiration, as was the search for a 'new man'. After Hitler's follies and the horrors of the Second World War, those who had shared in this hopefulness found it difficult to explain. They tended to rewrite, remain silent about, or completely refuse to confront, much less overcome, their past.

Notes

1. This could well be the first time 'personalism' was adopted as a revolutionary discourse in a document for public circulation in France.
2. Recollection of Alexandre Marc.
3. Marc tricked Mounier by inventing 'Otto Neumann' ('O.N.') to present Marc's own ideas in *Esprit*, but neither Mounier nor his group ever discovered the spurious identity of this 'New man'.
4. In March 1933 Mounier depicted de Becker and Henri Bauchau's new *L'Esprit Nouveau* as remarkably similar to Mounier's own *Esprit* (Mounier, 'Les événements et les hommes', *Esprit*, (6 March 1933) 1027).
5. He published it with Arnaud Dandieu and Robert Aron. Dandieu, a friend of Georges Bataille and considered a genius by his peers, would be dead in a matter of months. Aron would, after the war, publish the first influential history of the Vichy regime – based on first-hand observation and information garnered from *Ordre Nouveau* people at Vichy such as Pierre Laval's administrative secretary Jean Jardin, with whom Aron stayed during his visits there.

6. Cf. the concluding section of Alexandre Marc and René Dupuis, *Jeune Europe* (Paris, 1933).
7. Robert Loustau and his close comrade Robert Gibrat were recruited for the *Ordre Nouveau* movement in 1933 by Robert Aron from *the Centre polytechnicien d'études économiques*, better known as *X-Crise* – a sophisticated discussion and planning group of technocrats with authoritarian leanings trained at the elite *Ecole Polytechnique* (nicknamed '*l'X*' by its students). I am grateful to Jackie Clarke, University College, Cork, for ideas from her forthcoming dissertation.
8. Flamand informed Marc's group that their communitarian personalism was interesting but insufficiently religious. Paul Flamand to Alexandre Marc and *Ordre Nouveau* (24 and 29 November 1934).
9. Considered an expert in a new field, Marion would become propagandist for Doriot's PPF, publishing a book called *Leur combat. Lénine, Mussolini, Hitler, Franco* (1939).
10. On 22 June 1935 *La Flèche* announced a meeting of the new *Front social* to draw in disgruntled former members of the *Volontaires nationaux*.
11. Aron and Chevalley *Ordre Nouveau* minutes sent to Alexandre Marc, 22 June 1935.
12. It was to be called the *Mouvement Travailliste Français*. Cf. Edmond Lipiansky, *Ordre et démocratie* (Paris, 1967): 76; Gérard Brun, *Technocrates et technocratie en France 1918 1945* (Paris, 1985): 39; Hellman, *Emmanuel Mounier and the New Catholic Left 1930–1950* (Toronto, 1981): 314n43.
13. On 17 October 1935 Loustau and Gibrat went to call on Mounier, claiming to have been 'formed' by *Esprit*, and that it should become the 'spiritual laboratory' of their whole generation. Mounier confessed to finding their thinking rather 'elitist', but had already been pondering such a project ('*Entretiens VIII*, 24 October 1935', in *Oeuvres*, IV (Paris, 1963): 576).
14. François Perroux, 'La personne ouvrière et le droit du travail', *Esprit* 42 (March 1936), 881.
15. Robert Loustau, *Justice sociale, économie humaine* (Saint-Denis, 1936).
16. 'Le camp international de Zoute', *L'Avant-Garde*, 16 July 1936. These discussions were not reported in *Esprit* or the *Journal Intérieur* of the *Esprit* groups, as was normal practice.
17. Cf. Mounier to Madame Guittet, 15 August 1936, in his *Oeuvres* IV: 597.
18. For example, that same month Catholic activist Paul Flamand opened

an apartment in the Latin Quarter as the new Parisian headquarters of various communitarian initiatives. Paul Flamand to Alexandre Marc, 13 August 1936.

19. The succession of mimeographed *Journaux intérieurs* of the *Esprit* groups recorded this development.
20. It was reported in Otto Abetz's bilingual, lavishly illustrated *Deutsch–Franzosische monatshefte/Cahiers Franco-Allemands*: 11.
21. Mounier published an abstract of his Manifesto – 'Was ist der Personalismus?' *Monastshefte* XI (1936) – in the same *Sohlbergkreis* in which Abetz recounted de Becker's talk.
22. Raymond de Becker, in Paul-Henri Spaak's *Indépendance Belge*, described 'the enormous possibilities for personalism in Belgium': 'Manifeste au service du personnalisme', *Indépendance Belge*, 21 January 1937.
23. *Sept* followed up its successful issue on communism in December 1936 (110,000), with one on 'Le Christ et l'ouvrier' in February 1937 (150,000). Henri Daniel-Rops of *Ordre Nouveau* contributed a romantic portrayal of Christ as a working person (cf. Aline Coutrot, *Sept* (Paris, 1961): 141).
24. *Esprit* groups' *Journal intérieur* XXIV (March 1938): 5.
25. Raymond de Becker, *Livre des vivants et des morts* (Brussels, 1942): 229. Exiled from Belgium after the war, de Becker wrote several books and articles in a self-analytical mode about his itinerary to self-understanding through his discovery and analysis of his homosexuality.
26. Cf. *Le Soir* 16, 18–21 July 1939.
27. Cf. Francis Bertin, *L'Europe de Hitler* I (Paris, 1976): 154; J. Gérard-Libois and José Gotovich, *L'An 40: La Belgique occupée* (Brussels, 1971): 48.
28. In January 1938, for example, Mounier urged his people to work with Jean Coutrot and his *X-Crise*, with *La Flèche*, with the trade-unionists of *L'homme réel*, and with the *Nouveaux cahiers* people such as Denis de Rougemont, Simone Weil, and Raoul Dautry, head of the railway system, *X-Crise* initiate, and boss of *Ordre Nouveau*'s Jean Jardin. After the declaration of war in 1939, Dautry, the new Minister of Armament, summoned Georges Lamirand, the future youth director of Vichy, and facilitated his becoming director of the Renault factories in Billancourt.
29. Alexandre Marc to Pierre Prévost, 1 July 1936. The *Ordre Nouveau* activist Pierre Prévost played an important role in this initiative.
30. René Belin, *sécretaire conféderal* of the CGT, was the head of the

anti-communist and *munichois* element of that organization. He would serve as Minister of Labor in the Vichy regime.

31. The individuals involved were Izard, Galey, André Déléage, Georges Duveau. Cf. Mounier's review of *Bataille de la France*, *Esprit* 76 (January 1939): 621–2.
32. 'Letter from France', *The Commonweal*, XXXIII 1 (25 October 1940): 11.
33. Mounier's classic essay to launch the *Esprit* project called on his generation to 'Refaire la Renaissance' (the lead essay of the first *Esprit*, October, 1932), and attacked modern individualism in the name of communitarian values. Berdyaev's most influential book in the period was his prophecy of *A New Middle Ages (Un nouveau Moyen-Age*, Paris, 1927) in which a merging of communist and Christian communitarianism would create a new era.
34. Edouard and Lucienne Didier, Hendrik de Man, and Léon Degrelle.
35. After the war Carette would change his name to 'Félicien Marceau', publish a large number of books, and enjoy a distinguished career as an *académicien*.
36. William Irvine, *French Conservatism in Crisis* (Baton Rouge and London, 1979): 208.
37. 'Par la jeunesse, la culture se répandra dans tous les milieux et tous les métiers, par elle se reforgera une communauté nationale': *Archives départmentales de la Gironde, Directives générales du Secrétariat général à la Jeunesse transmises aux préfets de la zone occupée.* This directive is cited at greater length in Michel Bergès, *Vichy contre Mounier* (Paris, 1997): 46.
38. Cf. Roger Leenhardt, *Les yeux ouverts. Entretiens avec Jean Lacouture* (Paris, 1979).
39. For example, a key July 1941 *Jeune France* declaration was ornamented with pre-war Mounierist texts on culture: *Jeune France, Principes, Directions, Esprit* (official statement of *Jeune France* given to Michel Bergès by the head of *Jeune France* in Bordeaux, cited in Bergès, *Vichy*: 52; Mounier, 'Entretiens' (28 July 1941), in *Oeuvres*, IV: 711). I am grateful to Professors Bergès and Jean-Louis Loubet del Bayle for their sharing information on this subject.
40. On the importance of *Jeune France* for the notion of French state culture see Marc Fumaroli, *L'État culturel. Essai sur une religion moderne* (Paris, 1991).
41. Cf. Bergès, *Vichy:* 56, 81–93; recollections of Alexandre Marc.
42. See John Hellman, 'Les intellectuels catholiques et les origines idéologiques de la Révolution nationale de Vichy', in *L'engagement*

des intellectuels dans la France des années trente, ed. Regine Robin and Maryse Souchard (Montréal, 1990): 69–80.

43. Like Schulze-Boysen or Otto Strasser. The manifesto of Strasser's Black Front had been published in *Plans* (10 December 1931) and a long exposition of his positions in three successive issues of *Esprit* in early 1933.
44. Cf. Schulze-Boysen to Claude Chevalley (7 March 1935) (Marc archives).
45. The 'personalism' of Uriage school training is recorded in the dossiers in the school archives relating to school doctrine (*Archives départmentales de l'Isère*, 102 J 12–13). The archives do not reveal the fact that the Vichy government seems to have confiscated the château from its hereditary proprietors in a rather impersonal, even brutal, way. Personalism continued being taught at Uriage until the school provoked the jealous hostility of Pierre Laval, who closed the original school at the end of 1942 as a result of a power struggle for control over youth institutions among members of the Vichy government, allowing the castle's transformation into a leadership school for the notorious Milice.
46. See his book *Vers la plus grande Allemagne* (Paris, 1939) and favorable description of Portuguese youth movements in the Uriage publication *Jeunesse . . . France!* ('Jeunesse Portugaise', *Jeunesse . . . France!* No. 25 (1 December 1941): 6–7).
47. Most of them were in agencies concerned with the training of youth, as is demonstrated by the addresses of the alumni in the Uriage archives.
48. *Archives départmentales de l'Isère* (102 J 142–146: *Ecoles régionales de cadres*).
49. Ibid., 102 J 14–22: *Ecole nationale des cadres: doctrine*; 102 J 23–25: *Ecole nationale des cadres: bibliothèque et documentation.*
50. For more detail see Michel Bergès, *Vichy contre Mounier* (Paris, 1997): 112–13.
51. Hubert Beuve-Méry himself was concerned about this (interview with the author).
52. Vincent had been one of the most original inter-war non-conformists and personalists, as co-founder, with Fabrègues, of the student review *Reaction* in 1929, and a contributor to *Combat* (1934–9).
53. On Vincent's role in employing propaganda to create a totalitarian France see Denis Peschanski, *Vichy, 1940–1944. Contrôle et Exclusion* (Brussels, 1997): 45.
54. In a 1965 interview with Jean Louis Loubet del Bayle, the contents

of which we have only recently learned, Fabrègues recalled that Mitterrand had zealously distributed *Combat* in the Latin Quarter from 1937 to 1939 from the Marists' student residence at 104 rue de Vaugirard. Since Mitterrand provided resistance credentials for Fabrègues after the war, the latter had no reason to undermine the former's reputation.

55. In January 1943 the SOL would be transformed into the Milice. One of Mitterrand's heroes, the romantic mystical Catholic Antoine Mauduit, founded *La Chaine* in the castle at Montmaur with Vichy subsidies – as an Order with a special devotion to French interests and the 'true' Pétain. Mauduit volunteered to fight the British and Free French 'invasion' of Syria.
56. Mitterrand letter (22 April 1942) cited in Pierre Péan, *Une jeunesse française* (Paris, 1994): 187.
57. For examples recently come to light see John Hellman, 'Vichy France/Québec, 1940–1950: Monasteries, *Miliciens*, War Criminals', *The Journal of Contemporary History*, Vol. 32, No.4 (Fall, 1997): 539–54.
58. Henri Azeau and André Ulmann, *La Synarchie* (Paris, 1968): 106–7; Bergès, *Vichy:* 330–1; Alexandre Marc recalled several anecdotes from Robert Aron's wartime *séjours* in Jean Jardin's residence on the outskirts of Vichy.
59. Archival sources cited in Bergès, *Vichy:* 360.
60. The *Archives départmentales de l'Isère* contains a dossier on the Uriage Order that includes provisional constitutions, annexes, and directives (102 J 150).
61. It seems plausible, as Jean Moulin's former secretary Daniel Cordier has claimed, that Henri Frenay, the head of *Combat*, had gone so far as to propose his old friend Dunoyer de Segonzac to succeed the betrayed and assassinated Moulin as head of the National Council of the Resistance. Cf. 'Interview: Daniel Cordier' by Pierre Assouline, *Lire*, No. 169 (October, 1989): 43.
62. For the story of the Left-Catholic contribution to the Socialist Party see Jean-François Kesler, *De la Gauche Dissidente au nouveau parti socialiste* (Toulouse, 1990). Mitterrand made a personal effort to dissuade Bernard-Henri Lévy from attacking Mounier's historical reputation: Bernard-Henri Lévy, 'Fascisme français, je persiste et signe', *L'Evenement du Jeudi*, No. 718 (6–12 August 1998): 40.
63. For example, Jacques Delors, when leader of the European Community, spoke at length of his debt to Mounier on the occasion of a meeting celebrating the 40th anniversary of Mounier's death at the

Lycée Emmanuel Mounier in Châtenay-Malabry, France (30 November 1990). In answer to a question from the author as to the suitability of identifying with a tradition so hostile to American liberal democracy, Delors responded that Europeans were tolerant of Americans but wanted to be themselves.

64. See Zeev Sternhell (ed.), *The Intellectual Revolt Against Liberal Democracy, 1870–1945* (Proceedings of the Conference in Memory of Jacob L. Talmon, 1990) (Jerusalem, 1996.).

–8–

Vichy Singular and Plural

Denis Peschanski

If there is indeed a legacy widely attributed to Robert O. Paxton by many historians who have followed him, it is that, in a certain sense, he 're-naturalized' the French State at Vichy. Far from being a mere antenna of the occupier, as was commonly written when Paxton's work first appeared, he reintroduced Vichy into the national space not, as its admirers had predicted, by integrating it into the vast enterprise of the Resistance, but rather by highlighting the originality of its political and ideological project, along with the connection between this double project and the choice of collaboration. In that same work, *Vichy France,* Paxton devoted a lengthy chapter to distinguishing the various strands that made up the leaders at Vichy, thereby showing that the new state could not be reduced to its project alone.

I intend to explore several areas of investigation in the light of the most recent historical research, whether that research emphasizes the unity or the diversity of the regime, because it is impossible to understand Vichy without grasping it both as a unity and as a plurality, and also without considering how Vichy fits into the larger historical context.

Vichy in the Singular

The Evidence

Although cobelligerence with Germany was several times on the agenda, especially early on, from Laval's plans in December 1940 through to the signing of the Protocols of Paris (allowing Germany to use French bases in Syria against the British) in May 1941, the idea never took hold. The refusal to go to war indeed formed, from 1940 to 1944, a constant of Vichy policy, which for a long time rested on the assumption of Germany's victory and later on the desire to neutralize the conflicting forces. This logic emerges in Laval's 22 June 1942 declaration that he hoped for a

German victory. Although it is often pointed out that Laval went on to weigh the pros and the cons of a Bolshevik victory, a recently-discovered document reveals that as early as the autumn of 1940, at the height of German-Soviet relations, Laval expressed the same hope and offered the same analysis. Indeed, at the end of September 1940, he spoke to several journalists, one of whom was Angelo Tasca, who reported Laval's remarks:

> Journalists talk way too much. And without rhyme or reason. They say that 'President Laval brought nothing back from his trip to Paris.' What do they know? Such comments only favor de Gaulle's movement. But the only people who wish for his triumph are former supporters of the Popular Front (Jews, bankers and Freemasons). It is important to see the situation without taking into consideration public opinion 'which is female'. The desire for immanent justice would make us hope that England alone would pay for the war costs. That hypothesis can be dismissed. So then?
>
> Since an English victory could never be complete enough to be useful to us, we can really only consider two solutions:
>
> a) The best for England – the worst for us: a peace by compromise leaving France to pay the costs of the war.
>
> b) *A total defeat of England* – Everything leads us to believe that this is what will happen, as England is clearly on its last legs. In this scenario the war costs would be borne by both France and England. Therefore, much less burdensome for us.
>
> Conclusion. From a practical point of view, the only policy is to collaborate with Germany. In terms of our wishes, we must hope for a German victory.[1]

Vichy's unity resided, quite simply, in its authoritarian political system. Joseph Barthélemy, Minister of Justice for two years, tersely summarized the change of regime: 'the design of the authoritarian regime is perfectly realized by Constitutional Act no. 2':

> Article 1: §1. The Head of the French State has complete governmental power; he appoints and dismisses Ministers and Junior Ministers, who report only to him.
>
> §2. He exercises legislative power within the Council of Ministers 1) until the creation of new Assemblies, and 2) after their creation, in the event of external tensions or a serious internal crisis, upon his decision alone and in the same manner. In such circumstances, he can decree all arrangements concerning budgetary and fiscal matters.
>
> §3. He promulgates the laws and assures they are carried out.
>
> §4. He fills by appointment all military and civil service jobs where the law has not specified another manner of filling the position.

§5. He has the armed forces at his disposal.
§6. He has the right to pardon and declare amnesty.
§7. He gives accreditation to the envoys and ambassadors of foreign powers. He negotiates and ratifies treaties.
§8. He can declare a state of siege over one or several portions of the nation.
§9. He cannot declare war without the prior consent of the legislative assemblies.
Article 2: All stipulations of the Constitutional laws of 24 February 1875, 25 February 1875, and 16 July 1875 are repealed, being incompatible with the present Act.

This regime's authoritarian quality found immediate expression in an obsession with order that remained a constant from 1940 to 1944. Another constant of the regime, the relationship between the National Revolution and the choice of collaboration with the occupier, lies at the heart of the 'Paxtonian revolution'. The National Revolution was more than simply the framework of a governmental program whose results were quite limited, as we know, by the constraints imposed by the Occupation, the World War, and the varying levels of conviction successive leaders exhibited. The National Revolution provided the new regime with a constitutive ideology, and as such played a major role both in terms of adhesion and cohesion. Furthermore, the National Revolution, rather than being the brainchild of a specific group – the Ultras – during Vichy's early days, must be conceived of as the synthesis of several currents of thought *and*, as Jean-Marie Guillon reminds us, as a process.[2]

As for the choice of collaboration, there is no need to insist here on Jean-Baptiste Duroselle's confirmation via the French archives of what Robert Paxton and Eberhard Jaeckel had emphasized on the basis of their work in the German archives. We simply point out that recent research has stressed a key motivating factor for many of the acts of government officials and senior civil servants: the desire to affirm the sovereignty of the French State over the entire national territory, even if it meant fulfilling the occupier's objectives. This motivating factor applied to repression and persecution as much as to economic and financial matters. A 'Note on French–German economic relations since the Armistice', written in the fall of 1941, clearly illustrates this point.

> One cannot understand the policy followed by those who, for over a year, have been responsible for discussing economic matters with the German authorities if one loses sight of the fact that it is entirely dominated by the desire to maintain the government's sovereignty over the entire territory and the economic unity of the country . . . This attitude is the very reason and

> principal justification for the Marshal's acceptance of the Armistice conditions and for his willingness to remain on French soil despite the enemy's presence.

But as historian Michel Margairaz has written, 'the double submission of the "free" zone to economic control and to supplying the Reich represents the price paid for maintaining the *economic unity* of the country'.[3]

André Lavagne, Deputy Director of Pétain's civil Cabinet, put the matter more bluntly in notebooks that remain unpublished today. On 12 August 1942, he testified to his feeling of repulsion at the round-ups and deportations of Jews occuring at the time, and at the French State's role in this. 'The Germans are acting more or less freely here, although in appearance France maintains a certain autonomous sovereignty and is self-governing. We only dishonor ourselves by being instruments of the Germans. Far better to leave to the Germans the responsibility for carrying out their own decisions'.[4]

The Policy of Exclusion

Despite Lavagne's hesitations not only about racial persecution, but also from 1941 on political repression, Vichy's fundamental policy of exclusion reinforces an impression of its continuity and unity. This has certainly been one of the most heavily researched issues since the early 1980s and the publication of Michael Marrus and Robert Paxton's *Vichy France and the Jews.*[5] By placing state antisemitism into a larger political context, my work, like that of other scholars, confirmed that the policy of exclusion was at the heart of the French State, that it was consubstantial with it. The exclusionary core of Vichy resulted from an interpretation of the defeat that saw its explanation not in military errors or short-term political misjudgments, but in the decay of the Republic, necessarily leading to decadence and hence defeat. To use Pétain's own August 1940 terminology, this rot, this decadence, was the result of a plot by 'anti-France' forces: Communists, Jews, foreigners, Freemasons. There was no point in trying to save the country by fighting the occupier, since the defeat was a symptom and not a cause. The first priority was to regenerate French society from the inside by excluding the 'impure' elements considered to be responsible, and by bringing together the 'pure' elements around such traditional values as work, family, fatherland, order and piety. This analysis explains why, starting in the summer and fall of 1940, and without the slightest pressure from the Germans, Vichy issued exclusionary legislation aimed at foreigners (public services closed to the children of foreigners, a commision to review naturalizations), Communists (the repressive law of 3 September), Freemasons (dissolution of their lodges), and Jews (the first law on the internment of foreign Jews). We are familiar with the ways in which German pressure increased to the point that the French State finally accepted close and official collaboration linking its own policy of exclusion to the policy of extermination, the occupier's new goal, put into effect in France in 1942.

On this subject, the Jewish question has come to play a key role in both the historiography and in the collective memory of the past decade. This has happened in part owing to the marginalization of anti-Communist repression in contemporary thought. Once a major issue, it is now hardly ever brought up. The collapse of the Soviet system is certainly a major factor, preceded and then amplified by the extended crisis of French communism since the late 1970s. Although the French Communist Party has re-established a place for itself in the national political landscape, regaining a measure of appeal if not voting strength, it has nonetheless been subjected to recent and recurrent attacks centering on several key personalities of the French Resistance, such as Jean Moulin or Raymond Aubrac. Although the phenomenon in relation to antisemitic persecution follows exactly the opposite trend, it also results in a decline of memory. The paradigm of Jewish suffering has shifted from Buchenwald to Auschwitz-Birkenau, from Fresnes to Drancy. The recent memory shift is tied, first and foremost, to the importance of the subject and, correspondingly, to its low position among the various forces of collective memory until the early 1980s. Other authors have analyzed this process, pointing out the awakening of Jewish identity at the time of the Six-Day War (1967), the Eichman trial in the early 1960s, the role of Serge Klarsfeld and his judicial, historical and political struggles, and the implications of the 1964 law establishing the imprescriptibility of crimes against humanity.[6]

Today, however, the scale has tipped too far in this direction for us to be able to perceive the Vichy regime in all its complexity. Recent trials, hamstrung by the very limitations of the law, provide almost a caricature of this simplification. Consider the case against Paul Touvier, a Milice leader prosecuted and condemned for crimes against humanity. Thanks to news and media attention during the trial, the Milice found itself portrayed as an instrument of the Final Solution in France. While it certainly was not averse to this kind of work, in fact the Milice was principally an instrument of civil war against resisters. And if one notes that prosecutors changed the charges completely after the preliminary phase of Touvier's trial, in order to conform better with a Court of Appeals ruling, one can only question the pedagogical value of such judicial proceedings.[7]

Avoiding the pitfalls of memory's chronology requires inscribing the French State's antisemitic policies into the larger logic of exclusion at Vichy's heart, delimiting the parameters of the system at work, and – as with any subject – acknowledging the Germans' role, given the extent to which Laval's policies, after his return to power in April 1942, were above all a management of constraints.

Vichy in the Plural

Although I prefer the phrase 'plural dictatorship', Stanley Hoffmann's description of Vichy as a 'pluralist dictatorship' provided us with an expression as striking as it is innovative.[8] It cleared the way for extensive reflection on the diversity of elements that made up the regime, and on the importance of the time factor. One must also take geography into account, or more precisely, the division into zones where the balance of power varied appreciably according to location. As geographical variation has been studied extensively, we shall limit ourselves to a discussion of the first two parameters of diversity and 'plurality'.

The Elements

In his chapter on the leaders at Vichy, Robert Paxton established a basic framework by distinguishing between the experts, the traditionalists, and the Left. Since that time, we have seen deeper analyses in at least three areas: the Catholic scouting movement, 'the spirit of the thirties', and the Vichyist Left.

Thanks to Bernard Comte's thesis on the *Ecole de cadres d'Uriage* (Uriage Leadership School), we better understand the Catholic scouting movement, a meeting-place of sword and holy water.[9] Scouting emphasized themes of leadership, social mission and traditional values (as opposed to secularism, liberal democracy and class struggle) that defined a conservative, if not not Maurrassian, discourse. This movement sought supporters from two breeding grounds that had many points in common, the *Route des Jeunes* (scouts) and the Officers' Social Circles (*Cercles sociaux d'officiers*), which had developed under the Popular Front. We need only recall the colonial activist Marshal Louis-Hubert Lyautey, who not only served as Honorary President of the French scouts when they were established, but was also the inspiration for the Officers' Circles. In the war years, we note the influence of the priests Paul Doncoeur and

Marcel-Denys Forestier (the latter, chaplain of the *Scouts de France* since 1936, became chaplain of the *Chantiers de la Jeunesse*, a quasi-military association of young men Vichy's Youth Secretariat organized as a subsitute for mandatory military service), of officers like commandant Frédéric de la Chapelle and General Joseph de la Porte du Theil, and the major role played by a politician like Paul Baudouin in the early years of Vichy. In fact, Catholic scouting circles' influence peaked between 1940 and 1942, especially in the administration of Youth Services. But for the most part, up to 1944, these men remained equally devoted to Marshalism and Pétainism, that is, to the man himself and to the values underlying the regime, to adopt Jean-Pierre Azéma's distinction.

Historical studies of the 'spirit of the thirties' began earlier and have been more numerous. Without delving into the 1930s, when a complex movement reflecting on the state and the economy coalesced around a shared ideology of rallying around the nation, I simply mention that men coming from this movement were equally likely to become Parisian collaborationists or to join the Resistance, even if most of them flocked to Vichy and especially to the monthly magazine *Idées*. It is symptomatic that the first issue of *Idées*, published under the auspices of Vichy's Information Services, came out in November 1941, the year when Admiral François Darlan headed the goverment. Neither 'synarchy' nor a myth, the Banque Worms 'team' surrounding Gabriel Leroy Ladurie, including a number of important ministers from the Darlan government, shared the conviction that parliamentary democracy was in serious decline, and that France needed both active military and political collaboration with Germany and internal regeneration. The distinctly collaborationist commitments of Paul Marion or Jacques Benoist-Méchin lead us to nuance the break between Paris and Vichy, real as it was.[10]

The Left at Vichy

Although Marion, a member of the French Communist Party in the 1920s, did indeed originally come out of the Left, the fact that from its inception in 1936 he associated as head of propaganda with Jacques Doriot's fascist *Parti Populaire Française* (PPF) makes it impossible to label him a member of the 'Left at Vichy', even if, in terms of political experience, Marion stands well apart from the *Action Française* traditionalists surrounding Pétain's civil and military cabinets. On the other hand, men at Vichy with a background in Confédération Générale du Travail (CGT) labor unionism, the socialists and radicals around René Belin who had generally opposed the Popular Front, clearly belong in the 'left at Vichy' category. A complex alchemy operated that combined the strength of legacies with the weight of exceptional circumstances to impel some members of the pre-war Left to Vichy: the strength of legacies at the SFIO (the French socialist party), for example, where revisionism, pacifism and anti-Communism created bridges with Vichy, although there was no necessary, predestined connection; and the weight of circumstances when the trauma of the Republic's defeat combined with the loss of the instruments of collective reflection.

The collapse of 1940 is of prime importance in understanding the remarkable itinerary of a man like Angelo Tasca, who played a major role in launching the newspaper *L'Effort,* which brought together Vichy socialists in the fall of 1940. Tasca's journey is unusual: a co-founder of the Italian Communist Party along with Antonio Gramsci, member of the Secretariat of the Communist International in 1928 before breaking with Stalin over the German question and the 'class against class' strategy, he made it to France, where, after working for a long time on Henri Barbusse's paper, *Monde,* he played an important role both in the Italian Socialist Party and in the SFIO. He occupied an anomalous position on the political spectrum, challenging the pacifism but sharing the anti-Communism of Paul Faure. Tasca's stupefaction at France's collapse combined with his peculiar political position in the 1930s explains his ambiguous position at Vichy, where he became one of the key people in Information Services. He shared the view of those in power that the solution to the crisis required above all an internal regeneration of French society, and for a long time considered both useful and necessary his contacts with those in the upper reaches of the Vichy regime, and especially with Henri Moysset, a minister and Darlan's *éminence grise.* Yet, beginning in February 1941, Tasca was nothing less than the chief intelligence agent of a Belgian resistance network based in London, to which he furnished detailed reports on the political situation. He did not do one to cover up the other: in this respect, he corresponds very well to the 'Vichyist–resister' label devised in the mid-1980s to describe those who joined the Resistance while remaining convinced that they should and must act in and with Vichy. Tasca clarified his position in these notes from 1946:

> What was the mistake of July 1940? [. . .] I don't recall knowing the exact wording that we argued over just prior to July 9. I do, however, have a very precise recollection of my state of mind: the legal texts seemed to me of no importance; it was necessary to make a clean break from the past and to rebuild from scratch on new foundations. Aside from neglecting the need for a certain

> continuity which no revolution or counter-revolution can do without, our position represented too much of a belief in the value of rupture *per se,* separated from the forces and tendencies that would have to overcome it. As with any revolution, the value of a rupture is the spirit with which it is accomplished; it does not have within itself a lasting effectiveness. [. . .] As to the critique of the past and my idea of national revolution, there is nothing I would change. On the other hand, I was thoroughly mistaken about the means required to achieve the new construction.

Another excerpt, from a letter sent to Bertrand de Jouvenel on 3 August 1940 again underscores the critical importance of that brief moment of collapse in the summer of 1940:

> I would like you to leave Vichy with the impression – which I believe to be justified – that it is perfectly possible to remove the incrustation of the past and give France a thorough cleaning from top to bottom, to change its face and its structures, to integrate France into the new Europe, if we can simply work in relative freedom for a few months. In order to prove movement, we need to be able to walk; in order to walk, we need to have a path in front of us, and not a dead end.[11]

The Time Frame

Two periods have attracted the particular attention of scholars in the last few years: the spring and summer of 1940, and the so-called Darlan year (February 1941–April 1942).

In the months following Germany's launching of war in the west, the trauma of France's defeat combined with the illusion of a *tabula rasa.* It is impossible to understand Tasca's attitude, or Henri Moysset's (his idea of 'the call of the void') or Emmanuel Mounier's toward the new regime without considering the impact of the defeat, so well expressed by Jean Giraudoux's searing analysis of the exodus:

> Everyone can see that it is not so much the fear of invasion that had brought him there, but rather the abdication of each Frenchman in favor of another Frenchman, of each province in favor of another province, the desire to stave off disaster by reaching toward whatever might appear more French than oneself . . . Because Picardy was emptying itself into the Paris region, which was emptying itself into the Beaune region, which was emptying itself into the Rouergue region, everyone thought that the secret was for each Frenchman to merge into another until there remained only one, inaccessible and invincible, who would save everyone.[12]

Pierre Laborie has recently suggested that it is more the memory of the collapse than of Vichy *per se* that has been and remains to a large extent forgotten. Alongside the Armistice of June 1940, a host of organizations materialized that expected finally to be able to carry out their ideas on social, political or economic renewal. Although they came from differing ideological backgrounds, some examples of this tendency include the Uriage Leadership School, Gaston Bergery and Marcel Déat's fight for a single party, and the control of radio news broadcasts by convinced collaborationists. At the same time, the political and ideological policies of the regime were fully congruent with the legislative development of a logic of exclusion and coalescence, which we mentioned earlier.

But the greatest progress has been made in our knowledge of the Darlan year. Following in the footsteps of Robert Paxton, who had inverted the hierarchy by contextualizing the 'Flandin interlude' that followed Pierre Laval's dismissal on 13 December 1940 and ended with Pierre-Etienne Flandin's resignation on 9 February 1941, a period the historian Robert Aron considered key, research has emerged that underscores the principal characteristics of Darlan's year in power, from February 1941 to April 1942, a crucial year that witnessed:

- the emergence in the administration's upper ranks of an administrative and economic-financial elite, who, in the thrall of technocratic illusion, believed they could finally put their long-stifled ideas into practice, now that they were finally rid of the constraints of parliamentary democracy;
- reforms of the police (such as national control of municipal police forces) and of the prefectorial administration (such as the establishment of regional prefectures) that show an accelerated centralization of state powers, as well as attempts by the French State to control all areas of society, such as Information, with Paul Marion, or Youth, with Marion and Pierre Pucheu;
- the height of French initiatives in collaboration. The Protocols of Paris Darlan signed in May 1941 and the advanced negotiations of January 1942, reveal the willingness within certain government circles to go to the point of cobelligerence with Germany;
- a considerable increase in repression and persecution, in order to counter the double threat of the public's increasing rejection of the regime and the French Communist Party's commitment to armed struggle. At the same time, German pressure was increasing in response to the situation in France and the evolution of the war;

- a turning-point in public opinion in 1941. Pétain's awareness of that shift appeared in a speech he gave on 12 August 1941 complaining of an 'evil wind'. Many parameters must be linked to explain changing public opinion. One key factor was the noticeable decline in the socio-economic situation during the spring and early summer of 1941.[13]

Although Vichy went through several easily distinguishable phases, there were not several wholly distinct Vichys. Studies on the 'native' origins of policies of exclusion in 1940 or on the characteristics of the Darlan year have already refuted that traditional view. Along with Philippe Burrin and several other scholars, I reject the notion that there was a difference in kind between the 'first Vichy' and the largely Milice-dominated state of early 1944. Rather, there was a difference of degree, as the regime became more radical in carrying out the repressive policies that were contained within Vichy from the very beginning, with the Milice gaining in aggressivity thanks to German support.

Vichy in Diachrony

Historians always debate the validity of chronological demarcations. Recently, the question of periodization has systematically been asked of those who study Vichy France or France under Vichy rule. Periodization has a definite heuristic value, since it allows us to test, or even to qualify or challenge paradigms; but it is not a way to postulate the specificity of the period being studied. Chronology poses two series of problems. On the one hand, our conceptual tools are not very good, whether we are talking about the rupture/continuity pairing, the archaism/modernity pairing, or the triptych consisting of parenthesis/catalyst/embryo. We shall examine three examples from recent or ongoing research.

Economy and Finance

Considerable progress has been made in the last twenty years thanks to Richard Kuisel, Alan Milward, Henry Rousso, and especially the recent thesis by Michel Margairaz on state financial planning and the economy from the 1930s to the 1950s.[14] The chronological demarcations Margairaz established already offer an initial answer to the questions by placing Vichy in a medium-term perspective. The case is fascinating for the complexity of Margairaz's answers.

In questioning the discourses and practices under Vichy, Margairaz notes that while Vichy's economic discourse was largely archaic, its practices were resolutely modern. If we consider the regulation of supply and demand from a macroeconomic perspective, from a technical point of view, Vichy policy represented a clear break from the 1930s and continuity with the post-war period. Vichy's policy consisted of two components, austerity created by cutting the money supply (the policy forced down demand to adapt it to a limited supply) and an unprecedented degree of state control over the economy. Three groups largely carried out state control: organization committees for each economic sector sponsored by Vichy, the Central Office for the Distribution of Industrial Products (OCRPI), and the Ministry of Industrial Production, all of which were in place by 1940. State control of the economy was all the more obvious in that the Minister of Industrial Production appointed the presidents of the organization and distribution committees. If there was any debate, it was between corporatists and advocates of state control, and was won by the statists. However, corporatist spokesmen like the economists François Perroux or Maurice Bouvier Ajam cannot be placed on the archaic side without running the risk of anachronism.

We note no fundamental changes among the actors, especially at the middle and lower levels. But to speak of continuity is absurd, given that the same men did not make the same policies and that the political and economic context changed radically. Margairaz's analysis leads him to reject the overly facile rupture/continuity pairing and subtitle his thesis 'History of a Conversion'.

There has been quite a bit of interest in these areas of research for some years, for they highlight the importance of the constraints acting upon a given event, the flexibility of the actors, and the weight of the ideological and political context (under different regimes, technically comparable measures have different meanings), and they allow us to establish new chronological demarcations.

The Police

If repression and persecution have been the subject of numerous studies, the police as an institution remains the neglected child in the historiography of the dark years. It could be claimed that this is due to the obvious difficulties, now diminishing, in obtaining access to the documents needed for such a study. But an equally important factor is the relative lack of a tradition of recent administrative history. A collective study is now under way, directed by myself and Jean-Marc Berlière, to fill in some of the gaps.[15]

In terms of structure alone, the war years represented a major turning-point in the history of the police and police forces. The French State inherited a dual system of national police forces (such as the *Sûreté générale*, which became '*nationale*' in 1934, and the *Gendarmerie*, a branch of the Ministry of Defense) and local police forces (municipal for the most part, with the exception of certain large cities like Lyons and Marseilles that had state-controlled municipal police forces, and the very powerful Paris police). A transformation occurred in two steps: a series of laws enacted in the spring of 1941 provided for state control of municipal police in cities with more than 10,000 people, while the national police would maintain order in the country through its Mobile Reserve Groups (*Groupes mobiles de réserve*) (GMR). In 1942, under the supervision of René Bousquet, appointed secretary-general of the police when Laval returned to power, a process of concentration was added to state control when the central administration reabsorbed most of the recently established parallel police forces. Although the context changed completely after the war, there was no going back on this double process of state control and centralization. The 1941 reforms thus marked a major turning-point in the history of the police. These reforms endured because they addressed long-standing concerns of the profession, not because they provided a short-term answer to an exceptional situation. In 1911 *Sûreté* director Hennion called for just these kinds of reforms, which then became the principal demand of the Association of Police Chiefs (before unions were authorized) after the First World War.

At the same time, personnel policies were in some respects surprising. We note, of course, a certain degree of specialization, with the most ardent believers assigned to shock troops (such as the *Brigades spéciales des Renseignements généraux*, in Paris), while the less committed men received more marginal assignments (like the Third Section of the *Renseignements généraux*, in Paris). We also note a spectacular career boost for the most zealous police officers. Finally, the law of 17 July 1940, a sword of Damocles over the heads of all civil servants, including the police, provided for dismissal at will. In actual fact, however, purges of police were very limited under Vichy. The duty to follow orders, at the heart of police culture, imposed a double transgression upon anyone choosing to resist: the act of resistance itself, which, as we know, only a minority of French people chose, and the act of disobedience to the authority of one's supervisors. This duty to follow orders combined with a broadly shared conviction that the struggle against foreigners and Communists represented merely a continuation of police duties carried out during the 'phoney war' and in the years before the 1936 Popular Front. It is against this standard that one must measure the shock (and genuine change) represented by the purges of the Liberation, significant in police circles: purges that challenged the lack of responsibility and thus the impunity associated with the duty to follow orders.

Local Elites

Much like the police, local elites have long been neglected by historians. A recently concluded study at the department level, carried out by several dozen researchers, allows us to take stock of the situation.[16] From the perspective we have privileged in this third part, the common perception is that the dark years constitute a kind of parenthesis, a dual break in French history occurring in 1940 and again in 1944. Two points – at the very least – need to be made, however: the first demonstrating the limits of French State interventionism, and the other suggesting that if there was indeed a significant break, it occurred at the Liberation.

As soon as it came to power, the new regime made known its desire to create new local elites. This found expression in the law of 16 December 1940, which handed over to administration authorities (from the Prefect to the Interior Minister, depending on the size of the city) the responsibility of appointing mayors in cities and towns of more than 2,500 inhabitants. As a result, the southern zone municipalities led by the Popular Front were to a large extent purged. In order to keep in touch with the local population, however, the prefects most often relied on conservative local notables, many of whom had lost their former political positions, especially following the 1935 elections. After his return in April 1942, Laval increasingly sought out former office-holders, for the most part centrist and center–right, who retained some credibility in the population; but he often had difficulty finding what he wanted.

Vichy's initial desire to re-establish control was further limited by external constraints that pushed things in an opposite direction. The availability of men and their willingness to serve had to be taken into account. The gaps left by the absence of 1.58 million French prisoners of war created serious problems, especially in rural areas where the mayors were absent either because they were prisoners themselves, or, more frequently, because the mayor was a prisoner of war's father and had to work the family farm in his son's absence, leaving little time for the increasingly heavy workload at the mayor's office. Managing food, fuel and other shortages made the job unusually demanding, and often put those mayors who remained on the job in an awkward position.

And then there were the Germans. In fact, their attitude did not correspond to the image that exists today in our collective memory, for a simple reason related to their strategic objectives: their priority was to create the conditions for a rational and efficient exploitation of the occupied country, while assuring the security of the occupying forces. The Germans very quickly realized that, for this purpose, it was preferable to rely on traditional, recognized intermediaries rather than Paris extremists or National Revolution ideologues who were cut off from the population at large. Thus can be explained their willingness to engage in negotiations with French Communists in Paris in the summer of 1940. In the context of the Nazi–Soviet pact still in effect, these negotiations provoked the ire of French authorities and were briefly interrupted by an ill-timed Paris police intervention. But Germany's need for efficiency and security applied more enduringly to elected officials in the occupied zone, including the departments of the Seine, Nord, and Pas-de-Calais, although these departments were dependent on different military authorities (the first on Paris, the other two on Brussels). The communists had disappeared from the legal political landscape owing to Prime Minister Edouard Daladier's banning the French Communist Party in 1939, as well as the subsequent dissolution of communist municipalities. But the socialists were still very much in evidence, and like many others, wanted to adopt a 'policy of presence' even though most of them had no sympathy for the occupier and his ideology. The Germans for the most part let them be, which could only be irritating to Vichy's desire for change, especially in the Seine, a department where collaborationists hoped for a measure of official recognition even though Jacques Doriot's PPF could never extend its reach beyond its strongholds in the northeast suburbs.

We cannot therefore speak of a true break in 1940, even when Vichy managed to enforce its desire for control, for there often reappeared at that point traditional notables ready to return to the political scene. If there was a true break, it was at the Liberation, a period of enormous turnover in elected officials, as the generation that had served between the wars largely disappeared, especially in the urban areas, worn down by the struggles of the war and by old age. The Liberation also witnessed significant sociological changes: in rural areas, there was a near-total disappearance of landowners who did not farm their land. In cities and towns, there was a considerable increase in the power of skilled workers and mid-level salaried employees, especially schoolteachers. In this latter case, we must of course bear in mind the influence of related factors, such as the spectacular growth of the French Communist Party and the SFIO. The diagnosis of discontinuity at the Liberation can be qualified, however, by considering the process of feminization that was just starting, the instances of reclassification (even the RPF upheaval in 1947 needs to be qualified), or aspects of the political structure. The diagnosis of discontinuity, or the limits one would place on that diagnosis, also require that considerable geographic variation be taken into account.

The three areas that we have all-too-rapidly explored illustrate a new relationship to this history. We no longer assume the specificity of the Vichy years; instead, the chronological shackles are thrown off, and even with the possibility of re-establishing that chronological specificity within a broader perpective, more often than not a different tempo emerges, punctuated by different breaks. Likewise, the usefulness of the rupture/continuity model must be re-evaluated to avoid oversimplification.

To this broadening of the historian's territory, we must add the historiographical change that occurred in two stages, as the focus shifted from the state to society, from Vichy France to France *under* Vichy: first the 1980 publication of Pierre Laborie's thesis on public opinion, and second the 1990 conference on 'Vichy and the French People'.[17] Necessarily, other questions will emerge, other temporalities will be brought to light. Rather than ending reflection on the fundamental unity of the regime, this enriches it.

Notes

1. 'Déclaration à la presse de Pierre Laval', quoted in the annexe to notebook B of Angelo Tasca, quoted in David Bidussa and Denis Peschanski (eds), *La France de Vichy. Archives inédites d'Angelo Tasca,* Annali Feltrinelli no. 31 (Milan, 1996): 160.
2. Jean-Marie Guillon, 'La Philosophie de la Révolution nationale', in Jean-Pierre Azéma and François Bédarida (eds) in collaboration with Denis Peschanski and Henry Rousso, *Le Régime de Vichy et les Français* (Paris, 1992): 167–83.
3. 'Note sur les rapports économiques franco-allemands depuis l'armistice', National archives F37 20, and Michel Margairaz, *L'État, la direction des finances et l'économie en France 1932–1952. Histoire d'une conversion,* doctorat d'Etat (Paris, 1991): 57.
4. André Lavagne, Notebooks, 12 August 1942, Archives Nationales. His notebooks refer on several occasions to his rejection of this policy, but also to his inability to convince others in the upper echelons of the regime of his view, despite his credentials as solid Pétainist and militant Catholic with an *Action Française* background.

5. Michael Marrus and Robert Paxton, *Vichy et les Juifs* (Paris, 1981); Serge Klarsfeld, *Vichy–Auschwitz,* Paris, 2 vols, 1983 and 1985. More recently, see the survey by Renée Poznanski, *Les Juifs en France pendant la Seconde Guerre mondiale* (2nd edn) (Paris, 1996).
6. See Henry Rousso, *Le Syndrome de Vichy* (1st edn) (Paris, 1987); Annette Wieviorka, *Déportation et génocide. Entre la mémoire et l'oubli* (Paris, 1992).
7. On the Touvier trial, see the chapters in Eric Conan and Henry Rousso, *Vichy, un passé qui ne passe pas* (Paris, 1994) (2nd edn 1996, Folio, Gallimard).
8. Stanley Hoffmann, article in the *Revue française de science politique,* 1966, and reprinted in his collection *Essais sur la France. Déclin ou renouveau?* (Paris, 1974).
9. Bernard Comte, *L'Utopie combattante. L'Ecole des cadres d'Uriage 1940–1942,* (Paris, 1991).
10. Jean-Louis Loubet del Bayle, *Les non-conformistes des années 30* (Paris, 1969). See also Philippe Burrin, *La Dérive fasciste* (Paris, 1987), especially the chapter entitled 'La France dans le champ magnétique des fascismes'. The memoirs of Benoist-Méchin (*De la Défaite au désastre* (Paris, 1984–1985), 2 vols) and the memoirs of Drieu la Rochelle (*Journal 1939–1945* (Paris, 1992) – and see also Robert O. Paxton's preface to *Fragments de mémoires 1940–1941* (Paris, 1982) and the war journals of Tasca (published in two installments, in 1986 *Vichy 1940–1944. Archives de guerre d'Angelo Tasca*, ed. D. Peschanski, Milan/Paris: Feltrinelli Ed. and Editions du CNRS; and *La France de Vichy. Archives inédites d'Angelo Tasca,* ed. David Bidussa et D. Peschanski (Milan: Feltrinelli Ed., 1996) – have contributed to a better understanding of the group. For the Information Ministry, see Philippe Amaury, *Les Deux premières expériences d'un 'ministère de l'Information' en France* (Paris: LGDJ, 1969); my article entitled 'Vichy au singulier, Vichy au pluriel. Une tentative avortée d'encadrement total de la société 1941–1942' in *Annales ESC,* no. 3, 1988: 632–61; and an approach to the issue as it relates to the entire period, collected in *Vichy 1940–1944. Contrôle et exclusion* (Brussels, 1997): 39–58.
11. Angelo Tasca, Quaderno XV (1946): 59–61, and Quaderno A, 8, quoted in *La France de Vichy. Archives de guerre d'Angelo Tasca.* (Also included, aside from the 1940–42 notebooks, are an article by David Bidussa on Tasca during the war, and another by Laurent Douzou and Denis Peschanski on 'La Résistance face à l'hypothèque

Vichy'.) I had proposed the term 'Vichyist-resister' in the first volume of Tasca's war archives (see above).

12. Jean Giraudoux, *De pleins pouvoirs à sans pouvoirs* (Paris, 1950).
13. On the economy, see Michel Margairaz, *L'Etat, les finances et l'économie en France 1932–1952. Histoire d'une conversion* (Paris, 2 vols, 1991); on public opinion, see Pierre Laborie, *L'Opinion française sous Vichy* (Paris, 1990).
14. Richard F. Kuisel, *Le Capitalisme et l'Etat en France: modernisation et dirigisme en France au XXe siècle* (Paris, 1984); Alan Milward, *The New Order and the French Economy* (Oxford, 1970); Alain Beltran, Robert Frank and Henry Rousso, *La Vie des entreprises sous l'Occupation* (Paris, 1994); and Michel Margairaz, *L'état, les finances et l'économie.*
15. This is an investigation by departmental correspondents that culminated in a final meeting in December 1998, to be published by La Documentation française under the title *La police française entre bouleversements et permanences (1930–1960).*
16. An investigation by departmental correspondents of the Institut d'histoire du temps présent, led by Gilles le Béguec and Denis Peschanski, to be published by CNRS-Editions under the title *Les élites locales en France dans la tourmente. Du Front populaire aux années 1950.*
17. Pierre Laborie, *Résistants, vichyssois et autres. L'Evolution de l'opinion et des comportements dans le Lot de 1939 à 1944* (Paris, 1980); and Jean-Pierre Azéma and François Bédarida (eds), *Vichy et les Français* (Paris, 1990). See also the work of Dominique Veillon on everyday life, *Vivre et Survivre au quotidien* (Paris, 1995). My chapter was written before the publication of Marc-Olivier Baruch's *Servir l'Etat français* (Paris, 1997), an essential contribution to the history of Vichy France and of France under Vichy.

—9—

Rural France and Resistance

H. R. Kedward

For twenty years after the war any historical approach to peasant culture, regionalism or ruralism in the 1930s and 1940s triggered such an immediate association with the rural program and mythology of Vichy that it seemed quixotic to question it. The metaphoric windmills of Vichy's corporative structure for agriculture, the *Corporation paysanne*, continued to turn, breaking the lance of Cervantes' intrepid knight, in this case the disingenuous historian researching ideas and experience that might suggest an alternative rural France. For the same number of years the history of the *maquis*, the armed resistance in the hills and forests, remained undisturbed; it was left uncritically in the format of heroic stories dating from immediately after the Liberation, and it was largely ignored by academic historians.

In the last twenty years, however, the discursive monopoly of Vichy over the exploration of peasant culture, regionalism and ruralism in the 1930s and 1940s has been decisively broken: Bertram Gordon's chapter in this collection, for example, explores the problematic relationships between Vichy and the countryside. At the same time, the history of the *maquis* has been closely re-examined. The two developments are interconnected. Both derive vitality from recent research into the specificity of resistance – research that, in its turn, has gained new vigour from disciplines other than history.[1]

The effect of specificity

Two books, taken from many, can be seen as emblematic of this recent research: Jacques Canaud's *Maquis du Morvan* (1981) and the Club Cévenol publication, *Cévennes, terre de refuge 1940–1944* (1987), edited by Philippe Joutard, Jacques Poujol and Patrick Cabanel. The former presents detailed work done in the 1970s on every aspect of the *maquis*: their plurality, their varied roles of refuge and combat, their social composition, their leadership, tactics, and strategy, and their precise localization or mobility within the Morvan. Public and private documentation is examined alongside oral testimonies, from individuals but also from groups brought together by the author and allowed to discuss and argue among themselves. The selective history of the *maquis* established in the post-war period, what Jean-Marie Guillon calls 'its legendary status',[2] receives no less critical attention than the reconsidered attitudes thirty years later, and the result is a local history of the *maquis* that breathes and expands, a rich case study of rural resistance.[3] The portrait of the Cévennes during the Occupation is also a case study based on interviews and local histories, a careful reconstruction of the refuge and support given by the Cévenol peasant and village communities to Jews, refugees, resisters on the run and anti-fascists, in which the Protestant religion and Cévenol culture are thrown into sharp relief as diametrically opposed to the attitudes and behaviour that Vichy expected of its rural populations. Where most of the peasantry and rural opinion in 1940 and1941 are identified in prefects' reports with 'the sound elements of the population', the Cévennes are classified as difficult, independent and subversive.[4]

Taken together the two books are a model of the kind of research that has established the specificities of resistance. They are now so taken for granted that Jean-Marie Guillon could legitimately ask in 1994, 'Can the Resistance be defined outside the context in which it occurs?' His question prioritizes *context*, in particular the context of the village; but it could also be rephrased to ask whether resistance can be defined outside the *function* it is called on to fulfill, as François Marcot has consistently and persuasively argued.[5] The point is that however or wherever specificity is located in the national picture of French Resistance it presupposes heterogeneity, plurality, and difference. It also results in a contested but unavoidable enlargement of the meaning of resistance, as Michel Boivin and Jean Quellien discovered in their analysis of the sociology of resistance in Basse-Normandie. Having produced a number of social observations from the files of those who had been recognized as Combattants volontaires de la Résistance (CVR) they took stock of the narrowness of the category:

> Isn't the perception we have of the Resistance against the German Occupation during World War Two too narrow? Too often we tend to limit it to those men and women who belonged to an organized movement or network. To our way of thinking this definition is too rigid and too categorical . . . eclipsing those attitudes, and resulting actions, which clearly signified a state of mind . . . the 'spirit of Resistance'.[6]

The authors proceed to suggest suitable new categories, including 'peri-resistance' and 'infra-resistance', and make it clear that while they want to avoid the pitfalls of 'the Resistance myth' their research makes it obligatory for them to insist on the importance of 'this infra-resistance which was widespread and multifaceted'.[7]

Their conclusion is anticipated, echoed and refined in an abundance of case studies meticulously researched and presented in the last ten or so years, many of which not only revolutionize what had been an urban and often condescending approach to rural resistance, but also break through the gender barriers and bring knowledge about women's actions closer to the realities of the time. Without dissent from the notion of resistance as a minority phenomenon, an enormous amount of new material has been found on rural support networks; individual aid and refuge; the voluntary provision of food, lodging and clothing; participation in the elaborate staging of raids and thefts that covered rural collusion with a show of victimization; the recovery, transport and camouflage of parachuted arms and ammunition; the silence of whole families in the face of police and Gestapo inquisition, and the protective, decoy role of the woman at the doorway.[8] We know far more now about the rural adoption of certain *maquis* units as 'our boys', reflecting the fact that many of them contained local agricultural workers and village youths, and there are enough examples of whole village and rural communities involved in resistance in 1943 and 1944 to substantiate the existence of an 'outlaw culture' in specific localities.[9] The significance at the time of studies such as *Cévennes, terre de refuge,* and the conference and subsequent publication of *Le Plateau Vivarais/Lignon: Accueil et Résistance,* was to ensure that any adequate history of resistance would have to include the role of 'humanitarian resistance';[10] and in 1994, at the same conference as the proposals for a definition of 'infra-resistance', François Marcot produced his own generic solution by coining the term 'resistance-movement' to represent the actions, however small, of all those who helped the organized resistance when it needed them. This functional 'resistance-movement' was, François Marcot declares, of sufficient size to be called a mass phenomenon; and he states that 'The resistance-movement is not on the margin of organised resistance: it conditions the latter's existence.'[11]

The move towards a more inclusive understanding of resistance might appear to some a regressive return to pre-Ophuls complacency, an artificial mending of the 'broken mirror'.[12] In fact, it could not be more dissimilar. If the product of greater specificity is, paradoxically, a wider definition of resistance, its most obvious concern is the naming of names, the recovery of little-known events and the rediscovery of places; it makes distinctions, it suspects homogeneity, and it continues to disturb the placid surface of comfortable reflections. In the history of rural France it insists on a level of precision in time and place that defies the small-scale map and the generalities of chronology: it makes summaries (and short conference papers) almost impossible.

We should be clear that this localized research has not invariably discovered larger quantities of resistance, and it certainly does not turn negative indices into positive ones. It is apparent from the very precise research by Christian Font that the rural population of the Aveyron was, on any numerical scale of resistance, at the negative end. The endogenous reasons for this negativity are listed as isolation and parochialism, relative prosperity, economic self-interest, the absence of resistance leadership from village notables, xenophobia, traditional Catholicism and political adherence to the Right. In total, the image of this rural *département*, conservative and Catholic, was not modified by the experience of the Occupation, though Christian Font, true to detailed specificity, acknowledges local exceptions to each of his negatives.[13] In the Haute-Saône Jean-Claude Grandhay found rural willingness to provide the police with precious information on *maquis* units that were not specifically from the local area,[14] and in the Morbihan Christian Bougeard reports evidence of early hostility to the first FTP *maquisards* who came from outside, and the betrayal of the Groupe de Bubry by a peasant informer in December 1943.[15] Vichy authorities, writes Patrick Cabanel, found the rural population of the Catholic Lozère subservient, resigned, apolitical and incapable of resistance, and his research highlights the specificity of the area in comparison with the mainly Protestant Cévennes.[16] Work done recently in the villages of Burgundy that suffered German reprisals has disclosed what Angélique Marie calls 'a highly negative counter-memory of the armed struggle, which certain villagers hold responsible for the repression which they suffered'.[17]

Negative evaluations such as these, and many others, foreground rural experience of the *maquis* as a reign of terror. In both the Haute-Saône and the Chablais, as in many other rural areas, pre-war right-wing political affinities clearly conditioned the labeling of the *Francs-Tireurs et Partisans* (FTP) as bandits; but once the accusation, or experience, of banditry is closely investigated in any region it is apparent that some resisters are seen as bandits and others are not, and where this distinction prevailed the historian can arrive at categories of resistance that were more, or less, acceptable to rural societies.

Whether positive or negative, rural involvement with resistance has normally been seen to follow a slow evolutionary curve, with a noticeable turn upwards once the impact on farm workers of the *Service du Travail Obligatoire* (STO), the forced labor draft, became apparent in the early summer of 1943. Both Jean-Marie Guillon and Jacqueline Sainclivier in 1994/5 used terms of gradual or progressive ruralization of the resistance from a base that was strikingly low compared with that in the large towns; and although such a model chronology has been defensible in general terms it is now mainly useful as a comparative device for situating the specificities and calibrating the differences within a plural and localized time-frame. With any attempt at general measurement or chronology the relativity of the observer's perspective comes into play: Jean-Marie Guillon cites the words of Charles de Richter in 1945, who contrasts the external impression of a village judged not to have played a role in the resistance with the view from inside the village, which presents a quite different reality.[18] There are competing subjectivities at issue here, and the research of the moment is clearly inclined to give more priority to the rural subjectivity that has previously been marginalized, or in this case marginalized in the history of resistance, but centered within the history of Vichy. As both positions are reassessed, it is the special relationship between Vichy and the rural population that is most affected.

The Plurality of Rural France

The concept of 'the return to the land', as developed by the nationalist Right between the wars, drew on the ideological codes of a mythologized past: it was essentialist and anti-historical. By the time it becomes a main pillar of Vichy's *Révolution Nationale* its apostrophe to eternal virtues is already a cliché. The concept, alongside 'the woman in the home', had become a wide-ranging discourse of preferred values: country against town, provinces against Paris, peasant against industrial worker, family against decadence, tradition against modernity, and Catholicism against bolshevism, the Freemasons and the Jews. The discourse was aggressively polemical in the fascist-style action of the *Défense paysanne* led by Henry Dorgères, and was backed by the organizational drive of the corporatist leader Jacques le Roy Ladurie, who later became Minister of Agriculture under Vichy. Both of these self-appointed prophets of a new rural France contributed to the mythology with their own abstractions of the peasant, not least in the ostensibly concrete notion of the peasantry as an immutable fact of French life.[19] For Vichy it was an essential but increasingly dysfunctional myth, evidenced by numerous reports from Vichy prefects, starting in 1941 in some *départements*, which almost disbelievingly began to portray the peasantry as egoistic, avaricious, and rebarbative, the replacement of one abstract typology by another. Ideal-type or simple-minded propaganda, the abstractions persisted throughout the Occupation period and lasted well into the 1960s and beyond. They are now progressively fractured by the detailed research into local resistance, and the redefinitions that have followed.

The recuperation of particular rural histories under the Occupation is not just an extension of empirical knowledge: it is part of a cultural history that is flexible in its reference to *longue* and *courte durée* and that interweaves structures, ideas and events without the constraint of a formulaic determinism. It finds it easier than ever before to listen to the expressions of local attitudes that hitherto have been consistently dismissed as purely rhetorical. Taken as seriously as this, familiar cultural expressions open lines of exploration that recognize the plurality of rural attitudes to such recurrent signifiers as region, home, valleys, hills and mountains, attitudes on which shared, or conflicting, identities are based. The Protestant uplands of the Vivarais and the Cévennes constituted a paradigm of alternative rural culture well before the Occupation. The austere discipline of the Old Testament combined with folk and religious memory of persecution at the hands of Louis XIV's dragoons indelibly marked the mentalities of the Huguenot communities to the point where it should occasion little surprise that they resisted the 'Jew hunt' imposed by Vichy. The ramifications of Camisard culture in the Cévennes penetrate family and community dynamics, and govern the transmission of folklore, popular history, Anglophilia, and the knowledge of paths and caves in the hills. Patrick Cabanel underlines the everyday vitality of the tradition, which had not become ossified, and shows that the sacred place of Champdomergue, one of the focal references of Camisard memory, did not need to be successively re-invented during the nineteenth and twentieth centuries: it was a recurrent assembly point and a symbolic constant, to which the FTP were both military and cultural inheritors in 1943. In a number of accounts of the French peasantry under the Occupation weight is given to their xenophobia, which is seen to condition either a growing anti-German position or hostility to those *maquisards*, such as Spanish republicans or urban communists, who come from outside. In the case of the Protestant Vivarais and Cévennes, it has to be asked whether xenophobia was to any degree a cultural phenomenon in these areas? No history of rural France should assume its universality.

The fragmentation of the rural picture is the direct result of many such studies. For example, Christian Bougeard situates the Breton *maquis* of Saint-Goazec in an area marked by long-standing anticlerical culture and pre-war left-wing voting patterns, and he produces one of the many recent portraits of a specific area solid in its resistance; according to the oral evidence of numerous resisters in the area of the Trégor, organizers and members of the FTP action groups were regularly provided with refuge and food by familial friends in the small towns (café proprietors, merchants, artisans and schoolteachers) and in the countryside.[20] Writing on Brittany as a whole, Jacqueline Sainclivier also stresses the persistence of political temperament: 'people of the so-called "blue" regions, those that had been republican since the nineteenth century, were among the first to resist, particularly in the rural areas'.[21] In a recent interview Brooks Richards, one of the first British organizers of secret naval lines to Brittany, records that the political traditions of the Breton fishing ports were seen by the British Secret Services in 1940–41 as predisposing them to resistance. Later, in September 1943, when he was put in charge of the French Country Section of the SOE network 'Massingham' in Algiers, which was organizing operations in Corsica and southern France, he attached more importance to the political identities of different rural regions than Maurice Buckmaster in London, who always claimed that politics were of little significance compared with the capability of individual agents, wherever they were operating. Richards said he was assured, for example, by messages from the town of Dieulefit that the collective republican memory in the Drôme, not least of opposition to Louis Napoleon in 1851, together with Protestant defiance of Cardinal Richelieu in the seventeenth century, offered a cultural guarantee of widespread resistance sympathy in the local countryside – an evaluation that was entirely endorsed by the experience of Francis Cammaerts at the head of network 'Jockey' in the south-east.[22]

Vichy's rural ideology did, of course, promote the concept of regional difference, but within its unifying discourse of the peasantry and the land, which was archetypal. Research into rural resistance does not reveal a plurality that was totally unknown to Vichy, but rather one that was overlaid by this undiscriminating discourse. As Charles Maurras in his positivist guise should have realized, it was irrational to extol the traditional freedoms of different parts of the country and yet expect rural France to show single-minded, consistent support for an interventionist government, whatever its politics. He had curiously learnt little from the anti-Jacobinism on which his counter-revolutionary expectations were historically based. There was also within the Vichy ideology the rigid social polarization of town and country, a self-evident anachronism based on the simplistic identification of rural France with the peasantry. Perhaps the most open-ended result of the recent research has been the blurring of lines in many areas between peasantry and villagers, and between small towns (*petits bourgs*) and the surrounding countryside – an acceptance of Marcel Jollivet's observation that during the twentieth century the rural collectivity gradually ceases to be a village and becomes a rural space centered on a small town.[23] Just what point in this process had been reached at the time of Vichy, and whether or not the effects of the Occupation were to reintroduce behavioral patterns of an earlier time, are unresolved questions; but, to borrow from Jean-Marie Guillon, can there be any serious analysis of peasant resistance outside the contexts of village, of village notables and of family or commercial relationships with the local small town? The norm in the social exploration of all resistance is to use the term 'social environment'; but this has to be defined and refined according to both the structures and the dynamics of the locality. The consequence, yet again, is to break down the rural abstractions that dominated not only Vichy but much of the resistance historiography that followed.

For the local publication celebrating the fiftieth anniversary of the Liberation of the Lot, and aimed at the general public, Pierre Laborie chose to call his contribution 'The peasantry: beyond the myths'. Peasants in general, he states, 'have been crudely identified with a whole series of negative, often insulting, images' and to rectify this, while respecting the complexity and variety of peasant responses to the Occupation, he writes '. . . the peasant populations of the Quercy, like those of the Limousin, the Cévennes, the Haute-Loire, the Haute-Savoie, the Breton countryside and many other rural areas, provide examples of behaviour far removed from the grayness of the usual stereotypes'. He would acknowledge that his selective geographical categories are still too broad in themselves; but his vigorous rejection of what has passed for a general sociological truth was a timely popular summary of the state of research. He goes further by specifying certain details of peasant resistance and then adding, 'The majority contributed in their own customary manner, without fuss or flamboyance, within the anonymity of the ordinary course of events, in a multitude of obscure, everyday acts.'[24] This language opens up the whole area of theory about what is habitual and what is everyday, establishing close conceptual links with anthropology.

The Impact of Anthropology

There are two generalizations that specific research has tended to promote rather than undermine. The first is the remarkably consistent record of rural areas in the treatment of allied airmen shot down over France, whether hiding those who survived or burying those who were killed.

Numerous local studies mention a simple funeral of an airman as a significant and ritualistic show of rural solidarity, the equivalent of urban street demonstrations. Brooks Richards remembers attending a briefing of pilots before a bombing raid on the submarine pen at Saint Nazaire at the beginning of 1942, at which they were told that if they were shot down they should go to the smallest house in the landscape, where they would find no Germans and would be certain of help.[25] The escape society of the Royal Air Force estimated that 3,000 airmen escaped from France through Spain, and that it was ordinary rural families who normally provided the first refuge, action that in itself involved the collusion of many others in the immediate locality, and eventually a network of *passeurs*. As Jacqueline Sainclivier rightly remarks, in all these acts of clandestine passage, along the whole demarcation line and on the frontiers of France, there were peasants involved.[26] The second generalization is that peasant producers, almost regardless of region, did everything they could to subvert the enforced requisitions and low-priced quotas of goods demanded by Vichy – action that was again at source individual, yet collective in its scale and impact.

The two types of action are regularly compared and contrasted. Aid to airmen is categorized unproblematically as resistance, whereas economic subversion is held to be self-regarding and materialistic, though it is added that acts of passage nevertheless did present an opportunity for material gain and reward, and that escalating peasant recalcitrance over Vichy's agricultural pricing should not be ignored when charting the upward curve in the ruralization of resistance. The very process of comparison highlights the cultural and behavioral studies of anthropology, and elsewhere I have particularized the theories of James C. Scott on everyday peasant resistance, derived from local research in Malaya, the global range of material on protest and revolt in *Subaltern Studies* and the ideas of David Lan on oral transmission in the Dande district of the Zambezi valley.[27]

The stimulus of this canon of work is to propel the history of resistance into a more theoretical framework. Like Pierre Laborie, Hélène Dumora-Ratier is close to the language of Scott on the moral economy of the peasant when she writes of peasants in the Ariège that: 'Responsibility towards families with whom one was more or less related undermined the slogan of "everyone for themselves" and reawoke old solidarities', while Jean-Philippe Marcy also suggests the habitual nature of peasant economic protests when he quotes the reports of the *Renseignements Généraux* detailing the same peasant resistance to surrendering food in March 1945 as under the Occupation.[28] The comparative historian of rural resistance, Riki van Boeschoten, has suggestively utilized Pierre Bourdieu's cultural concept of the 'habitus' to contrast different cultural systems that operated within villages of the northern Pindus during the German Occupation of Greece, and she complements her archival and oral history with relevant indigenous theory, the equivalent of Guillon's view from the inside, quoting Eric Hobsbawm's dictum that peasant action and goals that are seen from the outside as conservative are often 'traditionalist formulations of revolutionary aspirations'.[29] Pastor André Bettex of the village of Le Riou in the Vivarais-Lignon confirmed that the hiding of Jewish refugees on the plateau was a direct expression of a religious culture in which parents taught their children through the Psalms to love the Jews, and transmitted the biblical imperatives to give food and shelter to those in need. Giving refuge was, in this sense, traditional and protective, and yet in its humanitarian aspirations revolutionary.[30]

The least the historian can do when evaluating the importance of peasant self-protection is to look at how it both empowered and disempowered resistance, and how it was both receptive and indifferent to Vichy. Here there must be cooperation between historians and anthropologists, with room for heuristic disputes over what is time- or place-specific and what is culturally innate or atavistic. For example, the rural aid to airmen appears episodic and time-specific; yet there is also the cultural dimension that stresses the age-old symbolism and special status of men falling from the skies. Conversely, the acts of economic foot-dragging, false compliance and dissimulation, which are prominent features of Scott's habitual, everyday peasant resistance, have their own specific history in Occupied France, which indicates that in 1943 some did, and some did not, provide fertile ground for *maquis* development.

If theory does nothing else, it at least keeps a diachronic history of rural protest as a sub-agenda in resistance studies. It asks what is generic about peasant and rural revolt that can illuminate the phenomenon of rural resistance and that habitually conditions action, or that stands as precedent, memory or inspiration. This must mean looking at any common aspects in all previous rural protests, whatever their political association or pedigree. If I read Robert Paxton on Dorgères correctly, it is precisely in the localized strategy of confrontation, disruption and subversion that the *Défense paysanne* was successful; not in the creation of a national peasant equivalent to the CGT that Dorgères desired, nor in the promotion of his ideal of a 'peasant nation', even if his movement played a part in re-creating the positive identity of the peasant in French society. His eventual marginalization under Vichy appears due to his image as a grassroots agitator, who could not, or would not, transcend what the notables of the *Corporation paysanne* saw as his movement's limitations, but that he regarded as the visceral strength of a militant peasant base.[31] Politically, Dorgères was too committed to his own brand of fascism to respond to the depredations of the German occupiers, and failed to recognize how far Vichy's statism, low prices and requisitions had alienated much of the peasantry, precisely in the domain of peasant self-interest. It is evident that one of the main successes of rural action in the resistance, whether at the time of the *maquis* or before, was the achievement of very local objectives. The creation of '*maquis* country' which the Germans and Vichy were unwilling to penetrate except in large formation, and which was maintained through the commitment, the voluntarism, the self-interest and often the fear of the peasantry, must be seen as exemplary of a strategy of local territorial control, of which the remnants of the 'greenshirts'of Dorgères must have been envious.

To take another example of historic peasant action: the defense of forest rights has propelled peasants into recurrent illegal occupation of forests against intrusive and unacceptable authority – action that is central to the formative period of the *maquis*. A comparison of the subterfuge of hiding *réfractaires*, who were on the run from the STO, with the inversionary acts of forest rites in the nineteenth century may verge on the fanciful; but the thrust of the comparison is once again to widen the reference points for rural action. Writing on the so-called 'War of the Demoiselles' in the Ariège in 1829, with an impressive mix of cultural theory and empiricism, Peter Sahlins concludes his account:

> To look back . . . is to see the War of the Demoiselles, not as the last gasp of a dying peasantry, but as the beginning of a different struggle over the mountains of the Ariège . . . In 1973 . . . men and women who still worked the land and earned their livelihood from stockraising . . . organized themselves and successfully opposed a governmental proposal to create a national park in the mountain communes . . . More than a century and a half after the War of the Demoiselles in 1829, peasants from the Ariège continue to battle the state and outsiders for possession of their forests.[32]

Drawing also on the Ariège, Hélène Dumora-Ratier approximates to the cultural analysis of Sahlins at one particular point, the indulgence towards youthful role-play. From oral evidence she finds that the resistance leaders came mostly from the most respected elements of village society, and as such stood at the head of a rural family whose younger members were the *réfractaires*: 'This resistance minority organized the *réfractaires* into small mobile groups whom they treated with the indulgence habitually shown to youth. They described their actions as pranks (one of the roots given to the word "*maquis*" is *maquiller*) or as petty pilfering. They accorded them no military value.'[33]

Conclusion

Trawling the history of rural protest for similar continuities could obviously lead to more rather then fewer essentialist statements about the peasantry, which certain theories from anthropologists would also encourage. The particularity of recent research has not yet addressed this as a problem; the essentialisms it has first addressed are those of Vichy and resistance historiography, with their origins in 1940–42 in the reinvigorated ideological conflict for 'true France'. With a remarkably similar iconography, Vichy's publication *La France Nouvelle travaille* of 1941 and the London-published *La France Libre* (15 January 1942) both lay claim to a unitary concept of the peasantry (see Figures 1–6).

Figure 9.1. 'La terre, elle ne ment pas', *La France Nouvelle travaille*, Vichy 1941.

Figure 9.2. '. . . l'époque des labours', *La France Libre*, London, 15 January 1942.

These are striking, positive rural images of the peasantry as the salt of the earth, as the fundamental embodiments of France; and it must be clear that *La France Libre* uses them in the same essentialist way as Vichy. Later there were remarkably similar urban judgments on the egoism and isolationism of the peasantry, again from both Vichy prefects and resistance historiography, producing Pierre Laborie's 'grayness of the usual stereotypes'. This chapter has attempted to analyze the ways in which such stereotypes are being dismantled by historians of the Resistance, and I have suggested that cultural theory and the history of peasant action provide new hypotheses for a more complex reading of both rural France and rural resistance. Specificity, however, remains at the center of any explanatory process, to which we should add the ambiguities that have emerged in the course of this chapter. As a project for the future,

Figure 9.3. 'Celui-ci remplace son père . . .', *La France Libre*, London, 15 January 1942.

Figure 9.4. '. . . les jeunes nous montrent le chemin', *La France Nouvelle travaille*, Vichy 1941.

Figure 9.5. 'Dans le foyer, bastion de la résistance . . .', *La France Libre*, London, 15 January 1942.

Figure 9.6. '. . . quatre générations de Françaises . . .', *La France Libre*, London, 15 January 1942.

the approach to rural France and the resistance can fruitfully be articulated through a number of polarities or tensions, some empirical and some theoretical: inside and outside; collectivity and individualism; local and central; individual and nation/republic; villager and peasant; silence and rumor; context and function; provisioning and payment; isolation and involvement; culture and politics; history and anthropology.[34] Research that moves within these tensions and between these polarities will continue to establish both cultural and historical diversity. A certain amount of virgin soil has been cultivated, as François Marcot claimed at Besançon.[35] Perhaps it should also be seen as a recovery of truths known at local level but abandoned for too many years, a sort of *Regain* in which the historian aims, with only a slight sense of irony, to re-enact the testament of Jean Giono, '. . . solidly planted in the earth like a column'.

Notes

1. This chapter makes particular reference to the research papers given at a series of six conferences, organized by the Institut d'Histoire du Temps Présent (IHTP) under the general title of 'La Résistance et les Français', which took place between 1993 and 1997: Jean-Marie Guillon and Pierre Laborie (eds), *Mémoire et Histoire: la Résistance* (Toulouse, 1995); Jacqueline Sainclivier and Christian Bougeard (eds), *La Résistance et les Français: enjeux stratégiques et environnement social* (Rennes, 1995); *La Résistance et les Européens du Nord* (Brussels, 1994); François Marcot (ed.), *La Résistance et les Français: lutte armée et Maquis* (Besançon, 1996); Laurent Douzou, Robert Frank, Denis Peschanski and Dominique Veillon (eds), *La Résistance et les Français: villes, centres et logiques de décision* (Cachan, 1995); *La Résistance et les Européens du Sud: Pré-Actes* (Aix-en-Provence, 1997).
2. Jean-Marie Guillon, 'La Résistance au village' (Rennes, 1995): 235.
3. Jacques Canaud, *Les Maquis du Morvan 1943–1944: la vie dans les maquis* (Château-Chinon, 1981).
4. Philippe Joutard, Jacques Poujol and Patrick Cabanel (eds), *Cévennes, terre de refuge 1940–1944* (Montpellier, 1987).
5. Jean-Marie Guillon in Sainclivier and Bougeard (eds), *La Résistance et les Français* (Rennes, 1995): 233; François Marcot, 'Les paysans

et la Résistance: problèmes d'une approche sociologique', ibid. (Rennes, 1995): 255.

6. Michel Boivin and Jean Quellien, 'La Résistance en Basse-Normandie: définition et sociologie', ibid. (Rennes, 1995): 166–7.
7. Ibid.: 169–71.
8. See Laurent Douzou, 'La Résistance, une affaire d'hommes?' *Cahiers de l'IHTP,* No.31 (October 1995): 11–14, and H. R. Kedward, *In Search of the Maquis* (Oxford, 1993): 91–2.
9. H. R. Kedward, 'The Maquis and the culture of the outlaw', in H. R. Kedward and R. Austin (eds), *Vichy France and the Resistance: Culture and Ideology* (London, 1985): 232–51.
10. François Bédarida, 'L'histoire de la Résistance, lectures d'hier, chantiers de demain', *Vingtième Siècle*, No.11 (1986).
11. François Marcot, 'Les paysans et la Résistance', in Sainclivier and Bougeard (eds), *La Résistance et les Français* (Rennes,1995): 255.
12. Henry Rousso, *Le syndrome de Vichy* (Paris, 1987): 111–46. 'Le miroir brisé' (the broken mirror) is the heading for the chapter on 1971–4, when Rousso argues that the post-war images of the Occupation were shattered, mainly by the Marcel Ophuls film, *Le Chagrin et la pitié* (*The Sorrow and the Pity*).
13. Christian Font, 'Les Paysans et la Résistance, le modèle aveyronnais?' in Sainclivier and Bougeard (eds), *La Résistance et les Français* (Rennes, 1995): 181–9.
14. Jean-Claude Grandhay, 'Les Maquis haut-saônois dans leur environnement social', in Marcot (ed.), *La Résistance et les Français* (Besançon, 1996): 283.
15. Christian Bougeard, 'Les Maquis de Bretagne dans leur environnement social', ibid. (Besançon, 1996): 297.
16. Patrick Cabanel, 'Les Eglises, les paysans et la Résistance. L'exemple des Cévennes et de la Lozère,' in Sainclivier and Bougeard (eds), *La Résistance et les Français* (Rennes, 1995): 223.
17. Angélique Marie, 'Mémoires des maquis et de la lutte armée en Bourgogne' in Marcot (ed.), *La Résistance et les Français* (Besançon, 1996): 468.
18. Guillon, 'La Résistance au Village' in Sainclivier and Bougeard (eds) *La Résistance et les Français* (Rennes, 1995): 234; Sainclivier in *La Résistance et les Européens du Nord* (Brussels, 1994): 347.
19. Robert Paxton, *Le Temps des chemises vertes. Révoltes paysannes et fascisme rural 1929–1939* (Paris, 1996): 271. For alternative images of the peasantry in the 1930s, and the involvement of the Popular Front in its own form of ruralism, see the important recent study by

Shanny Peer, *France on Display. Peasants, Provincials, and Folklore in the 1937 Paris World's Fair* (New York, 1998).

20. Christian Bougeard in Marcot (ed.), *La Résistance et les Français* (Besançon, 1996): 296.
21. Sainclivier, *La Bretagne dans la Guerre, 1939–1945* (Rennes, 1994): 171. The areas of republican sympathy were called 'blue' after the blue uniforms worn by republican soldiers during the revolutionary period.
22. Author's interviews with Brooks Richards at Durweston, 11 September 1997, with Maurice Buckmaster at Forest Row, 4 November 1990 and with Francis Cammaerts at Grane, 18 March 1991 (see Kedward, *In Search of the Maquis:* 275–9).
23. Marcel Jollivet, 'L'Analyse fonctionnelle-structurelle en question, ou la théorie nécessaire' in *Sociétés paysannes ou lutte de classes au village?* sous la direction de Marcel Jollivet (Paris, 1974), 195–6; see also Kedward, 'Le monde rural face au maquis' in Marcot (ed.), *La Résistance et les Français* (Besançon, 1996): 340.
24. *50ème anniversaire de la libération du Lot*, Cahors, Bulletin de Liaison ANACR/46 (1994): 62–3.
25. The briefing was given by Edward Shackleton. Author's interview with Brooks Richards, 11 September 1997.
26. Sainclivier, in *La Résistance et les Européens du Nord* (Brussels, 1994): 346.
27. J. C. Scott, *Weapons of the Weak. Everyday Forms of Peasant Resistance* (New Haven, CT, 1985); David Lan, *Guns and Rain. Guerrillas and Spirit Mediums in Zimbabwe* (London, 1985). See Kedward, 'La résistance, l'histoire et l'anthropologie: quelques domaines de la théorie', in Guillon et Laborie (eds), *Mémoire et histoire* (Toulouse, 1995): 109–18.
28. Hélène Dumora-Ratier, ibid. (Toulouse, 1995): 285; Jean-Philippe Marcy, 'La Résistance et les structures professionnelles agricoles dans l'Aveyron', in Sainclivier and Bougeard (eds), *La Résistance et les Français* (Rennes, 1995): 201.
29. Riki van Boeschoten, 'Pour une géopolitique de la résistance grecque: le cas du Pinde du nord', in *La Resistance et les Européens du Sud* (Aix-en-Provence, 1997), no pagination, and 'The Peasant and the Party: Peasant Options and "Folk" Communism in a Greek Village', *Journal of Peasant Studies*, 20, no.4 (July 1993): 625. The reference she gives is to Eric Hobsbawm, 'Peasants and Politics', *Journal of Peasant Studies*, 1, no.1 (1973): 12.
30. Oral contribution to a discussion at the 1990 Conference at Le

Chambon-sur-Lignon, published in Pierre Bolle (ed.), *Le Plateau Vivarais-Lignon. Accueil et Résistance 1939–1944* (Le Chambon-sur-Lignon, 1992): 434.

31. 'Alors que ses collègues ne parlaient que de grands principes généraux, Dorgères préférait rapporter des doléances locales ramassées dans quelque buvette de campagne . . .': Robert Paxton, *Chemises vertes*: 236–7. See also the memoirs of Dorgères, in which, for example, he claims that a typical local action, by *Jeunesses paysannes* in Algeria, was to throw 340 sacks of foreign corn into the sea, and that the 'greenshirts' adopted the traditional songs of each region to emphasize their local rootedness: Dorgères, *Au XXe siècle. 10 ans de jacquerie* (Paris, 1959): 95–107.
32. Peter Sahlins, *Forest Rites. The War of the Demoiselles in Nineteenth-Century France* (Cambridge MA, 1994): 134.
33. Hélène Dumora-Ratier, in Guillon et Laborie (eds), *Mémoire et histoire* (Toulouse, 1995): 287.
34. For the significance of rumour see Jean-Marie Guillon's perceptive article, 'Sociabilité et rumeurs en temps de guerre. Bruits et contestations en Provence dans les années quarante', *Provence historique,* Fascicule 187 (1997).
35. François Marcot, 'Pour une inscription de la lutte armée dans les stratégies de la Résistance', in Marcot (ed.), *La Résistance et les Français* (Besançon, 1996): 511.

–10–

The Countryside and the City: Some Notes on the Collaboration Model during the Vichy Period

Bertram M. Gordon

Introduction

In his work on the Green Shirts in France and their leader Henry Dorgères (Henri-Auguste d'Halluin), Robert O. Paxton argued that peasants had been an important element support in the early days of the Mussolini and Hitler movements in Italy and Germany, respectively, yet they had received relatively little attention in the study of French fascism.[1] Although most members of the wartime collaborationist movements came from 'the so-called "popular" classes of the cities and towns', Paxton's book suggested a reconsideration of the models, or paradigms, of peasantry, Vichy, and collaboration.[2]

There are many problems involved in drawing up such models. The brevity of the Vichy era, together with the constraints of wartime and occupation, gave long-term plans for structural social reform barely time to germinate, let alone grow. In addition, categories such as 'notable', 'fascist', and 'collaborationist' are more fluid than taxonomically-minded historians might like. During the four-year history of Vichy, political engagements changed rapidly both in groups and individuals with the evolving war situation. Finally, the diversity of rural France makes generalizations about peasants difficult. The term 'peasant' itself has evolved in France, referring in the 1930s, as Paxton indicates, not only to someone who cultivated the soil in the countryside but also to a complex of virtues associated with a rural culture, rich in roots and traditions.[3]

Change in rural France was not uniform. Some areas moved rapidly toward an optimal peasant dispersal, where some peasants moved away and others developed modern agriculture based on railways, refrigeration, and later trucking. Other areas, such as Brittany, were unable to take advantage of these infrastructural changes until the 1960s. However, by the 1930s and 1940s, peasants were less in debt than previously and institutions such as the *Office nationale du Crédit agricole*, created in 1920, worked to develop what might be called a middle-level rural society. By the end of the nineteenth century, clogs were replaced by shoes. Films of the inter-war and Second World War years that show well-fed peasant families and a head of family with no tie, but a black vest and pants to wear to church, indicate how far many peasants had come since the middle of the nineteenth century.

The creation of this intermediate class from the peasantry tended to concentrate political values in the center right as opposed to the mass of *jacquerie* leftist peasant agitators of the Middle Ages or even the French Revolution, a shift exemplified even in the rhetoric of Dorgères, who refrained from appealing to the 'ancestral *jacquerie*'.[4] By the 1930s the rural population included specialized shopkeepers and mechanics, all of whom traded with peasants and formed what Paxton has called 'a separate world' (*monde à part*) from urban culture.[5] It was a world that defended its independence in questions of social authority and family planning and child-rearing practice, including religion. Food formed a significant part of peasant lives. They lived on it, exchanged it and treated it as the basis of solidarity, taking a certain pride in being able to indulge in food and drink. Their world, whether at church or at home, was to a large extent a world of conversations about family, livestock, farm machines and prices. Most farm journals, according to Gordon Wright, 'were filled with a combination of complaints about farm prices and advice on how to avoid mildew'.[6]

Alliances between national urban fascist groups and the countryside, such as those Paxton discussed in the Po Valley in Italy and Schleswig-Holstein in Germany, were deceptive in that peasants and fascists had very different goals in mind, as Paxton elaborates in his discussion of Dorgères's critique of fascism in the mid-1930s.[7] Though the imagery of fascism and the countryside might approximate one another in the evocation of the hard-working state, the good farmer, and the upstanding family head, real congruence of interests was occasional. Peasants in the twentieth century were generally unenthusiastic about going to war or having their sons serve in the army. Fascists found out soon enough that the peasants were not the kinds of patriots they had hoped for.

During the Second World War, Vichy's determined effort at solidarity with the rural population ultimately failed not only because of the war's constraints but also because the peasantry disliked state officials, whom they saw as alien city people who neither went to church, nor had large families, nor ate big meals in common. To the peasants, visits by state officials meant increased requisitions for food and labor, especially as the war continued and Vichy became increasingly collaborationist. The remainder of this chapter addresses the changing fortunes of the peasantry during the Third Republic and the relationship of the Vichy state to the countryside, suggesting that Vichy achieved limited success only to the degree that it departed from the fascist model. Lastly, it offers as a model of Occupation era fascism the position of Marcel Déat, more articulate than many, but representative of the collaborationists in their lack of connection to the rural situation.

The Countryside under the Third Republic

The Third Republic ushered in a period of consolidation of peasant well-being, but at the same time increased the differentiation between land-holders and the landless in the countryside. Those who owned land became increasingly involved in the market-place, as tradesmen, whereas the landless peasants increasingly resembled the urban proletariat and fled in large numbers to the cities.[8] Job losses and failures in the agricultural sector during the depression of the late nineteenth century took a high toll in human suffering, as cultivated land in France fell by some 12 per cent between 1882 and 1912. A shift from grain to animal production fed into changing dietary patterns and helped reduce demand for agricultural labor. Improvements in mechanization, agricultural genetics, and chemical fertilizers all enhanced productivity, although such modernization affected only a minority of French agricultural producers.[9]

Changes between 1880 and 1910 included the extension of roads and railways connecting previously isolated villages to the market-places of the outside world. Schooling taught the peasants to speak and write French in addition to, if not instead of, their local languages.[10] Communal roads increased from 331,000 kilometers in 1871 to 539,000 in 1911. Bicycle usage spread, train service increased, and daily mail became commonplace in rural life, all favoring the diffusion of the press, spreading urban values into the countryside. Military conscription also took the sons of peasants away from their villages and exposed them to urban norms.[11] The turn of the century saw a take-off in per capita consumption of proteins as opposed to carbohydrates in France, as well as other European countries.[12] In general, the percentage of family income spent for bread declined from 40 per cent in 1800 to 20 per cent in 1850 to 7 or 8 per cent in 1919.[13] Newspapers such as *Le Petit Journal* and *Le Petit Parisian* circulated in the countryside and, through their advertisements, helped promote urban fashions. By the First World War, folklorists, eager to preserve the artefacts of what they saw as a peasant culture in danger of dying, sometimes dressed as peasants for a day, especially in Provence, under what Annie Moulin calls the 'bemused gaze of local peasants dressed in urban clothes'.[14]

The First World War produced a demand for foodstuffs that drove up the prices of agricultural goods and brought even many of the small subsistence farmers into the market. Many peasants were able to pay off their debts and even purchase some additional strips of land. Urban dwellers sometimes complained of the high price of food in the early 1920s and regarded the peasants as 'profiteers'.[15] The First World War moratorium on debt repayment meant that on resumption rural repayments were based on the nominal levels of 1914. After the 1928 franc stabilization, peasants repaid their debts in francs of one-fifth their previous value. By the inter-war period, some 75 to 80 per cent of farms relied on family labor, systems of tenure were relatively stable, and three-quarters of the farmers owned their own farms. In Annie Moulin's words, 'the myth of the small family farmer, a myth assiduously cultivated by the III Republic, began to approximate ever more closely to reality'.[16] Government policies also favored the peasantry, which many commentators saw as a bulwark of social stability in the face of a growing urban proletariat influenced by an active Communist Party. In 1920 *the Office nationale du Crédit agricole* was created as a public body serving as an umbrella organization for private credit groups. Electrification spread from 48 per cent of the communes in 1927 to 95 per cent eleven years later.[17]

The creation of a para-kulak class in the countryside, which then saw its aspirations disappointed with the collapse of agricultural prices in the 1930s, heightened public fears of peasants' leaving the countryside. Potential loss of the family farmer troubled virtually the entire spectrum of French political thinking in the 1930s, with even the Socialists worried. Farmers who remained in the countryside were often forced to a more subsistence production, a change resented by those whose lifestyles had changed since the eve of the First World War. Their anger produced the kind of peasant radicalism that Paxton describes in *Le Temps des Chemise Verts*. Renewed peasant radicalism was accompanied by a rediscovery of corporatist thought, articulated in 1937 by Louis Salleron, whose *Un Régime corporatif pour l'agriculture* inveighed against liberalism, Marxism, and the perceived urban bias of the state toward the urban population. Reacting to intensified peasant agitation in 1939, the government enacted a Family Code, extending family allowances, previously limited to urban workers, to farm families as well, with most costs borne by the state.

Vichy and the Countryside

The Vichy government faced a variety of problems in food supply, including the disruption caused by the May–June 1940 military campaign, the loss of more than a million men, first to the 1939 mobilization, and then to the German prisoner of war camps, and substantial losses of farm machinery, draught animals, and fertilizer.[18] Approximately 1,300,000 farmers had been mobilized, of whom 55,000 were killed and 500,000 taken prisoner in 1940. By 1944, some 400,000 men were still unavailable for agriculture.[19] In the Loiret, for example, the *Services de Contrôle mobile du Ravitaillement Général* estimated in January 1942 that, owing to decreased harvests and increased rural hoarding, only 30 per cent of the potato crop was reaching the official market.[20] In addition to these losses and the loss of Alsace-Lorraine, France suffered division into six occupation zones and difficulties in transporting goods among them.[21] War constraints also interfered with the shipment of supplies from North Africa, and ceased altogether following the Allied invasion of November 1942. Overall, the Germans took some 10 to 15 per cent of French agricultural production. Rouen and Lille faced meat and grain shortages as early as July 1940. The government responded by emphasizing distribution rather than production.[22]

Despite the constraints, the agrarian image became a key piece in Vichy's National Revolution. On 25 June 1940, Marshal Philippe Pétain spoke of the 'soil that does not lie . . . A field that falls fallow is a part of France that dies. A fallow field that is again re-sown is a part of France reborn.'[23] Pierre Caziot, newly installed as Minister of Agriculture in Vichy, tried to put into effect his long-standing goal of restoring the family farm. A law of 27 July 1940 provided state credits to farmers willing to take over land abandoned for two years or more. On 20 August 1940, a *Mission de Restauration Paysanne* was established to increase the number of family farms.[24]

Vichy's policy toward the peasantry was highlighted by the establishment of the *Corporation paysanne*, the sole agricultural professional organization allowed, on 2 December 1940. Created 'to promote and manage the common interests of peasant families in the social, moral, and economic domain',[25] the *Corporation paysanne* was a compromise resulting from different points of view, divided largely over the issue of how much independence the corporation's institutions were to have *vis-à-vis* the Ministry of Agriculture. Although nominally membership was voluntary, affiliation in any of the professional agricultural associations 'implied' membership in the corporation as well. Many such groups never submitted their membership lists to the corporation's local *syndicats* [local associations], or, if they did, left it to the latter to try to collect membership dues. The *Corporation paysanne* did not specify whether officials within the *syndicats* were to be elected or appointed. Salleron and others argued that 'natural' leaders would emerge. The relationship of the *Corporation paysanne* to the Ministry of Agriculture remained unclear and, as time went on, and the pressure of German requisitions and increased shortages became more harshly felt, the Ministry assumed more power, rendering the *Corporation paysanne* increasingly vacuous.[26]

The fledgling *Corporation* was quickly confronted by growing scarcity and the government's programs to control distribution. Its leadership consisted largely of the notables who had been active in the inter-war *Union Nationale des Syndicats Agricoles* (UNSA). By late January 1941, *L'Œuvre* of Marcel Déat, one of the more ardent collaborationists in Paris, denounced the new organization as hand-picked representatives of banking and landed interests.[27] Practical problems also emerged with putting Pétain's and Caziot's return to the soil program into effect. In many cases of denunciations peasants attempted to settle old personal scores. Forty-two dossiers examined under Caziotís law by the authorities in Aveyron resulted in only eight new grants of land, and none created new peasant families.[28] In a message to the peasants on 20 April 1941, Pétain continued to promise the consolidation of unproductive small farms, which he hoped would increase the number of successful family farms and reverse the flow of artisans from the countryside to the cities. Emphasizing the need to elevate the morality of the nation, Pétain warned against the black market.[29] Summarizing 'what one year of the Marshal's government' had brought to the peasants, Caziot could only refer to the joy of labor and evoke Pétain's references to the 'patience' of the peasantry.[30]

Indicative of Vichy's rhetorical attention to the peasantry, the book *France 1941, La Révolution Nationale Constructive*, celebrated the accomplishments of the first year of the National Revolution. Of the twenty-five articles covering most phases of French life in *France 1941*, three were devoted to the peasantry, a fourth article to artisans, and several others to corporatism and related economic reforms. Salleron defended corporatism, citing Frédéric Bastiat's social harmony theories and American theorist Henry Charles Carey's doctrine of land as the basis of value.[31] Salleron, like Pétain, addressed economic questions in terms of morality, arguing that agriculture was France's economic and spiritual 'calling'. Looking to the German system of barter, Salleron argued that a state-run policy of exchanges between agricultural and industrial sectors would so raise French economic output that it would enable France to double her population. Where, he asked – in a question curious for someone committed to autonomy for the *Corporation paysanne* – was the Colbert to take the economy in hand?[32] Henri Pourrat, in *France 1941*, depicted the peasant as a totally self-sufficient Robinson Crusoe, whose progressive disappearance needed to be reversed by a repopulation of the small towns, after the fashion of the medieval monks, who had established their monasteries around which the villages grew. Breathtakingly *rétro*, Pourrat wrote: 'Let's neither impose central heating on the peasants – benefits are dubious – nor even running water.'[33] A radiator, he continued, could not serve the same social centering purpose as an open hearth fire in the peasant's home. Pourrat defended the old ways, including clogs. For farm animals, muddy water was preferable to sterilized water provided by laboratories and the 'offices of urbanism',[34] in other words, by by urban municipalities.

Although it took only five months from the inception of the Vichy government until the enactment of the law creating the *Corporation paysanne*, it required the next two years to develop the *Corporation*; and even then problems remained. The corporatist movement itself divided over relations with the state. Caziot favored greater state power and Salleron more corporate autonomy. At the end of 1941, Salleron was released from his post in the *Corporation*, and his weekly journal, *Syndicats paysans*, ceased publication.[35] The *Corporation* also split over the degree to which specialized professional interests should be represented. Only in late 1942 was a regional network of corporations established.[36] Financing the *Corporation* presented a continual problem. The beginnings of Communist resistance in the countryside and the attempts of collaborationist parties such as Déat's Rassemblement National Populaire (RNP) to co-opt the *Corporation* placed the organization between two undesired alternatives. In addition, the Germans increased their pressure to bring the *Corporation*'s publications under the control of the Paris *Propagandastaffel* office.[37]

A law of 16 December 1942 increased the *Corporation paysanne*'s centralization and further reduced its autonomy, giving wide authority to the Minister of Agriculture to nominate *Corporation* officials on the regional and national level. The 1942 law also recognized the practical impossibility of grouping together in one organization all those engaged in agricultural production. Farm workers, small tenants, and share-holding tenants, who had shown little inclination to join the *Corporation paysanne*'s *syndicats*, were now to join special syndical subdivisions called *sections sociales* (special branches) at the regional level, and a new *Chambre syndicale* at the national level.[38] The increasing privations of the war, however, militated against successful operation as the *Corporation* became ever more involved in setting the levels of produce requisitions and as the peasants grew increasingly indifferent, if not hostile, to an institution that they saw as yet another bureaucratic arm of the state.[39] The *Corporation*'s failure to stabilize prices by 1943 had driven the price of a kilo of butter to 350 francs, while a bank employee earned 3,500 francs per month.[40]

By the beginning of 1944, Pétain was still evoking an unchanging essentialist image of the peasant, whose duty to marry young and create a family he emphasized as the traditional reality, stability, and solidity of France.[41] The tangle of organizations and associated regulations of the *Corporation paysanne* had grown to such an extent that even a pro-Vichy publication had difficulty sorting them all out, though it justified them on the grounds that they preserved order as opposed to liberty, meaning the open market.[42] Raymond Richard called for more 'grandeur and patriotic feeling' among the leaders of the *Corporation paysanne* to get through a difficult period.[43]

The Collaborationists and the Countryside

The Vichy of Pierre Laval, the Milice, a pro-fascist paramilitary police force, Philippe Henriot, and Marcel Déat in 1944 was, despite important continuities, not the same as that of the traditionalist notables of 1940. The collaborationists, whose perspective was predominately urban, developed an extreme version of the Vichy model of the countryside. There was no collaborationist follow-up after 1940 to the Green Shirt movement, most of whose supporters looked to Marshal Pétain and official Vichy after 1940. Dorgères himself became a fervent supporter of the Marshal, and when eventually he turned away from Vichy it was to the Resistance.[44] Urban middle-class youth in quest of spiritual values, which they believed lay in the countryside, were occasionally inspired by the pastoral writings of Jean Giono, a pacifist during the inter-war years. Although some of his followers found their way into the *Centre Laic des Auberges de Jeunesses* (Secular Youth Hostel Center) in the late 1930s and, later, under the Occupation, a few, such as Marc Augier and Philippe Merlin, joined the *Légion des Volontaires Français contre le Bolchevisme* and the French Waffen-SS, respectively, most urban youth showed scant interest in peasant realities.[45]

One of the clearest articulators of the urban collaborationist paradigm, Marcel Déat, chief editorialist for *L'Œuvre*, head of the RNP, and in 1944 Minister of Labor and National Solidarity, emerged as a leading spokesman for the New Order under the Occupation. Paxton notes that Dorgères had regarded Déat as an enemy of the peasantry before the war and continued to distrust him during the Occupation.[46] Déat's public positions regarding the countryside in July 1940 echoed those of official Vichy.[47] Déat, like Pétain and others in Vichy, argued that France had been defeated in 1940 because she had been living too well. The future, he wrote, belonged to the lean [*maigre*] peoples of Central Europe.[48] Solving what he called the 'peasant problem' was of the highest priority, he wrote; but he suggested nothing more specific than cooperation between peasant corporations on the one hand and labor associations on the other, which, he argued, would end the already burgeoning black market.[49] By late 1940 he accused the Vichy government of trying to sabotage Franco-German collaboration by impeding the transport of provisions to the capital in order to turn popular sentiment against Germany.[50]

In a 1941 article whose title, 'The Battle of Bread', evoked Mussolini's Battle of Grain, Déat supported a mobilization of manpower and cited utopian socialist Charles Fourier's argument that farm work needed to be made more attractive.[51] Returning to the battle motif four days later, in 'The Battle of Production', Déat called for state-supported agricultural cooperatives, based on 'coordination', national insurance, and credit.[52] By mid-1941, Déat was suggesting that Parisians, with their children, take their vacations in the countryside to work on farms, helping the peasants increase agricultural production.[53] Following the German attack against the Soviet Union, he urged the recruitment of the peasants as a 'military mass'.[54] In August 1941, when Pétain was complaining of a *mauvais vent* (ill wind) at Vichy, Déat argued that the English blockade, rather than German requisitions, created the real problem requiring greater production.[55] He subsequently blamed too much government bureaucracy while contradictorily calling at the same time for more coordination by the director of provisioning.[56]

By 1942, Déat welcomed the *Corporation paysanne*, but argued that it was too bureaucratic and that peasant organizations would be better off directing themselves. As had Salleron, Déat anticipated a 'true' peasant corporation giving rise to a new peasant elite through natural selection.[57] Déat welcomed Pierre Laval's return to power in April 1942; but the food problems remained, and, as Vichy turned increasingly toward police measures, Déat's tone against the 'inefficiency' of Vichy bureaucrats also became more punitive.[58] Anti-hedonic theory blended with wartime necessity in his September 1942 critique of refinement when he noted that the French complained most about their daily ration. Déat characterized the French as lovers of good food, which he viewed as a sign of elevated civilization but not a preparation for warrior virtues.[59] In the fall of 1942, he again argued for greater constraint and repression: prisons and concentration camps should be used to overcome the *psychose du profit.*[60] In May 1943, contradicting previous statements, he argued against forced requisitions, which, he wrote, merely pushed the peasants toward Communism.[61] Déat believed the peasants exhibited more bad will than any other social group. The fault, he argued, lay in a maladroit governmental administration, which, incapable of running peasant affairs smoothly, had resorted to heavy-handed requisitions. What France needed was a single party on the German model.[62]

With the war turning against the Axis in the summer of 1943, Déat warned that if 'Europe' lost the war either a brutal collectivization of French peasant land by Russia would follow, with opponents sent to Siberia, or an American takeover would force Europeans to buy American wheat. The French would be condemned in the latter case to unemployment and poverty, with France becoming just a tourist site for American millionaires.[63] Déat closed the year 1943 with an essentialist analysis of the 'French peasant', who, he said, had not changed since the 1789 Revolution. The peasant of 1943, just like his forebears of 1789, sought ownership of the land. Déat agreed with the Vichy traditionalists that the peasant served as a guarantee of social and political stability; but unlike Vichy, he concluded that only national socialism under a 'totalitarian state' could serve peasant interests. He also acknowledged that he was preaching to the deaf.[64] Nominated Minister of Labor and National Solidarity in March 1944, Déat continued to blame the Allies for French starvation, arguing that they wanted to reduce the French to slavery.[65]

Conclusions

The preoccupying hunt for food by urban dwellers and the existence of the black market during the Occupation turned many city people against the peasants, whom they accused of profiteering. Images from Jean Dutourd's *Au bon beurre* come to mind.[66] If the peasants were distinctly cool toward the collaborationists, however, relatively few peasants joined the ranks of the Resistance, whose requisitions, along with those of Vichy, alienated them. Apparent peasant indifference has led some to conclude that the peasants in general were fascists or collaborators.[67] Few of the 1930s peasant leaders from the Agrarian Party joined the Resistance. Most followed Pétain, at least in 1940, though, of course, this could be said of the French population in general.[68] As H. R. Kedward has shown, even in the south, where the Resistance was stronger, the relationship of the peasantry with the *maquis*, the Resistance fighters in the countryside, was complex, shifting toward the Resistance only in the beginning of 1943.[69] At first, the peasants were exempted from the *Service du Travail Obligatoire* (STO), Vichy's forced labor service that sent many Frenchmen to work in Germany. Vichy's increasing exactions, enforced by the growing police power supported by Déat, together with the changing fortunes of the war, pushed more peasants to support the Resistance. Fleeing the Germans and the STO, to which they had become subject in 1943, young rural men were frequently among the first to take to the *maquis*. They were often protected by villagers, to whom for the most part they were tied by family connections.[70] The collaborationists usually lacked the kinds of social links with the countryside that the Resistance successfully developed. In any event, by 1944, in Kedward's words, 'realism had changed sides'.[71]

In reality, the paradigms of countryside and collaboration, which bore superficial similarities, were very different at heart. In general the French popular rural communities have risen successfully over the past hundred years. Urban development, including railways and automobiles, and even the Second World War, has favored them in the areas of food and social life. Urban communitarian reform, such as the promotion of the art galleries and exhibitions so popular with collaborationist literati, meant little to the country people. On the other hand, pre-1940 Republican reforms in public health, the separation of clergy and state, and paid vacations, had been a great boon for the rural population. Viewed long-term, the peasants gained from the modernization processes initiated in the towns, and recognized this. Eugen Weber cites a peasant in 1907 as having said: 'We compare what the teacher gives us with what the priest can give. Well, he [the teacher] gives us more. It's the teacher that has taught us how to read, and that is useful in life. He has taught us how to reckon and that is even more useful . . . If we need advice for our taxes, for our business, we just go to see him. He's got books and papers about farming, about fertilizer.'[72]

The fascists in general, and the collaborationists in the particular circumstances of occupied France, were unable to appreciate the rural interests and lifestyle that might be encapsulated as eating well and buying a car. Consequently, fascist calls for self-sacrifice and volunteer labor, their readiness to take away the sons of the peasants for war, in short Déat's call for a leaner France, hardly endeared them to the peasants. In the First World War a peasantry with a rising standard of living disliked the Germans, who symbolized shooting their sons, destroying their families, taking away their food, and eliminating their automobile or the possibility of their ever acquiring one, and all for nothing. In the Second World War the Germans were no more popular than they had been during the First World War, which created serious difficulties for the collaborationist agenda in the countryside.

Historically, the peasants have been conservative when they owned what they wanted, radical when they did not.[73] There has been no famine in France in a more than a century, and peasant lifespans have grown longer. Peasants are better educated, and most are now trained in modern science. Weber's peasant of 1907, speaking for the French rural population, could see what worked for him. To the degree that Vichy's early corporatism corresponded to peasant interests and there appeared to be no realistic alternatives, the people of the countryside appeared willing to give it a chance. As the pressure of wartime circumstance and its own internal logic drove Vichy closer to fascism and collaborationism, the gulf between it and the countryside widened. The model of a fascist France exemplified by Déat, Darnand, and the Vichy of 1944 held little appeal in the countryside. With the Liberation, the purge was quite limited, and many of the pre-war peasant leaders returned. They would see a post-war France that, as Bertrand Hervieu of the *Centre National de la Recherche Scientifique* (CNRS), phrased it, ceased to be an agrarian society and became instead an agricultural power.[74]

Notes

1. Robert O. Paxton, *Le Temps des chemises verts: Révoltes paysannes et fascisme rural 1929–1939* (Paris, 1996): 251. See also Annette Lévy-Willard, 'Les chemises noires de la France verte', *Libération*, 24 October 1996, VIII.
2. On the collaborationists' urban background, see Bertram M. Gordon, *Collaborationism in France during the Second World War* (New York, 1980): 335 and Bertram M. Gordon, 'The Morphology of the Collaborator: The French Case', *Journal of European Studies*, 23 (parts 1 and 2): 89 and 90 (March–June 1993): 7.
3. Paxton, *Le Temps des chemises verts*: 286. As H. R. Kedward notes, in 'Rural France and Resistance' (Chapter 9 above), Vichy's 'discursive monopoly' over the exploration of peasant culture has been superseded

by the historical literature focusing on the peasants and the Resistance; see especially his footnote 1.

4. Ibid.: 273.
5. Ibid.: 270–1.
6. Gordon Wright, *Rural Revolution in France: The Peasantry in the Twentieth Century* (Stanford, 1968 [original edition, 1964]): 72. See also Paxton, *Le Temps des chemises verts*: 272.
7. Paxton, *Le Temps des chemises verts*: 255–6.
8. Gérard Walter, *Histoire des Paysannes de France* (Paris, 1963): 420 and 431–2.
9. See Annie Moulin, *Peasantry and Society in France since 1789*, trans. M. C. and M. F. Cleary (Cambridge and Paris, 1991): 99–100.
10. Eugen Weber, *Peasants into Frenchmen, The Modernization of Rural France 1870–1914* (Stanford, 1976): 493–4.
11. Moulin, *Peasantry and Society in France since 1789*: 116–18.
12. Marcel Aymard, 'Toward the History of Nutrition: Some Methodological Remarks', in Robert Forster and Orest Ranum (eds), *Food and Drink in History* (Baltimore, 1979): 5–6.
13. Weber, *Peasants into Frenchmen*: 137–8.
14. Moulin, *Peasantry and Society in France since 1789*: 121–2.
15. Wright, *Rural Revolution in France*: 29–30.
16. Moulin, *Peasantry and Society in France since 1789*: 141.
17. Ibid.: 143–4. By 1940, one out of three communes had been supplied with running water. See Wright, *Rural Revolution in France*: 34.
18. Directeur Régional de la Production Agricole, Région de Bordeaux, 'Annexe de la circulaire du 12 avril 1942', in a report to the Commissaire Général aux Ressources Agricoles, 21 May 1942; Archives Nationales, F10 5498.
19. Isabel Boussard, 'Peasantry under Vichy', in Bertram M. Gordon (ed.), *Historical Dictionary of World War II France: The Occupation, Vichy and the Resistance, 1938–1946* (Westport, CT, 1998): 280.
20. M. Gaudet *et al.*, 'Rapport sur la possibilité d'augmenter la commercialisation des produits agricoles', Annexe 2: 'Note sur la répression du marché noir,' 19 January 1942; in Archives nationales, F10/2184.
21. For a discussion of the problems caused by the division of France into zones and the loss of Alsace-Lorraine, see Michel Cépède, *Agriculture et Alimentation en France durant la IIe Guerre Mondiale* (Paris, 1961): 50–5.
22. M. C. Cleary, *Peasants, Politicians and Producers: The Organisation of Agriculture in France since 1918* (Cambridge, 1989): 92–3.
23. Philippe Pétain, *La France Nouvelle, Principes de la Communauté,*

suivis des Appels et Messages 17 juin 1940–17 juin 1941 (Paris, 1941): 25.

24. *Agriculteurs voici ce qu'en un an le gouvernement du Maréchal a fait pour vous* (Vichy: Edition du Secrétariat Général á l'Information et á la Propagande, 1941): 8.
25. Ibid.: 10.
26. Isabel Boussard, *Vichy et la Corporation Paysanne* (Paris, 1980): 42–3. See also Wright, *Rural Revolution in France*: 80–1. In a case unique under Vichy, the Corporation's permanent trustees were elected by their peers, see Moulin, *Peasantry and Society in France since 1789*: 152–3.
27. Boussard, *Vichy et la Corporation Paysanne*: 57.
28. Cleary, *Peasants, Politicians and Producers*: 100–1.
29. Pétain, *La France Nouvelle*: 139–40 and 142–3.
30. Pierre Caziot, 'Après l'orage . . .,' in *Agriculteurs voici ce qu'en un an le gouvernement du Maréchal a fait pour vous*: 5–6.
31. Louis Salleron, 'Agriculture et Industrie,' in André Bellesort *et al.*, *France 1941, La Révolution Nationale Constructive, Un bilan et un programme* (Paris, 1941): 407.
32. Salleron, 'Agriculture et Industrie': 411–15. 'Colbert' refers to Jean-Baptiste Colbert (1619–1683), Louis XIV's Finance Minister and Controller General, noted for his policies of strong centralized state leadership in the economy.
33. Henri Pourrat, 'La Question Paysanne', in André Bellesort *et al.*, *France 1941*: 422–3. 'Qu'on n'impose pas aux paysans le chauffage central, – sur ses bienfaits, on peut rester en doute, – ni même l'eau au robinet . . .'.
34. Ibid.: 425. Albert Dauzat regretted the disappearance of peasant folk dress in the countryside that he dated to the years before the First World War: see Dauzat, *Le Village et le paysan de France* (Paris, 1941): 139–40.
35. For his sharp critique of what he saw as an incipient *étatisation* in the ways in which the *Corporation paysanne* were being constructed, see Louis Salleron, *Naissance de l'État Corporatif: Dix ans de Syndicalisme paysanne* (Paris, 1941): 15–16 and 239–40.
36. Cleary, *Peasants, Politicians and Producers*: 97.
37. Boussard, *Vichy et la Corporation Paysanne*: 182.
38. Ibid.: 198–9. See also Wright, *Rural Revolution in France*: 84–5.
39. See, for example, Le Directeur Régional de la Production Agricole, Angers, 'Préparation du plan d'imposition pour la campagne 1942–3,' report to Ministère de l'Agriculture, Commissariat Général aux

Ressources Agricoles, Paris, 25 May 1942; and Direction Régional de la Production Agricole, Région de Poitiers, 'Rapport du directeur régional de la Production Agricole sur le plan d'imposition de la campagne agricole 1942–1943,' Poitiers, 15 May 1942; both in Archives nationales, F10 5498.

40. Christian Guy, *Histoire de la Gastronomie en France* (Paris, 1985): 127–9.
41. Henri Lacroix, 'Ce que le Maréchal a dit du paysan dans ses messages', *Cahiers du Monde Nouveau* (1 January 1944): 14.
42. Raymond Richard, 'Ce qu'est et ce que doit être la corporation paysanne', *Cahiers du Monde Nouveau* (1 January 1944): 7–8. On the need to eliminate the free market, see also G. Guillemette, 'Evolution de la législation agricole en France', ibid.: 62.
43. Richard, 'Ce qu'est et ce que doit être la corporation paysanne': 10–11.
44. Pascal Ory, 'Le Dorgèrisme: institution et discours d'une colère paysanne (1929–1939)', *Revue d'histoire moderne et contemporaine*, 22 (April–June 1975): 175 for a discussion of Dorgères's relations with Doriot before 1939, and ibid.: 182 for consideration of the peasant leader's strong *Maréchaliste* position after the armistice. See also Gordon, *Collaborationism in France*: 39–40.
45. For the relationship between fascism in general and the ideas of Jean Giono see Henri Pollès, *L'opéra politique* (Paris, 1937): 30–3, 48, 145 and 155; and a review of this book by André Billy, 'Naturisme et 'Fascisme' de Giono', *L'Œuvre*, 29 August 1937. See also Gordon, *Collaborationism in France*: 256.
46. Paxton, *Le Temps des chemises verts*: 239 and 242.
47. Marcel Déat, 'Ressources provinciales', *L'Œuvre*, 18 July 1940.
48. Déat, 'Les vraies richesses', *L'Œuvre*, 13 July 1940, reprinted in Déat, *Perspectives françaises* (Paris: Editions de 'L'Œuvre,' n.d.): 5.
49. Déat, 'Ceux des champs et ceux de la ville', *L'Œuvre*, 12 November 1940. On *syndicats*, see also Boussard, *Vichy et la Corporation Paysanne*: 94 and 336–7.
50. Déat, 'Saboteurs du ravitaillement', *L'Œuvre*, 29 December 1940. He returned to this theme again in Déat, 'Le blocus de Paris', *L'Œuvre*, 7 January 1941. For a denunciation of Caziot by Déat, see Déat, 'Formules creuses et ventres vides', *L'Œuvre*, 24 January 1941.
51. Déat, 'La bataille du pain', *L'Œuvre*, 6 April 1941.
52. Déat, 'La bataille de la production', *L'Œuvre*, 10 April 1941.
53. Déat, 'Pour une accueil rural des familles parisiennes', *L'Œuvre*, 5 June 1941.

54. Déat, 'L'accroge au sol', *L'Œuvre*, 7–8 July 1941. For the 'mauvais vent', see Robert O. Paxton, *Vichy France, Old Guard and New Order 1940–1944* (New York, 1975 [1972]): 225–6.
55. Déat, 'Répartir, c'est bien produire, c'est mieux', *L'Œuvre*, 8 August 1941. Pétain's complaint about an 'ill wind' was his public recognition of a growing popular alienation from Vichy and an intensifying Resistance activity, shortly after the German invasion of the Soviet Union.
56. Déat, 'La dictateur aux vivres', *L'Œuvre*, 26 November 1941.
57. Déat, 'Corporatisme paysanne', *L'Œuvre*, 26 March 1942. See also Déat, 'Le blé qui se cache', *L'Œuvre*, 8 April 1942.
58. Déat, 'Punir les affameurs', *L'Œuvre*, 16 June 1942.
59. Déat, 'Niveau de vie européen', *L'Œuvre*, 17 September 1942.
60. Déat, 'Le plafond est atteint', *L'Œuvre*, 16 October 1942.
61. Déat, 'Doléances paysannes', *L'Œuvre*, 10 May 1943.
62. Déat, 'Soudure et Marché Noir', *L'Œuvre*, 12 May 1943.
63. Déat, 'Perspectives agricoles', *L'Œuvre*, 8 July 1943.
64. Déat, 'Les paysans et la Révolution', *L'Œuvre*, 29 December 1943.
65. Déat, 'De la famine à l'esclavage', *L'Œuvre*, 17 July 1944.
66. A Church survey of sixty priests, published, as 'Problèmes missionnaires de la France rurale', (*Collection 'Rencontres,' no. 16*) in spring 1944 complained of peasant greed and licentiousness: cited in Walter, *Histoire des Paysannes de France*: 461–3.
67. See, for example, Anne-Marie Badourès and Maurice Bouyou, *La Paysannerie en Périgord* (Bordeaux, 1983): 77–8.
68. Moulin, *Peasantry and Society in France since 1789*: 158.
69. H. R. Kedward, *In Search of the Maquis: Rural Resistance in Southern France 1942–1944* (Oxford, 1993): 16. See also ibid.: 7, 9, and 28. See especially Robert Bonnafous, ibid.: 246.
70. Ibid.: 235, 239, 241, 244, 251, and 253–4.
71. Ibid.: 105 and 144–5.
72. Weber, *Peasants into Frenchmen*: 362. See also Moulin, *Peasantry and Society in France since 1789*: 144–6.
73. See Pierre Goubert, *La vie quotidienne des paysans français au XVIIe siécle* (Paris, 1982): 277–90.
74. Cited in Eric Fottorino, 'Bertrand Hervieu, directeur de recherches au CNRS', *Le Monde*, 22–23 June 1997: 14.

—11—

The Resistance and Vichy

Dominique Veillon

For a long time, historians of the Second World War have tended to focus on either the resistance movement or the Vichy regime, without dealing directly with the relationship between them. Yet recent inquiry has shown that all resisters and resistance organizations did not necessarily and unequivocally question the authority of Pétain, nor did they all distance themselves from Vichy policy and institutions. Consequently, those who did commit themselves to opposing the government early on appear all the more remarkable for having recognized the reprehensible nature of the regime from the very beginning.

Thanks to the breakthroughs of Robert Paxton's work, the historiography of Vichy France has evolved considerably (despite an early reluctance on the part of many French historians to consider scholarship produced outside France): certain aspects of the regime are now better understood, and a number of myths have been swept aside.[1] The same cannot be said, however, for the historiography of the Resistance. Recently, hitherto little-known facts have been revealed by the newly-accessible archives of the *Bureau Central de Renseignements et d'Action* (BCRA) and the documents presented by Daniel Cordier in his study of the resistance leader Jean Moulin.[2] Together with the findings of the past few years, these sources make it possible to nuance our appreciation of the Resistance by re-evaluating the attitudes that some resistance organizations had toward Vichy in their initial phase.

Although a number of those who led the fight against the occupier were quick to condemn both the Germans and the Vichy regime in the same breath, such resisters were very much in a minority. Others were certainly anti-Nazi and/or anti-German and committed to fighting the enemy, but had a generally favorable attitude toward Pétain. Beyond the existence of these two major tendencies however, little else is known. To what extent did the Vichy government fetter, or conversely, accelerate, the emergence of the Resistance? And within the Resistance itself, could an oppositional stance leading to illegal activities coexist with pro-Pétainist leanings? Put simply, could one be both pro-Vichy and a resister at the same time, and if so, under what conditions? What kinds of relationships existed between pro-Pétainist resisters and the existing government? How far could such resisters hope to go? And how was it that 'generations' of resisters of the pro-Vichy type, exemplified by François Mitterrand and his prisoner-of-war movement, entertained a relationship with Marshal Pétain over a considerable length of time? Sentiments, attitudes, and politics within resistance groups did indeed evolve over the course of the war: the timing of the break with Vichy in such groups is crucial, for it reveals the degree of consensus that existed among members of an opposition who did not reject the regime outright. For many in the pro-Pétain camp, the Allied landings of November 1942 marked the beginning of an important ideological shift.

This is a large agenda, and in the interest of opening a few avenues for future research, I will limit my discussion to the following three areas: (1) the impossibility of ignoring the relationship between some resistance groups and the Vichy regime; (2) the ideological basis of such relationships, as seen in the cases of Henri Frenay and Commandant Georges Loustaunau-Lacau; and (3) the institutional nature of such relationships, as exemplified by the Uriage leadership school and François Mitterrand's prisoner-of-war movement.

I. Vichy and the Resistance: A Reality that Cannot be Ignored

If the existence of the occupier weighed heavily on the development of the Resistance, especially in the northern zone, so too did the Vichy government, dominated by the personality of Marshal Pétain. In both zones, trauma following the defeat created major upset in all realms, including the moral one. Everything was called into question. This explains why certain values advanced by the National Revolution could have been perceived as necessary for the renewal of French society, which many French people, including some pioneers of the Resistance, genuinely desired. Resisters in both zones had to take Vichy into account, albeit in different ways and for different reasons. The existence of a government that practiced a policy of collaboration with the enemy was a reality that they could not ignore. Nor is it now possible to disregard the influence that Pétain and his regime had on some resistance groups. In the southern zone even more than in the northern, these early resisters factored Vichy into their thinking; they made their first moves in response to the particular political context in which they found themselves.

1. The hard-line anti-Vichy position

From the very beginning, a minority of resisters fully and unequivocally condemned Pétainism. For them, antifascism and antinazism were indissociable from a thorough rejection of the Vichy regime. Agreeing with the unambiguous positions of the Free French in this matter, certain early resisters did not hesitate to show their anti-Vichy sentiments by circulating small, virulent publications such as *La France Continue* and *Valmy*.[3] This anti-Vichy stance was the cornerstone of their revolt; it shaped their identity and provided a common ground. In this group we can include the *France-Liberté* circle (later to become *Franc-Tireur*), *Libération-Nord*,[4] and *La Dernière Colonne* (later to become *Libération-Sud*),[5] all of which also produced underground newspapers by the same name. These resisters denounced Pétain and his clique as enemies of freedom who had been working hand in hand with the Germans from the very outset.

In an appeal accompanying a letter of 20 February 1941 addressed to London,[6] the founders of *France-Liberté* did not hesitate to compare Vichy to Nazi Germany: 'The part of France that Vichy administers is no doubt privileged in that it is not under the boot of the German army, but that does not mean that it is free. The official media, the press, the radio are all controlled by Germany.' There follows a condemnation of the National Revolution, as well as a denunciation of exclusionary measures taken against Jews.[7] 'Thus have they destroyed traditions, customs, laws, and attempted, under the guise of a supposed National Revolution, to reduce the French people to sheep.' The conclusion is a call for a free France, the very antithesis of Vichy.

For the hard-line anti-Vichy resisters who were the leaders of *Libération* or *Franc-Tireur*, the consequences were clear: Pétain and his associates could not be counted upon to resist Germany, because they had chosen to make concessions to the victor. The hostility of these resisters toward Pétain and his government was such that any contact with those in Vichy's orbit was unimaginable. This was clearly the case of the *Franc-Tireur* group, whose anti-Vichy position was unmistakable. Even in 1942, when Jean-Pierre Lévy, the head of the group, agreed to meet with General B.-L. Fornet de la Laurencie[8] to seek financial support, many members disapproved of such a move. Despite the close bond between the leader of *Franc-Tireur* and his comrades, Lévy had not had time to consult the others first, which in the end produced tensions within the movement.

2. The Pétainist resisters

There were also many resistance pioneers who saw in Pétain a last resort or a guide. Although submitting to Germany was clearly out of the question for them, they still deemed it necessary, at least initially, to trust Pétain. And so there developed a form of 'resistance' that might be called 'Pétainist', one that saw no contradiction between committing to the struggle against Nazism, and maintaining hope in the head of state.[9] The *Liberté* group, organized in November 1940 by François de Menthon and Pierre-Henri Teitgen, two Christian-Democratic law professors, illustrates this tendency. In their newspaper of the same name, they were careful not to attack Pétain directly, and asked their readers to trust him: 'The Marshal must know that the French people unanimously support his resistance.' For many, trust in Pétain was a necessary first step. In their view, a head of state who had stood up to the enemy during the First World War had earned their loyalty; Pétain's leadership [collaboration] did not preclude all hope of liberating France from the Germans. After the war, the group's leaders suggested that tactics, not ideology, had led them to support the head of state; the fact remains that in the beginning, *Liberté* and its members leaned heavily in favor of Pétain.

3. General Gabriel Cochet

This Pétainist attitude also informed the actions of General Cochet, an Air Force general who belonged to the Deuxième Bureau prior to the war. As early as September 1940, he published a call for resistance, followed by several newsletters signed under his own name. He was in fact the first to write leaflets in the hope of creating a group that would operate on French territory. These leaflets were intended primarily for those in his own social and professional sphere, the army and his fellow officers. In the very name of patriotism, General Cochet believed that Pétain, because of his glorious past, was the best possible bulwark against the enemy. He said so explicitly in a letter dated 26 September 1940, parts of which show his support for Vichy policies. In appoving the reforms that had been undertaken, he emphasized,

> the unanimous will of the French people to remake, and thus liberate France by means of all the resolve, all the patience, all the prudence necessary to the task. [. . .] As former officers who have remained outside the political struggle, our duty is to focus all of our efforts on propaganda and actions that can unite all patriots, working side by side, behind the head of state, patriots who are

full of conviction and confidence, and ready to take vigorous action to redress the situation.

Despite his acceptance of the principle of collaboration, Marshal Pétain is represented as the occupiers' adversary. According to this line of thinking, Pétain knew what he was doing and why. If he negotiated with the enemy, then it was because he hoped to allay French suffering and obtain concessions from the Germans. Although Cochet was favorably disposed toward collaboration in the beginning, he became increasingly critical of it over time. By contrast, his distrust of Charles de Gaulle was constant.

Imbued with a deep nationalism, Cochet's movement grew in the south (Cannes, Toulon, Nice) and in the center (the area of Saint-Etienne and Clermont-Ferrand). A Vichy-led investigation in the spring of 1941 emphasized General Cochet's loyalty to Pétain, all the while acknowledging his hostility toward collaboration. Aside from propaganda activities judged 'inopportune and dangerous' and driven by a 'misguided patriotism', Vichy accused Cochet of dissident activities such as the establishment of armed groups in the Var region. On Darlan's orders, Cochet was arrested and imprisoned on 21 June 1941. A month later, he reaffirmed his allegiance to Pétain even from his prison cell.

4. *Défense de la France*

Although the *Défense de la France* movement can also be characterized as Pétainist, it is a different sort of group altogether, if only because of its context of operation. In the northern zone, young students led by Philippe Viannay aimed above all to change the thinking of the surrounding population. The establishment of a newpaper was conceived initially as a moral act; indeed, the group was originally founded to inform public opinion, not engage in direct action. The first issue of the newspaper *Défense de la France*, dated 15 August 1941, showed moderation toward Pétain. For these young people, the fight was above all a spiritual one: no victory could be possible without a moral recovery – a position consistent with that of the National Revolution.[10] Of all the members of *Défense de la France*, its leader Philippe Viannay seemed the most favorably disposed toward the head of state. Viannay's Pétainism can be explained by 'a family background characterized by antisemitism, conservatism, Catholicism', and a clear anticommunism, according to the historian of the movement, Olivier Wieviorka.[11]

If *Défense de la France* opposed Germany for patriotic reasons, its position regarding Pétain remained somewhat ill-defined through November 1942, but without causing frictions among its members. The young women students in particular, who were numerous in the group, seemed more critical of Pétain than their male colleagues, yet they were unable to change or influence the movement's positions. At least that is what emerges from their post-war testimony. Hélène Mordkovitch (later to become Hélène Viannay), Génia Gemahling, and Charlotte Nadel all gravitated around the group's leadership. By family tradition, they were profoundly attached to the republican values inspired by the Revolution of 1789. Their personal histories played a considerable role in this: all three were of Russian origin and had lived in France only a short while, their parents having emigrated to France after the First World War. Their democratic values did not allow any sympathy for a regime that repudiated the motto 'liberty, equality, fraternity', or for the old man running the country. But all three women made it clear that they had little influence in editorial matters at the time, even though they had been involved in the production of the underground paper.

Furthermore, it is essential to note that the activists of *Défense de la France* refused to break into factions over a problem they considered secondary: if the issue of the French State raised moral questions, especially in the southern zone, it had less relevance for activists operating in the northern zone: 'Whether a moral or a political question, the Vichy problem remains outside [our] sphere of action.'[12] The newspaper, profoundly anti-Nazi despite its Pétainist language, was by its very existence a response, indeed a form of opposition, to the resignation advocated by Pétain. The very fact of its regular publication was in itself a kind of challenge. Although *Défense de la France* rejected collaboration as a political option from the outset, the group continued to espouse a Pétainist line until November 1942. At that point, they finally broke with Vichy and advocated civil disobedience; the editors of the newspaper replaced their original Pétainist discourse with a pro-republican one. Nevertheless, the movement was more Giraudist than Gaullist through March 1943 – proof that the pro-Vichy period was more than a simple parenthesis in the movement's history.

II. Ideological Links Between Vichy and the Resistance[13]

To understand the relationships that emerged between certain Pétainist resisters and the Vichy government, one must begin by looking at the critically important role played by the army in the eyes of Marshal Pétain. He expected the men of the post-Armistice army[14] to become partisans of the new regime – which did not keep some of them from clinging to the hope of liberating France. While a number of officers who were stunned by the cataclysm of 1940 intended to continue the fight, most did not wish to become dissidents, since it was not their proper place to call into question the authority of the state, and therefore their own legitimacy. A culture of opposition based on protest and disobedience, which sets the stage for subversive activities, was altogether foreign to these men. And if a few soldiers agreed to hide arms or vehicles, or to help support British or French Resistance networks, they did so with only the tacit agreement of their superiors. The trajectory of Henri Frenay, career army officer, Pétainist, and founder of the *Mouvement de Libération Nationale* (MLN), is no different from that of a number of resistance pioneers. Yet his case appears more complex. Ideologically drawn to the National Revolution, Frenay moved in Vichy circles, which prompts questions as to the ties he established with the regime and the circumstances surrounding his break with the Marshal.

1. The case of Henri Frenay

Transferred on 15 December 1940 to the Second Bureau of the EMA (*Etat-major de l'Armée*) at Vichy, Henri Frenay, stunned by the defeat, had but one idea: to continue the fight. He used his position to publish *Bulletins d'Information*,[15] but his loyalty to Pétain was total, as evidenced in the text of the *Manifeste de Libération nationale*, which was presumably drafted in final form in November 1940. As Daniel Cordier reminds us, this text is important: of all the founders of the various resistance organizations, Frenay was the only one to offer a real resistance platform 'in which he pledg[ed] allegiance to Pétain and support[ed] the National Revolution'.[16]

His call to resistance, though cautious with regard to Pétain himself,[17] evokes the major themes of the National Revolution. The manifesto expresses ideas similar to those of General Cochet, in that it advocates bringing together patriots of good will, particularly those in the post-Armistice army. 'Since the defeat, men of all kinds, bound solely by their common love of country [*la patrie*], have organized to save France from foreign domination [. . .] in order to carry out the necessary program of the National Revolution.' But Frenay is adamant on one essential point: for this revolution to take place, 'we must first drive the Germans out of France'. The text ends with a glowing homage to Marshal Pétain: 'May the Marshal live long enough to sustain us with his great authority and incomparable prestige.'

How is it possible to explain Frenay's position in 1940, other than by assuming a certain ideological complicity with the Vichy regime? For Frenay to turn away from Pétain, he would have had to abandon a project that he supported and in which he deeply believed: the renewal of France.[18] It would have meant breaking from the army that had shaped him and in whose ranks he had many friends. The support of certain activists of the MLN who had joined him would also have been at stake, in part because of the loyalty the movement had shown the head of state. Finally, it would also have meant severing all ties to right-wing circles, specifically those Vichy supporters whom he still hoped to rally to the cause of resistance. Hence, the contact Frenay maintained with General de la Laurencie.

Frenay's break from Vichy and Pétain at the end of 1941 was brought on by a number of factors: the toughening of governmental policy; promises made by Vichy to the Germans; the increasingly explicit connection between the National Revolution and the policy of collaboration; and the influence of his entourage, specifically that of Claude Bourdet, who wanted *Combat* to affiliate with de Gaulle. Frenay's decision was also inspired by mergers with other resistance groups. Although the merger with *Liberté* was essentially complete by November 1941, Frenay came up against Emmanuel d'Astier's refusal to accept a position that did not condemn Vichy along with the Germans. D'Astier believed that 'the liberation of French territory and liberation from the Vichy government [were] part and parcel of the same problem'. Nonethless – and this is important, for it marks a change of position by Frenay – the leaders of the three movements who met with Laurencie in mid-December 1941 made a joint decision to turn down the General's offer to assume leadership of the united resistance forces. Conversations with François de Menthon, then in the anti-Vichy camp, and Emmanuel d'Astier, anti-Pétainist from the very beginning, no doubt had some effect on Frenay's final decision. For Frenay, the severing of all ties to Vichy was the price to pay for the alliance with de Gaulle. Although Frenay's change of heart between August and December 1941 was indeed genuine, the leader of Libération-Sud remained unconvinced.

Following a series of arrests within the *Combat* movement,[19] and at a time when his reservations toward the regime were becoming more pronouced, Henri Frenay met with several Vichy officials with the aim of securing the release of his imprisoned comrades. At the end of January 1942, he conferred with Commandant Rollin, Deputy Secretary General of the Ministry of the Interior, followed by talks on 28 January and 6 February 1942 with Minister of the Interior Pierre Pucheu. At this stage, the Frenay of 1940 had become both a critic of the regime and the leader of *Combat*. For him, these meetings were only means to greater ends. Be that as it may, as soon as the incident became known, it caused great consternation among those who had become his partners in the movement. It also contributed to a certain reserve on the part of Yvon Morandat, one of the first envoys of the Free French to arrive on French territory. After the war, Morandat accused the movement of loyalty to Marshal Pétain: 'I only half-liked *Combat* because its newspaper published articles with a somewhat fascist bent. The Marshal was treated with respect, and they still seemed to believe that Pétain wanted to be independent and to resist the Germans.'[20]

The mistrust of *Combat* and its leader's relationship with Vichy is noted in an analysis of the Resistance in the southern zone by 'Pierre' (Stanislas Mangin). Even after the merger, and before the Frenay–Pucheu encounter had taken place, the leaders of *Libération Nationale* reveal a surprising degree of confusion about *Combat*, which they still perceived as a Pétainist movement. Although the groups had already joined forces earlier that month (January 1942), the Vichy issue had yet to be resolved between them. Frenay was suspected not only of ideological complicity with Vichy, but also of maintaining relations with high-ranking army officers, as noted in the following excerpts.

From Roger Stéphane: '[. . .] *Libération Nationale* is a movement composed of military men and right-wingers – [people with] very different leanings than *Liberté*; [it is] a small group whose reactionary nature poses a problem for a merger with *Libération*[*-Sud*].'[21]

From de Menthon: 'It is true that Frenet [*sic*] is very suspect because of his relationship to the EMA [army leadership]. This situation is uncertain and requires that certain precautions be taken. At the very least, we must assume that the EMA is completely aware of everything relating to his movement. It is reasonable to assume that the same must also be the case for our own movement. It is true that this could all be explained by Frenet's friendships within the EMA and the recruitment [of the movement's members] from the officer corps.'

From 'Mercier' (Jean Moulin): 'Frenet [*sic*] can indeed be suspect. I am supposed to see him tomorrow [28 January 1941]. I expect my control of the budget will give me some leverage.'[22]

Only Morandat, who kept some distance from *Combat*, notes with honesty that Frenay's links to the army could have some advantages as well, such as providing ideal cover to resisters or facilitating acts of resistance against the Germans.

Despite their clear rejection of the Pétainist option, in a certain sense

Frenay and *Combat* always remained identified with their initial position. Albeit indirectly, the links Frenay maintained with Vichy enabled him to successfully mount one of the first, most important resistance groups. At the same time however, these same links would give rise to subsequent conflicts between *Combat* on the one hand, and Jean Moulin and the Free French on the other.

2. *Georges Loustaunau-Lacau*

Initially, Commandant Loustaunau-Lacau's position was similar in many respects to that of Frenay, but the official relationships he established with Vichy institutions led him to try other solutions.

Loustaunau-Lacau had clear right-wing political sympathies. Before the war, and in association with the *Cagoules*, he founded the Corvignoles network to identify and report Communist activities in the barracks. After the defeat, Loustaunau-Lacau condemned neither the Armistice, nor the new French State. He was released from active duty following the Armistice and appointed Secretary General of the *Légion Française des Combattants* in August 1940. He planned to use this position to rally around him anti-German war veterans, with the idea of forming a *revanchiste* army. In his speech of 12 August 1941, Pétain himself made a veiled allusion to men like Loustaunau-Lacau when he condemned those who used their Vichy connections to mask illegal activities.[23]

Thanks to the advantages of his official position, Loustaunau-Lacau was able to found an embryonic resistance group, publishing flyers and printing newsletters.[24] In October 1940 he authored *La Croisade*, a sort of declaration of principle of the resistance to Nazi barbarism, and established the anti-German and pro-British military intelligence network *Navarre*. In December 1940, he was able to make contact with his long-time friend Pierre Fourcaud, then an agent of the Free French, who wished to form an alliance with the *Légion*, and even to reach a secret accord with Pétain. In so doing, Fourcaud was acting against the orders of General de Gaulle, for whom repudiation of the Vichy regime was essential. When de Gaulle learned of the plan, he categorically refused to have anything to do with Loustaunau-Lacau, whom he considered to be too close to Pétain.

Loustaunau-Lacau, faced with de Gaulle's order to exclude him from any common project, turned instead to the British, to whom he sent intelligence acquired through his network. Although his institutional connections enabled him to engage in quasi-legal activities, the leader of *Navarre* remained nevertheless marked by his Pétainism and loyalty to certain tenets of the Vichy regime. In contrast to Henri Frenay, whose allegiance to de Gaulle was accompanied by a condemnation of Pétain, Loustaunau-Lacau's failed overtures to the Free French resulted only in fueling his anti-Gaullism and pushing him into the British camp.

III. Institutional Links between Vichy and the Resistance

A new generation of activists was unique in that they were both pro-Vichy and resisters (*vichysto-résistants*) at one and the same time. Members of the Uriage school and the prisoner-of-war movement experienced a genuine fascination with Marshal Pétain. They fully subscribed to the principles of the National Revolution, which had become an obligatory rite of passage in breaking with the Third Republic, then seen as the source of all evil. Many believed that a fundamental reform of society and political institutions as conceived by Vichy was a necessary prerequisite to action, and that it was not incompatible with the struggle against the Germans; on the contrary, working for the National Revolution and the Resistance were part and parcel of the same project. These pro-Vichy resistance organizations 'were integral parts of the state bureaucracy [. . .]. They did not call into question its basic premises because they were convinced of the quality of the principles that governed the establishment of the French State,'[25] and of the need to resist.

1. The National School of Uriage

The *Ecole Nationale des cadres d'Uriage* (National School for Leadership Training) was one of the most important institutions created under Vichy's auspices immediately after the defeat. The position of its founder, Pierre Dunoyer de Segonzac, was typical of that of other military men. Although Segonzac did not wish to remain in the post-Armistice army, which he considered to be under the control of the enemy, he too saw national renewal as indispensable. Looking ahead to France's need for an elite capable of rebuilding the country, he secured permission from the Vichy authorities to create his training center for the future leaders of France. The school was thus not a state initiative, but that of one man, Dunoyer de Segonzac, who showed 'absolute loyalty' and total submission to the person of the Marshal. For him, Pétain was the savior, a providential being, the flag, the last hope.[26] Institutional ties with General Secretary for Youth Georges Lamirand were such that the Vichy regime soon considered the school a state-sponsored accomplishment.

Under such conditions, how was it possible to reconcile hostility toward Nazi Germany with support from a regime that preached collaboration with the enemy? How could Uriage maintain its autonomy, at the same time that it was answerable to a ministry of the Vichy government? What were the consequences of this arrangement for Uriage's members?

Although Dunoyer de Segonzac repeatedly expressed his loyalty to the Marshal and embraced several principal values of the National Revolution, he distanced himself from the regime by proclaiming in November 1941: 'We serve the Marshal, yes. Do we serve his government? No.' Certain members of the Uriage group, speaking as educators and inculcators of moral values, expressed their reservations about the regime. Men as diverse as Abbé de Naurois, Emmanuel Mounier, and Hubert Beuve-Méry acknowledged the impossibility of reconciling Hitlerian reality with an accommodation of Nazism in any form. But until the end of 1942, Uriage's refusal to make a definitive break from the regime kept the school in an equivocal position. The school's leaders continued to devote all their efforts to their mission: the training of a new military and political elite. They chose not to address the question of the school's link to the state, leaving it up to Vichy to decide whether to maintain the relationship. From 1943 on, Uriage cooperated with the Resistance, but without aligning with any particular group: 'Without situating itself within the organized Resistance, the Uriage group counts among resistance forces.'[27] Almost to the very end, Segonzac remained faithful to some of the values associated with the National Revolution, preferring to work with General Giraud before joining the Gaullists just prior to the Liberation in 1944.

2. The Pinot-Mitterrand Group

This same political and ideological ambiguity characterized numerous official bodies charged with helping repatriated prisoners-of-war, in particular the *Commissariat Générale aux prisonniers de guerre rapatriés* (Repatriated Prisoner-of-War Commission), or CGPGR, headed by Maurice Pinot. In the spring of 1942, the young François Mitterrand, recently escaped from a prisoner-of-war camp in Germany, promoted initiatives to help his fellow military men still in captivity. He entered into contact with small groups associated with the *Commissariat*, ultimately taking a job himself at the CGPGR[28] under the direction of Pinot.

The political climate at the CGPGR was staunchly anti-German. Its leaders were almost all ex-prisoners-of-war with fresh memories of their captivity who were committed to helping escaped prisoners and furnishing them false papers, all under the auspices of an official agency of the Vichy government. At the same time, they viewed the National Revolution in a favorable light and were impressed with Marshal Pétain. Mitterrand's interest in his fellow escapees led him to contact other POWs and to establish a structure for receiving escapees once they had made their way back to France. In June 1942, a meeting of former escaped prisoners was held at the Château de Montmaur, where they decided to set up an operation called *La Chaîne*. The North African landing and the arrival of the Wehrmacht in the southern zone served to accelerate implementation of the plan. *La Chaîne* grew, expanding its clandestine activities within the prisoner community. This was the point of departure for what was to become a resistance organization consisting of former POWs, the *Rassemblement National des prisonniers de guerre* (RNPG). The anti-German and anti-collaborationist leaders of the Commission became ever more mistrustful of the French State, while necessarily maintaining their relationship to it. Although Maurice Pinot was dismissed by Laval in January 1943, François Mitterrand remained in place, running a relief operation that served as cover for his illegal activities.[29]

In the spring of 1943, the RNPG, or Pinot–Mitterrand group, established close ties to Giraudists in the army and obtained the support of the *Organisation de Résistance de l'Armée* (ORA), an offshoot of the *Organisation Métropolitaine de l'Armée*. The ORA brought together military personnel who had remained garrisoned after the demobilization of the army and who had gone over to the Resistance in November 1942.[30] Giraudist in nature, the RNPG also sought to become part of the unified Resistance movement. To that end, François Mitterrand met with Eugene Claudius-Petit[31] in the spring of 1943, and later with Emmanuel d'Astier and Henri Frenay. Pinot and Mitterrand did not completely sever their ties with certain members of Pétain's entourage, however; they remained in contact with men such as Paul Racine, who worked in Pétain's own office, and Jean Vedrine, of the CGPGR – both of whom were personally and ideologically dedicated to the Marshal.

By the time Mitterrand flew to London and then Algiers, arriving in early December 1943, de Gaulle had fully outmaneuvered Giraud. Mitterrand, himself then suspected of Giraudist and pro-Vichy sympathies, pleaded the case for 'a movement devoted exclusively to repatriated or escaped prisoners-of-war who found themselves on French soil'.[32] His appeal ran up against the existence of another, smaller group, the *Mouvement de Résistance des prisonniers de guerre et des déportés* (MRPGD) run by Michel Cailliau, General de Gaulle's nephew and an unconditional resister. With Henri Frenay's support, Mitterrand was able to meet General de Gaulle on 2 December 1943. The meeting went rather badly, with de Gaulle asking Mitterrand, as RNPG representative, to merge his movement with the MRPGD. Mitterrand categorically refused, arguing that his group had far more members,[33] as well as the support of the *Mouvements Unis de Résistance* (MUR). Despite Cailliau's strong opposition, Mitterrand prevailed, and a three-man committee was set up to head a single organization uniting all POW groups, now renamed the *Mouvement National des prisonniers de guerre et déportés* (MNPGD). Throughout the entire process, Michel Cailliau remained suspicious of Mitterrand on account of the RNPG's ties to Vichy and then to General Henri Giraud.[34]

Taking the lead from Robert Paxton, it is now time to consider the Vichy regime and its relationship to the Resistance. If certain matters concerning the Vichy regime are now clearer, thanks to Paxton's path-breaking work, we are only just beginning to challenge the image of an idyllic Resistance, implacable and pure, which derived its legitimacy from a total and spontaneous condemnation of the Vichy regime from the very outset. Historians must now turn their attention to the connections between the regime and the small groups of resisters who were active from 1940 to 1942. This is essential, for it can shed light on fundamental questions such as what constitutes 'resistance,' and what distinguishes an oppositional *stance* from oppositional *activism*. Finally, careful study of archival materials should also permit us to identify a range of responses and behaviors, and ultimately, to sketch a typology of resistance groups and the political positions they adopted early in the struggle to free France.

Translated by David Lake and Paula Schwartz

Notes

1. See in particular, Eric Conan and Henry Rousso, *Vichy, un passé qui ne passe pas* (Paris, 1994).
2. Daniel Cordier, *Jean Moulin, L'inconnu du Panthéon* (Paris, 1993).
3. *La France Continue* was written almost entirely by Paul Petit. The first issue, dated 10 June 1941, is violently anti-Pétain. The first issue of *Valmy* came out in January 1941. It condemned the Armistice and pleaded in favor of a return to the Republic.
4. Seven typewritten copies were produced of the first issue, dated 1 December 1940. There followed mimeographed pages written by

Christian Pineau, a government employee in the Ministry of Food Supply who, as editor of *Libération-Nord*, was one of the very first to distance himself from Pétain and his government.

5. On *Libération-Sud*, see Laurent Douzou, *La Désobéissance, histoire d'un mouvement et d'un journal clandestins: Libération Sud (1940–1943)* (Paris, 1995).
6. 3AG2 BCRA 332, Lyons, 20 February 1941. Source: BBC European Intelligence, FFL, EM of General de Gaulle, 32877/AR, p. 1, Archives Nationales (AN)
7. 'They have weakened the nation by attacking its unity through racial measures mimicking those of Germany and contrary to all the humane traditions of France' (ibid.).
8. Delegated by the government to the occupied territories, he was called back to the Free Zone after 13 December 1940. Reprimanded in April 1941 for 'Anglophile remarks', he wrote an open letter to Admiral Darlan in which he stated: 'I am hopeful for an English victory, and furthermore believe in that victory'; yet he remained faithful to Pétain.
9. Cf. Henri Frenay, *La nuit finira* (Paris, 1973): 118. On the subject of Henri Frenay, the founder of *Combat*, see Cordier, *Jean Moulin*, in which the author analyzes a series of documents, notably the *Manifesto*.
10. 'If all of France resists and refuses to be dominated, if it comes down to spiritual power, the source of all its power, then the barbarians will break', Indomitus (Philippe Viannay), 15 August 1941
11. Cf. Olivier Wieviorka, *Une Certaine Idée de la Résistance: Défense de la France 1940–1949* (Paris, 1995): 45.
12. Wieviorka, *Une Certaine Idée:* 157.
13. To supplement the analysis presented here, see Laurent Douzou and Denis Peschanski, 'La Résistance française face à l'hypothèque Vichy' in *La France de Vichy: Archives inédits d'Angelo Tasca* (Milan, 1996): 3–42.
14. See Robert Paxton, *Parades and Politics at Vichy: The French Officers Corps under Marshal Pétain* (Princeton, NJ, 1966).
15. These newsletters contain no allusion to Vichy and rarely mention Marshal Pétain. That is not the case for *Petites Alliés* (published in the Free Zone), four issues of which appeared between June and July 1941, which was followed by *Vérites* in August 1941.
16. Cordier, *Jean Moulin*: p. 149.
17. 'The war and the defeat have caused in our country a great soul-searching, which has resulted in a profound change in our political

institutions, putting into power an authoritarian government led by a respected man,' *Manifeste de Libération nationale.*

18. In his letter to President Roosevelt on 7 October 1942, Frenay goes over his path since the Armistice: 'I even believed in a truly human and social national revolution. Like all French people, I was cruelly disappointed, horribly mistaken.'
19. The arrest of a liaison agent allowed the police to trace part of the network and arrest close to forty members.
20. 'Yvon Morandat, Souvenirs inédits,' *Les Cahiers de l'IHTP*, no. 29 (September 1994): 78 (edited with an introduction by Laurent Douzou).
21. At this point, Roger Stéphane was in contact with Jacques Renouvin and linked to the *Libération Nationale* group, not all of whose ideas he shared.
22. BCRAM/ SR, no. 913 D/BCRAM-R, London, 7 March 1942. Source: Pierre, 'Libération nationale', 3 pp., 1–2. These papers were discovered by Laurent Douzou and Dominique Veillon during research on the origins of the Resistance in the Lyons region.
23. 'My patronage is invoked all too often, even against the government, to justify supposed projects of salvation, which in fact are only calls for insubordination.' Loustanunau-Lacau was eventually arrested in July 1941 on the orders of Admiral Darlan.
24. The *Alliance* network.
25. Laurent Douzou and Denis Peschanski, *'La Résistance française'*: 27.
26. Cf. *Jeunesse France*, no. 1, 22 May 1941: 'A long time ago, Joan of Arc accomplished the marvel of suddenly bringing alive a national community whose members did not know each other or had become dispersed. Now we have the unique opportunity of having the Marshal.'
27. Bernard Comte, *Une utopie combattante. L'école des cadres d'Uriage 1940–1942*, Paris, 1991): 550.
28. Mitterrand's title was Director of the Press Bureau in the Unoccupied Zone. This title was comfirmed 24 November 1942 by service note no. 1, series B, from the CGPGR, AN F9 2998, cited by Pierre Péan, *Une jeunesse francaise, François Mitterrand* (Paris, 1994): 201.
29. This position offered him the opportunity to meet with Marshal Pétain on 15 October 1942.
30. 'Situation de l'organisation de la résistance de l'armée française et des groupements civils similaires,' SHAT 14 P 15, cited by Laurent Douzou and Denis Peschanski, *'La Resistance française'*: 186.

31. Eugéne Claudis-Petit, a member of the Board of directors of *Franc-Tireur*, declared himself 'dumbfounded' by Mitterrand's pro-Vichy stance. Cf. Éric Conan and Henry Rousso, *Vichy, un passé:* 186.
32. Note for Colonel Passy, London, November 29, 1943, BCRA, 3AG2 378.
33. He learned at the same time of the existence of yet another resistance organization, a Communist one, led by Robert Paumier.
34. Letter from Cailliau to de Gaulle sent 1 February 1944, archives BCRA, cited by Péan, *Une jeunesse francaise*: 403.

Part III
Everyday Life: Culture, Institutions, Public Opinion under the Occupation

–12–

1940–1944: Double-Think in France

Pierre Laborie

> But we are, I know not how, dual in ourselves, so that that which we believe, we do not believe, and we cannot put out of our minds that which we condemn.
>
> – Montaigne[1]

Will the work of historians ever help the French sort out and judge, outside the realm of passions, those times when they 'did not love one another'?[2] How thoroughly can we know and understand this France of the dark years, entangled in the confusions of an identity crisis brought to a fever pitch? To what extent can we understand the true meaning of collective choices, when the confusion of a humiliated people affects the depth of its consciousness and the very foundation of its notion of nation and country?

Obsession and Deafness

Time and generations go by, witnesses fade away, but fascination and doubt remain, tightly intermingled. The ever-present and excessive glorification of refusal is starting to quiet down, as if nothing could soothe the scars of Vichy and the Occupation.[3] A portion of the present continues to write itself in the past; but the opposite is also true, and this dialectic increasingly gives structural depth to the syndrome analyzed by Henry Rousso. By stirring up almost obsessively the memory of those four interminable years, France keeps asking and repeating the same troubled questions about itself over and over, while ignoring or pretending to rediscover each time truths long ago established by scholars. The repeated expressions of surprise, exploited and amplified by the media, show the French to be stubbornly oblivious to the strangeness of their own deafness. They endlessly repeat that it is time to lift the time-worn taboos, that it is urgent to speak at last of those issues that are never spoken of. To be sure, we are far from having said everything about Vichy, collaboration, or the Resistance; we know even less about the various ways that French society made it through this period. But one is entitled to wonder what can be gained from the continual stutterings of a history/memory that is constantly being adapted to suit the changing trends of the moment. What remains of the civic dimension of reflecting on the past, when the whole process is being manipulated and distorted in successive reconstructions, when identity politics encroach on the logic of truth, when ideological agendas result in anachronistic interpretations that show scant regard for basic rules of method and concern for accuracy? Despite the professed intentions of those who uphold such a methodology, its effectiveness is open to question. It is not clear that these simplifications and reversals of perspective are the best means of persuading the French to look at their past without self-indulgence, and to look their entire history in the face.

The judgments passed on the collective attitudes and behaviors of the period between 1940 and 1944 are characteristic of this mixture of respectable intentions, fearfulness, and anxiety over all that is at stake in the realm of memory. The extraordinary variety of personal experiences passed on by friends and family, as well as the topic's sensitivity and its popularity – everyone has an opinion on the matter – limit the impact of the dispassionate perspective of historians and their efforts to explain what happened. When these efforts stray too far from that which is touchily guarded as 'memorially correct' to a particular group or community, they are poorly received, and sometimes even suspected of insidiously striving to justify the unjustifiable. The troubling question of behaviors during the Occupation is a recurring central theme in a debate that has been more about pronouncing judgment than about dealing with the issues and understanding their complexity.[4] Such questions are deeply relevant to our times because of their moral dimension, and yet too often they are reduced to the level of excessive generalizations, simplistic alternatives, or even summary judgments of the 'all guilty, all collaborationists'[5] variety. The question keeps coming up repeatedly, whether in relation to the extermination of the Jews, the early career of a French President, the trial of a senior civil servant, the paths followed by certain members of the Resistance, or the zeal of the administration . . . Using solidly established and over-rigid typologies – Pétainists, resisters, collaborationists, fence-sitters [*attentistes*], criminals, accomplices, etc.– people want to classify, categorize, and count. They also seek to blame or glorify, denounce, demand justice and seek reparations. In contexts where needs of the moment require the mental categories and cultural models of the present to be applied to our understanding of the past (at the risk of distorting its meaning), historians are nevertheless summoned for validation. The result is a persistent misunderstanding, further complicated by insistent injunctions as to the duties of memory, whose task is to carry the past into the future.

Collective Behaviors and the Complexity of the Social Sphere

The universality of the Holocaust's teachings, along with the imprescriptibility of crimes against humanity, have given a powerfully renewed momentum to the complex dialectic of the relationship between memory and history. The difficulties of the dialogue are not new; but they cannot be allowed to lend credence to the notion that all explanatory methods be considered by nature exonerating and relativistic. To pursue and investigate more deeply the nature and meaning of French collective reactions, which is the object of the hypotheses put forward in this chapter, serves but one purpose: to recover ordinary ways of thinking and to analyze their mechanisms in order better to understand the complexity of the social sphere. It is within this perspective that this essay on double think and the French people must be placed.

Before proceeding further, three points need to be made for the sake of clarification. The first states a fundamental fact: the social actors' way of being in the world constitutes an essential factor for understanding their relationships to the events and problems of the time. Only by attempting to recreate modes of reasoning and systems of mental representations (and these are rarely directly accessible) can the historian hope to uncover some of the essential mechanisms that inform behaviors. The second point is an extension of the first, and deals with methodology: one must break with that kind of political history that understands the movements of public opinion in terms of rational and self-evident explanation, that analyzes public opinion on the basis of its outward forms. The third point, though obvious, must not be ignored: it is important to remember that collective feeling is always expressed according to a scale of interests and a certain order of priorities, these being unstable hierarchies that are created from what individuals perceive, or think they perceive, of reality at a given moment. As mundane as it may sound, one must agree with Etienne Fouilloux that, immediately following the defeat, 'taking sides was not the major preoccupation'[6] of a population that was distraught, tired, and dogged by a lingering apathy.[7]

Ambivalence and Lost Cultural Codes

How can we know what ordinary French people of the time perceived, thought, and understood? How can we grasp how much they knew of history, and understand how they were living it? How should we read and experience, over half a century later, the words of 1940 or 1944, and how can we uncover and reconstitute the interpretative frames through which they were heard and understood? On 10 February 1941, Jean Guéhenno wrote in his *Journal:* 'What genius the historians of the future will need in order to recognize the true causes and true motives behind the events referred to in these texts, these communiqués in which not a word is either loyal or accurate!'[8] Once we sift out the portion of malice that lurks behind these words, we can see that the 'work of genius' to which historians of the future are called constitutes a kind of instruction manual. He foresees with clarity the considerable difficulties historians will encounter in trying to rediscover the collective sensibility of a disconcerting period, in seeking to reconstruct the era, to grasp what might have been going on in people's minds, and in attempting to piece together what most French people's ordinary understandings of the present might have been.

Despite the apparent proximity, the illusion that we might easily bridge the modest gap in time, the mental logic and cultural codes of French people in the 1940s have become largely foreign to us.[9] We must nevertheless investigate what their modes of operation may have been. This research underscores, among other things, the major role of ambivalent thoughts and feelings. So strong a presence and so much evidence inevitably lead some to wonder.[10] Before turning ambivalence into a major concept for the analysis of public opinion, or into a structural element of all forms of mass psychology, however, we need to determine whether we are dealing with an inherent characteristic of the fundamental nature of opinion, independent of environment and culture, or whether ambivalence constitutes a feature specific to certain particular cultures. We lack the elements of comparison that would allow for a credible answer. Should the phenomenon point unwaveringly to a French singularity, the example of the 1940s could reinforce certain stereotypes of a common Francophobia that puts a heavy emphasis on a natural propensity for artful maneuvering, for opportunism and subterfuge.

Ambivalence or Ambiguity

Whether a national particularity or a widespread feature of the relationship between occupying powers and occupied people, the considerable role of ambivalence is a major characteristic of French attitudes under Vichy. It is also one of the least-distorting mirrors for understanding the mutability of wait-and-see situations and their apparent contradictions. The simplistic alternatives of Pétainism and Gaullism, resistance and Vichyism, or resistance and collaboration, can only provide highly reductionistic images of what people went through at the time. We know, for instance, that a majority of the French lamented the defeat while wishing for the armistice, that they were able to applaud Marshal Pétain fervently while rejecting the Vichy regime, and could be implacably hostile to the occupying forces without ever becoming resisters; we even know that some of them helped save Jews while maintaining a loyal attitude toward the Head of State. These observations, noted by many, have given rise to varying interpretations, often accompanied by considerations of a moral nature.[11] One hears of the French people's schizophrenia, but also of their talent for adapting and shifting their loyalties, their ability to follow the prevailing winds, as well as their tendency toward indecisiveness. This has been interpreted as calculating opportunism, duplicity, cynicism, and spinelessness. In many people's minds, then, ambivalence and ambiguity were two sides of the same coin.

Without denying the potential validity of value judgments, the notion of ambivalence opens other doors to the historian, broadening the possibilities of analysis. It allows one to think about the contradictions in terms of more than mere antinomies – resisters *or* Pétainists, Gaullists *or* fence-sitters – to push past the familiar binary oppositions and seek to understand what they tell us beyond the half-truths of their overt meaning. Taking into account the ambivalence in people's minds helps us understand that the general evolution of the conflict and Germany's predicted defeat do not offer sufficient elements to explain everything. The majority of the French were not Vichy supporters initially and then resisters, or Pétainists who then turned Gaullist. Rather, they may well have been a little bit of both simultaneously, for varying lengths of time depending on the individual. In a recent interview,[12] Simone Veil repeated how difficult it is for us now to grasp the complexity of those times, and said of the French that 'some behaved well, others badly, many did both at the same time'. She added '. . . things weren't as simple as people portray them today'. By taking both sides of the matter into account, Simone Veil's judgment approaches the truth more closely, especially when considered in the light of the problems raised by the effort to pass an overall judgment on 'average' French behavior, which can never reflect the multiple singularities of lived experience.

A Culture of Duality

The image of the French people harboring within themselves opposing emotions, torn between contradictory impulses rather than entrenched in hostile camps, cannot be reduced to a mere manifestation of double-dealing. It refers back to the notion of a dual man,[13] who is both one thing and the other, more as a result of external pressures than out of self-interest. Double think belongs to the mental universe of the French under Vichy: it is one of its realities, it reveals one of the modes of operation of systems of representation, and underscores its importance. Further study of double think might help to illuminate the prominent place that ambivalent modes of thought occupy in public opinion. Their characteristic features might be seen to spring from the broad development of a kind of culture of duality and its accompanying effects. Hence, the culture of duality was not a feature of clear conscience, nor was it experienced as an agonizing contradiction; rather, duality was a form of acculturation that came to shape everyday thinking, whether in the mundane activities of daily life, or in extraordinary situations where one had to weigh the risks of taking sides. In order to survive, the French had to learn very quickly to live with two images of themselves: one public face for the sake of appearances and survival, and one hidden face to preserve a certain way of being and to take action.[14] Traces of duality were everywhere; they became a familiar feature of the landscape and created a pattern of dual living, examples of which come easily to mind. The two main zones that made up the nation resulted in a double mental representation of the country, and there were two ways of conceiving of France, the London way and the Vichy way. Within the narrow confines of the Vichy realm, there were still two more ways of being French: Pierre Laval's way and that of Marshal Pétain. A majority of the French people saw the old Marshal himself as a double man, identified with the secret strategy – insistently attributed to him – of playing a double game. Until November 1942, the press and authorized magazines in the free zone were read through a subtle deciphering of a double language.[15] Finally, choosing to go underground meant living a double life, with double days and double identities, while the shortages of everything imposed a double market . . .

The Gray Areas of Double Think

Despite its murkiness and confusions, double think came about as a means of getting around a reality that had become unbearable, as a fitting response to an exceptional situation, as one element of a larger process of adaptation. However, let us not be naive: it is clear that the gray areas of ambivalence entail the risk of falling into compromising positions. To make a reasonable judgment, one must use chronology as a first gauge. Until the fall of 1942, it was possible for two concepts of France to coexist in the same mind. Beyond that point, however, with the multiplication of ever more obvious signs of collusion between Vichy and Nazi Germany, it goes without saying that ambivalence took on a whole new dimension. One could no longer claim to be simultaneously a resister and a Vichy supporter without turning a blind eye and a deaf ear to the realities of collaboration, or deliberately playing into the machinations of the double game. Double think then became a 'matter of splitting oneself in two'; as Georges Bernanos wrote in 1943 of the behavior of those government bureaucrats who refused to resign: 'their consciences cross oceans to fly to freedom's rescue, but their civil-servant bodies stay put'.[16]

The uncertain waverings of ambivalence and the safety of fence-straddling shed additional light on the real resources and great strain of a harshly tried people.[17] Far removed from heroic behaviors and loud refusals, double think emerges as a form of social response to alternatives deemed insurmountable. A response specific to that time that must be considered as such, and as a poignant attempt to negotiate between desire and the attainable. Although its meaning seems to elude any single interpretation, it may have had a pedagogical function in helping people mentally prepare to accept other harsh contradictions imposed by the necessities of war. Hence, despite the number of victims and the exploitation of the situation by the German and Vichy propaganda machines, the violent 1944 Allied bombings of the country were endured with dignity – and this at a time when the German army's reprisals against civilian populations were steadily intensifying. Simone de Beauvoir refers to this in one of her emotional letters to Nelson Algren, after bluntly describing the horror of a train machine-gunned by British and American planes: 'It was all happening at the end of the war, as *you* were trying to stop the trains and destroy the locomotives, as you had to; no one was indignant about it, we were just a little scared.'[18]

In breaking down the mechanisms of the society of the spectacle and of the practice of pseudo-simulation, Guy Debord issues the powerful injunction: 'Political? Social? There has to be a choice. What is one cannot be the other.'[19] The double think of the French people, their strain and their confusion remind us how difficult it is to press the thick texture of the social into the narrow strictures of a binary culture.

Notes

1. *Essais*, book II, chapter XIV, 'On Fame' (Paris, 1962).
2. To quote the words of President Georges Pompidou during his 21 September 1972 press conference: 'Isn't it time to throw off the veil, to forget these times when the French did not love one another, tore one another apart, and even killed one another . . .' See *Le Monde* of 23 September 1972, and Henry Rousso, *Le Syndrome de Vichy de 1944 à nos jours* (Paris, 1990).
3. 'Everything today contributes to the obsessive recollection of Vichy', observed once again, and like so many others, Pierre Nora in the 1 October 1997 issue of *Le Monde*.
4. One can only quote, once again, Marc Bloch's famous apostrophe, which he wrote after realizing that empty rehabilitations were only following hollow prosecutorial speechifying: 'Robespierrerians, anti-Robespierrians, we beg you for mercy: please, just tell us who was Robespierre': *Apologie pour l'Histoire ou métier d'historien* (Paris, 1974).
5. One opinion among many: on Sunday, 20 March 1994, Jacques Attali, a former special adviser to President François Mitterrand, was thus able to assert on Radio J's 'Forum': '. . . since the war, we have been living a double lie personified by two presidents of the Republic . . . De Gaulle made the French believe they were resisters, when in fact they were collaborationists. Mitterrand made the French believe that they were leftists, when in fact they were right-wing. This double façade . . . has been hiding a reality: France was collaborationist' (*Le Monde,* 22 March 1994).

   For a differing viewpoint on a debate the French never seem to tire of, one might also consult, for example, François Maspero's article 'Tous coupables?' [All guilty?], published in the same newspaper on 11 December 1997.
6. Etienne Fouilloux, *Les chrétiens français entre crise et libération, 1937–1947* (Paris, 1997).
7. In the spring of 1939, looking back on his publication's hostility to the Munich Accords, Emmanuel Mounier wrote: 'If our reaction was so violent last October . . ., it is because we suddenly felt a kind of deathly languor in our country, that first blackout of the will that foreshadows its upcoming surrender.' (*Esprit*, no. 80, May 1939).
8. Jean Guéhenno, *Journal des années noires, 1940–1944* (Paris, 1947).
9. Many contemporaries of the period admitted, only a few years after the end of the Occupation, that they had become incapable of

deciphering the meaning of the allusions and subtleties that had fed their need for daily protest. Cf. for example Charles d'Aragon's testimony in *La Résistance sans héroïsme* (Paris, 1977). The *Esprit* case is exemplary, as its editors were to confess, at the Liberation, their inability to understand their own writings: '. . . sometimes only in the furthest recesses of our memory can we now find the event, so well-known to all at the time, that gave this commentary its edge . . .' (*Esprit*, January 1945).

10. Chronicles or memoirs of that period are full of examples. This is particularly true of Léon Werth's *Déposition, Journal, 1940–1944* (Paris, 1992), edited and introduced by Jean-Pierre Azéma. Much of my work points to this characteristic feature of the modes of thought during the years of occupation.
11. It is occasionally the case, in matters of history, that moral judgments may hide a surrender in the face of the effort necessary to understand.
12. Interview with journalist Eric Conan, *L'Express,* 9 October 1997.
13. In January 1937, in Toulouse's *La Dépêche,* Emile Vandevelde titled his review of Aragon's novel *Les beaux quartiers* 'Les hommes doubles' [the dual men]. One of the book's characters states: 'we are living through historic times that will maybe one day be known as: the time of dual men'. In the preface he wrote for the book's 1965 reissue, Aragon goes back to the dual men theme, which, according to him, was only picked up on at the beginning of the 1960s. Cf. Roger Garaudy, *L'itinéraire d'Aragon* (Paris, 1961). My gratitude goes to Edouard Ruiz, to whom I owe this information.
14. These observations are inspired by Joffre Dumazedier's testimony, in the May 1981 *Esprit.*
15. On this, consult 'Des revues sous l'occupation', *La revue des revues, Revue internationale d'histoire et de bibliographie,* Paris, no. 24, 1997. In addition to other contributions, the study of the positions taken by the periodical *Esprit* in 1940 deals with the matter of camouflaged language.
16. Georges Bernanos, 'Réflexions sur le cas de conscience français' [Reflections on the French moral dilemma], October 1943, non-collected texts, 1938–1945, in *Essais et Ecrits de combat,* Vol. 2 (Paris, 1995): 892.
17. Reflecting back on the weaknesses of the French, the resister Jean Cassou said, after the Liberation, that it was better to speak of 'average cowardice than of average villainy': *Une vie pour la liberté* (Paris, 1981). Nearly 40 years earlier, in April 1944, the resister Jacques Bingen wrote in his letter-testament: 'not to forget, after the glorious

victory, that if France is a great lady, the French will be quite tired'. One will need to have for them 'not only a lot of ambition, but also a lot of forgiving tenderness'.

18. Simone de Beauvoir, *Lettres à Nelson Algren* (Paris, 1997): letter dated Tuesday, 16 December 1947.
19. Guy Debord, *Commentaires sur la société du spectacle,* followed by *Préface à la quatrième édition italienne de la 'Société du Spectacle'* (Paris, 1992): 37.

–13–

Vichy and Abortion: Policing the Body and the New Moral Order in Everyday Life[1]

Miranda Pollard

Vichy's policies on abortion are often viewed at either end of an interpretative spectrum. On the one hand, gender is erased and abortion becomes a 'woman-less' narrative. Antoine Prost has argued, for example, that the majority of French people [*sic*] had overwhelmingly opposed abortion in a pre-war opinion poll, and that Vichy's infamous abortion policies were unsurprising. Vichy was worried about depopulation. Abortion was one of the worst French 'social scourges', against which a conservative, pro-Catholic regime inevitably reacted.[2] On the other hand, abortion is represented as, more or less exclusively, a story of women. Women, as both clients and professional abortionists, were the targets of Vichy's repressive policies; it was a woman who was guillotined in 1943 for performing abortions; it was women who were to be re-introduced to the joys of maternity – persuaded or coerced – by the National Revolution's *femme au foyer* (return women to the home) agenda to renounce the egoistical *jouissance* (pleasures) of the inter-war years. As Célia Bertin comments in her survey, *Femmes sous l'Occupation*, abortion really was women's business because 'the problem uniquely affected women; men never experienced it'.[3]

In the first version of Vichy's anti-abortion history, abortion is a disembodied historical phenomenon and women are a meaningless category (they are the invisible object of social policy); in the second, women are an overloaded category (they are the hapless victims of zealous laws directed against them; they are the subjects of a uniquely sexed experience). Perhaps neither approach does justice to the complex history of Vichy's policies, jurisdictions and power, nor to the complicated ways in which women, men and children lived state repression. Can the story be retold? Using the records of the Tribunal d'Etat, a special court created in September 1941 to deal with Resistance cases that was given jurisdiction in February 1942 over abortion cases, I would like to suggest some fresh perspectives on Vichy's abortion story. While primarily a 'story of women' – in the sense of both representing women's business and being about female sexuality – abortion was also a multifaceted narrative about social existence under the Occupation. The history of abortion and Vichy illuminates the dynamic relationship of state policy, local policing, community discourses and personal lives; repressive abortion policy renders visible and public the taboo, the intimate and the personal. It imbricates women and men in a complex heterosexual social matrix that problematizes the very nature of social experience.

Discipline and Punish

At 5.25 a.m. on Friday 30 July 1943, Marie-Louise Giraud, a thirty-nine-year-old washerwoman from Cherbourg was guillotined in the courtyard of La Roquette prison in Paris. Her body 'being claimed by neither the family nor the Academy of Medicine' was buried in a prison plot. Her coffin cost forty-four francs, according to the records. Her crime: performing twenty-seven abortions, twenty-two of which were after the enactment of the so-called 300 Law against abortion.[4]

At 5.45 a.m. on Friday 22 October 1943, forty-six-year-old Desiré P——, from the Sarthe, was beheaded in the prison of La Santé in Paris. P—— apparently 'learned with calm and courage that his appeal had been rejected and was only surprised that one got one's head cut off for abortion'. He took communion and proceeded to the scaffold. Buried at the cemetry in Ivry, P—— was also laid to rest in a state-supplied 44-franc coffin. His crime: performing three abortions.[5]

Although, by mid-1943, Vichy had presided over thousands of deaths and deportations, these two judicial murders were unique. The accused had no knowledge of the new 1942 law that they had transgressed and neither belonged to any political party, organization or racial/ethnic group targeted by Vichy. The crime to which they both admitted – performing illegal abortions – had been so widespread in the years before the war that some commentators had estimated that there were as many abortions as live births annually in France.[6] Although the justification for the harshness of the 300 Law against abortion was precisely its deterrent effect, neither case received widespread attention. The sentences were posted at the homes of the accused and a few newspapers carried small articles.[7]

In both cases, prosecutors called for the maximum severity in sentencing because of the character of the crime: numerous abortions undertaken for profit; three abortions undertaken for profit, with one in particularly repugnant circumstances. It is worth contrasting these two stories, the story of a woman and the story of a man, both mixed up in the business of abortion.

In February 1942, the 300 Law made abortion a capital offense synonymous with treason, '*de nature à nuire au peuple Français* (harmful to the French people)', and brought it within the jurisdiction of the new Tribunal d'Etat. Most abortion cases were still heard by the civil courts – as they had been under the Third Republic, when the number of backstreet abortions supposedly matched those of live births. But between February 1942 and July 1944, the Tribunal d'Etat heard forty-two 'special' abortion cases. Apart from the executions of P—— and Giraud, fourteen people were condemned to life imprisonment, and twenty-six others to prison terms of twenty years or less (the majority with hard labor) and fines ranging from 5,000 to 200,000 francs. From Paris to Cherbourg to Bordeaux, hundreds of people were questioned by police in elaborate investigations that involved the accused abortionists, their clients, and their neighbors and friends, as well as local notables and officials.

Madame Giraud, the monster 'femme au foyer'

The case of the thirty-nine-year-old Marie-Louise Giraud was heard in June 1943 and involved 196 interviews conducted between October 1942 and May 1943 with neighbors, clients, and accomplices. Thirty-eight others were charged in this case, with three women 'accomplices' being sent to the Tribunal for referring women to Madame Giraud under the guise of fortune-telling.[8] Although well-known in the neighborhood, both for performing abortions and for renting out rooms to prostitutes, Madame Giraud was arrested following a denunciation, apparently by her husband, Paul, who had been heard to say that he would have her thrown in prison. For some time he had been aware of her 'business' and her relations with other men; indeed these took place within full view and knowledge of her husband, children and neighbors.

Madame Giraud had performed twenty-seven abortions (using an injection of soapy water into the uterus), charging pregnant women between 500 and 2,000 francs, apart from her neighbor, Gisèle, from whom she received a record-player and some records. It was calculated that she earned 13,000 francs in total from abortions – roughly equivalent to the annual salary of a civil servant or office worker, but less than her husband's annual 18,000 franc Navy pension.[9] However, it was not the amount of money, the large number of abortions involved, or even the death of one of her clients, that attracted the attention of the Tribunal. Rather it was Madame Giraud's lifestyle, her flagrant immorality and disconcerting cynicism that outraged the prosecution (led by Colonel Farge, the government representative to the Tribunal).

This mother of two children, aged five and seven, who stated that she did not work outside the home, was herself the third child in a family of six children, three of whom had died young. Her father was a gardener, her mother a housewife. She stayed at school until she was twelve and worked as a domestic servant before her marriage in 1929. She had five children, and like her mother before her, had three die in infancy. Working-class, unemployed, this *faiseuse d'anges* ('angel maker', a widely-used term for abortionist), far from being Vichy's ideal *femme au foyer,* was her very inverse image. Accused of 'the worst conduct and morality' – adultery, abortion, prostitution, conspicuous consumption, poor mothering – she was a domestic 'monster',[10] an 'unnatural' woman, *disconcertingly cynical*, publicly flaunting her disregard for her husband, the law, social convention and propriety.

Desiré P——, 'incorrigible abortionist'

If Madame Giraud's case involved an excess of story-telling, that of Monsieur P—— has left little trace in the archives, history books or cinema. A forty-six-year-old, divorced father of two, P—— had previously been convicted of performing abortions by the Tribunal Correctionnel in 1935 and 1939. The latter conviction, for 'involuntary homicide', involved a jail sentence of eighteen months following the death of a pregnant woman. P—— was accused by Vichy in August 1943 of performing three abortions, for which he received 120, 300 and 500 francs respectively and/or sexual intercourse as payment. P—— was a blacksmith and also a gelder [*hongreur*]. He worked around the area of Bourg d'Yvre Le Polin, in the Sarthe, carrying a bag of instruments, ever-ready to ply his trade/s. In the case of Eugénie, a pregnant farm worker from the area, who was a widow, P—— had offered and performed an abortion 'in a field, on some straw' in conditions that the *Tribunal* considered 'particularly repugnant'. P—— was having an affair with one of his (married) clients; he had a prior record; he was not especially discreet about his activities. But it was the open, public, and utterly shameless nature of his actions that caused the court to sentence him to death. P—— was dangerous and criminal because of his 'incorrigibility', the fact that he was always ready to 'undertake his disgusting practices'. P——'s story thus comes to be told in terms of obduracy and disregard for public decency.

Abortion thus involved prohibition and punishment, but also a multi-layered production of 'truth'. Many of the stories told in these abortion cases resemble secular confessions. Women and men, old and young – lovers, parents, friends – come before the law as part of a criminal investigation. They are obliged to tell a story. But their answers speak to the need to be understood, to have their explanations heard, to be given a 'pardon'. They tell their own stories, not always centered on criminality or legal culpability. Particularly when a woman has died or been hospitalized following an abortion, her family and those 'in the know' want to retrace the story, rationalize their actions, articulate their guilt and grief beyond even the immediate juridical framework. In this abortion history, there are multiple voices and frames of reference; but I am choosing to highlight just three: the stories of the women accused of having had illegal abortions, the stories of their families and lovers, and the stories of the abortionists. Each set of stories illustrates the ways in which Vichy's masculinist narratives 'penetrated' French women's lives. They show not only how inadequate 'women' is as a category to encompass abortion history, but also how gender and sexuality were interwoven – and intrinsically politicized – discourses.

Confessions I: The Stories of Women

A twenty-three-year-old married shop assistant, Ernestine, explained that she met a man, a French chauffeur working for the Germans, while her husband was a POW: 'I got to know him and finally was so weak that I became his mistress.' She had an abortion in May 1942 because she was distraught at the idea of having a child while her husband was in captivity: 'I have always got along very well with him but of the five years since we've been married, I've barely had one with him because he did his military service, then he went off to war and was taken prisoner.'[11]

A twenty-six-year-old domestic worker, a mother of two children aged four and six whose lover worked in the aircraft industry and whose husband had been a POW since June 1940, told the investigators, 'I never got on well with him. He's brutal and violent and doesn't give me enough money to run the house.' When she realized she was pregnant she worried that her husband would learn of her misdeed and could take away her two children whom she adored.[12]

A married secretary, mother of two children aged fourteen and fifteen, said that when her period was two weeks late, the idea of being pregnant so alarmed her – given that she had two children already and her parents to look after on her husband's and her own income of 2,800 francs per month – that she had sought out an abortionist. She was 'so upset' to learn that she was pregnant that she couldn't remember whether the decision to go ahead and place the catheter had been hers or the nurse's.[13]

Material and emotional factors were connected. Mme B——, whose lover, a German soldier according to a friend, stopped seeing her when he learned she was pregnant, explained: 'Afraid of losing my job at the Banque de France, I decided to get an abortion and . . . went to Mme M——. I never told anyone what happened and I went back to work on the following Tuesday.'[14]

The war and occupation gave special intensity to these material/emotional connections and heighten our awareness of a certain voyeurism – and historical undecidability – re-hearing these stories. In this time of restrictions, potential narratives of romance and sex were largely re-centered around needs (for affection, company, food . . .). Was this a 'feminine' device, an acceptable alternative story to that of active sexual desire and pleasure? For example, Odette, a twenty-three-year-old café worker from Evreux, told the police that one day the grocer had made sexual advances to her: 'I accepted because he had been nice to me, mostly he gave me credit . . . and sometimes a gift of produce . . . I had sex with him several times at his home.'[15] She was unmarried and already had a two-year-old child. Her lover, who was married, arranged for the abortion, which took place above his shop.

Mother of a four-year-old girl, Mme I——, a twenty-nine-year-old farmer from Equeurdreville (Côteville), whose husband was a POW, also explained her actions in terms of the war: 'In my husband's absence, I was lonely and thus, for the past eight to ten months, I have been having affairs with soldiers of the Occupying Army.'[16]

Mme P——, a twenty-nine-year-old day laborer, was rumoured to have had an abortion but denied it. She admitted however that, 'it is true that since the departure of my husband, who is now a POW, I have had a German soldier friend, currently out of the area, with whom I have had an affair . . . however, I have never been pregnant, despite the gossip; I had no need of an abortion or of abortifacients.'[17]

Confessions II: The Stories of Family

In three different and particularly harrowing accounts, three women died from botched abortions and their families were the surviving interpreters of what had happened.

Roubaix, January 1943. An autopsy concluded that a twenty-nine-year-old woman, Thérèse L——, died from septicemia. She had told her mother that her lover, Emile, a returned POW with whom 'she had been doing black marketeering', forced her to get an abortion, 'or else he'd leave her for good'. Thérèse had asked her brother, Henri, to be present while the abortion was performed and he alerted a doctor when she went into a coma. Henri confessed to police that he had not 'realized the seriousness of the operation'. He had given way to his sister because she was threatening to commit suicide.[18]

Croisy-sur-Seine, January 1943. A father of two children aged nine and eleven, didn't know that his five-month-pregnant wife, Marie, had gone to get an abortion until the woman abortionist called on him. She told him that his wife had visited her at home and that 'her heart had given up'. Marie was dead. Her husband brought her body home, wrapped in a mattress, on a hand cart 'because of the current difficulties of finding transport'.[19]

Bayeux, January 1943. Twenty-two-year-old Marcel had written to his girlfriend's parents, knowing that they detested him, but asking for their daughter's hand in marriage. He was spurred on by her impatience to leave home and then her discovery that she was pregnant. He had received no reply from her father. A few days later he found out that his girlfriend, Adrienne, eighteen years old, was dead:

> I was dumbfounded by the news and didn't know what to think; my first thought, without having any evidence, was that her father had killed her . . . I didn't dare go to her house . . . The following Sunday I read what had happened in the papers . . . I never knew what my girlfriend had intended and if I had I would have certainly dissuaded her.[20]

This girl's father initiated a complaint against the abortionist. He admitted, at the investigation after her death, that he had disapproved of his daughter's boyfriend and would not have consented to their marriage willingly because 'this young man did not seem suitable [*un parti intéressant*] for my daughter'. He couldn't understand 'the unfortunate decision' taken by his daughter because, although he had taken issue with her a few times about the relationship, he had done so 'without any harshness at all', adding only that she would have to wait until she was twenty-one.[21]

Adrienne's thirty-three-year-old aunt, Rachel, who had accompanied her to the abortionist, confessed that she was not in the room when the operation was performed. She recognized her mistake in not having stopped Adrienne from going ahead with the abortion or in alerting her family: 'If I regret this so much it is because my niece, whom I loved deeply and whose death affected me terribly, would still be alive today.'[22] Rachel had handed over the 7,800 francs demanded by the abortionist, an exorbitant sum which apparently her niece had stolen from her father.

But notions of duty and responsibility took different forms within families and relationships. In Evreux, in September 1942, Edmond B——, a train driver with the SNCF, coming home from work one day, was presented with a *fait accompli.* His wife had decided to have an abortion. Although they had both agreed that they should not have a third child 'given the current difficulties', he vehemently opposed her having an abortion because 'such an act risked having her thrown in jail and me thrown out of my job at the railway, destroying the life of our two children'. Nonetheless, as she was going ahead anyway, he took care of his wife 'as was my duty'.[23] (He was charged with complicity and with his wife sent before the Tribunal Correctionnel.)

Confessions III: Stories of the Abortionists

Abortionists did not necessarily see themselves the same way their clients or the law saw them. Their stories ranged from defensive, self-serving or naïve, to cynically incredulous of the charges and the accusations against them. It is not hard to imagine why many women with unwanted pregnancies felt hostile or ambivalent about abortionists who profited from their miseries. Gabrielle, the thirty-eight-year-old midwife from Bayeux, whose teacher husband was a POW, was suspected of performing abortions regularly. Her last 'client' (the eighteen-year-old, Adrienne, who paid 7,800 francs for the abortion) had died. She expressed her deep regrets about what had happened:

> I deeply regret what I have done and I swear in all sincerity that this is the first time . . . I have always refused up until now . . . but I was so short of money because of the current circumstances having members of my family to look after. That's why I let myself be tempted. I still can't explain how I let myself go that far.
>
> I took all the usual hygienic precautions . . . there's always a mystery in death that escapes science. Mlle C—— perhaps infected herself, just as the infection that caused her death may have been completely unrelated to my intervention.
>
> Just because I have admitted performing one abortion does not mean that I should be saddled with so many others.[24]

A sixty-one-year-old midwife from Arcachon near Bordeaux admitted that she performed abortions for the money, although she already made a good living. But also perhaps because, 'I wanted to help those who sought me out. I was very wrong to act as I did.'[25] This justification was echoed by Madame Giraud who claimed, 'if I did [abortions] on such a large scale, it was to help out women in trouble whether they were unmarried or married to prisoners'.[26]

But economic hardship also played a part in abortionists' narratives. One woman who was accused of having performed over forty abortions claimed to police that she did so 'to meet the needs of my household and the upkeep of my children'.[27] Pro-family discourses were not the exclusive prerogative of Vichy: women and men appropriated the language of care, protection, and material need to explain their recourse to the very actions that Vichy was criminalizing as anti-family.

These confessions speak to a complex web of social relations, the interconnectedness of desire and duty, the conflicts and anxieties specific to wartime France, as well as to the more generalized eruptions of conflict within families and between lovers. These men and women were not just voicing a pre-formatted confession. They were – albeit often in a language that suggests a template of bureaucratic correctness – sketching out the rationale, the story, the fabric of their own local and complicated lives. These were stories that existed within and alongside Vichy's discourse on abortion, women and family. Ordinary people caught up in unexpected and frightening events explained and narrated their actions and attitudes in images and language that re/produced commonsensical and normative values – with regard to illegitimacy, adultery, poverty, heterosexual romance, parental authority, etc.

How did people 'know' what they knew about abortion? The Tribunal stories reveal what Foucault called a 'grid of moral order', exercised by medical and legal professionals, the police, the judiciary, networks of pharmacists, bourgeois notables and merchants, and women and men on the streets and in the cafés of urban and rural France during the Occupation. Nearly all dossiers include information about those accused of performing or undergoing abortions that reveals this moral/sexual surveillance and the common language of proper order. Previous legal convictions – for anything from theft to abortion – were recorded. But more consistently and more vividly present were contemporaries' observations and local reports about behavior: women were assigned classifications – 'a loose woman', 'of dubious morality', 'given to vice', 'the subject of bad reports', 'notorious', etc. This moral surveillance brings into focus a wider set of social relations and presumptions about how women and men should behave. As abortionists, prostitutes, POW wives, unmarried mothers and/or lovers of Germans, women (and the few men whose incorrigibility was unmasked) were observed as transgressing and flouting certain conventions of propriety. These Tribunal stories reveal a 'gaze' constituted by police, doctors, grocers, mayors and neighbors that defined women as promiscuous, unfaithful, immoral – that indeed created the very category of 'woman' as 'other'. But these same women, these women who stepped 'out of line', also articulated their *own* lives within and against these dominant discourses of sexual difference; they narrated their own identities as lovers, mothers, wives, abortion-givers and abortion-seekers.

There was no univocal discourse on/of abortion. Pregnant women, for example, experienced abortion in ways that overlapped but were not coterminous with legal or medical knowledge. Their language and metaphors reveal the unevenness of knowledge, and its situational character. One young woman remembered going to Arcachon: 'In the course of a conversation, I learned that Mme B—— did abortions. The word wasn't spoken but it wasn't hard to guess . . .' After the abortion, this young woman's father buried the fetus, which was 'more like clots of blood'. Another woman miscarried: 'it was like a ball of blood which I threw in the WC'. Marcel H, the twenty-five-year-old lover of a POW wife, admitted 'It was the *gendarmes* who told me that it was called a fetus because I didn't know what it was.' Women tried mustard baths, quinine, specula and tubes, bicycling and various concoctions to bring on miscarriages. In most cases women talked to other women to get addresses, loans and support. These women created and circulated what Gayatri Spivak has called 'subjugated knowledges'.

What was at stake for Vichy? A 1942 *circulaire* to Prefects about the 300 Law noted 'it's a question of interning individuals who are harmful to society . . . You will, by your energetic involvement [in this struggle], help to rid France of this deadly peril.' Yet, what we find in the evidence of the Tribunal d'Etat hardly constituted an all-out war on abortion, a state crusade against this 'deadly peril'. Despite its powers and its mandate, the Tribunal only heard forty-two abortion cases. While these cases cover a seemingly large number of abortions – about 267 – they in fact represent a small proportion of the abortions and infanticide that we can imagine was taking place in France during the Occupation. Most conspicuously, these cases come not from the length and breadth of France: these forty-two cases come from nineteen departments in all, the vast majority from areas like the Manche, Calvados and the Nord with high concentrations of German soldiers.

Neither were these cases 'ferreted out'. Thirty-four of these cases came to the attention of the police – and were prosecuted – because of either a death (6) or hospitalization (7), or because of rumors (8) and denunciations (13). There was no state-initiated campaign to suppress abortion 'on the ground'. The government financed an anti-abortion propaganda campaign that made clear Vichy's political position. But Vichy allocated no resources to create a special anti-abortion section of the police, for example, or to apply the 300 Law rigorously, through investigations of clinics, hospitals and medical/midwifery practices liable to facilitate this 'treasonable' activity.

Some sex, some abortions, were more frowned upon, more liable to be 'criminalized', than others. Conversely, some sex and relationships were 'passed over'. Bourgeois women, for example, fell entirely outside the apparatus of surveillance (as were their bourgeois lovers/husbands). The forty-two cases overwhelmingly involved working-class women and men, with some *petit bourgeois* women also accused of performing abortions. The abortionists and their clients were primarily factory workers, domestic workers, waitresses, agricultural day laborers, seamstresses or midwives. Their social status, their geographic location and the weight of moral evidence assembled against them suggest that these women [and men] were not just prosecuted 'for abortion'. They were prosecuted for sexual criminality, where abortion *stood in for* the most heinous and unthinkable flouting of the Law.

Abortion represented treason: these women (42 defendants?) were the symbolic *saboteuses* of France; their crimes attacked the maternal/reproductive body of France. This attack was both physical (anti-natalist) and profoundly symbolic/moral (sleeping with the enemy meant betraying France doubly). So, it was not the literal phenomenon of abortion that Vichy felt the most urgent need to suppress (despite the enthusiasm of private anti-abortion groups like the *Alliance National Contre la Dépopulation*). The very acts (adultery, infidelity to a POW husband, sleeping with German soldiers, 'living it up' under the Occupation), the activities that might be 'hidden' by abortion had to be attacked. (Of ninety-nine women accused of having abortions for which there is reliable information from the Tribunal, forty-four were POW wives – ten of whom were involved with Germans – and fifteen were single/married women involved with Germans). The authority of *chefs de famille*, husbands and fathers, had to be reinstated and reinforced. If POWs were rendered powerless, 'cuckolded', for example, then so was Vichy. If individual women took it upon themselves to flout or redefine conventional sexual mores in wartime, to collaborate 'horizontally' with Germans, then Vichy's 'vertical' (and/or complete) seduction by and collaboration with Nazi Germany was made all the more apparent . . . and morally questionable.

Anti-abortion policies were contradictory, implementation uneven. The 300 Law, under the guise of 'national interests', gave the state the ability to intervene in the private lives of women – where German soldiers were present, where French women were conspicuously transgressing 'national' codes of sexual propriety, where the honor of French prisoners of war might be upheld. But, ironically, in policing women's private lives, Vichy generated and widened a more diffuse negative discourse. Abortion stories articulated women's identities as sexual actors. But these abortion stories also narrated family hardships; they detailed the everyday struggle for survival and decency in working-class homes where the war was ever-present; they laid bare the myths of the national renewal (*renovation nationale)*, especially that of the captive *femme au foyer*.

So Vichy was not just another conservative, antifeminist regime. The French State at Vichy was profoundly different. Vichy's anti-abortion laws and actions were construed as matters of *war*, when France was actually in the midst of a *world war*. Requiring few resources to police, aberrant women represented a new constituency to target. If Vichy had failed in its plans to return women to the home, to bring back the prisoners of war, to return families to the land or to foster new social harmony, it could at least declare war on (some) women who were conspicuously 'of dubious morality'. Perhaps this was the real treason: abortion stories re-narrated social existence, revealing how Vichy could not protect French men, French homes or French families.

Notes

1. This analysis is part of my larger study, *Reign of Virtue: Mobilizing Gender in Vichy France* (Chicago, 1998). I thank Laura Lee Downs and Sarah Fishman for their helpful comments on this article.
2. Remarks by Antoine Prost, 'Le Régime de Vichy et les Français', June 1990 Colloque Internationale du CNRS, Paris (1990). See, also, for example, Jean-Pierre Azéma, *From Munich to the Liberation, 1938–1944,* trans. Janet Lloyd (Cambridge, 1984) who mentions on page 58 that 'abortion was severely repressed' and footnotes this comment on page 222 with the statement, without attribution, that 'At least one woman "who despatched a little soul to heaven" was guillotined.'
3. Célia Bertin, *Femmes sous l'Occupation* (Paris, 1993): 244. For a critique of feminist historians' use of the concept of 'experience',

see Joan Wallach Scott 'The Evidence of Experience', in *The Lesbian and Gay Studies Reader*, ed. H. Abelove, M. Barale and D. Halperin (New York, 1993).

4. The 300 Law, passed 15 February 1942, made abortion a capital offense synonymous with treason and placed it under the jurisdiction of the Tribunal d'Etat. The law was the three-hundredth law enacted by the regime; hence its nickname. Archives Nationales (AN): 4 W 13 dr5.
5. AN: 4 W 15 dr5.
6. 'Dr Serge Huard du Commissariat Générale à la Famille commente devant la presse la nouvelle législation sur l'avortement' (6 March 1942) AFIP; Georges Pernot 'La lutte contre l'avortement, 1939–1940' AN: F60 606; D. V. Glass, *Population Policies and Movements* (Oxford, 1940).
7. The sentencing was announced in *Aujourd'hui* on 17 November 1942, for example. The *Alliance Nationale*, noting that no woman had been executed before the war, no matter how odious her crimes, applauded the capital punishment of Madame Giraud, 'an inveterate criminal'. The sentence, it was hoped, would be a deterrent to others who might follow Madame Giraud's example. See *Revue de l'ANCD*, Number 359 (September 1943): 143.
8. These women received sentences of 10 years in prison (a lenient sentence because the accused was 60 years old); 5 years with forced labor and a 6,000 francs fine; and 8 years with forced labor and a 6,000 francs fine. AN: 4W 22 dr2; 4W 13 dr15; 4W 13 dr5.
9. For a detailed breakdown of wages in Clermont-Ferrand, for example, during 1942–3, see John Sweets, *Choices in Vichy France* (Oxford, 1986): 18–19.
10. I take this expression from Anna Lowenhaupt Tsing's anthropological study of women accused of prenatal endangerment and infanticide in the contemporary US. See 'Monster Stories: . . .' in Faye Ginsburg and Anna Lowenhaupt Tsing (eds) *Uncertain Terms: Negotiating Gender in American Culture* (Boston, 1990).
11. AN: 4 W 13 dr5 côte 205.
12. AN: 4 W 13 dr5 côte 238.
13. AN: 4 W 8 dr5 côte 15.
14. AN: 4W 9 dr5 côte 6.
15. AN: 4 W 9 dr7 côte 194.
16. AN: 4 W 13 dr5 côte 65.
17. AN: 4 W 9 dr7 côte 219.
18. AN: 4 W 15 dr4 côtes 16,77,81.

19. AN: 4 W 14 dr5.
20. AN: 4W 15 dr7 côte 28.
21. AN: 4 W 15 dr7 côte 29.
22. AN: 4W 15 dr7 côte 33.
23. AN: 4 W 12 dr8 côte 61.
24. AN: 4 W 15 dr7 côtes 19,30.
25. AN: 4W 8 dr5 côte 14.
26. AN: 4W 13 dr5 côte 62.
27. AN: 4W 9 dr5 Req. defin.

–14–

Youth in Vichy France: The Juvenile Crime Wave and its Implications

Sarah Fishman

In 1942, police near Le Bourget stopped 'T', a 16-year-old apprentice metal worker and his 20-year-old friend, and found 25 kg of apples in each one's bicycle sack. When questioned, 'T' used the oldest excuse in the book – everyone else was doing it. He claimed they had just gone out for a ride in the country when they saw other people gathering apples in a field and decided to 'gather some up for our brothers'. His adult companion thought up a more compelling reason, 'I didn't know we weren't allowed to take apples because I thought they belonged to the whole world.'[1]

This case nicely mirrors the uncertainties of the era. Were other people taking apples too? Did his older friend lead 'T' astray? Did they mean to eat the apples, share them with their families, or sell them on the black market? One thing is clear – none of what these young men said reflected Vichy propaganda.

In 1940, leaders at Vichy had hoped that through contemplation and self-criticism born of the defeat, the French people would internalize values they thought the Third Republic had nearly destroyed. Because in theory young people remain impressionable and not completely corrupted by the previous system, any regime working to remold its citizens focuses attention on children and adolescents, the best hope for the future. No exception in this regard, Vichy directed considerable attention to children. Through songs, posters, the school curriculum, a 'purified' teaching corps, youth groups and leadership schools, Vichy promoted a vision of the kind of French man or woman children should strive to be. Schools, the *Compagnons de la Jeunesse*, the *Chantiers de la Jeunesse* and leadership schools like Uriage tried to instill loyalty to Pétain, honesty, discipline, respect for authority, and the desire for hard work, clean living, early marriage and large families. Scholars like W. D. Halls, Pierre Giolitto,

John Hellman and Bernard Comte have covered many aspects of Vichy's youth policy, considering not just Vichy's agenda, but also trying to discern how young people at school or in youth groups responded to the barrage of propaganda. Other scholars, like Roderick Kedward, Emmanuelle Rioux, or Jean-Claude Loiseau, have studied young people who clearly rejected Vichy, in the *maquis* for example, or who mocked its desires, the *zazous*.[2]

My work on juvenile delinquency provides another window onto the relationship between the Vichy regime and the young people of France. Certainly, rising juvenile crime rates alone indicate the limits of Vichy's ability to reshape adolescent behavior. The number of minors appearing in court tripled by 1942 from the pre-war averages. In the 1930s, the number of minors appearing before juvenile courts hovered between 10,000 and 12,000. In 1937, 11,917 minors appeared before the juvenile courts. By 1940, that number had risen to 15,911, in spite of the disruption of the courts during the Battle of France, and it peaked in 1942 at 34,751, a 192 per cent increase from 1937[3] (see Table 14.1).

Using the dramatic upsurge in youth crime to learn about the attitudes and behavior of young people requires more than aggregate crime statistics. First, crime statistics always present certain problems of interpretation. Increasing crime rates can reflect more aggressive policing, or the addition of new crimes to the penal code. The authoritarian nature of the Vichy regime meant increased police surveillance, and Justice Department publications indicate an attempt in 1942 to 'crack down' in response to rising rates apparent by 1941.[4] Also, the institution of rationing in September 1940 entailed new regulations and enforcement mechanisms, thereby creating new categories of illegal behavior. The Vichy years also generated nearly double the total number of criminal complaints, verbal crime reports and denunciations (see Table 14.1), augmenting the number of cases that appeared in court.

In addition to their statistical shortcomings, Justice Ministry crime figures provide little beyond aggregate information about the category of the crime or misdemeanor, the age/sex breakdown, conviction rates and other general information. Thus, understanding juvenile crime requires detailed information impossible to glean from Justice Ministry statistics. Records generated directly by the courts add depth and detail to the aggregate statistics. For the Seine Department, which included Paris and its nearby suburbs, I compiled information on 667 cases taken from sixty-five *Penalty Registries* generated by the Fifteenth Chamber from 1938 to 1946. The registries present summary information that includes the minor's age, address and occupation, parent's occupation, and general

Table 14.1. Juvenile Court Cases and Complaints of Crime under Vichy and the Third and Fourth Republics

Year	Juvenile Court Cases	Complaints, Denunciations, Crime Reports
1937	11,917	642,939
1938	13,310	672,016
1940	15,911	725,019
1941	30,894	1,084,052
1942	34,751	1,191,781
1943	30,347	1,099,600
1944	22,393	1,120,125
1945	17,502	1,235,748
1946	29,526	1,152,690
1947	23,844	1,079,917

Source: Justice, *Compte-général*, xix, xx, xxiii.

details about the charge, such as what was stolen, where, when and from whom. Supplementing those summary data, case files are available for the 1943 in the Seine Department and for the entire war period in the three provincial departments chosen for this study: the Nord, Indre-et-Loire, and the Gard. The case files include arrest reports, investigation reports, depositions, material evidence, informational sheets on the families, and social case reports, which provide a huge amount of information about the minors, their families and the circumstances of the crime/arrest/investigation. My findings include material from forty-six case files in the Seine, forty-five in the Nord, thirty-four from the Gard and twenty-eight from Indre-et-Loire.

It might be tempting, given the recent tendency toward more fluid definitions of resistance, to read rising delinquency as a manifestation of some form of resistance to Vichy. Yet active resistance contributed very little to the Justice Ministry's aggregate youth crime statistics for two main reasons. In August 1941, Vichy passed a law establishing special courts to handle the repression of communism. Young people arrested in connection with resistance activities could also be turned over to the German authorities. Of the 165 cases from June 1940 through to August 1941 in my Paris database, nine minors were charged with communist propaganda. Only two additional cases in Paris clearly indicated anti-Vichy sentiments, though they do not suggest organized resistance activities. One office boy, seventeen, was charged in 1942 with insulting a police officer, violence and drunkenness for yelling obscenities at police he claimed represented the 'new order'.[6] Another 17-year-old boy, charged in 1943 with insulting an officer, drunkenness, rebellion and 'insulting the Head of State' had called the police 'Pétain's manure'.[7] The disrespect these two boys expressed for Vichy may have reflected generalized anti-authority sentiments unrelated to the specific regime in power. Yet, as their arrests and hearings clarify, the context of an authoritarian regime radicalized their behavior.

One incident in the Gard also clearly revealed anti-Vichy sentiment. A 17-year-old student was accused of 'remarks liable to exert an unfortunate influence over the public state of mind'. According to the police report, in response to one woman's denunciation of British air raids near Paris, an altercation broke out amongst the group of women standing in line for milk. The accused minor jumped into the fray, claiming that if she could, 'she would happily go with the English'.[8]

Still, these thirteen cases were rare exceptions to the rule, making it difficult to argue that rising juvenile crime rates represented an intentional rejection of Vichy. What kinds of cases did find their way into the Courts for Children and Adolescents? The overwhelming majority involved small-scale property crimes, primarily theft. Of the nearly 700 Paris cases, 72 per cent involved theft.[9] National statistics here illuminate a significant trend. In the pre-war years, the vast majority of juvenile trials involved petty theft. In 1937, 60 per cent of the nearly 12,000 juvenile offences tried involved theft. But, as the total number of juveniles in court increased in the 1940s, the already high proportion of cases involving theft increased. In the peak year, 1942, some 75 per cent of all juvenile cases involved theft.

While the new, authoritarian political system certainly contributed to rising theft cases, information from the case files points away from attributing too large a share of the increase either to police tactics or to the denunciatory practices encouraged by an authoritarian state. Of the forty Seine case files that involved theft, twenty-one arrests resulted from complaints filed by the victims of theft. Under circumstances of rationing and severe shortages, theft victims are more likely to report even minor losses. On the other hand, there were no random denunciations by third parties.

The remaining nineteen minors from the Seine case files were caught by policing. Three cases involved police surveillance set up in response to theft complaints; seven minors were caught in the act either by the police (3) or by department store guards (4); three were nabbed as a result of police control points (in train stations, for example); and finally, the police stopped six minors simply for looking suspicious. However, the random stopping of people without probable cause did not result from new police powers accrued during the Vichy regime. French law, from Napoleon I on, has placed only weak limits on police power to conduct searches in France. In other words, aggressive policing and an increased tendency to report crimes contributed only a share to the rising crime rates.

Further, the fact that petty theft acted as the leading edge of juvenile crime, alone accounting for the overall increase during the war, points strongly to the driving force of wartime economic hardship, shortages and the black market. Vichy propaganda promoting self-sacrifice and hard work held little attraction. Minors who found themselves in court, the ones who got caught, responded rather to France's dire economic circumstances and in some cases to opportunities the black market presented.

Family and social status information attests to the economic hardships faced by nearly all minors who found themselves in court. In the Paris area and in the provinces, the minors overwhelmingly came from working-class backgrounds. The 17th–20th *arrondissements* alone accounted for one-third of the cases from Paris proper. Of the 344 from suburban municipalities, two suburbs, (Montreuil-sous-Bois and Drancy), had fifteen cases each, Aubervilliers had thirteen, Saint Denis ten, and Boulogne-Billancourt had eleven – all of them working-class suburbs.

Supplementing the geographical information in the Paris registries, case files from all four departments provided detailed occupational information about accused minors and their parents. In the Paris area, virtually all the parents were working-class. Families headed by mothers often made do on marginal, low-paid employment. Several mothers worked as rag pickers, cleaning ladies or apartment *concièrges*, and a number of the minor girls also worked as domestic servants. The provincial records echo those of the Paris region. Most minors and their parents were listed as manual laborers; some were higher-status tradesmen, such as carpenters, masons, or employees of the SNCF, France's national rail system. There were also a few rag pickers, cleaning ladies and domestic servants, and one family of gypsies who re-caned chairs. In rural areas, most minors came from the landless rural proletariat. Only five potentially middle-class families appeared; two of them had fallen on hard times. Typical monthly incomes hovered around 2,000 francs. A few of the skilled adult males earned as much as 4,000 francs a month; employed mothers usually earned considerably less than 2,000 francs.

The working-class background of most of these adolescents and their families could hardly be considered surprising. More striking from case files was the number of families living on the edge, their resources barely keeping up with their expenses. For example, one boy's mother worked as a rag picker earning 120 francs a month. His stepfather brought in 672 francs a month in unemployment benefit. A charity provided them with an extra 100 francs per month.[11] Another boy's father had died prematurely as a result of being gassed during the First World War. The mother remarried, but the stepfather had disappeared. As a *concièrge* she earned 500 francs a month, supporting three children without family allowances. The social worker wrote, 'One wonders what this family lives on.'[12]

The minors who found themselves in court came from working families of very modest means, precisely the group hardest hit by the war economy's rapid inflation and Vichy's wage freeze. More insights about arrested minors emerge from studying the circumstances of the delinquent act. Of 479 cases of theft in Paris, 107 minors were charged with stealing money, from small sums of ten francs up to a few cases of 10,000 francs or more. Next came food, with 83 cases, and bicycles, with 82 cases. Finally, there was a fairly steep drop to the next most frequent category, shoplifting, with 54 cases. The interesting twist here is that girls made up a much larger proportion of the cases of shoplifting. Fifty-three per cent of the shoplifters were girls, whereas for the three categories above, money, food and bicycles, girls represented about ten per cent of the total number accused. Shoplifters almost always stole non-essential personal items, like scarves, perfume, handbags, make-up, watches or pens. Occasionally shoplifters took food.

In a few extreme cases, the minors who stole food were starving. The court in Nîmes was inundated in the late summer of 1940 by cases involving adolescent boys, mostly Belgians who could not speak French, warehoused in refugee camps, usually charged with stealing food from the fields. Belgian refugees in the Gard faced a local population indifferent, if not hostile, to refugees from a nation that had betrayed France. One Belgian boy who stashed his stolen 20 kg sack of potatoes so he could eat them as needed explained, 'Hunger forced me to behave that way because the everyday fare is not enough.'[13]

However, with a few exceptions, even the minors accused of stealing food may have been hungry but were not starving. First of all, nearly all the minors in my study worked for wages. In fact, the vast majority of adolescents in France, 95 per cent, left school at the age of thirteen, and many of them found jobs. Adolescent wages were extremely low, but they did prevent starvation. Employment also provided opportunities for enrichment apart from wages.

One-third of the minors from the forty-six Paris case files had stolen from their employers. Working around food presented powerful temptation. 'P' worked for a biscuit maker. He stole a 40 kg sack of flour and was arrested with several young co-workers as they were dividing it up. The boys claimed that 'if they got enough to eat' thanks to biscuits provided on the job, 'their parents didn't have enough bread'.[14] One 17-year-old boy stole four liters of cooking oil and three packets of margarine from the cooking oil refinery that employed him, but he insisted that the oil was, 'meant for cooking potatoes for my personal consumption'.[15] It is impossible to verify whether stolen food was meant for personal or family consumption rather than the black market.

Other materials young workers took could hardly have been used for personal consumption and therefore were probably meant for sale. 'D' stole lead pipes from the job. 'G' claimed that the washers, electric wire and screws he took from his workshop were merely perquisites of the job, yet they were worth, according to the complaint, 15,000 francs, more than his annual income.[16] A delivery boy for a soap factory altered a receipt to read that twenty-nine kilos of soap had been paid for instead of twenty, and sold two kilos under the counter (*sans ticket*) for fifty francs.[17] 'A' stole meat, cooking oil, noodles, and cheese from a warehouse in Paris over a period of several months. He sold it to several people, including his own mother, who claimed she did not know it was stolen. The father in this case admitted that his son routinely brought home extra food, but since the boy worked at a cafeteria, the father, indiscreetly, explained, 'I assumed he was involved in a little black market activity just like everyone else these days.' The minor spent his 3,000 franc earnings of crime on movies and other 'miscellaneous pleasures'.

Several teenage girls who worked at abysmal pay as domestics or maids stole money or jewelry from their employers. 'W' took clothing, a watch and some jewelry; 'R' took forty francs and jewelry worth 15,000 francs. 'M' took 1,600 francs in order to buy herself a bicycle.[19] One 16-year-old boy placed at a transit center for young French labor volunteers on their way to Germany, took his work jumpsuit (*bleu de travail*) and sold it at a café for 400 francs, 'to get myself a little pocket money'.[20]

Adolescents who stole from the job, whether for personal consumption or for sale, gave in to a combination of temptation and opportunity. Most of them were not professional thieves. On the other hand, some adolescents were involved in complex theft rings. Several bicycle theft rings relied upon boys to steal the bikes. For example, the police learned from an 18-year-old butcher's assistant accused of stealing three bicycles about 'traffic in stolen bicycles' regularly taking place at a café in Boulogne. The boys stole the bikes and were paid by the café owner, who disguised and then resold the bikes, often for double what he paid the boys.[21]

A cargo theft ring developed in St Ouen, a Paris suburb. 'B', fourteen, and his stepbrother were part of a gang that stole coal, clothing, food and alcohol from packages held in SNCF storage. He admitted he had been stealing from the SNCF for about a year and that the goods were sold at the Clignancourt Flea Market. According to the social worker, 'an entire organized gang stole from the warehouses, even from POW care packages'.[22] Eight theft rings emerged from my Paris data, and only two from the provincial courts.

Most minors did not steal to make huge profits on the black market. The grinding hardship of the occupation years created a strong sense of deprivation. The temptation was too strong for 'D', a 17-year-old girl working as a packer at 6.60 francs an hour in a pastry shop. She was accused of shoplifting two blouses and a blush from La Samaritaine, a Paris department store. The father worked irregularly as a plumber to support his family of four on 1,600 francs a month. The mother, a housewife, wrote, 'I admit I am not rich and cannot satisfy my children's needs, but I never would have stood for my daughter's doing such a thing!'[23] The items stolen strongly suggest that 'D' wanted nice things she could not afford.

In other words, Vichy's moral prescriptions proved irrelevant to many adolescents. Juvenile delinquents were, to a certain extent, behaving as rational actors, responding to the same economic cues as adults. Adult crime statistics followed an almost identical curve to juvenile crime statistics. Between 1937 and 1942, theft trials increased 267 per cent for juveniles and 245 per cent for adults. Charts 14.1 and 14.2, based on aggregate national figures and therefore subject to all necessary caution, juxtapose the increase in theft cases for minors and adults, which are of two different orders of magnitude but follow very similar curves.[24] Indeed, by 1943 the virtues Vichy promoted, hard work, honesty, and loyalty to Pétain, earned few real rewards, and could land a young person in a labor convoy to Germany.

Juvenile delinquents and other young people who in some way refused to follow Vichy's marching orders can be divided into four separate but overlapping groups: resisters, labor draft evaders, *zazous* (France's swing kids) and delinquents. Neither the law nor the authorities could always accurately separate young people who broke the law out of political motives from minors who stole food either to eat or to sell on the black market. However, aside from the few cases cited above, political motivation appears infrequently in cases from the juvenile courts. Admittedly, resisters caught stealing would have every reason to conceal their politics; but the circumstances of the cases in juvenile courts usually make a resistance connection highly unlikely.

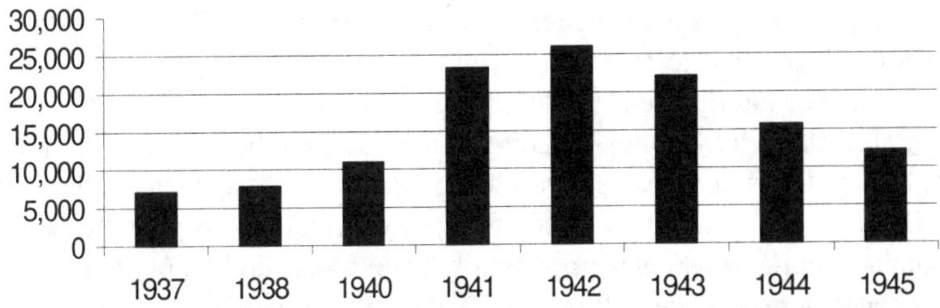

Chart 14.1. Juvenile Theft Cases

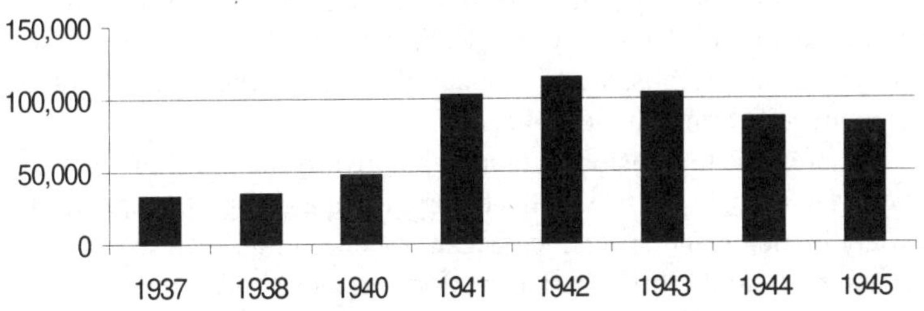

Chart 14.2. Adult Theft Cases

Zazou culture, clothing, musical preferences and language did not constitute resistance in the strict sense, but did explicitly reject Vichy's cultural values. Much as certain collaborators would have liked, *zazous* could not be arrested simply for being *zazous*, but only for breaking a law. Furthermore, arrest records do not describe the dress of accused minors, making it difficult to determine whether some juvenile delinquents were also *zazous*. However, the *zazou* lifestyle, defined by dress and consumption, demanded spending money well beyond the means of the vast majority of the minors who found themselves in court.

Given the repression directed initially at labor evaders and especially at youth in the Resistance and the furious reaction of conservatives in Vichy and fascists in Paris to the *zazous*, the regime's response to juvenile delinquents is somewhat surprising. An authoritarian regime like Vichy might be expected to respond harshly to criminal youth. But juvenile justice policy illustrates the Paxtonian theme of continuity. The movement away from a punitive and toward a therapeutic system that began early in the twentieth century and intensified under the Popular Front continued through the Vichy years.

In part, Vichy's lenience reflected its decision by 1942 to crack down on traffickers but to spare those who violated rationing laws to satisfy personal or family needs.[25] More pertinent to youth crime, however, was the fact that Vichy policy-makers did not interpret the alarming increase in juvenile crime rates as a youthful rejection of its agenda. Rather, on the basis of the writings of contemporary specialists in juvenile delinquency, policy-makers blamed family breakdown, and, in particular, the absence of nearly one million POW fathers.[26] The 1940s experts assumed a connection based not on careful study but on extrapolations from prewar studies and gendered assumptions about family life. In fact, my research fails to verify a connection between war captivity and juvenile crime. But attributing youth crime to the absence of POW fathers allowed delinquent youth to be portrayed as victims of forces beyond their control, furthering the reformist agenda espoused by nearly everyone who wrote about juvenile crime in the 1940s.

The pressure to transform France's punitive system into a therapeutic one began early in the twentieth century, when a group of people from a variety of fields and specialties began to concentrate their attention on the issue of child criminals. Their efforts resulted in the law of 22 July 1912 that created France's first juvenile courts and instituted a probation system. However, many experts remained unhappy with certain aspects of the 1912 law, and grew increasingly dismayed by the dismal condition of penitentiary colonies for young offenders. By the 1930s, a virtual juvenile delinquency establishment had crystallized around the issue of reforming the system. Leading voices included the pediatric neuropsychiatrist Georges Heuyer, the wealthy philanthropist Olga Spitzer, the social worker Madame Guichard, the Quaker activist Henri Van Etten, the legal expert Henri Donnedieu de Vabres, the scouting advocate Henri Joubrel, Judge Jean Chazal, and the public administrative inspector Jean Bancal.

In contrast to the specialists' desire for reform, in the early years of the century the broader public reacted with fear and anger toward children who committed crimes. Spectacular press coverage aroused hysteria about the so-called *apaches* – bands of dangerous young men who roamed city streets with cruel disregard for other people. The pressure to transform France's punitive system had little success in convincing the public that criminal children deserved lenience until after the Great War, when public fear of child crime waned, replaced by a new mass hysteria: fear of demographic collapse.

If, as was commonly assumed in France, the size and vigor of a nation's population indicated national strength, then the slower population growth rate apparent since the mid-nineteenth century endangered France's world position. Demographic anxiety peaked in reaction to the massive loss of young men during the Great War. Pro-natalists finally convinced politicians and the public that France faced a serious population crisis. By successfully redefining the problem of juvenile crime in demographic terms, children's activists countered the portrayal of juvenile delinquents as fearful, evil, precociously perverted children. France needed the contribution of its entire population, and could no longer afford to waste a portion of its youth. Writings in the field emphasized that the vast majority of the children in trouble with the law came from broken or otherwise 'defective' families. The media, in a major shift from its earlier *apache* paranoia, echoed experts' ideas, denying that society could distinguish between 'victimized children' and 'guilty children'. Most minors who broke the law were troubled and in need of protection rather than repression. 'The young delinquent, in effect, is both the guilty party and, most often, a victim too.'[27] Given France's demographic crisis, throwing away children would have disastrous consequences.

As for the institutional treatment of delinquent youth, nearly everyone in the field, even people who worked for the penal administration, condemned existing public institutions for delinquent youth as ineffective and cruel. Books and articles consistently referred to state-run correctional houses or penitentiary colonies for minors as *bagnes d'enfants* (children's penal camps), an explicit comparison with adult penal labor camps (*bagnes*) renowned for harsh conditions and cruel wardens.[28] Sending young people to such institutions represented a waste of people France could no longer spare. Press campaigns in the 1930s described in vivid detail the horrors of life in these 'children's penal camps' and raised public sympathy for juvenile delinquents. State institutions for minor boys were rocked by a number of scandals in the 1930s involving the serious mistreatment and even the death of juvenile inmates. The press campaigns eventually made it impossible for the government to ignore the situation.

The Popular Front's first Minister of Justice, Marc Rucard, highly sympathetic to the juvenile justice reform movement, attempted unsuccessfully to rewrite the 22 July 1912 law on separate juvenile courts and procedures. Rucard also undertook a major effort to reform the worst of the institutions. However, the attempt to rewrite the juvenile code got nowhere in the Assembly, and institutional resistance limited the effectiveness of correctional school reforms. What progress had been made at public juvenile institutions was completely undone by the general mobilization of 1939, which removed nearly all the dedicated reformers.

However, by the winter of 1940, demobilized reforming educators returned to their positions, specialists concerned with juvenile justice resumed their efforts, and the movement picked up where it had left off. Throughout the occupation years, the same group of experts active in the 1930s continued to press for change. Reforms initiated by the Popular Front were maintained and in some cases even extended during the war. Ironically, because working for the Penal Administration provided young men with an exemption from forced labor in Germany under the *Service de Travail Obligatoire* (STO), boys' institutions in 1943 witnessed a major influx of young, often well-educated and idealistic men, many of whom came from the scouting movement. Because STO evaders themselves were thwarting the system, these new monitors often felt more affinity for their wards.[29] While public institutions for girls, less violent but in most ways bleaker than the boys' institutions, had received no public attention in the 1930s, the first reformer, Dominique Riehl, was sent in 1943 to survey the girl's Preservation School at Cadillac, and in October 1944 she became its director.[30]

Finally, the Vichy Minister of Justice Joseph Barthélemy appointed Jean Bancal and Fernand Contancin to produce a completely revised juvenile legal system. They intended the resulting law of 27 July 1942 to serve as a code for delinquent youth. It began with something reformers had pressed for since the early twentieth century, the presumption of the complete penal irresponsibility of minors.[31] In some critical ways the 27 July 1942 law reflected the authoritarian nature of Vichy, limiting avenues of appeal, making the court's appointment of a defender optional, and most shocking of all, removing the attenuating excuse of youth in certain capital crimes. However, the code's preamble outlined in great detail the new, therapeutic system to be established at public institutions. Discipline would operate through positive reinforcement rather than physical punishment. Also, after setting up a preliminary court to deal quickly with the less serious cases, the July 1942 law mandated a stay in an Observation Center for the more serious cases, where minors could be observed and tested to determine if they suffered from any identifiable conditions requiring treatment.

The law of 27 July 1942 never had an application decree, and therefore its new criminal procedures never entered into effect. However, immediate funding of Observation Centers resulted in three functioning centers in the Paris area and several others across France by war's end.

The Provisional Government in Algiers studied Vichy's 1942 law and rejected its authoritarian provisions, but determined that a return to the status quo was unacceptable. Hence a committee began working on reforming juvenile law in Algiers, enabling passage of another major reform shortly after the Liberation. The 2 February 1945 ordinance reversed the 1942 law's authoritarian procedural aspects, and rather than requiring a stay in an Observation Center made it an option at the judge's discretion. However, two of the most basic elements of the 1945 law bore a strong resemblance to the 1942 law: a triage system and the presumption of penal irresponsibility. Passage of the 2 February 1945 law that established the juvenile justice system still in effect today has ever since the war been presented as a virgin birth. The Liberation furnished reformers concerned about delinquent youth with a *tabula rasa*. In fact, the continuities from the Third Republic through to the Provisional Government are striking, both in the state's response to juvenile delinquency and in the work of specialists in the field. The spectacular jump in juvenile crime statistics between 1937 and 1942, followed by a minor decrease and then another upswing between 1945 and 1948, did not perturb the legal, scholarly or institutional developmental curves, which moved continuously in the same direction. The Vichy regime did not reverse, but encouraged, those developments.

Pre-war reformers had successfully redefined delinquent minors as victims of bad families or of psychological conditions. Thus, even though delinquents, like resisters, labor draft evaders and *zazous*, failed to live by Vichy's moral standards, Vichy responded very differently, hoping to repress resisters/labor evaders and spank *zazous*, but rehabilitate delinquents. I have argued that adolescent behavior was not entirely irrational under the circumstances, and could really be seen as an extension of the *système D*, a term denoting the variety of methods (legal and illegal) for coping with wartime hardships. As with many of Vichy's goals, exhortation could only go so far, especially when so strongly contradicted by self-interest.

Notes

1. Archives Départementales de Paris (ADP) 221/73/1/0001. I shall refer to people from case files by a single initial.
2. W. D. Halls, *The Youth of Vichy France* (Oxford, 1981); Pierre Giolitto, *Histoire de la jeunesse sous Vichy* (Paris, 1991); John Hellman, *The Knight-Monks of Vichy France, Uriage 1940–1945* (Montreal, 1993); Bernard Comte, *L'Ecole nationale des Cadres d'Uriage*, 2 vols (Lille, 1989); Roderick Kedward, *In Search of the Maquis* (Oxford, 1993);

Emmanuelle Rioux, 'Les zazous. Un phénomène socio-culturelle sous l'occupation', *Mémoire* (Paris X, 1987); Jean-Claude Loiseau, *Les Zazous* (Paris, 1977).

3. Ministère de la Justice, *Compte général de l'administration de la justice civile et commerciale et de la justice criminelle, Années 1944 à 1947*, Melun, 1953: xxii.
4. A 1946 Justice Ministry study explained, 'devant l'accroissement de la criminalité juvénile, les tribunaux avaient exercé une répression nettement plus sévère' (Ministère de la Justice, *Rapport quinquennal sur l'application de la loi du 22 juillet 1912 sur les Tribunaux pour Enfants et Adolescents et sur la liberté surveillée*, *Journal Officiel*, Annexe Administrative, 16 April 1946: 2); the Joubrels' study of the Paris juvenile courts revealed that the per centage of juveniles who faced trial after an initial appearance rose from 33 per cent in 1938 to 43 per cent in 1942 (Henri and Fernand Joubrel, *L'Enfance dite 'coupable'* (Paris, 1946): 10–11).
5. In the late 1930s, criminal complaints, denunciations and verbal reports averaged 650,000 a year, rising to nearly 1.2 million in 1942, dropping back slightly, and rising again to slightly above 1.2 million in 1945 before slowly declining (Justice, *Compte général*: xvii).
6. He called them 'shits, bastards, buggers' (*fumiers, salauds, enculés*) but was acquitted without discretion and returned to his parents (ADP D1 U6 3993).
7. 'fumiers à Pétain'. He was sentenced to 15 days, 30 francs (ADP D1 U6 4117).
8. Although the investigating magistrate noted, 'La famille H est considérée comme professant des idées "gaullistes" and one member of the family had already been convicted of antinational propaganda, this minor's case was dismissed (*Non lieu*) (Archives Départementales (AD) Gard, Nîmes, 6 U 10 354).
9. The 1946 Justice study reported that *vols* in the 1930s accounted for 68 per cent of all cases and rose during the war to 80 per cent (Justice, *Rapport Quinquennal:* p. 2). Of 165 cases from 1942 through to1944, Crémieux found 116 *vols*, 70 per cent; and Henri Van Etten's survey claimed that 72 per cent of the cases in the Paris Children's Courts in 1942 involved *vol* (Crémieux, *L'Enfant devenu délinquant:* 27; Henri Van Etten, 'Au tribunal pour enfants de la Seine, Statistique 1942' *Pour l'enfance coupable:* 53 (March–April 1944): 7). My provincial court data included 109 cases of theft, or 76 per cent.
10. Eight of the 21 complainants were also employers of the minors charged.

11. ADP 221/73/1/0008.
12. ADP 221/73/1/0001.
13. He and his friend got suspended sentences. AD Gard, 6U 10/262.
14. ADP 221/73/1/0001.
15. ADP 221/73/1/0043.
16. ADP 221/73/1/0004 and 0015.
17. ADP 221/73/1/0015.
18. ADP 221/73/1/0047.
19. ADP 221/73/1/0045, 0009 and 0045.
20. ADP 221/73/1/0015.
21. Another ring operated in Tours. AD Indre-et-Loire, Tours 127 W 230.
22. ADP 221/73/1/0008.
23. ADP 221/73/1/0015.
24. Justice, *Compte général,* xxii, xx.
25. The law of 15 March 1942 set penalties of two to ten years and 2,000–10,000 francs for infractions of rationing decrees; but, 'ne sont pas toutefois soumises aux dépositions de la présente loi, les infractions qui ont été uniquement commises en vue de la satisfaction directe des besoins personnels ou familiaux des délinquants'.
26. The Justice Ministry reported, 'Le défaut d'éducation, de surveillance et d'autorité résulte souvent de l'absence du père, retenu en captivité ou parti travailler en Allemagne.' (Ministère de la Justice, *Rapport quinquennal sur l'application de la loi du 22 juillet 1912 sur les Tribunaux pour Enfants et Adolescents et sur la liberté surveillée, Journal Officiel,* Annexe Administrative (16 April 1946): 2); see also Pierre Flot, *Constatations médicales et sociales relatives à la délinquance juvénile en Bretagne* (Paris, 1945); Albert Crémieux, *L'Enfant devenu délinquant* (Marseilles, 1945).
27. René Luaire, *Le rôle de l'initiative privée dans la protection de l'enfance délinquante en France et en Belgique* (Paris, 1936): 4.
28. Henri Danjou, *Enfants du malheur. Les bagnes d'enfants* (Paris, 1932); Germain Despres, *Bagnes d'enfants* (Paris, n.d.,); Henri Wallon, *Une plaie de la société: Les bagnes d'enfants* (Bourges, 1934).
29. Jacques Bourquin, 'Le temps de la réforme: 1934–1936–1950', *Journal de Sologne* 83 (January 1994): 44; Bourquin, 'Sur la trace des premiers éducateurs de l'Education Surveillée: 1936–1947', *Cahiers du CRIV* 2 (October 1968): 33. Jacques Bourquin kindly provided copies of articles and showed me photographs and a documentary filmed at Mettray with two former wards. His research group (CFES-PJJ) at Vaucresson is doing excellent and very important work on these institutions.

30. Béatrice Koeppel, 'Les temps forts de la rééducation des filles (de Cadillac à Brécourt): 1935–1950', *Cahiers du CRIV* 2 (October 1986): 69; Dominique Riehl, 'L'institution publique d'Education surveillée de Cadillac', *Sauvons l'enfance* 64 (May–June 1946): 2–4.
31. Pierre Giolitto, *Histoire de la jeunesse sous Vichy,* labeled the penal irresponsibility clause repressive, since previously even guilty minors could be acquitted. Yet minors acquitted as acting without discretion could be sent to penal colonies, and in fact all young people in public Supervised Educational Homes (the official name after 1927 for penitentiary colonies) had been acquitted, yet could spend up to seven years in those highly repressive institutions.

–15–

Everyday Culture in Occupied France

Jean-Pierre Rioux

In November 1987, l'Institut d'Histoire du Temps Présent organized its first conference, attended for the most part by young and adventurous scholars whose work on a variety of topics – fashion, young people, sports, theater, the movies, books, or music – opened a different and in many respects new approach to the Occupation in France, one that focuses on culture. The aim was to show both the breadth and originality of the area of research that had been sketched out, and to suggest that a focus on culture could profitably add to our knowledge of the period and reinvigorate the field. The proceedings of this conference were published in 1990 in a volume I edited. I later wrote a kind of summary of the conference for a book edited by Jean-Pierre Azéma and François Bédarida, published in 1993.[1] In that same year, 1987, a French version of cultural history was taking its first tentative steps.[2] Now, ten years later, it seems worthwhile to try to assess this enterprise within the context of this tribute to Robert O. Paxton, who succeeded in waking us from dogmatic slumber. Thanks are therefore due to all our American friends, at Columbia and elsewhere, for affording us the opportunity to discuss calmly a question that had never once been asked a quarter-century ago, in 1972, at the dawn of the Paxtonian revolution – a question that, like so many others, rises directly from that revolution.

On the whole, the work of the past decade has been neither so plentiful nor so rewarding as one might have hoped. We must acknowledge this problem, try to understand the reasons for it, and think how to proceed from here. What was our starting-point in 1987, what did we envision? First and foremost, the examination of the very close relationships between the political, the ideological, and the cultural – understood here in the strict sense of cultural policy – brought to light two paradoxes noted at the time by Henry Rousso.

The first was the relative autonomy of the cultural sphere. Hence, while the Germans and Vichy both exerted a deliberate, stifling, evil, and repressive force in the areas of censorship and exclusion, this policy did not take the extreme path of propagandistic totalitarianism, nor did it set out to create the image of a new man that would challenge traditional ones. Indeed, there continued to exist social and cultural spaces where the freedom to create, to consume, to explore one's private world were scarcely undermined at all, where they were even encouraged. This observation not only reveals a great deal about the very nature of Nazi policies implemented in France – policies that, from the end of 1941, fueled impatience and despair among the propagandists and theoreticians in Berlin – but also about the extent of the National Revolution's ideological reach, measured largely by its limitations and contradictions. For this relative impotence of Vichy runs not only through the history of its stated ambitions, but also through its institutions and its specific programs. For example, many of those who persevered or prospered in these spaces of freedom – the *Esprit* circle, for example, or the activists for a 'people's' education – were undoubtedly caught up at some point within the 'magnetic field' of Vichy, as Philippe Burrin would say; yet the numerous official cultural initiatives of the regime often could not be realized, for they contained at their core a relative freedom that proved either ruinous or subversive. It is in these failed initiatives that the continuity with the pre-war period becomes clear, at the very moment when the regime proclaimed with such arrogance that it had broken with the past and ushered in a new era of salvation. *Jeune France* and the radio and film industries of the unoccupied zone illustrate this incompleteness and impotence, which one finds even where one might least expect it, in the heart of occupied Paris, notably at the Comédie-Française.

'In other words', according to Henry Rousso, 'the cultural dynamism can be attributed in part to the opportunities offered indirectly by defeat, the Occupation, and the installation of a regime with the ambitions and illusions of reform.'[3] This 'indirectly' formed a launching pad for cultural history, which thrives on perspectives that, rather than directly contemplating the real, would rather examine the world of representation. It also gives broad support to the importance of an 'oppositional culture', of the maintenance of the French flame, of which it was said at the Liberation, though not as 'mythologically' as people think today, that it would have enlightened all, justified all, as in Antigone's eternal revenge upon Creon.

The second paradox, noted a long time ago by Pascal Ory, was summarized in this provocative statement: 'Vichy left its mark in those areas where it pursued the policies of the Popular Front.'[4] Sports policy, popular education, youth programs, the launching of a people's theater, the establishment of a 'cultural affairs' administration: the analysis of these areas, well under way for some time now, indeed reveals more mimesis than rupture, more symbolic borrowing than revolution, as the constraints inherited from a France wounded since 1918 were too great to be overcome. The paradoxical result is that the only observable rupture is internal. For in the mood of general indifference, broadly diffused from 1942 on, it was the very impotence of Vichy's management of these affairs that eventually broke a continuity that was never acknowledged at the time but that seems very clear in retrospect. We could thus legitimately state, ten years ago, that to relate the cultural to the political and the ideological was interesting, but would not take us very far: in the course of our research, we would simply confirm and clarify things that we already knew, or that we were planning to establish more solidly, about the nature of the German Occupation and the Vichy regime. The endeavor was an appealing one, but its benefits seemed limited.

On the other hand, the exploration of the culture of everyday life seemed potentially more fruitful, once it became clear that a true rupture had indeed occurred in the minds of most French people, at a moment when, as the painter Jean Bazaine stated in 1942, 'all that remains is man confronting life. Innocent to the point of awkwardness.'[5] It is this wartime innocence that interested us, with its attendant sufferings and privations, its string of all-too-obvious tragedies and ruined hopes, its nomadic wanderings and cacophonies, along with its relationship – still to be evaluated – to Sartre's famous existential assertion, 'Never have we been freer than under the Occupation.' In the vast galaxy of cultural creations, of practices and consumption, we sought to find a series of correspondences with that secret freedom that nourishes any conscious being plunged into such difficulties, and to develop a kind of historical psychoanalysis of the trauma affecting the values and commitments, the affections and hopes of this country as it reeled from the double blow of defeat and exodus in 1940. We also sought to relate this 'ingenuous' rupture, this secession within the mind that followed the collective disaster, to the withdrawal of the majority of French people into their inner worlds as they waited for better days, the possibility of good times ahead. At first, we uncovered only stubborn ambivalences, for we had neither the conceptual key nor the comparative perspective that would allow us to sort through these ambivalences and give them a more unequivocal meaning.

But our initial findings were already clear enough. Cultural life, it seemed to us, had indeed been simultaneously a refuge and an awakening, a distraction and a reflection, an accommodation and an evasion, a rumination and a revenge; but it did not acquire its contradictions and ambivalences with impunity. On the contrary, we felt very strongly that this wartime 'innocence' was set within a continuum, that it was consistent with fundamental trends observed in the thirties and the fifties: the broadening of cultural consumption, the power of the media – and of radio in particular – in inaugurating mass culture, the search for specific audiences in true social agitation outside of or in opposition to this embryonic mass culture, the irruption of cultural matters into the sphere of public policy, the fragmentation and search for a recomposition of cultural space, both nationally and internationally, the breach of the old republican boundaries between believers and secularists, the transformation of generational relationships through the public recognition of the relative autonomy of youth, the search for a new relationship between the elites in need of regeneration and the disoriented masses who were bypassing the old rules of republican meritocracy and advancement, even at school, a renewal of secessions both artistic (in painting, for example) and intellectual in attempting an impossible return to order, one that would reconfer a meaning to both words and signs. Within this avalanche of disparate expressions of the authentically new, to which the war gave an extra appeal and color – and which, as a whole, continues even today to contribute to the 'French exception' – we have singled out the most visible, and consequently the most accessible, along three lines of investigation: the broadening of consumerism and hence of cultural curiosities; the decentralization of cultural practices increasingly freed of Parisian domination; and the militant insistence on culture for all.

Ten years and several books later, these initial approaches have not, in our estimation, been called into question. The validation of these approaches, however, seems to have run out of steam and lacks conviction. For this state of affairs, I see two explanations, one stemming from the course of collaborative works on the years of Occupation, the other from cultural history itself.

It is understandable that the history of Vichy France has been in the spotlight principally in other contexts, placed there both by the internal dynamics of scholarship and by the interests of society at large. This latter factor produced a situation we know too well: caught in the crossfire between the media coverage of the most recent trials, from Klaus Barbie to Maurice Papon, the obligations of memory, and the pinpricks of the revisionists, the history of Vichy France has become in some sense subject to the jurisdiction of the courts, as well as the occasion for a collective form of therapy. In a world deprived of the ideologies that shaped its old post-war antagonisms, in a France where national identity is open to question, the only ideal that has survived with particular force is that of the Rights of Man, flouted by our century's barbarism, and what has become an obsession is the blind spot of our history, the genocide of the Jews, the Shoah.

Moreover, the survivors and witnesses, haunted by impending death, will not rest until they can transmit the responsibility to bear witness, even if they must skip a generation, to take up again not the thread of time, but that of memory, whose 'duty' is considered imperative and whose debt is inextinguishable. The social activism of the former deportees in particular has no other motive, especially in the context of educational establishments, than to force the hand of destiny by making the very youngest into new witnesses, without a presumption of innocence.[6] Without wishing to enter here into any sort of debate, one must admit that the history of the Second World War, in its scientific renewal launched so vigorously in the seventies by the Paxtonian revolution, was well-armed and quite ready to go boldly beyond the social prescriptions of the present day.

Advances in the study of the exclusions and repressions of Vichy, final excavations of the ideological reasons underlying them, refined analysis of the governmental mechanisms that had zealously put them into action, the lively beginnings of a study of the Resistance free of mythologizing, a refined knowledge of the evolution of public opinion, a return to the systematic study of material and daily life conceived as a strategic vector, of the evolution of public opinion and the course of politics generally, slow digestion by a history of memory of the collective guilt fostered by *The Sorrow and the Pity*: all the great working themes of the past twenty years easily found their place and role in the chorus of investigations which the era demanded. The cultural, considered as an area of its own providing a sharper perspective, entered this concert on the off-beat, sounding all the wrong notes, for it seemed to identify too many areas of ambivalence, too many private acts of limited public import, too many transformations that set the stage for another turn of events, the post-war period: it sat ill with the historical fatalism the period is so often credited with today, with its attendant teleological temptations. Hence, despite numerous contributions by individual historians, the cultural has not been a prime field for research.

As for the field of cultural history, it has not wholly succeeded in making clear the need for a specific study of the war years. Here again, one must take into account research priorities, which are methodological in nature and have attempted to determine the most favorable windows of historical opportunity. It is thus not by chance that, despite the foundational exemplarity attributed to Second World War, the cultural history of the First World War has succeeded, slowly but surely, in making remarkable progress unmatched in the study of 1939–1945. By the same token, the period of the Dreyfus affair has been considered richer than Vichy in its long-term consequences for the structural analysis of political engagement, intellectuals, or the influence of the media on public opinion. Similarly, it is only too clear that, on the major themes of cultural history, at least for the French – history of mediation, history of mass culture, history of cultural institutions and policies, history of signs and symbols – research into the specifics of the Second World War has been marking time, from the moment when we considered, perhaps too lightly, Vichy as a simple link in a chain of continuity that surrounded it and consequently diluted it, when it would doubtless have been preferable to start from a study of the different temporalities experienced at the time by the French people.

Let us put a stop here to thematic and methodological introspection, for we need to look ahead. And to do that, we must be certain that we have at our disposal a few concepts to work with and some useful comparisons to make. First of all, one can say that the cultural history of the Occupation would do well to follow the lead of studies of daily life during wartime. These studies certainly do not constitute an isolated area of research: it has been shown convincingly that matters related to rationing and food supply had their fighters who soon moved into the political, ideological and social arenas, and that these matters were, by their very nature, basic elements of the conflict. Perhaps everyday life can also serve as a good gauge of cultural maturations, evolutions, or ruptures. This approach is rarely brought to the cultural field, even by scholars who, like Dominique Veillon, straddle both fields[7] – as if rutabagas didn't also affect certain understandings of the world and of life!

It is also true that the two approaches – the everyday and the cultural – are so closely allied that the sources to consult in order to understand their interrelationships are often the same: that poorly inventoried, little-explored and under-utilized mass of eyewitness accounts, letters, notebooks and diaries, literary traces and journalistic crumbs, packed into attics and closets, which could also be used to organize the last plausible large-scale oral investigations. The abundance of this documentation, and problems of access, have tended to block or discourage its use, while the well-sorted boxes of the public archives are much more tempting. Nevertheless, I believe that we must not give up on building a history that begins without presuppositions in its encounter with the everyday life of the French, for ultimately, it will doubtless prove to be more cultural than one had suspected.

Two other concepts will also be of use. The first is Philippe Burrin's notion of 'accommodation', in all its cultural richness of adjusting to a new reality, with its many social, generational and regional variables, and all its modes and degrees of structural constraint, opportunity, voluntary service and complicity. For this accommodation, in all its forms, ultimately brings into play representations of the world that are at the heart of cultural history, and shows that ways of living, thinking, and dreaming are subject to the temper of the times; specifically, for 1939–1945, the memory of previous struggles, the unbearable impossibility of mastering the course of such events, produced a powerful sense of ideological, social and national decomposition, and nourished hopes of surviving the ordeal in the best possible condition. And Burrin has himself shown the operational value of his concept of 'accommodation' especially as it related to scientific institutions, and specifically the one directed by Frédéric Joliot-Curie at the Collège de France; in the discussion following his analysis, he made it very clear that the history of major institutions under the Occupation could no longer hide in the 'darkness of curfews'.[8]

The second operational concept, conversely, could be that 'civil resistance', which Jacques Semelin has taken up retroactively, on the basis of his study of the cultural reconstructions and rebellions that preceded the recent disintegration of communism in Eastern Europe.[9] That resistance indeed confirms the necessary de-ideologicalization, which had perhaps already progressed further than we imagined in 1940–44; it obliges us to re-examine the force of law in its relationship to power in unstable societies, it asserts the importance of the struggle for values that lie at the heart of daily life, it reveals the importance of obscure actors who prefer to remain obscure, it rehabilitates a contemporary form of the mediated event. Better yet, it attempts to weigh a cultural force replete with protests and testimonies, it emphasizes the high stakes that memory bears in all its forms – resignation, defiance and resistance, it helps us understand the reality of the social synergy of media messages, and, as a result, forces us to reread the press, re-listen to the radio and re-view the cinema of the Occupation.[10] This civil resistance could well be the happy counterpoint to accommodation.

But experimenting with concepts will not suffice: a vigorous comparative campaign must also be launched. A comparison, first of all, with other democratic nation-states at war, Great Britain and the United States especially, to try to show that, despite enemy occupation and the unusual, if foreseeable, installation of the Vichy regime, France may or may not fit into the framework of a comparative study of a deconstruction, reconstruction and renaissance of the nation-state threatened by fascism. In other words, under cover of the defense and victory of the 'anti-fascist' form of the civic contract against Nazism, what was the deep-rooted role of the critique and the defense of the normative function of the state, which seemed inevitable if one were to manage a society and bring it back together? To what extent were republican values put at risk, and with what success and what consequences? For the Vichy period is clearly inscribed within a continuous evolution of state and social management of the republican contract, within the course of a new writing of the 'grammar of the Nation', as Philippe Burrin put it.

Finally, a detailed comparison with the Great War of 1914–1918 would in all likelihood yield the most striking results. The entire cultural history of that first conflict can be grasped in the awareness of the extraordinarily painful gap between a cause so valiantly defended and the devastating magnitude of the sacrifice undertaken to assure its victory, between the mobilized force of national tradition and that of modern death, a death whose survivors dimly felt opened out onto the unknown and that would allow only a memory, ardent and perhaps impotent; between a defensive acquiescence and a violence both evil and unbearable. If we compare point by point all these terms – cultural means mobilized in defense of a cause, consent to a defensive position, 'brutalization' (Georges Mosse) accompanying the eruption of a hitherto unknown level of violence – 1939–1945 immediately takes on a stronger relief, a more singular profile, the analysis of which would confirm many of the points we started from ten years ago: the unbearable spectacle of the national territory dismembered and put into sudden competition, a far cry from the classic give-and-take that lends cultural vigor to the separate parts; the absence of defensive strength caused by the defeat and the collapse, without a rectilinear front to protect received ideas or a mental Maginot line able to resist the virus of decomposition; sacrifices scattered to the far corners of the theater of operations, subject to horrible sufferings spread out among the camps and torture chambers; a hopefulness whose presence on the national territory is not readily evident, in the long, reciprocal misunderstanding between the internal Resistance movement and the Free French. One could easily extend the list of questions that a comparative approach might renew or make more topical. But four seem decisive: the relationship to the Great War, the trauma of defeat and the exodus of 1940, the moral and mental response to material shortages, and the new growth and decentering of cultural activity.

We may conclude from all this that a history of the culture of everyday life, if properly executed, could be thought-provoking in a broad range of fields. And to restart this thought-machine, any American aid of the sort provided by Robert O. Paxton in 1973 would be most welcome.

Notes

1. Jean-Pierre Rioux (ed.), *La Vie culturelle sous Vichy* (Brussels, 1990), and Jean-Pierre Rioux, 'Ambivalences culturelles (1940–1941)', in Jean-Pierre Azéma and François Bédarida (eds), *La France des années noires,* vol. 1 (Paris, 1993): 515–36.
2. See Pascal Ory, 'L'histoire culturelle de la France contemporaine: question et questionnement', in *Vingtième siècle. Revue d'histoire,* November–December 1987, and Jean-Pierre Rioux (ed.), *L'histoire culturelle de la France contemporaine. Bilans et perspectives de la recherche* (Paris, 1987), 4 vols. For an overview, see Jean-Pierre Rioux and Jean-François Sirinelli (eds), *Pour une histoire culturelle* (Paris, 1997).
3. Henry Rousso, 'Vichy: politique, idéologie et culture', in Jean-Pierre Rioux (ed.), *La Vie culturelle sous Vichy* (Brussels, 1990): 34.
4. Pascal Ory, 'La politique culturelle de Vichy: Rupture et continuité', in J.- P. Rioux (ed.), *La Vie culturelle sous Vichy* (Brussels, 1990), 229.
5. Jean-Pierre Rioux, 'Ambivalences en rouge et bleu: les pratiques culturelles des Français pendant les années noires', in Jean-Pierre Rioux (ed.), *La Vie culturelle sous Vichy* (Brussels, 1990): 45.
6. Most recent example, dated 12 September 1997: the Annie and Charles Corrin Foundation for the struggle against the trivialization and forgetting of the Shoah wants to better 'make known the history of the Shoah', 'thus carrying out the work of memory' with the support of the Ministry of Education, since 'the duty to preserve historical memory falls to the present generations'.
7. It is paradoxical that her work in *Vivre et survivre en France (1939–1947)* (Paris, 1995), contains no account or further discussion of what she had shown in her earlier book on *La Mode sous l'Occupation* (Paris, 1990).
8. Philippe Burrin, *La France à l'heure allemande (1940–1944)* (Paris, 1995), and Michel Pinault, 'Frédéric Joliot, les Allemands et l'Université aux premiers mois de l'Occupation', in *Vingtième siècle. Revue d'histoire* no. 50, April–June 1996.
9. See Jacques Semelin, *Sans armes face à Hitler. La résistance civile en Europe (1939–1943)* (Paris, 1989).
10. See Jean-Pierre Rioux, 'Remarques historiennes au service d'une cause commune', in Jacques Semelin (ed.), *Quand les dictatures se fissurent: résistances civiles à l'Est et au Sud* (Paris, 1995).

–16–

Catholics, the Vichy Interlude, and After

W. D. Halls

Was the impact of the Vichy regime upon the Church *decisive* in effecting long-term change? Whilst acknowledging that finalities hinge also on factors other than an ephemeral government, to attempt an answer to this question one must first examine the state of the Church during and immediately after the war and then investigate certain religious, political and social phenomena that followed.

In a hierarchical Church much depended upon its leaders. The Assembly of Cardinals and Archbishops (ACA) shaped Church 'policy' through its pronouncements. In this the three diocesan cardinals, Suhard, Gerlier and Liénart, predominated. Like many of their fellow-prelates, as young priests they had experienced the separation of Church and State in 1905 and borne the brunt of anticlericalism. Bishops had grown old as 'internal *émigrés*' in their relationship with the Republic. Some had served in the First World War, and held Pétain in high esteem. Little wonder therefore that the 'divine surprise' – Charles Maurras's description of Pétain's assumption of power – of a new dispensation renewed their hopes of a national and religious 'revival'. Suhard, archbishop of Paris, welcomed the new regime and was prepared to sit out the Occupation. He temporized with the Germans and collaborationists – perhaps too much so, for at the Liberation he suffered humiliation. Cardinal Gerlier, archbishop of Lyons, one-time lawyer and Catholic youth leader, showed little disaffection towards the regime until September 1942, when he spoke out against the persecution of the Jews; he was censured for not having done so earlier. Liénart, bishop of Lille, remained virtually unreproached in 1944, despite continuing to be a staunch supporter of Pétain.

The comportment of the higher clergy, with one or two exceptions, had been ambiguous. Their loyalty to Vichy, even when in early 1942 they realized all hope had died of accomplishing the much-vaunted Révolution Nationale, was excessive, and is often contradicted by their private actions. Thus, for example, they succoured refugees and Jews wherever possible. In any case, was not the enterprise of effecting a national 'renaissance' in an occupied country amid a global war patently preposterous? Although most had kept the Germans at arm's length they were overly timid, as a German historian has confirmed.[1] Public and frank criticism might have achieved more positive humanitarian, social and even political results.

At the Liberation the cardinals figured on anonymous lists drawn up of diocesans whose conduct was judged unworthy of their high office. Their real crime lay in propping up a collaborationist regime at the end, in not confronting the Nazis as had their Dutch and Belgian counterparts, in a reluctance to come out against persecution, and in condemning the Allies for 'terror bombing', the Resistance for terrorism and the Free French for disloyalty, and failing to use their influence to mitigate the defeat.

Part of the responsibility for this indictment lies with the Vatican. The bishops took their lead from Pius XII, whose wartime silence has aroused such controversy. There is an apparent logic in their position. They mistrusted Nazism but viewed communism – wrongly, in the event – as the greater danger, as did the Pope. Moreover, the bishops saw the Vichy regime as offering opportunities for restoring the nation to its one-time Christian culture and the Church to its former position. 'Dissidence' would prevent their vision being realized. Rebellion ran counter to the traditional Church stance of submission to the established political order.

After the war the Vatican refused to condemn its accused prelates: only three metropolitan diocesan bishops were dismissed. Nevertheless, most of the hierarchy had been guilty of miscalculating the situation, partly because of ill-founded aspirations and apprehensions, and even more so because of lack of leadership from Rome. The upshot was a diminution in their influence, only partially redeemed by the major resistance role played by Catholics.

The consequence of this loss of authority by Church leaders was crucial in 1946. But the 'official' Church was not the whole body. There were others: Social Catholics, whose time came after the Liberation; armed resisters who risked life and limb, and spiritual ones as well (many of whom also endangered their lives), such as those who produced the clandestine publication *Témoignage Chrétien*. All these helped to improve the situation for the Church, whereas the bishops merely reluctantly submitted once more to a republican regime. However, the bogy of communism they perceived did induce them to exhort their flock, especially women, the main churchgoers and now voters for the first time, to support a new Christian Democrat party, the MRP (*Mouvement Républicain Populaire*), which initially enjoyed success, as will be seen, at elections. By 1948 Pope Pius XII could welcome France again as a major player in the Catholic world. A mass was said in Rome 'Pro felice statu gallicae nationis (For the happy condition of the French nation)'.[2] The Pope even approved of the left-of-center MRP, regarding it as a countervailing force to French communism and its social policies, and as another way of winning back the workers to Christianity.

What of numbers? Religious leaders enjoyed a higher profile at Vichy than the number of practicing Christians justified. Re-conversion, particularly of the masses, became the priority. The publication in 1943 of Godin and Daniel's *France, pays de mission?*[3] stimulated Cardinal Suhard to set up the *Mission de Paris* and later to send worker-priests to Germany,[4] and Abbé Godin to start a *Mission de France*. These formed a precedent for the worker-priest movement, which flourished ephemerally after the war: by 1951 some hundred worker-priests were working in factories. Some, however, plunged into trade union activities and sympathized with those Marxist ideas that Pius XII again condemned in 1949, a phenomenon that represents a prime case of what might be termed 'centrifugality', a moving away from official Church policy. An alarmed Vatican forbade further recruitment, and the movement was suspended in 1954. Meanwhile Suhard's proselytizing chimed with that of the *Jeunesse Ouvrière Chrétienne* (JOC), the *Jocistes*, to 'rechristianize' France – 'nous referons chrétiens nos frères' ('we shall make our brothers Christians again'), they sang.

What success did the rechristianization campaign have? In the working-class 'red belt' around Paris before the war the number of practicing Catholics was under 1 per cent. In 1939 a quarter of all Frenchmen attended Sunday mass and a third made their Easter communion. The war heightened religious observance, but the effect was not lasting. By 1947 26 per cent of the population attended mass and 31 per cent made their Easter communion.[5] Thus pre-war figures had scarcely changed. By 1980 Easter attendance had fallen to 14 per cent. This decline is mirrored in the number of vocations: in 1944 1,058 men entered the priesthood. By 1963 the number had dropped to 573.[6] During the war the number of younger priests increased.[7] Yet by 1965 some 60 per cent of priests were over the age of forty-six.[8] There was in any case a growing indifference to religion.

Did the war help to promote Christian unity? Catholics had not participated in the formation in 1938 of a World Council of Churches, a Protestant-inspired organization, but events were to draw the two branches of Western European Christianity closer. Thus, for example, in German prison camps Catholics, Protestants and Jews had lived cheek by jowl and learned to respect each other's beliefs.[9] A striking illustration is provided by Mgr Piguet, of Clermont-Ferrand. Arrested in May 1944 for helping a priest on the run, the bishop, hardly notable for speaking out against Jewish persecution, landed in Dachau. Liberated on 3 May 1945 by members of the French special services, he took an after-lunch glass of champagne with Léon Blum, his fellow-prisoner. Such fraternal gestures would have once been inconceivable.[10]

In assistance to Jews, Christians had collaborated in the relief organization, *Comité Inter-Mouvement auprès des Evacués* (CIMADE), which was initially Protestant but which eventually combined with Catholics in *Amitié Chrétienne* and extended its activities even to helping resisters. Protestants such as Madeleine Ribot and Catholics such as Père Chaillet and Père Glasberg buried their differences in the common cause (as indeed mainly did the Resistance as a whole) – another example of practical ecumenism.

After the war inter-denominational relations, although improved, made slow progress. Some Protestants felt that what was demanded of them was their conversion to Catholicism.[11] Twenty years passed before the Catholic Church (which, as one Catholic said, has eternity on its side) fully accepted the 'separated brethren'. A Frenchman, Père Congar, was invited by Pope John XXIII to participate in drawing up an agenda for ecumenism for the Second Vatican Council (1962–5), supported by Cardinal Liénart at the Council, from which body eventually emerged the decree *De Œcumenismo*, proclaiming that all Christian faiths were united by one baptism. War did bring about a practical ecumenicity; but ecumenism in the narrow sense of reconciliation of doctrine and agreement on ecclesial structures did not progress.

The Vichy period threw up at least three important theological questions. The first concerned St Thomas Aquinas's theory of the 'just war': it is legitimate to fight if the cause is just. The practical corollary is that it is a duty to take up arms against injustice. ('Integral' pacifism made a few proselytes among Catholics, and the Reformed Church had condemned pacifism as early as 1932.) After the defeat the 'just war' doctrine was invoked by those Catholics who opted for active or spiritual resistance. For them it overrode all admonitions of Church leaders to accept the situation, and is a further example of a seepage of Church authority.

Another issue concerned the right of the individual Christian to decide his own course of action. The Church had long asserted the paramountcy of its *magisterium*, the teaching dispensed by the bishops. They had exercised it in religious and even in secular affairs, such as forbidding the faithful to vote for left-wing parties. But it was recalled that Cardinal

Newman, one-time Anglican priest and Oxford don, had much earlier reasserted the supremacy of the individual conscience, against whose dictates no authority on earth could prevail. For Christians who resisted, thus disobeying the Church's injunction to accept the status quo, conscience became the final arbiter of all their actions. (Exceptionally, however, when young Catholics were faced with compliance with the forced labor draft laws, the Church had cautiously accepted liberty of conscience as decisive.)

The third issue concerned the obedience Catholics owed the state. In his tract *Le Prince-Esclave*, Père Gaston Fessard postulated[12] 'the common good' (*le Bien commun*) as the supreme law of society. The state's duty is to ensure the elementary common good of its citizens, defined as ensuring their security and very existence. Also, a higher common good exists, consisting of the values that a society must be willing to fight to retain. A state is only legitimate if it can ensure both forms. The Vichy regime was barely able to preserve the elementary common good. The Gaullists, Fessard argued, could fight only for the higher common good. Thus neither was entirely legitimate. Vichy was therefore in the position of a *Prince-esclave vis-à-vis* the Germans, who were acting against French interests; hence '. . . the more the *Prince-esclave* is reduced to proceeding along the path of "collaboration" the more its people must stand firm in stubborn resistance'.[13] Such is the only patriotic course. This theological position profoundly modifies the relationship between Church and State, and was another justification for resistance.

What emerged from these three propositions after the war were new principles regarding the interlocking demands on the individual, Church and state power. Such perspectives represent a major break with the past. They can be represented as yet another example of challenging traditional Church authority.

'Work, family, country' was Vichy's new national motto. It was one to which all the bishops could subscribe; but it did not survive the Liberation. Moreover, most Church leaders endorsed at least some of the following concepts: hierarchy, authority, communitarianism, the family, and paternalism. (They opposed materialism, individualism, parliamentarianism and extreme republicanism.) Again, the tide of history was against them. Little of substance in the way Vichy conceived such terms survived under the Fourth Republic. The same held good for such abhorrent legislation as the anti-Jewish statutes or the anti-freemasonry measures, which the bishops, with few exceptions, condoned.

Laval's return to the government in April 1942 came as a shock to the Church. The rehabilitation of the 'horse trader' signified a loss of power by Pétain to the Germans, whose nominee Laval was. It marked the end of the bishops' dreams. Yet they clung to Pétain not only from personal loyalty, but also because of a forlorn hope that he would be an interlocutor acceptable to the Americans and, like some *deus ex machina*, would, with the Pope, mediate a compromise peace, thus saving France from being overrun by the Bolshevik hordes. When Pétain was later put on trial they mostly lapsed into indignant silence. An exception was Cardinal Liénart, who was a character of different mettle. Joining with a motley crew of former military men and Maurrassians, he pressed for the rehabilitation of the Marshal. In 1948 he headed a National Committee (*Comité d'honneur*) founded to free Pétain from banishment on the Ile d'Yeu.

Since the separation in 1905 a definitive statute to regulate the relations between Church and State had been lacking. The episcopate trusted the Vichy regime to propose a settlement, with the ultimate aim of achieving a new Concordat. This ambition was doomed to failure, because the Vatican first wanted an end to the war. The bishops also failed to retain Vichy laws allowing religious orders to acquire a legal personality, and to be free to teach and deal with property in their own right. The legislation was declared null and void at the Liberation.

During the war, initial financial advantages obtained from Vichy by its confessional schools were gratifying to the Church.[14] In July 1945 subsidies to these schools were abruptly stopped. Nevertheless, the bishops insisted that Catholic children should be educated in their own schools. The Protestant and Socialist André Philip chaired a parliamentary commission to seek a way to maintain aid, but failed to convince an implacable front of parliamentarians, particularly Socialists and Communists. A loophole was sought. The Poinso-Chapuis decree (22 May 1945), emanating from the Ministry of Health, allowed family associations, in which Catholics predominated, to distribute funds to needy families to finance their children's education (i.e., in Catholic schools) but was scarcely implemented, because the mandatory ministerial orders were interminably delayed. However, Vichy had set a precedent for state assistance: the *loi Marie* (1951) and the *loi Barangé* (1951) paved the way for more comprehensive subventions given in the *loi Debré* (1959) and subsequent efforts to resolve the 'schools question'.

The terrible fate of the Jews under the Vichy regime is discussed elsewhere, and is therefore only dealt with summarily here. Many excuses have been advanced for the long silence before the Church spoke out against Vichy's anti-Jewish measures. Thus, for example, the ACA, as usual underestimating its power to influence events, may have thought it was protecting French Jews by tacitly assenting to the deportation of foreigners and those recently naturalized. Furthermore, by then there was fear of German reprisals if the policy was thwarted. The enigmatic silence of Pius XII was also a factor. But all such reasons do not really hold water.

The case of Cardinal Liénart illustrates the ambiguity and discontinuity inherent in this issue. After the Paris round-up of Jews in the Vél d'Hiver in July 1942 the members of the ACA in the occupied zone, headed by the cardinal, protested to Pétain. However, the protest was never made public; nor were diocesan clergy informed of its contents. This may have been due to the prudence that was considered wise in the occupied zone or, as one authority has hinted, out of unfailing loyalty to Pétain.[15] In the Nord department – Cardinal Liénart's diocese – Jews were comparatively few in number: under 2,000 in all.[16] Marrus and Paxton comment on the 'curious silence'[17] of the cardinal, who nevertheless after *Kristallnacht* in 1938 had backed the protest action in his diocese by Abbé Catrice. Arrests of Jews *en masse* from the diocese began in September 1942, and of the 461 deported, 336 perished.

Liénart may have felt disquiet at his wartime passivity. His opportunity to redress the balance came much later, when he played an important role at the Second Vatican Council in the formulation of a declaration on the Jews, which, it was alleged, was made at the express wish of Pope John XXIII. Yet his 'Remarks' on the schema 'Ecumenism', in which the draft declaration originally appeared, argued nothing new: that the sacred books of the Jews were sacred to Christians also; Christ, his family and his apostles were Jews; Jews had been chosen as the people of God. Christians, he asserted, had now to be made more aware of these facts 'in order to reject utterly the anti-Semitism that has inspired so many crimes against the Jews up to the present day'.[18] The declaration, which was welcomed by Dr Nahum Goldmann, then president of the World Jewish Congress, did not expressly acknowledge any culpability on the part of the Church.[19] That had to wait till much later when, on 17 March 1998, the Vatican finally made a statement repenting of the Church's passivity during the Holocaust. It refrained, however, from open condemnation of the silence of Pope Pius XII. Meanwhile, earlier on 30 September 1997, sixteen French bishops, in whose dioceses during the war Jewish internment camps were located, meeting in Drancy, made what *Le Monde* called 'The "Declaration of Repentance" of the Church of France', which expressed 'regret' for 'the errors of the past'.[20] Thus the hierarchy made belated amends for its earlier silence, and internationally it was Cardinal Liénart who was partially the instrument of closing the tragic rift between Catholics and Jews that had subsisted since the Middle Ages.

The varying political 'engagement' of Catholics both before and after the war provides a classic example of continuities and discontinuities. The tradition that the Church was above politics was more honored in the breach than in the observance, particularly in 1940 and 1941.

Some of the bishops recognized, as the war drew to a close, that social reform was necessary. Archbishop Saliège of Toulouse, who incidentally had championed the Jews throughout, drew up a 'social plan' that addressed the plight of the workers, seeking an end, as he put it, to their being considered as a mere factor in capitalist production.[21] Cardinal Suhard wrote in January 1944 to Cardinal Liénart: 'The French Church must be ready not to shrink from reforms in the social structure',[22] a declaration echoed by the ACA in the following month. These moves from a conservative body were significant.

However, the end of the Vichy regime signaled also the virtual collapse of the political Right, which had been routinely backed by Catholics. (Simone de Beauvoir once remarked, 'religion is not on the right, it is the Right'.[23]) Many had supported *Action Française*, the monarchist right-wing organization (at least until it was condemned by the pope.) But in 1944, as René Rémond succinctly puts it, the Right was 'convicted, its esteem diminished, demolished, cast into the outer darkness'.[24] Thus there was room for a new Christian-oriented grouping to counterbalance the socialists and communists.

Continuity with pre-war politics was represented by Georges Bidault, one-time member of the *Parti Démocrate Populaire* (PDP), the small pre-war Social Catholic party. After Jean Moulin's death, Bidault had become head of the *Conseil National de la Résistance*, whose *Comité d'Experts* (later, *Comité d'Etudes*), charged with planning political and social changes after the Liberation, included a number of Christians. From such Catholic resisters sprang in January 1944 the idea of a Christian Democrat party. In November 1944, headed by Georges Bidault, it was formally constituted as the *Mouvement Républicain Populaire* (MRP).

The new movement (it shunned the appellation 'party' as too reminiscent of the discredited pre-war parties), whilst not being overtly confessional, would be linked, like its predecessor, to 'social' and 'reformist', as opposed to 'integrist' and traditional, Catholicism. It aimed at establishing a democracy based on Christian principles; thus it sought the elimination of capitalist 'fiefdoms' – Vichy had also claimed it was against these[25] – the nationalization of monopolies, worker participation and job security. It benefited because it was *new,* whereas other parties of the Left had to bear the burden of their past. In the event, at the first post-war elections of October 1945 almost half of those elected for the MRP had once been members of the PDP; one-sixth had been members of the *Confédération Française des Travailleurs Chrétiens* (CFTC), the Christian trade union, and others active in *Action Catholique*, the umbrella body for all lay organizations associated with the Church. The Social Catholic credentials of the MRP were therefore impeccable.

Since the bishops and the Catholic bourgeoisie continued to fear a communist takeover, the eclipse of the old right-wing parties left them no option but to throw their weight behind the movement. If the party favored 'socially venturesome actions' that displeased most higher clergy, they drew comfort from the fact that the party had 'spiritual concerns'.[26] Another factor in the MRP's meteoric rise was the new female franchise. It was assumed that women would vote as their confessors told them – and far more women than men attended church.

By June 1946 the MRP emerged as the largest party, winning 28 per cent of the votes, and in November it was only narrowly beaten into second place by the Communists. Thus for a brief period an unlikely triple alliance of Communists, Socialists and Christian Democrats governed France. The MRP, whilst supporting nationalizations, nevertheless rejected a wholly monolithic statist economy. Richard Kuisel describes its main aim as 'to humanize the economy and subordinate it to the service of the family and the nation'.[27]

As traditional conservatives rallied and once more gained Catholic support the MRP was also obliged to move to the right and back Gaullism, a difficult move for a strongly republican and parliamentarian party after France's Cincinnatus himself had retired to Colombey-les-deux-Eglises, declaring a plague on all assemblies. In any case, the church-going MRP voter could not accommodate himself for long to an anticlerical SFIO. Had not the bishops continually denounced socialism almost as vehemently as communism?[28] Quarrels about subsidies to Catholic schools meant that, as in the bad old days, the 'schools question' again became the touchstone of political allegiance. The upshot was that by 1951 the MRP share of the vote dropped to 13 per cent, and in 1956 to 11 per cent.[29] If five and a half million electors had voted MRP in 1946, by the end of the Fourth Republic this number had more than halved. In 1967 the party formally disbanded. Thus ended in failure one of the more significant initiatives to emerge from the Resistance. The Church had missed a golden opportunity. The cohesion of pre-war Social Catholicism, prolonged during the Occupation through the Resistance, proved in the end politically unsustainable.

The hierarchy's condemnation of socialism and communism was worrying to some Catholics. Christians and Communists who had cooperated in the Resistance had developed a mutual respect, and saw no reason not to continue a dialogue begun in war. But as the new form of Social Catholicism waned, so did the contacts. The original pre-war dichotomy of Right and Left re-emerged. The interlude of Vichy had brought about no permanent change.

The decision of the Vichy regime to dissolve existing national trade unions and force their members into a *syndicat unique* had aroused much opposition among Catholics. It had been represented as a move towards corporatism, but could also be interpreted as one step towards a fascist state. The specifically Christian union, the CFTC, founded in 1918, had always enjoyed Church backing. Especially strong in northern France, it was supported by Cardinal Liénart. Its struggle to resist being incorporated nationally in the new organization outlined in the *Charte du Travail* has been recounted elsewhere.[30] Suffice to say that it was one that almost set Liénart, that most loyal of prelates, at odds with Marshal Pétain, although eventually he fell into line. This did not deter the union during the closing years of the Occupation from working with the *Confédération Générale du Travail* (CGT), the largely communist congress of trade unions, in the *Conseil National de la Résistance* and from drawing up a blueprint for nationalizations, the extension of union rights and social security. Its later fortunes provide an indication of the war's effect on it. Eventually the bishops became alarmed at the Christian unions' close cooperation with the CGT. Some CFTC members were for secularizing their union and accepting socialism. In 1945 the ACA had pointed out to Christian workpeople where their duty lay: 'We emphatically remind Catholics that their place is in the Christian unions, which, genuinely professional and free, are inspired by Christian morality and the social doctrine of the Church, as opposed to other unions, socialist or communist, motivated by materialist conceptions of life, work and society.' The declaration was patently aimed at the CGT, which the bishops considered as being in the pocket of the Communist Party.

However, like the *Jeunesse Ouvrière Chrétienne* (JOC), the Church's young workers' organization from which many of its members were drawn, and other Catholic organizations after the war, the CFTC may be characterized as subject to the centrifugal tendency already mentioned. Before 1939 its decisions had broadly conformed to Church doctrine and papal encyclicals.[31] To this end in 1937 it had set up consultative theological committees, with members nominated by the archbishop of Paris. These bodies were not reconstituted at the Liberation. Appointments of *aumôniers de travail* – workers' chaplains – were allowed to lapse. After the bishops reinforced their disapproval of Catholics' joining the

CGT, Gaston Tessier, the CFTC leader, pointed out that even before the war Pius XI (notably more liberal than his successor) had allowed Catholic membership in secular unions. Although many in the CFTC remained practicing Catholics, by 1947 the deconfessionalization of the union was already practically complete. Final links were broken in 1964, when the name was changed to the *Confédération Française Démocratique du Travail* (CFDT), although a small union continued under the old auspices.[32] The new organization was overtly anti-capitalist and anti-bourgeois. Undoubtedly the bishops' acceptance of Vichy's corporatism was a contributory factor to the CFTC's break with the Church. For Catholicism it represented losing another valuable link with the industrial workers it had hoped to convert.

Before the war many Christian youth organizations flourished. The largest was the Catholic one, the ACJF (*Association Catholique de la Jeunesse Française*), an 'umbrella' for a number of specialized movements. The most successful of these, the JOC, targeted young workers; its primary objective was rechristianization, although, taking a leaf out of the book of the Young Communists, it also dealt with practicalities such as wages and factory conditions.

Under the Occupation the ACJF's movements functioned with difficulty. Extremists at Vichy such as Pierre Pucheu, when Interior minister, sought to unite them with secular movements in a fascist-like *jeunesse unique*, a single youth organization. After ACA opposition, Pétain ruled against any single youth movement. Meanwhile the JOC also justified German misgivings. Many of its members plunged into Resistance activities. Jocist *réfractaires* – defectors from the *Service du Travail Obligatoire* (STO), the forced labor draft – took to the *maquis* or continued subversive activities if deported to work in Germany.

However, the parent body, the ACJF, which dated back to 1886, did not survive for long after the war.[33] In 1957 it was disbanded, although its member organizations were allowed to continue operating independently. It was alleged that ACJF leaders had attacked French policy in Indochina and Algeria. In particular, JOC political activity proved its undoing, because after the Liberation it continued to advocate links with the Left. The Church's position was ambivalent: it wanted its youth to reach out to non-Christians, but jibbed at the political dialogue that inevitably ensued. Yet again, it proved itself unable to control the centrifugal forces in its organizations, which sought greater freedom.

The second term of the French State motto, the family, was a concept the Church set great store by. The Vichy regime continued the policy of the Third Republic, which had inaugurated a Family Code in 1939, and set up additional structures to promote the family in the *loi Gounot* of November 1941. A prime mover since 1935 in this field was the *Ligue Ouvrière Chrétienne* (LOC), a workers' Christian league started by former members of JOC. But by 1941 LOC became concerned that its outreach touched only the Catholic working class. It widened its clientele and renamed itself *Mouvement Populaire des Familles* (MPF), becoming a 'people's family movement', but still proclaiming its aims included 'the organization of the conquest of the workers to Christianity'.[34] Prominent in it were future ministers such as Robert Prigent and Paul Bacon of the Fourth Republic, which maintained the substance of Vichy family legislation. But the MPF's working-class ethos was not viewed favorably by the Catholic bourgeoisie, who ran rival family movements. Gradually the MPF cast off its Catholic affiliations, and eventually the ACA pronounced that it no longer formed part of *Action Catholique*, the umbrella organization for all Catholic movements. In 1950 it transformed itself into the *Mouvement de Libération du Peuple* (MLP), a 'people's liberation movement' with a distinctly leftist bias, concerning itself with causes such as poor housing and workers' health. One notes again a move away from the Church, so that by 1946 the MPF, although still led by lay Catholics, had already become deconfessionalized.

The events of 1940–1944 set in train great changes in Christian culture and institutions. Some would doubtless have occurred in any case; but for others the Vichy interregnum served as a catalyst. As we have seen, regarding religious observance the balance was negative: the Church failed in its attempts to 'rechristianize' France, and in particular the working class. Before the war Church leaders had denounced antisemitism (but with reservations). In wartime, late in the day, they reiterated their denunciation; but only many years after did they arrive at a blanket condemnation. There was a crisis in Church authority, undermined by the very existence of a Catholic resistance and Catholic Gaullists in London, and, to some degree, the presence of the collaborationists, many of whom professed to be Christians. The breach was never closed because the sovereignty of the individual conscience even over ecclesiastical authority had eventually to be tacitly acknowledged. Politically, Social Catholicism for the first time found expression in a mass party, which, although it played a key role in the early Fourth Republic, eventually collapsed. Institutions that had flourished before the war and that the Church had cherished gradually loosened their ties. Not only youth, but family organizations and Catholic trade unions shook off the ecclesiastical yoke.

Nevertheless, whether the Vichy experience 'made the difference' and was *decisive* for Christians must, all in all, remain an unproved hypothesis, although perhaps the hostility engendered by the regime pointed developments in one direction rather than another.

Notes

1. Hans Umbreit, 'Les services d'occupation allemands et les églises chrétiennes en France', *Revue du Nord,* Lille, vol. LX/237 (April–June 1978): 308.
2. Philippe Levillain, 'Pie XII et la France', in: Jean Chelini and Jean-Baptist d'Onorio (eds), *Pie XII et la Cité. La pensée et l'action politiques de Pie XII,* Actes du colloque d'Aix-en-Provence (Aix–Marseille, 1988): 192ff.
3. Henri Godin and Yves Daniel, *La France, pays de mission?* (Paris, 1943).
4. For how they fared, see Père Perrin, *Journal d'un prêtre-ouvrier en Allemagne* (Paris, n.d.).
5. Emile Poulat, *Une Eglise ébranlée* (Paris, 1980): 31–2.
6. Jacques Maître, *Les prêtres ruraux devant la modernisation des campagnes*, (Paris, 1967): 295, annexe 4.
7. See François Isambert, '*"Nouveaux prêtres" ou "aggiornamento" du clergé français*', in *Tendances et volontés de la société française,* Société française de sociologie (Paris, 1966): 323 ff.
8. Investigation carried out by Brigitte Vassort-Rousset for a Yale Ph.D., 1983, entitled *Politics and the Catholic Hierarchy in France.* See also her *Les évêques de France en politique* (Paris, 1986): 9 (Table).
9. Etienne Falloux, 'Une épreuve tonique pour l'œcuménisme?', in *Eglises et Chrétiens dans la II^è guerre mondiale*, Actes du colloque de Lyon, 1978 (Lyons, 1982): 528–9.
10. Roger Faligot and Pascal Krop, *Les services secrets français, 1944–1984* (Paris, 1985): 19–20.
11. Pastor Boegner, reacting to a general campaign for conversion by Catholics, expressed doubts in an article, 'Le catholicisme, l'emportera-t-il?' *Réforme* (7 July 1945).
12. Gaston Fessard, *Au temps du prince-esclave. Ecrits clandestins, 1940–1945*, presented by Jacques Prévotat (Paris, 1989): 99–108.
13. Ibid., 107.
14. For a discussion of these see Nicholas Atkin, *Church and Schools in*

Vichy France, 1940–1944 (New York and London, 1991), and W. D. Halls, *The Youth of Vichy France* (Oxford, 1981).

15. Intervention of François Delpech 'Débats sur les relations entre Chrétiens et Juifs,' *Revue du Nord*, Lille, LX/237 (April–June 1978): 458.
16. Danielle Delmaire and Yves-Marre Hilaire, 'Chrétiens et Juifs dans le Nord–Pas-de-Calais pendant la seconde guerre mondiale', ibid., 451 and 455.
17. Michael Marrus and Robert O. Paxton, *Vichy France and the Jews* (New York, 1981): 273.
18. Cardinal Liénart, *Vatican II*, Facultés Catholiques (Lille, 1976): 107–8.
19. The passage relating to the Jews forms part of a declaration on the relationship of the Church to non-Christians. The text is given in Georges Richard-Moland, *L'Hiver de Vatican II. Un pasteur au Concile* (Paris, 1965), Annexe II: 171. See also Hubert Roux, *Détresse et promesse de Vatican II* (Paris, 1967): 117–19. The passage never formed part of a formal decree. Representatives of the Eastern Uniate Church, from Moslem countries, thought it impolitic.
20. The full text of the declaration is given in *Le Monde* (1 October 1997).
21. Reported in the journal *France* (London, 9 December 1943). See also various 'Notes' in Archives Nationales (AN) file F.60.1674.
22. Archives diocésaines, Lille, carton 2B1, 'ACA 1942–1945. Letter from Cardinal Suhard to Cardinal Liénart (Paris, 28 January 1944): 'The Church of France must be prepared not to shrink from reforms of the social structure.'
23. Simone de Beauvoir, *Les mandarins*, quoted in René Rémond, *Les Droites en France* (Paris, 1982): 407. The writer wishes to acknowledge his debt to Rémond's outstanding account of immediate post-war politics given in his Chapter 12.
24. René Rémond, *Les Droites en France* (Paris, 1982): 241–2.
25. L. Liebmann, 'Entre le mythe et la légende: "l'anticapitalisme de Vichy"', *Revue de l'Institut de Sociologie* (Brussels, 1964): I, 109–48.
26. Rémond, *Les Droites en France*: 406, and Andrew Shennan *Rethinking France. Plans for renewal, 1940–1946* (Oxford, 1989): esp. 34–52, 287–96.
27. Richard F. Kuisel, *Capitalism and the State in Modern France* (Cambridge, 1981): 130.
28. AN 72 AJ 1863. A document reports the formal reiteration of the denunciation of socialism by Cardinal Gerlier and Mgr Delay, bishop

of Marseilles, on the occasion of the fiftieth anniversary of the Encyclical *Rerum Novarum* (May 1941).

29. Jean Chapsal, *La vie politique en France depuis 1940*, 2nd edn (Paris, 1969). Annexes, pp. 603ff., give details of election results over the period.
30. W. D. Halls, *Politics, Society and Christianity in Vichy France* (Oxford, 1995): 247–55. More specialized studies are: Gérard Adam, *La CFTC 1940–1958* (Paris, 1964), and P. Delon, *Le syndicalisme chrétien en France* (Paris, n.d.).
31. Jacques Lautmann and Annie Jacob, 'Rôles du syndicalisme patronal et évolution économique' in *Tendances et volontés de la société française,* Société française de sociologie (Paris, 1966): 307.
32. In the early 1980s the CFDT had 1.1 million members. The rump of the old union, strongest in the most Catholic areas, numbered only some 250,000.
33. Shennan, *Rethinking France*, 31.
34. See Groupement pour la recherche sur les mouvements familiaux (GRMF), *L'Action familiale ouvrière et la politique de Vichy,* Cahiers du GRMF, 3 (Lille, 1985).

Part IV
Myth, Memory and Representation

–17–

Out of the Picture: Foreign Labor in Wartime France

Sarah Farmer

I was led to the subject of the use of foreign labor in Vichy France by way of studying French commemoration of the experience of the war and Occupation. Reflection on the intersection of private remembrance and public recollection of the past made me well aware that the organization of public remembrance entails choices to recall certain events while remaining silent about others. Yet it was a discovery made after my work on commemoration had been published in France in 1994 that brought this home with a jolt.

I had traced the emergence of the 1944 massacre of civilians at Oradour-sur-Glane as a national symbol of French experience during the Second World War. In 1946, following the initiative of survivors and local notables, the national government expropriated the ruins of Oradour and preserved them as a national monument to French suffering under the Nazis. Approximately 300,000 visitors a year come to walk through the vestiges of the old town. A local man employed as an official guide by the National Monuments Service tells the story of an innocent French village, a haven during the war, which became the target of Nazi atrocities.[1]

In the summer of 1994 I dug further into Oradour's history and uncovered an aspect of its past that changed my mental picture of the town during the war. I discovered that in the area, foreign refugees had worked as conscripted laborers. Although the conscripted foreign workers were no longer in Oradour, and thus escaped the massacre, twenty-four of the 642 victims of the massacre had been members of their families, twenty of them Spanish refugees. A comprehensive history of foreign labor under Vichy remains to be written. What I could establish through archival research for the case of Oradour went against the grain of the commemorative story. My experience in the departmental archives also illuminated the differences between the professional writing of history, commemoration and personal memory. These distinctions bear noting at a moment when interest in memory is exerting such a pull on historians as well as on the general public.

I discovered the first clue when, to my utter surprise, someone who came from Oradour and had survived the massacre referred to a contingent of foreign workers who had been in the area from 1940 to 1942. He did not mean the women refugees from the Spanish Civil War who had found menial jobs in local hotels when they came to this town as early as 1938. During the many hours of interviews I had already conducted, no one had mentioned the existence of foreign workers (other than these refugee women and their children, who died in the 1944 massacre, and whose names appear on plaques in the cemetery). Nor had any of the archival records I had searched made reference to any foreigners other than refugees. My informer, a retired postal worker, who had been twenty years old at the time of the massacre, was referring to men performing conscripted labor. He did not know where these workers had lived. But he remembered that they had assembled periodically for roll call in the market-place under the supervision of a retired military officer. Most of them had left in 1942, when, he believed, they had been sent into the occupied zone to work for the Germans fortifying the Atlantic coast. That was all he knew. He could recall no mention of these foreigners by his parents or his grandfather, who was the wartime mayor of Oradour.

This finding caused me to go back to the archives in order to piece together a story that lies outside the commemorative narrative of the massacre and has not been treated in any account of wartime Oradour. At the archives I found a new entry in the card catalogue for registers listing the members of the '643rd Foreign Labor Battalion' (*Groupement de Travailleurs Etrangers*, or GTE). The title on these documents suggested that the unit had been administratively attached to Oradour-sur-Glane and Aixe-sur-Vienne.[2] The registers, it turned out, had remained uncataloged and therefore unknown to researchers until the retirement in 1993 of the man who had managed the archives for the previous thirty years. After his departure, a new director, more liberal toward access to records from the war period, made these materials available.

The registers of the 643rd Foreign Labor Battalion indicate that its members were Spaniards and foreign Jews from eastern Europe (Romania, Lithuania, Poland, Czechoslovakia, Hungary, and the Soviet Union), many of whom were stateless. These registers made it obvious to me for the first time that many more outsiders – other than those whose names we know because they were victims of the massacre – had been present in or around Oradour during the war years.

Learning of these people underscored the discrepancies between the historical circumstances of the war years and the image of Oradour portrayed in the commemorative accounts established after the war. It also drove home the simple truth that what the historian learns depends on what questions he or she asks and of whom.

Commemorative accounts of Oradour portray the town as untroubled, self-contained, and quintessentially French. In fact, a large number of Spanish refugees had been sent to Oradour in the last year of the Third Republic. After the fall of France in June 1940, foreign Jews fled to this *bourg* and its outlying hamlets in the unoccupied zone. Others came later as members of a foreign labor battalion. Contrary to the descriptions of Oradour in the commemorative narrative, the town, like the rest of France, shared in the complexities of life under the Vichy regime and the Occupation.

The village or small town as the locus of essential Frenchness has a long history and strong political valences – whether it is presented as the cradle of the secular republic or as the heart of an eternal France of conservative values and morals. At the end of the war, a time when the French were rebuilding the nation and national pride, the image of an ideal French town proved compelling. The mythic small town, in its French version of the late 1940s, was a place inhabited by insiders only. Foreigners would have been a disruptive element in a story of French victimization.

Those who write about memory of the war in France often use the word 'forgetting' to describe gaps in what is recalled, recollected or commemorated. But the foreigners at Oradour were not 'forgotten'; rather the commemorative process did not register those not considered part of the national or local community. Local people were concerned with mourning their personal loss and had little interest in the fate of a group of transient outsiders who had been marginal to the community. For politicians and administrators involved in creating the memorial at Oradour, recognizing the presence of foreign workers would have required seeing Oradour as part of a world buffeted by the dislocations of the war and occupation. It would also have demanded turning attention to the Vichy regime and its treatment of foreigners and Jews. This chapter describes the nature and scope of these battalions and reflects on what their existence might indicate for how the story of Oradour might be told more fully.

The use of conscripted labor in France from 1940 to 1944 originated even before the defeat of France. During the last months of the Third Republic, the French created companies of foreign workers, the GTEs, as part of their war effort. Approximately 400,000 Spaniards crossed into

France following the defeat of Loyalist forces by Franco's insurgents in January 1939.[3] The first GTEs consisted of Spanish men who had been interned in southern France.[4]

After the French defeat in 1940, the newly-founded Vichy regime inherited these labor battalions and also took control of the numerous internment camps that dotted the unoccupied zone.[5] The law of 27 September 1940, by which the Vichy regime took control of the GTEs, assigned to labor battalions all able-bodied male foreigners between the ages of fifteen and fifty-five who were unable to return to their country of origin and were considered 'superfluous in the national economy'.[6] This meant that male refugees without means of supporting themselves were obliged to serve in a labor battalion under the direction of the Vichy government acting through its Commissariat for Unemployment Relief (*Commissariat à la lutte contre le chômage et le travail* [CLC]). The labor battalions were intended to help French workers by preventing competition with foreigners for jobs.

The Vichy regime also used foreign labor battalions to further its goal of excluding Jews and foreigners from French society and economic life. In 1941, the government began to transfer men between the ages of eighteen and fifty-five from the internment camps to the labor battalions. Jews who had illegally crossed from occupied France to the southern zone were routinely assigned to a GTE.[7] By July 1941, a third of the approximately 60,000 men assigned to GTEs in the southern zone were Jews.[8] During that year the government also created all-Jewish labor battalions.[9] For many internees, entry into a GTE promised an improvement over life in the camps and even the chance to earn enough to enable their relatives to follow them out of the internment camps.[10] So when offered the possibility, many internees volunteered to join a GTE.[11] What began in the last years of the Third Republic as an effort to recruit labor developed under the Vichy regime into a structure that, for many, led to deportation and death in extermination camps.

In the unoccupied zone, most foreign labor battalions consisted of 250–300 men overseen by French administrators. Workers were frequently shifted from place to place and were often stationed in remote areas. In the summer of 1941 and 1942, some of these laborers were transferred from the authority of the CLC to the Germans' *Organisation Todt* – the body in charge building a chain of U-boat bomb shelters and fortifications along the French Atlantic coast.[12]

By 1942, the CLC for the southern zone was following a policy of spreading conscripted labor among different sectors of the economy, but with a strong emphasis on agricultural work.[13] In the case of the 643rd

GTE, of its 262 members in 1941, 160 worked in a tile works forty kilometers to the east of Oradour in the hamlet of Fontafie (Charente). Most others were spread out in the commune of Oradour, working as agricultural laborers on small farms.

At first, members of the foreign labor battalions in the southern zone led a reasonably safe existence. However, the Vichy government's pronouncements on GTEs took on an ominous tone for Jews at the end of 1941. On 10 December, Admiral François Darlan, the most powerful member of the Vichy cabinet, issued a statement announcing that 'all Jews resident in France who entered the country after 1 January 1936 will be . . . grouped in a Foreign Labor Battalion [those without financial means] or in special centers [for those who could pay]' – whether or not they had acquired French citizenship.[14] The following day, the Minister of the Interior Pierre Pucheu specified that Jews entering the labor battalions were not to be spread out but to be grouped in 'homogeneous' units. These 'operations' were to be completed for the southern zone within two months, by the end of March 1942.[15]

The Vichy government soon moved from a policy of isolating Jews to arresting and deporting them. The first mass arrests began in the occupied zone on 16 July 1942 in Paris; the French police rounded up and confined 12,884 Jews and then sent them to Drancy for deportation to the east. In the unoccupied zone the onslaught began a month later and lasted into the fall, as the Vichy police pursued those who had managed to evade the first wave of arrests.

In preparation for the round-up in the southern zone, the office of the prefect of the Haute-Vienne drew up a list of those targeted: 442 foreign Jews who had entered France since 1 January 1936. The number rose to 500 when, on 18 August, the order came to include those who had arrived since 1933.[16] The list from the prefecture and a report from the local police of Rochechouart indicate that at least twenty-five foreign Jews assigned to the GTE at Oradour-sur-Glane were slated for arrest.

In the early morning hours of 26 August, forces of the police carried out their assignment – which had been organized down to the details of turning off the gas in the residences of those they arrested and giving their livestock to the neighbors. An undated, handwritten note in the archives of the prefecture tallied the results of the round-up for the whole region:

> Limoges 17/91 [17 out of 91 anticipated]; Dordogne no trouble (*pas d'incident*) 80 per cent, Indre no trouble 60 per cent, Creuse perfect 93 out of 102 anticipated; . . . Confolens no trouble 42/38; Montmorillon no trouble 31/11; Corrèze 65/165 (15 non-transportable 2 absent) 60 per cent one attempt at escape . . .[17]

These results were deemed insufficient. On 30 August a telegram from police headquarters at Vichy to the regional prefects and the departmental prefects in the 'free zone' noted the 'palpable divergence' [*écart sensible*] between the number of Jews on the census and the number arrested. The authorities called for an intensification of police operations 'with all the personnel . . . available'.[18]

A few days later, the director of the Section of Investigations and Control for the Limoges region gave a partial explanation for the inadequate results; members of the foreign labor battalions had been forewarned and had fled.[19] The yield for the labor battalion attached to Oradour was particularly low. Of the twenty-five workers belonging to the 643rd GTE, only four were arrested and deported to the occupied zone.[20] On 17 September 1942, the office of the prefect of the Haute-Vienne reported a total number of 528 foreign Jews being held in camps for deportation.[21] It appears that warning of the round-up was passed along by administrators within the CLC. Both Henri Maux, CLC director for the unoccupied zone, and Gilbert Lesage, who ran the *Service Social des Etrangers*, a Ministry of Labor organization that provided social services for foreigners, are known to have sympathized with foreigners caught in the web of Vichy persecution.

The registers from 1943 and 1944 of the Jews in the 643rd GTE indicate that police round-ups resumed after the winter; in the last days of February and the first days of March 1943 twenty-six more members of the 643rd GTE were arrested. Over the course of that spring, fifty-five men were reported as having deserted. By the time of the Allied landings and the June massacre at Oradour, most members of the GTE had been sent elsewhere or had managed to escape. However, a handful survived until the end of the war working on farms not far from Oradour.

Records of the individuals who made up the GTE at Oradour remain frustratingly incomplete. Yet I was able me to track down the son of Jankiel Jakubowicz, a member of the 643rd GTE from 1942 to 1944, with the help of a member of the family for whom Jakubowicz had worked. The story of the Jakubowicz family provides a glimpse into the experience of foreign Jews who left occupied France for the Limousin.

In 1923 Jankiel Jakubowicz arrived in France from Poland with his wife and settled in Metz. Twenty-seven years old at the time, he and his wife never became French citizens or learned the language. They spoke only Yiddish with their three French-born children. In August 1942, within a few days of each other, the members of the Jakubowicz family all tried to cross into the unoccupied zone. Only four of them made it. Jakubowicz's wife and fourteen-year-old son, Samuel, traveled together by a train that was stopped and searched by French police. Madame Jakubowicz was arrested and deported to Auschwitz. Samuel was not apprehended. In a separate attempt, the youngest child was taken across the demarcation line by a French social worker and reunited with her father and siblings a few days later. Jankiel Jakubowicz traveled on his own. The *chef de gare* of a small railway station hid him in the water tank of a steam train that traveled from Angoulême, in German-occupied France, to Limoges in the unoccupied zone. Finding it too dangerous to try to hide underground, Jakubowicz joined a labor battalion. At the end of 1942 he was transferred to the 643rd GTE at Oradour and sent to the tile works at Fontafie. A few weeks later he was assigned to work on a farm in a hamlet outside Limoges, where he was joined by his son, Samuel. As a foreign Jew, Jakubowicz was still in danger; early in 1944 he received notice that he was to be sent to work for the *Organisation Todt*. Jakubowicz deserted his farm job and hid out for one month before returning to his employer. At the end of the Liberation he was formally freed by a prefectoral decree.[22]

The registers of the 643rd GTE at Oradour reveal the presence of Spanish and foreign Jewish laborers in the region of Oradour during the war years. But not all the persecuted show up on that list. Others, either hidden or living a semi-clandestine existence, were doing all they could to avoid attention. Fragments pointing to their presence exist when records remain of individuals who were investigated, pursued or otherwise noted by the authorities. For example, a twenty-one-year-old Jewish man born in the Paris region who had been living with his aunt, a refugee from Tours, in the town of St Victurnien five kilometers from Oradour: on 17 September 1943, the police came looking for him because he had failed to appear for a compulsory medical check.[23]

There were other Jews hiding at St Victurnien. Marguerite Lederberg, now a psychiatrist in New York City, remembers being concealed with her parents in the loft of a barn provided to them by Antoine Bardet, the wartime mayor of St Victurnien. Lederberg's father, a medical doctor named Adam Stein, was born in Poland in 1910. He had received his medical education in France and became a French citizen in the early 1930s. In early 1942 he and his wife and four-year-old child took refuge in St Victurnien. Lederberg has some distinct memories of those days. She recalls her parents going off periodically to provide medical services for the *maquis*, leaving her in the care of an elderly couple or a local schoolteacher. Lederberg also remembers standing outside with many of the villagers in St Victurnien and watching the sky turn red as Oradour burned. 'I was out looking at it. Mother came to get me and brought me home. She says I was screaming.' She remembers that, over the next several weeks, the townspeople of St Victurnien evacuated the entire village on several occasions for fear that the Germans would return and set upon their town. Lederberg was aware of another Jewish family also hiding at St Victurnien – a couple with an infant. Though her parents never explicitly discussed their circumstances, Lederberg knew intuitively that these people were in the same straits as her own family: 'They were extraordinarily sad. They had the same look as my parents did.'[24]

According to Bardet's daughter, Valerie Billes, her father sheltered others too: refugees from Lorraine and two Spanish refugees. Billes, who was in her early twenties at the time, also remembers three other Jewish families in town, as well as a rabbi who came every day to procure milk.[25] Lederberg says that she 'always felt that everyone must have known [we were Jewish]'. She attributes an incident of her mistreatment by local boys to this fact. Yet, although she may have felt uneasy there as a child, she makes the fundamental point that no one in St Victurnien collaborated by denouncing them to the police. 'We may not have been accepted, we may not have been liked, but we were not turned in.'[26]

The people in Oradour were also not unaware that a few of the families who had come there during the war were Jewish. Best remembered is the Pinède family – mother, father and three children. 'We played with the children. We referred to them as *les petits juifs* – there was nothing mean about it', recalled André Desourteaux. Robert Pinède, a tanner from Bayonne, had brought his family to Oradour at the suggestion of one of his business contacts in St Junien.[27] The Pinède parents died in the massacre while their three children hid under the steps of the Hôtel Avril. The children managed to escape when a German sentinel let them pass as they fled the burning town. Jacqueline Pinède became a member of the National Association of the Families of the Martyrs of Oradour (ANFM) and often comes to the commemorative ceremony of 10 June.

Foreigners who may have been Jewish did not fit in as easily, and seem to have been less welcome in Oradour than French Jews. The residents of Oradour today know practically nothing about the Kanzler family that came to Oradour in September 1939 with the other evacuees from Schiltigheim, a suburb of Strasbourg, when parts of Alsace were temporarily evacuated at the outbreak of the Second World War. They remain in the shadows today as they did during their stay in Oradour. Still, the archives reveal a bit of their story.

In April 1943, the mayor of Oradour-sur-Glane responded to a confidential inquiry from the prefecture asking for information about the Kanzlers. The mayor responded with basic information concerning their nationality (the parents were not French, the children were) and how long they had resided in the community. He declined to cause trouble for them or himself by refusing to speculate about their religion: 'The real religion of the family is not known. It is not possible for us to give fuller information about these refugees, the parents speaking French only with great difficulty and being uncommunicative; perhaps it would be more useful to proceed with a police inquiry on this subject.'[28]

The *Renseignements généraux*, the French internal security service, provided more detail. According to their report, Joseph Kanzler was born in Budapest and came to Strasbourg in 1923, where he married Maria Goldmann, who had been born in Warsaw. Kanzler worked as a hat cutter (*coupeur de casquette*) before setting up his own business in Schiltigheim. The *Renseignements généraux* concluded that the parents were 'doubtless of the Jewish race' despite the fact that the husband 'claims to be of the Protestant confession'. They noted that the Kanzlers kept to themselves: '. . . the members of this family have not been the object of any unfavorable notice and they live in a withdrawn manner seeing very few people. Nevertheless, because of their being foreigners, and most of all Jewish, they do not enjoy the sympathy of the population.'[29] The Kanzlers and their children died in the massacre with the long-time residents of Oradour.

The massacre revealed other foreign-born refugees: fifteen-year-old Sarah Jakobowicz (no relation to the Jakubowicz family), who had been lodging in Oradour, and Jean Jackow, age thirty-eight, who had been living in the nearby hamlet of Le Mas Ferat, were among the dead. Examining the list of the victims alongside the GTE register for 1941 reveals that the twenty Spaniards among the victims (all but one, women and children) were relatives of men in the labor battalion. As far as I know, these victims have never before been identified as wives and children of conscripted laborers.

In recent years, the French government has renewed its commitment to the memorial at Oradour by providing half the funding needed to create a 'Memory Center' (*Centre de la Mémoire*) at Oradour. The groundbreaking for this museum project took place in April 1997. The creation of the 'Memory Center' at Oradour now offers an opportunity to modify the telling of Oradour's story. More than fifty years after the massacre, the majority of those taking part in creating this museum are members of a generation that did not live through the war. Now there are historians of Vichy France to be brought into decisions concerning the interpretative presentation for the new museum.

It remains to be seen if the makers of the Memory Center choose to move away from the narrative established in the late 1940s by the organization of the families of the victims of the massacre. A museum offers possibilities, hardly imaginable at the ruins, to set the story of Oradour within the context of life in the Limousin under the Vichy regime and German occupation. Here one could address such subjects as the regional resistance, the existence of foreign labor battalions and French policies that led to the arrest of Jews in the Limousin and their eventual deportation. The history of the town would appear more fully and with greater complexity.

Rather than standing out as exceptional, the victims of the massacre would appear no better or worse than their compatriots, only more unlucky. This might well seem a loss to the descendants of the survivors who have committed themselves to the defense of their 'martyrs'. Such an effort would also go against the grain of a commemoration that stresses the unique horror of a horrible event. As in much of the commemoration of the Holocaust, one sees in the memorialization at Oradour the desire to keep certain events unexplainable, beyond words. In the logic of these forms of remembrance, to understand seems a step toward accepting inhumane behavior, to a lessening of moral outrage and to letting the event become forgotten. Yet, if not moored in historical understanding, the massacre at Oradour risks slipping into the realm of disasters remote in time that speak little to the concerns of the living.

Notes

1. See Sarah Farmer, *Martyred Village: Commemorating the 1944 Massacre at Oradour-sur-Glane* (Berkeley, CA, 1999) or *Oradour: arrêt sur mémoire* (Paris, 1994).
2. Archives Départementales de la Haute-Vienne (ADHV), 643e Groupement de Travailleurs Etranger [GTE], Oradour-sur-Glane, Aixe-sur-Vienne: état nominatif 1941–1944. So far, I have not been able to find any records or traces of the 643rd GTE that might illuminate the nature of its connection to Oradour. The archives for the body in charge of foreign laborers for the southern zone remain in private hands and are not accessible.
3. Michael Marrus and Robert Paxton, *Vichy France and the Jews* (New York, 1981): 64.
4. Jacques Desmarest, *La politique de la main-d'oeuvre en France* (Paris, 1946): 121. A decree of 12 April 1939 required all able-bodied

foreigners benefiting from a right to asylum in France to perform work service equivalent to the military service demanded of French men.

5. In September 1940 there were thirty-one internment camps in southern France; the major camps were Rivesaltes (Pyrénées Orientales), Le Vernet (Ariège), Rieucros (Lozère), Argèles (Pyrénées Orientales), Les Milles (near Aix-en-Provence), Gurs (Basses-Pyrénées), Noé (Haute-Garonne), and Récébédou (just south of Toulouse) (Marrus and Paxton), *Vichy France*: 165.
6. Loi du 27 Septembre 1940, *Journal Officiel*, 1 October 1940. This description was deemed to include Poles, Czechs, and Belgians demobilized from national fighting units that had fought alongside the French Army.
7. Christian Eggers, 'L'internement sous toutes ses formes: approche d'une vue d'ensemble du système d'internement dans la zone de Vichy', *Le Monde Juif* 153 (January–April 1995): 24.
8. Marrus and Paxton, *Vichy France*: 171. Paxton and Michael Marrus cite the figure for Jewish members of the GTE from a document from the General Commission for Jewish Questions. Christian Eggers considers this estimate too high, on the basis of the figures from the numbers of Jews deported from the GTEs one year later. Eggers, 'L'internement': 62.
9. Eggers, 'L'internement': 33.
10. The workers' salaries were to be paid by the state. The local body that benefited from the work performed was to provide lodging, food and any equipment or supplies (*Centre de Documentation Juive Contemporaine* [CDJC], Fonds Lesage. 'Le Ministre, Secretaire d'Etat à la Production Industrielle et au Travail à Monsieur le Prefet de . . .', Vichy, 12 October 1940).
11. Eggers, 'L'internement': 23.
12. From its inception in 1939, the *Organisation Todt* (which took its name from the man in charge of construction and armaments for Nazi Germany, Fritz Todt) continuously drafted laborers into its vast army of workers.
13. Henri Maux, 'Chômage et reclassement', *La Revue des hautes études politiques, sociales, économiques et financières* 6 (June 1942): 8.
14. CDJC, Fonds Lesage, Le Ministre, Secretaire d'Etat à l'Interieur à Messieurs les Préfets Régionaux de la zone libre, Vichy, 2 January 1942. The special centers (*Centres de résidence assignée*) had been formally created on 3 November 1941 (Eggers, 'L'internement': 50).
15. ADHV 185W 1/149, Ministère de l'Intérieur, circular no. 76, 2 January 1942.

16. ADHV 185W 251.
17. ADHV W 1/149.
18. ADHV W 1/149.
19. ADHV 185 W 1/73. Le Directeur de la Section d'Enquête & de Contrôle, Délégué pour la Région de Limoges à Monsieur le Directeur de la Section d'Enquête et de Contrôle en Z.N.O., Limoges, 1 September 1942.
20. ADHV W/251 and ADHV 646 W 251. On August 29, three others were arrested and then released (one because he had served in the French Army and two because their wives were pregnant), seven were on the run [*en fuite*], there were no records of two, six had been transferred to other GTEs, and two had been on leave from their units that day.
21. ADHV W 251. Monsieur le Préfet de la Haute-Vienne, Service des Etrangers, Limoges, 17 September 1942. 'As regards your telephone call today, I have the honor of transmitting to you, see attached, the statistics of . . . foreign *israélites* "housed" [*hébergés*] at Nexon [concentation camp south of Limoges] and transferred to either the occupied zone or the camp of Rivesaltes. Total transferred to the Z.O.[occupied zone] 451. Transferred to Rivesaltes: 77.'
22. Telephone interview with Samuel Jaquet (son of Jacob Jakubowicz) by author, 20 August 1996. Jaquet provided all the information concerning his family except for the date of his father's transfer to the 643^e^ GTE and formal exit from the group in June 1944. These details are noted in the register for the 643e GTE held in the ADHV.
23. ADHV 1374 W 21.
24. Marguerite Lederberg, telephone conversation with author, 13 September 1995.
25. Notes from a telephone conversation between Marguerite S. Lederberg and Valerie Billes, née Bardet, 13 September 1998.
26. Marguerite Lederberg, telephone conversation with author, September 1998.
27. André Desourteaux, interview by author, Oradour-sur-Glane, July 1995.
28. ADHV 187 W 19, 'le Maire d'Oradour-sur-Glane à Monsieur le Préfet de la Haute-Vienne (Service des Réfugiés à Limoges).
29. ADHV 187 W 199, Renseignements Généraux de la Haute-Vienne, le Commissaire Principal, chef de service, à Monsieur le PREFET – Service des Réfugiés, Limoges, 15 May 1943.

–18–

Tragédies bulgares et françaises: Tzvetan Todorov and the Writing of History

Robert Zaretsky

Of the multiple meanings that can be read in Tzvetan Todorov's work on Vichy, one of the most telling is largely implicit and autobiographical. To recall Krzysztof Pomian's notion of history as a 'screen', Vichy is the occasion for Todorov to replay and reassess his experience as a child and young man in Communist Bulgaria.[1] Hence the title of this article: *Tragédies bulgares et françaises*. But the use of the word 'tragedy' also points to the explicit and didactic aim of Todorov's history writing. As with the historians of antiquity, tragedy for Todorov is both a genre of narrative discourse and a tool of moral education. Historians of Vichy are aware of the tendency – especially during the first three phases of the syndrome elaborated by Henry Rousso – to deliver moral lessons.[2] This has always made us uneasy. Yet one of Robert Paxton's great accomplishments was to undertake an objective and documented moral accounting of the period. This is Todorov's approach, too, but it is one undertaken from a different professional and national perspective. This chapter will suggest that this approach represents a new and provocative contribution to our moral and historical understanding of the period.

I

Tzvetan Todorov had begun work in semiotics and language theory in Sofia, Bulgaria, and upon arriving in Paris in 1963 pursued these interests under the guidance of Roland Barthes. He soon became a leading theoretician, and helped to establish the study of poetics. Poetics, for Todorov, entails a science of literature that supplies a coherent body of knowledge grounded in specific epistemological axioms. It seeks to generate general principles or laws that explain (and perhaps govern) certain kinds of texts. Poetics is not, as Todorov notes, the 'the description of the particular work, the designation of its meaning, but the establishment of general laws of which this particular text is the product'.[3]

Though Todorov eventually turns to moral philosophy and history, he nevertheless retained the desire for a grounding that would permit him to make judgments of universal validity. The genres have changed, but not the concern with the coherence and sovereignty of truth. As Peter Brooks has observed, Todorov's work in literary theory moves from the specific to the general, 'from meaning to the conditions of meaning'.[4] Todorov makes a similar effort in his work on Vichy: namely, maintaining that the investigation of specific historical events, if it is to make sense, requires conditions of *moral* meaning. The acts of the participants and the understanding of the historian must both be grounded in a common ethical code.

Todorov's preoccupation with an objective account of language was largely a response to the abuse of language he encountered not just among Bulgarian Communists, but also among the French Left. Both were guilty of separating public and private meanings, words and deeds, facts and values.[5] Repelled by the hypocrisy and contradictions that bled into language itself, Todorov constructed a linguistic counterworld independent of the corrupted one in which he lived. By the late 1970s, however, he came to realize that what he had till then believed to be 'neutral tools and purely descriptive concepts now appeared to be the consequences of precise historical choices – choices that could have been different'.[6]

As a result, Todorov gradually abandoned poetics and focused with growing insistence upon two themes: the historical evolution of the concept of otherness and the nature and purpose of historical narrative. In other words, the ways in which history forms humanity, as well as those in which humanity freely forms both the course and telling of history. As for the latter, Todorov's reassessment of literature applies to history writing as well: 'Though some may be disturbed by such grand words, it is a discourse oriented towards truth and morality'.[7] This evolution in Todorov's thought is manifest in *La Conquête de l'Amérique,* in which he examines the texts of conquerers and conquered with his habitual analytical rigor, but now too with a sense of moral urgency.[8] Todorov affirms that the 'discovery' of America was the prelude to history's greatest genocide, and that his book is driven by the 'necessity of "seeking the truth" and the obligation of making it known'.[9] The nature of truth has been re-evaluated; no longer is it self-referential or limited to objective statements concerning narrative structures. Instead, truth resides in man's relations to his fellow men, and how these relations are justified, maintained or resisted.

In fact, Todorov's argument echoes that of the early modern philosopher of history Giambattista Vico: namely, that man best understands, morally as well as cognitively, what he himself has made rather than that which exists independently of him. In *Nous et les autres,* Todorov makes this assumption explicit, and in a deliberately provocative manner. Rather than situating the discussion in a historical context, as he did in *La Conquête de l'Amérique*, he engages in a discussion – or, as he describes it, a 'dialogue' – with notable French thinkers who have written on this subject.[10] Moreover, Todorov declares that he seeks to know 'both how things were, as well as how they ought to be'.[11]

What are we to make of this moral imperative? In part, it seems to be directed at himself, for Todorov dwells on the ways he, along with other thinkers, has violated this imperative. No less disturbed by the way in which Communist Bulgaria polluted the use of language than he was by the inconsistencies among French intellectuals between theory and life, Todorov now insists upon the parity between acts and words, facts and values. In part, as well, this affirmation reveals that Todorov has retained his earlier universalist concerns in poetics. Just as he had previously sought a 'science' of literature that provided the objective context for interpretation, he now insists upon a universal footing for his historical and moral evaluations. His earlier 'objective' concerns have carried over into an insistence upon a universal standard by which the moralist or historian can judge the welter of human acts over time and space.

It is for this same reason that Todorov's sympathies lie with Montesquieu and Rousseau. Both these thinkers, while aware that customs are many, insist that basic values are one. These values guarantee the flourishing of custom, while safeguarding the fundamental and common dignity of man. Todorov thus approves of Montesquieu's declaration in *Les Lettres persanes*: 'Justice is eternal and does not depend upon human conventions'.[12] Todorov is not content to leave matters there, however. His interpretation of moral life under Vichy, not to mention the Nazi and Soviet death camps, requires a further refinement of these formulas. Todorov suggests a universal foundation for morality in humankind's inherent capacity to *refuse* the variety of limitations that we encounter. To reject is to choose, and to choose is to exercise one's liberty: 'Liberty is the distinctive characterisic of human beings. Clearly, my milieu pushes me to reproduce the forms of behavior of which it approves, but the possibility of repudiating these influences also exists'.[13] Rather than promoting the universality of a specific characteristic, or group of characteristics, Todorov affirms that there are certain *capacities* or *potentialities* that are universally human and desirable.

Todorov's affirmation of human freedom informs his work on Vichy and on the experience of the death camps. Yet before we turn to that, one last issue requires discussion: namely, the proper perspective of the historian. We have already had occasion to refer to Todorov's engagement, which implies that indifference to the present risks reducing history to antiquarianism.[14] Yet, at the same time, he insists upon the necessity of perspective that either time or a different background provides. For Todorov, as for Montesquieu's Rica and Uzbek, such alterity comes naturally. His life, divided between East and West, totalitarianism and democracy, permits the acquisition of a new culture without the loss of the older culture – a status Todorov describes as 'transculturation'.[15] Though too much can be made of 'the view from afar' (*regard éloigné*), it nevertheless remains a *sine qua non* of historical understanding.[16] This, in part, explains his interest in the Russian literary theorist, Mikhail Bakhtin, who introduced the concept of 'exotopy', or the condition of non-belonging to a culture, as an effective condition of understanding that same culture.[17]

The terminology may be new, but less so the idea behind it – at least to the historians of Vichy, among whom non-French historians have played so important a role. Yet Todorov seems to be suggesting something more that potentially contradicts the theme of exotopy – namely, his familarity with the experiences of those who experienced Vichy or the '*univers concentrationnaire*'. In his growing preoccupation with autobiography, Todorov returns repeatedly to his adolescence and early adulthood in Bulgaria. The omnipresence of the state and the rule of terror, the collapse of civic institutions and institutionalization of concentration camps, the *dédoublement* of the self and the internalization of censorship: Todorov knew this world for the first twenty years of his life. As he observes in *Au Nom du peuple*, which presents the accounts of several Bulgarians imprisoned in the Lovetch concentration camp: 'I was unaware of this camp's existence. I was an adult and did not try to close my eyes to what surrounded me, yet the fact remains: though horror and I lived side by side, I did not know it and did nothing to stop it . . . I do not now seek to defend myself, and realize that I have little reason for self-reproach. Nevertheless, I recognize that, owing to these coincidences, I can never tell myself that these accounts do not concern me'.[18]

As a result, though Todorov neither lived in France nor through the war, he would never accept the familiar warning of the French generation that had: 'Young man, you will never know what it was like'.[19] On the contrary, he *did* know it: the experiences of Vichy and Sofia, though specific to their times and places, share fundamental traits. As such, they fall under the same category of exemplary history – namely, that though these histories may be singular, they are not unique. They help establish models that allow for generalization. Exotopy is, as it were, turned inside out, and the historian reveals the common experience that binds him to those who thought their pasts unique. It is through his experience in Bulgaria, Todorov writes, 'that I have sought to understand [Auschwitz and the Gulag] . . . That experience also gave me my first intimate encounter with political evil, but as something done by me, not to me. Nothing spectacular, merely the common lot – docile participation in various public demonstrations, acceptance of the code of social behavior without protest, mute acquiescence to the status quo'.[20] This docility and passive acceptance are essential elements to the Arendtian formula for evil – one that Todorov seems to make his own – and made for the tragedy of his adolescence and homeland.[21] And it is his own encounter with the tragedy of post-war Bulgaria that leads him to similar tragedies, such as the one that occurred in the department of the Cher in 1944.

II

In *A French Tragedy: Scenes of Civil War, Summer 1944* Todorov arranges his material into three acts: Uprising, Negotiation, Punishment.[22] In Act 1 we discover that confusion, principle and passion mostly account for the uprising on 6 June 1944 in Saint-Amand. Led by Daniel Blanchard, René Van Gaver, Hubert Lalonnier and Fernand Sochet, the resistance fighters succeed – if only briefly – in gaining their goal, which is to liberate Saint-Amand in advance of the anticipated arrival of the Allies. They storm the town, besieging the headquarters of the Milice (the paramilitary outfit created by Vichy in 1943, assisting the Germans in the repression of the Resistance and the hunt for French and refugee Jews). The Milice members surrender and are taken prisoner, including Simone Bout de l'An, the wife of the Milice's national leader. Upon learning the news in Vichy, Francis Bout de l'An immediately gathers a number of *miliciens*, wins German logistical support and heads toward Saint-Amand.

Todorov elegantly follows the snowballing of events: the short-lived celebration in 'liberated' Saint-Amand, the mad rush of civilians to join the *Forces françaises de l'intérieur* (FFI), the drunken excesses, and the contradictory attitudes of the various resistance leaders. The festivities quickly give way to confusion and fear when a German reconaissance plane flies over the town. The resistance fighters quit town as quickly as they arrived, taking with them the captured *miliciens* and Simone Bout de l'An, and leaving the civilian population to explain themselves to the arriving Germans and *miliciens*. Saint-Amand is rapidly retaken, and the members of the Resistance who remained behind are either captured or killed. Nearly two hundred hostages are rounded up and, locking the tragedy into place, Francis Bout de l'An then places Joseph Lécussan in effective control of the town and sub-prefecture. A violent anticommunist and antisemite, Lécussan was an associate of Paul Touvier in Lyon and counted among his crimes the murder of Victor Basch, the elderly leader of the League of the Rights of Man (*Ligue des droits de l'homme*). His arrival marks the end of Act 1.

In Act 2, Todorov introduces René Sadrin, the mayor of Saint-Amand.[23] A local winegrower, Sadrin had been appointed by Vichy to his post. Neither with the Resistance nor the collaborators, Sadrin belonged, Todorov would say, to the camp of humanity. Indifferent to ideology, Sadrin's actions were motivated solely by the desire to 'relieve the pitiful sufferings' of his fellow men and women.[24] In the company of two other 'just men', François Villatte and Bernard Delalande, Sadrin undertakes an epic quest to secure the release of the hostages taken by both sides. In a borrowed car (which trailed white sheets in order to identify themselves to both the German troops and the French Resistance), the three men barrel across the backroads of the Creuse over the next few days, working against repeatedly postponed deadlines and the mutual suspicions, hatreds and pride of the two camps. Through the intervention of the local leaders of the Resistance Blanchard and Van Gaver (who miraculously re-enter the story at this point), Delalande and Villatte persuade 'François', the leader of the regional FFI, to exchange Simone and the other women captives against the hostages taken by the Milice. Both sides keep their word, and the exchange takes place. Yet the fate of the *miliciens* held by the *maquis* is still undecided, and before it can be broached, the Germans attack the resistance hideouts. The curtain then falls on Act 2.

The third and final act is terrifying. Convinced that the captured *miliciens* risk the lives of his own men, one of the Resistance leaders, Georges Chaillaud, orders that they be executed. The order is carried out, and the thirteen men are hanged by men who had known many of the condemned men since childhood. Lécussan, now installed in Saint-Amand as subprefect, learns about the executions and immediately contacts the Gestapo headquarters in nearby Bourges. The commander, Fritz Merdsche, agrees to help avenge the dead *miliciens*. Inevitably, the target of their reprisal is the local population of refugee Jews. Seventy men, women and children are rounded up and sent to Bourges, where twenty-six of the men are eventually killed at an isolated and abandoned farm, where they are pushed one by one into dry wells. One prisoner, Charles

Krameisen, manages to escape and recounts the story. A short while later, in response to the assassination by the Resistance of the local Milice leader, eight of the women (and a lone Jewish man) are also plunged into a well. And so ends Act 3.

Toward the beginning of his account, Todorov argues that it was with 'the best of intentions' that the Resistance leaders stage their uprising; and that is why, 'instead of being wrong, the decision is tragic'.[25] The element of the tragic points to Todorov's principal concern: morality in the guise of history. This becomes clear in the Epilogue. Todorov first insists on an approximate moral equivalence between Francis Bout de l'An and 'François', the FFI leader of the Creuse. Though their principles are radically different, both men are blinded to the cost in human lives entailed by adherence to these principles. Both consider the enemy to be unworthy of life; both are preoccupied by pride and principle. As a result, the life of an entire town hangs in the balance: Bout de l'An threatens it with destruction (an all-too-real menace, given the destruction of Oradour-Sur-Glane a few days before), while 'François', who can easily resolve the crisis by releasing Simone, is quite willing to see the threat carried out. And both men are equally astonished by the efforts of Sadrin and especially Delalande, who eventually assumes the leading role in the negotiations. Why, they both seem to wonder, is he so interested in the lives of these hostages? As 'François' insistently asks Delalande, 'Whose side are you on?'

This is a crucial point. Bout de l'An and 'François' understand human motivations exclusively in terms of self-interest. They are blind to the motivation of those 'individuals who put the dignity and lives of human beings . . . above the ideals that drive the *maquis* and the militia alike'.[26] Both men think first of their image, next of their ideals, and rarely if ever of the lives of others. As a result, though there is an 'irreducible asymmetry' at the core of their respective ideologies, there is an unsettling parallel in their blind attachment to principle and indifference towards human life. As for Blanchard and Van Gaver, they acted on behalf of the honor and dignity of France. They died so that France would actively assist in its own liberation. As such, they 'work[ed] for the public good'.[27] Yet, though Blanchard and Van Gaver's actions are praiseworthy and good, they cannot be judged exclusively in these terms. Recall that these men acted in the public sphere, and that the actions had public and deeply unfortunate consequences. When this is the case, Todorov argues, the ethical principle that must be applied is the assurance 'that the good that should ensue from this will be greater than the bad that could come from it'.[28]

In other words, we confront the distinction made by the German sociologist Max Weber between the ethics of conviction and the ethics of responsibility. The former is the context of heroes; they act in the public sphere on behalf of ideals that may cost them their own lives, as well as the lives of others. The ethics of responsibility, on the other hand, spurs the actions of rescuers, not heroes.[29] As Todorov notes in *Face à l'extrême,* rescuers act on behalf of individuals, not abstractions. Their actions attend to the humanity of their fellow men and women. Into this category fall Delalande and Sadrin, as well as the local bishop who offered to replace the hostages with his own person, a bicyclist who covered hundreds of kilometers in order to deliver a crucial message, and the local peasant who took in and hid a half-crazed Charles Krameisen. Heroic action entails a morality of sacrifice – i.e, the belief that one's own death, or the death of others, is required for personal or collective redemption. Responsible action, however, carries a morality of risk. There is no call for violence or sacrifice, but a concern for the ordinary virtue of dignity and an 'intimate awareness of the community of men'.[30] It is such a concern that prodded Delalande to work for the release not only of the original hostages, but the Jewish hostages subsequently taken, as well as to testify on behalf of certain *miliciens* after the liberation.

III

There is undoubtedly a monument to the martyrs of the resistance in Saint-Amand, but one wonders if Delalande is remembered. Todorov does not say.[31] Delalande's relative isolation, in any case, seems to leave Todorov little cause for optimism. Like the chorus at the end of a Greek tragedy, Todorov has assumed a difficult task: to find meaning in a story rent by evil. At times, Todorov seems to believe that the writing of history in the tragic mode is itself a moral act. This is reminiscent of certain Roman historians, such as Sallust and Tacitus. For the former, the historian of the *Conspiracy of Catiline*, writing history is an act as virtuous as those accomplished by the statesman or general, whereas for the author of the *Agricola*, history writing explains and justifies the individual's silence during evil times.

Moreover, for both, history serves to prod others to emulate models of virtue. Similarly, in *Nous et les autres*, Todorov affirms the power of such ideals: 'If this wasn't my belief, why would I even have written this book, whose aim is to influence the behavior of others?'[32] He enters the specifics in *Face à l'extrême*, where he insists that goodness is more common than is commonly supposed. He asserts that 'a code of ordinary moral values and virtues, one commensurate with our times, can indeed be based on the recognition that it is as easy to do good as to do evil'. He proposes that Hannah Arendt's notion of the banality of evil might, in fact, be turned on its head: the banality of good is no less rooted in our lives. 'We need not imitate saints. Nor need we fear monsters; both the dangers and the means with which to neutralize them are all around us'.[33]

At other times, however, he seems far less sanguine. At these moments, Todorov's understanding of the tragic seems closer to the Greek tragedians and Thucydides. There surfaces a certain fatalism in his work, especially when it turns autobiographical. For example, while discussing the nature of onlookers, Todorov berates himself: 'If I had stayed in Bulgaria, I would have spent the next thirty years writing half-truths, trying to beat "them" at their own game, seeing who could outsmart the other. That is one of the most striking characteristics of totalitarian regimes: everyone becomes an accomplice; everyone is both inmate and guard, victim and executioner'.[34] Yet Todorov's severity is not limited to a self-critique. Entire peoples are, at times, implicated: 'The French, I think, ought to be grateful to Eichmann and his colleagues for having chosen Poland as their extermination ground, a choice made for "practical" reasons and not at all because the French would have refused to collaborate in the endeavor or because they would have been troublesome witnesses. Had the decision been otherwise, we might have learned yet again that, as Naploeon said, the word impossible is not French'.[35]

This may strike us as harsh, but it is not far removed from the judgment delivered to his American readership by Robert Paxton more than twenty-five years ago.[36] Implicit in Paxton's approach is the belief, reminiscent of Thucydides, that human nature is unchanging and perhaps unchangeable. It is possible that both Thucydides and Paxton would agree with Todorov's response to a Bulgarian peasant who, having lived next door to the concentration camp at Lovetch, claimed to have seen and heard nothing: 'This is how it was, and how it again will be should history repeat itself. Let us not risk ridicule in reproaching others for their lack of heroism'.[37]

With his concluding remarks, Paxton ultimately, if indirectly, makes a case for his account's exemplarity. (One of the consequences of such exemplarity is that the criticism made by a number of French readers of Paxton's moral balance sheet – namely that he was too harsh on the French – is beside the point. Paxton *is* harsh, perhaps rightly, on humankind, and not just the French.) Todorov makes this issue explicit, for it goes to the heart of his claim for a critical humanism, a creed that is necessarily universalist. The particular cases of France or Bulgaria are, finally, of import not because of what they tell us of France or Bulgaria, but because of what they reveal of human nature. Unlike 'literal history', which refers exclusively to itself and defines a single individual or group, 'exemplary history' acknowledges the *singularity* of these same events, but not their *uniqueness*. Instead, it serves as a model: 'this memory lends itself to analogy and generalization: it serves as an *exemplum* from which I can draw a lesson. The past thus becomes a principle of action for the present'.[38]

For Todorov, the quest for exemplarity is not exclusive to the historian. It is an ethical principle, and lives devoted to it are lives that 'acknowledge our common ties to those who fall outside our specific ethnic, linguistic or religious grouping'.[39] This explains, of course, a Bernard Delalande, who not only fought on behalf of imprisoned resistance fighters, but the Jewish hostages as well (and even on behalf of those *miliciens* confronted with the rough justice of the post-war purge of collaborators). It also explains the exemplary value of Todorov's work and life. As he writes, there is, in the end, 'an indisputable merit in turning from one's own misfortunes, or the tragedies of those close to oneself, to the misfortunes of others, thus refusing the exclusive status of former victim'.[40]

In the long transit from Sofia to Paris, from the analysis of Joseph Conrad's *Heart of Darkness* to the darkness of the wells at Guerry, Todorov has repeatedly confronted the fundamental questions of history: how and why is it written? At times, as in his critique of the growing cult of memory, Todorov seems to criticize implicitly those historians who refuse to teach the general lessons of the past. This position occasionally slides into provocation, as when he asserts that the historian's work is 'necessarily directed by the search for the good and not the truth'.[41]

But how far is his position from that of other historians of Vichy? As I have already suggested, the moral imperative inherent in Todorov's historical work is partly fueled by the memories of his own past. In a moving passage, Todorov confesses, 'Alone in the middle of the night, one suddenly understood all the damage and self-mutilation caused by the constant and relentless need of adaptation. One felt rising from within the desire to run out into the street and, like a madman, cry out the truth, the simple truth, at the top of one's voice. But you knew at the same time that you would not do it'.[42] Happily, most historians of Vichy France are not burdened by such memories. Is it possible, however, that some of us chose this field for the same reason that this field chose, as it were, Tzvetan Todorov? Namely, that it entails a study of oneself? Do we not ask ourselves the same questions asked by Todorov? How would we have reacted? What would we have done? The difference is, that for Todorov, these questions change tense from the conditional to the simple past: How *did* I react? What *did* I do? But, of course, no past is simple: neither for Todorov or us. There is, for him, no clear demarcation between the history of Vichy, the history of his youth and the history of this very moment. How clear is the demarcation for us? How clear are our motivations behind the writing of these histories? Todorov offers less a model of *how* history ought to be written, than *why* it ought to be written. As he would wish to have it, the matter is now open to dialogue.

Notes

1. Krysztof Pomian, 'Les Avatars de l'identité historique', *Débat* (July–August 1980). 'Tzvetan Todorov and the Writing of History', a special issue of the *South Central Review* (Fall–Winter, 1998) contains essays by both Todorov and various scholars, including this author, on a number of issues raised in this article, but appeared too late to be incorporated.
2. Henry Rousso, *Le Syndrome de Vichy de 1944 à nos jours*; 2nd edn (Paris, 1990).
3. Tzvetan Todorov, *Introduction to Poetics* (Minneapolis, 1982): 6. See also his introduction to *French Poetics Today* (Cambridge, 1982).
4. Peter Brooks, introduction to *Introduction to Poetics*: xviii.
5. While the totalitarian nature of Communist Bulgaria forced him to develop two personalities, 'one that was public and submissive, the other private and rebellious', the political and intellectual milieu in Paris was no less hypocritical: acquaintances 'led petit-bourgeois lives while claiming to follow a revolutionary ideal'. As a result, the introduction to evil he experienced in Bulgaria was effectively compounded after his arrival in France. See Tzvetan Todorov, *Nous et les autres* (Paris, 1989): 7ff. Unless otherwise indicated, I have translated all quotations from those works cited in their French version.
6. *Critique de la critique*: 182.
7. Ibid.: 188.
8. He declares that his 'main interest is less a historian's than a moralist's; the present is more important to me than the past': *The Conquest of America* (New York, 1982): 4.
9. *The Conquest of America*: 247.

10. *Nous et les autres*: 16.
11. Ibid.: 12. This is a form of engagement that recalls the position of Jean-Paul Sartre. In fact, Todorov appovingly comments on Sartre's notion of intellectual engagement: 'The writer is both "engaged" in the sense that he closely participates in the history of his time – that he is "situated" (*en situation*) – as well as in the sense that he assumes the role of liberty's guide, helping us surpass this same situation' (*Critique de la critique*: 57).
12. Quoted in *Nous et les autres*: 488. Todorov has more recently and forcefully echoed this sentiment, declaring that 'the sentiments of justice and injustice are born spontaneously within each one of us. They may lie asleep, but can be easily awakened': *L'Homme dépaysé* (Paris, 1997): 66.
13. *Nous et les autres*: 513–14.
14. He candidly acknowledges that much work on the discovery of the Americas has been already done, in greater detail and depth, by others. Yet this is a minor matter: 'I wish to address my work to a public more interested in the present than the past. If there is anything new in my interpretation, it is solely due to the perspective from which I am questioning the facts': *Les Morales de l'histoire*: 21.
15. He discusses this issue in a somewhat elusive manner in *L'Homme dépaysé*: 24ff.
16. The phrase is, of course, Claude Lévi-Strauss's, and Todorov is careful to recall that though the foreigner may be exempt from the prejudices of other cultures, it does not mean that he is exempt from the biases of his own. See the section he devotes to Lévi-Strauss in *Nous et les autres*: 95–129.
17. See his discussion in *Les Morales de l'histoire*: 26ff., as well as his book *Mikhail Bakhtin: The Dialogical Principle* (Minneapolis, 1984), especially pp. 99–107. In *L'Homme dépaysé* (Paris, 1996), Todorov alternatively describes this essential quality as *dépaysement*, which has the double meaning in English of 'change of scenery' and 'sense of strangeness'.
18. Tzvetan Todorov, *Au Nom du peuple* (Paris, 1992): 12.
19. The phrase '*Tu n'as pas connu ça, jeune homme*' is found in Pascal Ory, *Les Collaborateurs, 1940–1945* (Paris, 1986).
20. *Facing the Extreme* (New York, 1996): 28.
21. In defending Hannah Arendt's controversial notion of the banality of evil, Todorov recalls that Arendt did not imply that there is a little of Eichmann on in each one of us, for this would erase 'the distinction, basic to the notion of justice, between the capacity to act and the

action itself' (*Facing the Extreme*: 137). In short, simply because murderers are like us does not mean that we are all murderers (or victims).

22. *A French Tragedy: Scenes of Civil War, Summer 1944* (Hanover, NH, 1996), translated by Mary Byrd Kelly, edited and annotated by Richard J. Golsan: xvii. One is struck by the coincidence that this history occurs in the same region as does Alain-Fournier's *Le Grand Meaulnes*. Both stories deal with the lost innocence of adolescence, and the effort, ultimately successful, to assume responsibility for the acts committed as adolescents.
23. Sadrin wrote down his account of the period, which Todorov published in the original French version – *Une tragédie française: été 1944, scènes de guerre civile* (Paris, 1994) – alongside his own narrative. The account is not included in the English translation, which is unfortunate: Sadrin's souvenirs provides the means for a dialogue between the historian and his object – a dialectic that Todorov considers essential to a viable humanism.
24. *A French Tragedy*: 49.
25. Ibid.: 12.
26. Ibid.: 72.
27. Ibid.: 127.
28. *A French Tragedy*: 127. Todorov echos this concern in his discussion of the impact of 'scientific' theories of human nature. For example, he deals harshly with Gobineau's work, not only because it is bad science, but because 'he was naive enough to believe that one could have a passionate interest in what one held to be the truth, without worrying over the political and moral consequences of this same passion' (*Nous et les autres*: 179).
29. Max Weber, *Wissenschaft als Beruf und Politik als Beruf*, translated as *Le Savant et le politique* (Paris, 1959).
30. *Facing the Extreme*: 134.
31. Immediately after the war, Delalande wrote and published his own account of the events, *De la milice au maquis* (Saint Amand, 1945). The narrative is based, in part, upon the notes provided by Sadrin, who published his own version ten years later. Sadrin's description of Delalande may be the best of memorials: 'The task he was to undertake dovetailed with his rather adventurous spirit and overflowing energy. During these two weeks, he gave his all to this mission. Nothing checked him: neither temporary failures nor overwhelming exhaustion. To the contrary, the accumulation of obstacles actually stimulated him. It also reinforced his stubborn desire that

led to a happy conclusion to the negotiations between the milice and the resistance' (*Souvenirs d'un maire*, in *Une Tragédie française*: 204).

32. *Nous et les autres*: 14.
33. *Facing the Extreme*: 291.
34. Ibid.: 247.
35. *Facing the Extreme*: 249.
36. *Vichy France: Old Guard and New Order, 1940–1944* (New York, 1972).
37. *Au Nom du peuple*: 40.
38. Tzvetan Todorov, *Les Abus de la mémoire* (Paris, 1995): 30–1.
39. Ibid.: 45.
40. Ibid.: 43.
41. Ibid.: 50 (italics mine). A few pages later, Todorov reaffirms that 'far from remaining prisoners of the past, we must instead make the past serve the present, just as memory – and forgetting – must be enlisted in the service of justice' (p. 61).
42. *L'Homme dépaysé*: 46.

–19–

Why Be So Cruel? Some Modest Proposals to Cure the Vichy Syndrome

Pascal Ory

I consider Anglophone readers as friends, but from experience I know many of them to be quite critical when it comes to France during the 'dark years' of the Occupation. This being said, I would like to defend a thesis. The problem of this particular occupation raises a specifically French question. To answer this question, however, one must bear in mind that it is not a single but a double question. Moreover, this double question, in its very 'doubleness', has but a single answer. My explanatory model applies both to Vichy itself and to the Vichy syndrome.

1. The Problem

Vichy poses the same problem to the historian and to the citizen, to the French and to foreigners. Vichy is not limited to the four or so years of physical occupation of the national territory, even if one extends the time-frame and the problem to include the purges. To Vichy's 'contemporaneous' dimension has been added a retrospective dimension, one governed by the French *fin de siècle,* which I suggested a long time ago began in the 1970s,[1] the decade of Marcel Ophuls's *The Sorrow and the Pity* on one side of the Atlantic and of Robert Paxton's *Vichy France: Old Guard and New Order* on the other. It is evident that the contemporary and retrospective aspects of the problem remain fundamentally distinct. One must clearly distinguish the 'immediate' question of whether Vichy constituted either a unique regime in French history or a unique collaboration in the European setting, from the 'media' question created by the recurrent and theatrically dramatic questioning of Vichy in public opinion and in the collective memory of France. On the one hand, we have the events of 1940; on the other, we have Henry Rousso's 'Vichy syndrome'.

To put it another way, here, Vichy in itself (the events of 1940 to 1944); there, Vichy as specter (the Vichy syndrome) – a duality, or doubling, familiar to us at least since *Hamlet*.

1.1

Now, let us be a bit more specific. The year 1940 was in itself 'double'. Externally, it was characterized by the official choice of collaboration. Clearly, we must concede that the mere presence of the word 'collaboration' in the text of the Armistice of June 1940 did not necessarily determine all the policies that followed. Yet we must first consider the Armistice itself. It is not by chance that the rupture, the bifurcation, between Philippe Pétain and Charles de Gaulle occurred over the question of the Armistice.

France was the country of armistice. An armistice constitutes a civil rather than a military act. Surrender would have been a military act, as indeed it was for the King of the Belgians in 1940. In contrast, the politics of an armistice involve a logic of cooperation between unequals. Above all, an armistice is a document signed between two legitimate governments, one of which – without getting involved in legal wrangling – in this case was the government of continuity, the nascent French State, one and indivisible. This was the case neither for Yugoslavia (which ceased to be indivisible), nor for Greece, whose legitimate government opted for exile, like the governments of Belgium, the Netherlands, and Norway. Therefore, there was a striking singularity in the French question of 1940, present from the outset and further emphasized by Pétain's meeting with Hitler at Montoire in October 1940. In France, the armistice led to official collaboration, which concerned first and foremost state collaboration.

The French particularity is further highlighted by the choice of the National Revolution in domestic politics, the linking of a Franco-German armistice to a Franco-French settling of scores. Therein lies the difference between France and the only other country to engage in state collaboration, Denmark, where no link existed between defeat and internal revolution.

At this stage of the analysis, the key point involves the issue of sovereignty. Even the smallest of Vichy's acts carried with it a seal of legitimacy. Self-evidently, and even in collaborating with the occupier, this seal bound the 'French State' (so-named) to all the institutions dependent upon it. In addition, and I will return to this, Vichy's seal of legitimacy bound the state to the elites and other established groups that structured French society. The recent publication of Marc-Olivier Baruch's book[2] and the trial of Maurice Papon have helped to focus attention on the civil servants. But other scholars and other 'affairs' have shown the extent of the problem. Conversely, and to make my point clearer with an international comparison, the affair at the Université Libre de Bruxelles (Brussels Free University or ULB), could serve as a metaphor. The ULB, secular and anti-clerical, was the Belgian citadel of free thinking. Unlike the universities in Ghent or Liège and unlike French universities, it was independent of the state. The ULB could thus stand in clear opposition to German pressure, to the point that the entire university went on strike in 1941, an episode that is still celebrated there each year. One would search in vain for a single French establishment attempting a similar gesture of resistance. French universities were bound to the state. The French state was a state of continuity and collaboration, unlike its Belgian counterpart, which, with the exception of the king, had taken refuge in England.[3]

But to my mind, French particularity does not stop there. It takes on its fullest dimension if one considers the Vichy syndrome, that is to say the chronic national debate about the 'dark years'. We have an abundance of scholarship, or work claimed as such, but also a recurring presence of the issues of the Occupation in the media, the arts, and the everyday life of French people. Indeed, the term 'debate' does not really suffice. In one sense, the term 'polemic' works better, because it is certainly a question of a small Franco-French war of symbols. But in another, the Vichy syndrome, rather than remaining purely a war of words, has emerged in solemn initiatives taken by all three branches of government (executive, legislative, judicial), and even in collective and individual public acts ranging from petition to assassination.

1.2

It is important to stop here for a moment, to establish a few basic points that narrow the field of investigation, and that distinguish more precisely the main issues from secondary ones.

The problematic nature of Vichy's reality is not the radical nature of ideological change, but rather the continuity of men and institutions, who then underwent in turn a violent ideological conversion. As an object, Vichy can be turned and manipulated endlessly. But it is nevertheless true that France, and above all its elites, experimented in 1940 with new rules of operation in a practical sense and with new values in a theoretical sense. This experiment radically opposed the rules and values of the liberal and democratic republic previously in place. It is not the extremists, fascist or traditionalist, that warrant investigation. For them, Vichy was about taking revenge on the republican regime. Rather, we need to understand politicians from the republican side such as Pierre Laval, a full-blooded scion of the union of republican meritocracy with the parliamentary regime. The same can be said of like-minded civil servants such as Maurice Papon, who had Radical Party origins and who, before the war, had belonged to a left-wing student organization. To investigate theory, we should concern ourselves not with publications like ultra-right-wing or fascist newspapers of the 1940s, such as *Action française* or *Je suis partout*, but, by way of example, with conservative publications such as *Le Temps* or *Le Figaro*. Analyzing the contents of these publications is fascinating because one finds a rallying to a system that ran counter to this elite's original values. To apply concepts such as 'opportunism' – that fragile mix of psychologism and moralism – seems completely insufficient, though people have used such ideas in the past and will always be able to use them in the future.

This being said, the problem of collaboration, which lurks in the shadow of the problem of Vichy in itself, remains one of agreement in practice rather than in theory. The 'Paxtonian revolution' brought this into focus. State collaboration based itself on the conviction that France under Vichy operated in accordance with a self-generated continuity. Yet even at the outset, this continuity occurred only at the price of a certain distortion, and of an autonomy that Vichy maintained only sporadically, and increasingly as a hollow façade.

The principal problem of Vichy as specter is less the availability of information about the history of Vichy than the ways in which it has been filtered. It is an ethical issue bound up with the shifting gaze of public opinion. In 1945, the issue was the *patrie*, and hence treason. By 1995, the issue had become humanity, and crimes against it, and hence (by 1997, the year of the Papon trial), infamy. The criminal charges have changed, certainly in writings but above all in people's minds. Underlying scholarly and technical debates about the archives or about this or that aspect of Vichy politics, one does not have to be a great mind to uncover value judgments concerning the degree of responsibility of the group or individual under investigation.

2. The Interpretation

We can begin to respond to the duality of the question posed by Vichy. Context and historical time make Vichy in itself understandable, but Vichy as specter not at all. I mention here, only as a reminder, a contextual interpretation that, while it is very clear – and I have used it myself on several occasions – remains insufficient. This contextual interpretation places at center stage a 'spirit of the 1930s', which I would extend to 1970. This was an interventionist, organicist, and statist age, with deep roots in the experience of the First World War. Similarly, the rise of the Vichy syndrome was linked to, and was perhaps provoked by, the end of this era and by the period of economic, social, and cultural crisis that followed it.

2.1

Here I want to highlight another reading that complements the preceding one. It concerns not so much national historical time as the conceptual field of the nation. The specificity of the Occupation of France has its source in another well-known particularity of France: the image of France as the archetype of the nation-state, or one could even say, the model of the nation-state pushed to its highest degree of sophistication.

This is not the place to enumerate the elements and attributes of France as the archetype of the nation-state. Let us simply say that it is based on the combination of two factors that stem from an ancient and continuous political experience: the Capetian monarchy, and the foundational choice of Catholicism, which later and in turn directly contributed to the influence of secularism. France is 'the oldest Catholic country in the world', if one wishes to attribute this characteristic to King Clovis's choice, made 1,500 years ago. But France is also 'the oldest secular country in the world', according to a certain point of view that portrays French secularism as the child, via internal and external crises, of a strong and centralized power. Secularism brought into being its own secular clergy, destined bit by bit to replace the entrenched and formidable Catholic clergy.

Simply put, French Catholicism determined a certain type of relationship between the French people, politics and culture. One can also find more or less this type of relationship in Italy or Spain. But the depth of secularism in France, which distinguishes France so clearly from the United States, where the founding covenant was intrinsically religious, explains sufficiently the importance respectfully accorded to civil servants and the intelligentsia. The intelligentsia constitutes the regular clergy, adapted to modern values and structured around individualism and free-thinking. In addition, state administration and the intelligentsia meet in a particular profession, that of teaching. What does this have to do with 1940? Quite simply, France has pushed to an extreme degree both the reality and the myth of national unity based on a state that is strong both in its universality and its autonomy. Both of these characteristics were acquired under the traditional tutelage of the Church, the dynasties, and the two privileged orders, the clergy and the nobility. In short, a country centered on itself and with the help of a powerful intelligentsia, created a culture characterized by its brilliance and its boisterousness. And now, if we place such a model by way of experiment into the trials and tribulations of 1940, we get simultaneously the political reality, Vichy in itself, and an imaginary reality, Vichy as specter.

We will attribute to Vichy in itself the rigidity of the French system, its lack of flexibility, the centralism of its culture. None of this prepared France as a collectivity for dissent. In the name of a continuity dating back many centuries characterized by a strong state and an integrated nation, both of which guaranteed universalism, collaboration seemed a far more rational path to take than de Gaulle's path of stubborn resistance. French national history allows us to place 1940 on the list of alternating 'revolutions' and 'reactions', such as 1814, 1830, 1848, 1851, etc. We can add to this list another typical trait, as in 1792, 1814, or 1870, of a national defeat bringing about a change of regime. But the quality unique to Vichy, at least at the beginning, resembles that of La Fontaine's fable ('I am a bird, see my wings, I am a mouse, see my paws'). Vichy claimed not that it was playing a double game (the thesis of Pétain as shield versus de Gaulle as sword not bearing close scrutiny) but that it embodied both the Restoration *and* the Revolution. Vichy offered the restoration of an old, spiritualist, corporative and authoritarian France. But it also offered a revolution that would transform the masses, beginning with the young. As with each change of regime since 1789, the force of national continuity was such that it provided justification and practical continuity to all social groups, without disrupting anybody's state of mind and, at first, without debate. Vichy offered continuity of institutions from above (the Papon model), and as Philippe Burrin has argued, 'individual accommodation' from below. The strength of national continuity gave an intellectual coherence, if not a moral pretext, to the paradoxical zeal of collaboration at the outset, as Robert Paxton aptly pointed out for the first time.

Let me add here two points that, although they opposed each other, reinforced the impulse toward national continuity. On the one hand, diverse reformers and movements that crystallized during the 1930s around the theme of modernizing the state rallied to Vichy, from Anatole de Monzie, to Pierre Pucheu, to *X-Crise*, the *Centre polytechnicien d'études économiques*, a planning group of technocrats). This mixture produced a milieu that, as Dominique Veillon reminds us in this volume, could produce as many resisters as Vichyites. Above all, this milieu produced Vichyist resisters, notably Pucheu, whose tragic fate provided the most striking example.[4] On the other hand, there was the acclaim, the structuring, the 'spiritual assistance' given to Vichy at the beginning by the anti-secular Catholic intellectuals. This was a final testimony to the separation of Church and State, and thus to the limits of the republican system, which had consciously marginalized a 'Counter-France' as a product of a 'Counter-revolution'. It has reached the level of mythology that there was simultaneously the Resistance 'that believed in Heaven' as well as the Resistance that pointedly did not, in the words of Paul Eluard's poem, a mythology that permitted the definitive fusion of these two cultures.

One more observation should be made at this stage. The impulse toward national continuity postulated here was essentially situated in varieties of representation produced by contemporaries – actors and witnesses, agents and those they acted upon, torturers and victims – and not necessarily in the reality of their acts, their initiatives, and their programs. A solitary and simple example will clarify what I mean by this. The impulse toward national continuity explained and justified Vichy's defense of French Jews. This defense was relative, and not absolute, and is meaningful only in comparison to the fate reserved for foreign or stateless Jews, including children, who were abandoned to the Germans. I must add immediately that among these Jews excluded from the national community in October 1940 figured numerous denaturalized Jews, who were still French in June 1940.

But this configuration of French national unity and continuity also produced a delayed effect, the Vichy as specter effect, which began to crystallize in French public opinion during the 1970s. We can assume the idea of national continuity to have reached its zenith by the end of de Gaulle's presidency in 1969, though even then it was seriously wounded by the accelerating processes of globalization. But I directly associate national continuity with the duration, extent and violence – in short, the depth – of the Vichy syndrome. The model of the highly integrated nation-state helps explain the questioning directed toward 'the establishment' by new generations, and is therefore indirectly linked to the phenomenon we have been studying. This indirectness may come through age and generational status, but remains clearly linked to national and sometimes institutional continuity, if we recall the prominence of studies written by members of this or that profession on their own hidden memory of the Vichy past. Recently, we have seen, in addition to Robert Badinter's book on the legal profession,[5] a great deal of attention directed toward the study on the French civil service written by Marc-Olivier Baruch, himself a civil servant who eventually devoted himself to working full-time on historical research.

No doubt, the quasi-biological effect of time enters into this generational questioning of Vichy. It was, after all, the same children of de Gaulle rebelling against their fathers in May 1968 who, over time, gradually discovered that they were also children of Pétain. But the effect of place seems more pertinent to me, because it allows us to understand the differences of scope and chronology of the Vichy syndrome compared to its analogs, distant though they may be, in Sweden, Switzerland or Spain.

2.2

Many observers, including myself, have set *The Sorrow and the Pity* alongside Robert Paxton's *Vichy France* as parallel, foundational events. Twenty-five years after my first publications on the 'Rétro Satanas',[6] I have no reason to question this conclusion, on the condition that for our present purposes we emphasize two complementary dimensions of these two works. First, Paxton's book deals primarily with the state, though in a very broad sense and in the most comprehensive manner possible, while Marcel Ophuls's film seeks to tell us about the nation. The disruptive effects of the book and the film thus converged. Second, *The Sorrow and the Pity,* an essay told in images, also participates in the fictionalization of Vichy. This film, the work of Max Ophuls's son, tells the story, one way or another, of untold numbers of other sons and daughters. *The Sorrow and the Pity* takes over from a work that does not claim to be anything but fiction: *La place de l'étoile,* the first of Patrick Modiano's novels, published precisely in 1968.[7] And it is within the context of this centralized cultural life, as noted above, that one can situate the abundant and even self-propelled cultural production on this topic, meaning all the books, movies, articles, television shows, etc. devoted to the Vichy period, in media ranging from novels to films, from plays to songs. If the importance of times of cultural upheaval is measured by the extent of their inscription in the realm of fiction, then Vichy – meaning here posthumous Vichy – must be counted among the most violent and long-lasting of such times.

As often happens in such a situation, the machine of 'social demand' will consume just about any kind of fuel once it gets going. To a great extent, the rigidity of French cultural structures has tended to promote piecemeal analysis, which has meant slicing up the memory of Vichy into the university, the churches, businesses, the civil service, etc. But alongside this, assimilationist ideology came under scathing interrogation in the 1980s by, among others, voices coming from a hypothetically unitary 'Jewish community'. This spoke to a broader communitarian crisis that at the time had crystallized around the slogan of the 'right to difference'. Against this backdrop of investigative rigidity and cultural upheaval, it is no surprise that the Vichy syndrome took shape alongside a general crisis of French identity. This crisis showed itself both in cultural production (for example, Pierre Nora's project *Les lieux de mémoire*) and in political debate on questions such as immigration. To be sure, the Vichy syndrome is much more of an effect of this crisis than a cause, and we must add immediately that not all its effects are harmful. It is precisely because of this crisis that our time has witnessed two important and nearly simultaneous symbolic admissions – Jacques Chirac's official recognition of the French state's responsibility in the persecution of the Jews, and the army's official recognition of the innocence of Captain Dreyfus. It is never too late to do the right thing . . . .

We have seen the difficulty of putting Vichy in itself and Vichy as specter on a critical, or rather moral axis, or on a scale from positive to negative. For example, Vichy in itself was seen positively by the elites at the time and negatively by elites of subsequent generations. In contrast, while I imagine Vichy as specter to be negative in its image, it ultimately could have a positive effect on the evolution of French identity. Simply put, for me, it is 'the same France', meaning the same configuration of cultural structures, that assured continuity in 1940 and embarked upon retrospection in the 1970s. It is the same France that assured and assumed two declensions of the word 'responsibility', political responsibility and moral responsibility. One could criticize the model explained here – the highly integrated nation in combination with the Catholic/secular nation – for its excessive generality. But it does have the advantage of allowing scholarly analysis to include a moral dimension. French culture, so accustomed to self-analysis, has finally discovered the paradox of the continuity (rather than the rupture) of 1940. This continuity need neither be seen as a logical contradiction nor, as a result, an ethical scandal, as it allows the nation–state a certain duality.

I wish to conclude with this moral dimension. If, like others before me, I have been practicing 'egohistory', I must remind readers that my scholarly work on the 'dark years', as objective as it has striven to be, has never been part of a university cursus. My research specialty has always been elsewhere, even if that 'elsewhere' – cultural history and particularly the history of cultural identities – has an obvious relationship to the subject that concerns us here. I wrote about Vichy twenty-five years ago for ethical, and hence very bad, reasons. We all know, according to the classic formula, that historians' biographies should have nothing to do with their choice of research topics, and that historians should come to the subject, as they say, 'from no time and from no place'. We all know that, in both the old and recent controversies that have stirred up the hypothetical 'community of historians', the moral and political genealogies of individuals were not supposed to have played any role, were they? But for myself, I remain fond of the idea that we should not exercise the profession of historian with impunity. And since I have mentioned the 'profession', I should like to end by recalling a figure who, during the Vichy years, used the term 'profession of the historian' as the title for a work cut short by his death. I refer of course to Marc Bloch, a great scholar as well as a great resister, who lived *for History* (as he explained in his *Apologie pour l'histoire*) but who also, as the official phrase, now obsolete, goes, *died for France.*

Translated by David Lake and Leonard V. Smith

Notes

1. 'Du bon usage des salauds,' *Nouvelle revue socialiste,* 1 (April 1974): 76–9.
2. Marc-Olivier Baruch, *Servir l'État français: l'administration en France de 1940 à 1944* (Paris, 1997).
3. Pascal Ory, 'Les Universités belges et françaises face à l'occupation allemande', *Revue du Nord*, vol. 498 (1987): 51–9.
4. An industrialist before the war, Pucheu served as Minister of Interior at Vichy. Responsible for creating the anti-communist Sections Spéciales in Paris, he left Vichy, disillusioned, in 1943 but was arrested when he arrived in Casablanca. The *Comité français pour la libération nationale* tried, convicted and condemned Pucheu to death, executing him on 20 March 1944 (editor's note).
5. Robert Badinter, *Un Antisemitisme ordinaire: Vichy et les avocats juifs 1940–1944* (Paris, 1997).
6. 'Retro Satanas' refers to the Latin version of the words Jesus spoke to the Devil, 'Vade retro, Satanas'. For further explanation, see Ory, 'Du bon usage'. Other works by Ory also illuminate this point.
7. Patrick Modiano, *La Place de l'étoile* (Paris, 1968).

–20–

The Historian, a Site of Memory

Henry Rousso

Let me begin with a personal tribute to Robert Paxton. In 1975, when I was still a student, I was seeking a research topic and had already become interested in the period of the Occupation. Reading *Vichy France: Old Guard and New Order,* which had just been translated into French, persuaded me to work on that difficult period of recent French history. The shock of reading that book, and even more, the sense that it was having a considerable impact on French cultural life of the 1970s, played an important role in my choice of vocation. This is the debt I owe Robert Paxton, and I wanted to acknowledge it from the very outset.

The book itself, along with the reactions and debates it inspired, constituted a kind of double event. Robert Paxton had offered a clear step forward in the academic writing of the history of 1940 to 1944, one that served as a major boost to the historiographic renewal that began in the late-1960s. But its publication was also an event in itself, one that emphasized how much the French people's relationship with that aspect of their past was in the process of changing. The book thus provided the opportunity to raise questions not only about the history of Vichy, but also about a phenomenon still dimly perceived – the existence of a long history of the memory of the Second World War, a history in which Robert Paxton occupies a unique place.

A 'Site of Memory'?

In the minds of many French people, whether or not they have read his works, Robert Paxton is more than just a renowned historian. He has become a kind of 'site of memory' [*lieu de mémoire*], meaning a 'signifying unit, either real or imagined, that has become, through human agency or the effects of time, an element symbolic of a given community'. Pierre Nora quotes this definition, from the *Grand Robert de la langue française,* in the last volume of his monumental work.[1] A 'site of memory' is thus a symbolic entity, one that emerges from the imagination. It is the crystallization of a vision of the past onto a specific place, whether real or symbolic, onto a ritual, or even onto a remarkable individual. A site of memory refers back to the past and serves as a marker, a more or less permanent point of reference in the continuum of social and historical time. It also refers to a particular narrative, an interpretation or a vision of history, usually dated. Sites of memory also have a history, as does collective memory itself. In this sense, there is nothing fanciful or impertinent about speaking of a historian as a site of memory.

First of all, Pierre Nora himself devotes a part of his *Lieux de Mémoire* to 'historiography,' and includes as sites of memory the medieval *Chroniques,* Augustin Thierry, Ernest Lavisse's *Histoire de France,* and the *Annales* school. In this sense, it is only fitting – and true to historical reality – to offer a small place in this prestigious pantheon not only to Robert Paxton, but to the many issues surrounding memory and historiography that constitute the debate over Vichy in France.

Furthermore, the name of Robert Paxton, outside a small circle of specialists, spontaneously evokes the rupture that occurred between the historiography and the memory of the Occupation. His name is almost always associated with the idea that the French (historians included) have been incapable of 'confronting their past', from the Liberation of 1944 through to the Papon trial of 1997. This idea has become a persistent cliché, repeated in France as well as abroad, especially in the United States. It has given credence to the idea that the taboos and official silences that weighed so heavily during the 1950s and 1960s were broken only very recently. That cliché, although completely unfounded, is interesting in that it shows the extent to which Robert Paxton's work has given rise to ambivalent reactions. He is credited with having caused a true awakening, and with having taken on a task that native historians would have been incapable of carrying out. At the same time, the idea persists that this awakening had only very limited effects, since the supposed 'taboos' continue to this day, to the late-1990s.

Robert Paxton has thus become a character in the national novel of France. He is the messenger, come from afar to deliver the unpleasant news to a country that was steeped in its past and, until that point, proud of it. As a well-known scholar, invited to testify at the trials of Paul Touvier (1994) and Maurice Papon (1997) for crimes against humanity, his word has served almost as a kind of gospel for an entire generation. The theses developed in his works have been widely disseminated, and have contributed to an interpretation of that period that is now dominant among specialists and the public at large, even though Paxton's writings occasionally (and despite his best efforts) have been distorted or caricatured.

Before going any further, we must bear in mind that the impact of his work, and especially *Vichy France: Old Guard and New Order,* is much greater than its actual dissemination. Approximately 12,000 copies of the French edition of that book were sold in the first year of publication, 1973–4. While this is considerable, it is nonetheless a small number if one compares it to other works on the same subject or to the substantial sales of French history books in the 1970s, boosted to high levels thanks to the popularity of the *nouvelle histoire*.[2] Between 1973 and 1997 (and before the revised edition published in 1998), approximately 100,000 copies of the French edition of the book were sold, most of them in paperback. This is equivalent to a single year's sales for certain historical works of a more sensational nature, whose quality and longevity can be highly inconsistent.

Robert Paxton is therefore better known than he is read. In this respect, he resembles Marcel Ophuls. 'Only' 230,000 moviegoers saw Ophuls's film, *The Sorrow and the Pity,* in the weeks following its initial release in April 1971 – a very small number, given the film's notoriety and its impact on the collective consciousness, quite considerable even before the film was finally shown on French television in 1981, after having been banned for a decade.[3]

The American historian's book helped put forward a different image and a different kind of public discourse on occupied France, in much the same way as Ophuls's film did. It certainly was not the sole element to trigger this change in the nation's memory, but it did play a role in the process of profound cultural change that had its roots in the spirit of May 1968 and in the questioning of a new generation as it reached adulthood. This change of perspective on the recent past was later to be extended more broadly within the context of a crisis that has gone beyond the economic sphere and is profoundly altering traditional French culture, including the way the French see their nation's history. The heroic reading of the past – the glue that held together French identity – has slowly been giving way to critical readings, 'plural' readings, readings with strong moralizing tendencies, and readings that do not lack a certain masochism. Tragic episodes of recent history, such as Vichy or the colonial wars, have become recurrent contemporary debates. These debates have been fueled by the ethical questioning of a new generation in search of a concept of citizenship different from the one defended by the wartime generations, imbued as it was with a Gaullist or Communist perspective, and even more by the weight of the tragedies that these generations lived through.

A New Historiographical Perspective

Paxton's *Vichy France* was an all-encompassing interpretation of the regime, its ideology and its specific acts – one that brought to light the underlying coherence of the Vichy project. This was focused around the central idea that the ruling elites of the regime had a fairly clear understanding of the link between the 'external policies' and 'internal policies'. The men of Vichy understood the relationship between 'state collaboration' (a term initially proposed by Stanley Hoffmann and now generally accepted), which sought to give back to France part of the sovereignty it lost in the defeat, and the 'National Revolution', an ideology and practice whose goal was the establishment of a regime that would break with the republican tradition. The great originality of this book was that it explained in a specific and amplified way how state collaboration constituted a necessary, if not sufficient, condition for the realization of the National Revolution.

This thesis was a complete break from the pleas consistently argued by the men of Vichy since 1944, especially during the purges. These men insisted on the weight of the constraints placed on them, on their limited range of maneuver, and on the fact that most of the acts later judged to be the most damning for the regime proceeded from the Occupation and not from deliberate choice. With the antisemitic policies emblematic in this regard, Paxton's analyses allowed for clear distinctions between what had been Vichy's own decisions and what had resulted from the racial policies of the Nazis. As Stanley Hoffmann emphasized at the time, Paxton proposed an interpretation diametrically opposed to the one that saw the Vichy regime as buffeted by circumstances, lacking a clearly expressed ideology.[4] Yet the older interpretation, the one Paxton opposed, has remained a durable one. For example, the magistrates of the Paris court of appeals, in its refusal in April 1992 to prosecute Paul Touvier, referred to the Vichy regime as a 'constellation of "good intentions" and political animosities'.[5]

Robert Paxton thus created an opening in the dominant discourse, not simply from an ideological point of view, but because he proposed a different kind of analysis, one that went beyond a judicial view of the issue. That is in fact the key criticism Paxton directed at Robert Aron in 1996:

> Robert Aron worked almost exclusively from documents of the High Court of Justice, which was convened after the Liberation to judge the men of Vichy. Obviously, these officials tried to defend themselves against charges of having

violated Article 75 of the Penal Code – contact with the enemy during wartime. This brought everything back to the question of German influence, to the Germans' position of strength with regard to Vichy.[6]

Prosecutors and scholars both operated under the influence of a judicial paradigm in interpreting the Vichy years. For reasons that reflected both judicial convenience and the culture of the Liberation, prosecutors stressed the idea of treason – and thus *ipso facto* French dependence upon the occupier – rather than the idea of autonomy. Collaborators and the men of Vichy were to be seen first and foremost as traitors, rather than as elements of a *French* dictatorship.

One of the major problems posed by Paxton's book concerns the role of the principal historical actor in the drama, the Nazi occupier. Paxton's goal was to deal with the Vichy regime itself, an actor that up to that point had remained somewhat in the background – at least in the public's perception, if not that of historians. Not the least of the apparent paradoxes of Paxton's approach is that he put the 'French State' at the center of his analysis while using a great many German archival sources, because of the lack of access to French archives.[7] Despite the criticisms of this strategy, the choice to analyze the French point of view through German (and to some extent American) archives allowed for a reading that remains valid to this day. But even more importantly, Paxton's approach provided a crucial change in perspective that consisted – from a heuristic point of view – in training the spotlight on the background action (Vichy). Paxton did so not by casting the lead actor (the occupier) into the shadows, but by himself taking the place of the occupier, in the physical sense of the term. This is what Alain-Gérard Slama, one of Paxton's fiercest critics at the time, called 'the eyes of Abetz [the German ambassador to Vichy]'. Slama did not, however, see the merit in this strategy.[8]

An 'Event'

The impact of *Vichy France* cannot be attributed solely to the originality of the approach and to the reversal of perspective from occupier to occupied. Robert Paxton explored in greater depth and systematized with considerable acuity insights that other historians had developed before him, notably Eberhard Jaeckel, Yves Durand, and Henri Michel. But none of these historians enjoyed the same degree of success. Without minimizing its intrinsic merit, *Vichy France* is interesting because this particular historian of the exceptional episode that was Vichy would himself become exceptional. Indeed, Paxton would become an 'event'.

Part of this can be explained by a convergence of circumstances. The book was published barely two years after the release of *The Sorrow and the Pity*. Rightly or wrongly, the book seemed to propose a scholarly interpretation that echoed Marcel Ophuls's themes. Paxton maintained the same focus on the occupied rather than the occupiers, the same desire to decode the political and sociological workings of collaboration, the same attention to homegrown antisemitism, etc. His book thus brought into focus, with the authority of scholarship, a number of ideas and recollections that were once again in the public arena. Furthermore, the book was published shortly after the considerable commotion brought on in 1971 by President Georges Pompidou's pardon of an obscure member of the Milice named Paul Touvier. This pardon unintentionally marked the beginning of a decisive phase in the history of the memory of Vichy. Although it was intended to promote 'forgetting', the pardon of Touvier in fact kept alive the memory of this episode for the next quarter-century. Sentenced *in absentia* to death in 1946 and 1947, Touvier was pardoned in 1972 by President Georges Pompidou. But after a lengthy renewed judicial procedure beginning in 1973, Touvier was indicted in 1981 for crimes against humanity, for which no statute of limitations exists under French law. The new accusations relied on the testimony of former resisters and Holocaust survivors. And so began a new and complex judicial process that ended with Touvier's condemnation to life in prison in 1994.

Ophuls's film, Touvier's pardon, and Paxton's book thus fortuitously combined to create the 'accident', that is to say the initial event. From that point on, commentary on Robert Paxton's interpretations, whether from actually reading the book or just from reading or hearing *about* it, became an unavoidable feature of all manner of discussion on the Vichy past, sometimes at the cost of misunderstanding and distortion.

Because of this, Robert Paxton was no doubt one of the first historians to have been confronted with the renewal of public debate on very recent history of France. His interpretations met a need perceived vaguely at the time but much more clearly in retrospect. This need corresponded to the desire, especially of younger generations, to 'shine a light' on this hidden part of the past. But Paxton's work also highlighted the search for a discourse that is coherent, that synthesizes, that explains, that designates the 'guilty parties', and that breaks away from the discourse on the fatalism of the war and the contingency of events. In short, Paxton's work crystallized a response to the perspective of the generation whose youth was marked by the drama of Occupation, a perspective well expressed by the popular writer Henri Amouroux.

If French academic historians were initially unsure how to react, the 'Paxtonian revolution' very soon had an impact on the French imagination. Independently of its author, Paxton's book supported a kind of vulgate with deep roots in French public opinion, sometimes at the highest levels – intellectuals, political elites, and especially magistrates, these last because they needed to pursue the trials for crimes against humanity. It should be added that this vulgate emerged not only from a more or less faithful reading of Paxton's work, but also from the broad public consumption of the historical writing on Vichy that developed in France beginning in the 1970s.

'Where Did the Germans Go?'

What had been a heuristic choice on Paxton's part – highlighting French responsibilities rather than those of the Nazi occupiers – has become a foundational point of analysis. Indeed, the principal actors, the Germans, have progressively disappeared from the dominant discourse about Vichy. This tendency can be seen especially among the younger generations, who are inclined to consider the history of Vichy as emanating almost exclusively from an internal political and ideological history. In so doing, they misunderstand the true hierarchy of responsibilities.[9] Among the recent examples of this tendency is a speech given on 20 July 1997 by the newly-installed Prime Minister of France, Lionel Jospin, in front of the monument that commemorates the round-up of Jews at the 'Vél' d'Hiv'. Two years earlier, President Jacques Chirac had given a speech under similar circumstances, though a more accurate one. Jospin in his speech stated that 'this round-up had been *decided,* planned, and carried out by French people',[10] a reversal of the hierarchy of responsibilities that hides the main criminal – the Third Reich, architect of the 'Final Solution' – behind its accomplice. In a way, reversed responsibilities was one of the principal problems with the Papon trial, where the Nazi occupier numbered among the prominent absentees. The few German officers stationed in Bordeaux during the Occupation and still living were not even summoned to appear in court, as if their testimony were superfluous. Only the final verdict corrected this inversion of history by rejecting the murder conspiracy charge.

The important thing here is not so much to denounce this error from a position of 'scholarship' as to question the necessity of such a switch in perspective. A variety of explanations have already been proposed: the need to take the opposite view from the dominant interpretation of the early post-war years; the fact that the very notion of a German occupation no longer constitutes a particularly contested point in French memory, in contrast to the notion of a 'Franco-French war'; the idea – mostly erroneous – that German war criminals were brought to justice far more than the French, etc. We could add one more, almost in jest. After *The Sorrow and the Pity* was released, Stanley Hoffmann complained that a dark myth of an entirely 'Pétainized' France was replacing the golden myth of a France made up entirely of resisters.[11] This represents a classic swing of the pendulum, but also a recurring characteristic of French culture, frequently denounced by Hoffmann[12] – the tendency to believe that France, and every aspect of France, can only be understood in terms of its 'exceptionality'. In the years that followed the war, the majority of the French easily accepted the idea that they had been 'exceptional' in their resistance to the occupying forces. In more sophisticated versions, the idea that the French Resistance was by its very nature intrinsically 'different' from the others – 'exceptional' in the historical sense of the word – continues to have wide circulation, even among certain French historians. Similarly, when the collective consciousness came to rest on collaboration, the dark side of the story, so too France had to be 'exceptional', this time in crime. France had to differ from all the other nations subjected to the yoke of the Third Reich. Of course, there is a certain historical truth to this way of thinking, since the Vichy regime was in many ways unique within occupied Europe. But highlighting French exceptionality, whether in resistance or in collaboration, is almost never accompanied by the essential comparative analysis that would provide some sort of foundation for the argument. The absence of comparison, one of the major deficiencies of French historiography, which remains a largely 'national' historiography, serves only to show the extent to which the explicit or implicit affirmation of French exceptionality reveals less an objective historical situation than an ideological bias.

A 'French Ideology'

Robert Paxton, like many other historians before and especially after him, clearly brought out the ideological roots of the Vichy regime, and its place in the tradition of the French counter-revolutionary and reactionary Right, as well as in the history of the experiences, attempts, and temptations of French fascism. In this context, and in continuing the kind of analysis that seeks to determine the social impact of a historical work rather than its intrinsic value, we must link Paxton to Zeev Sternhell. Sternhell's books have contributed to the development of a second recurring theme: that 'fascism' is a long-underestimated and deeply ingrained ideology in

French political culture. Moreover, for Sternhell, fascism must be considered, both in retrospect and in prospect, a serious and permanent alternative to universalist, democratic and republican ideology.

Bernard-Henri Lévy best articulated this cliché in his famous and fanciful book *L'Idéologie française,* published in 1981. One of the consequences has been a frenetic rereading of the great names of French literature, thought, and politics by the standards of this axiom. Charles Péguy, Louis- Ferdinand Céline, Maurice Barrès, Maurice Blanchot, the anti-Dreyfusards, the Poujadists – how many writers, intellectuals, politicians, and ideologues have been summoned to the Court of History to show the extent to which the very foundations of French culture have been contaminated by fascist ideology? 'Vichy' then became a necessary manifestation of something that already existed in latent form and that could at any point re-emerge, independent of the contingent historical circumstances of the defeat of 1940. But this view neglects an essential historical fact. Fascism in France, however deeply rooted politically and intellectually in certain milieux, and even if it is far more than a mere 'impregnation', as certain French historians for a long time believed, was never a credible political alternative. Nor did it constitute a real threat to the Republic before the defeat of 1940. The defeat alone allowed it to accede to a measure of power.

The belief in fascism as a serious past and present threat to democracy, based to some extent on historical reality, clearly owes its strength to the recently renewed influence of xenophobic and populist ideologies in France and elsewhere in Europe. People lacked an explanation for the relative novelty of these movements, which began with Jean-Marie Le Pen's National Front. Unable to perceive him as part of an *emerging* phenomenon of the 1980s and 1990s, people simply found it easier to portray Le Pen as a *resurgence* of Vichy, or of French fascism. The result was that certain historical moments were retrospectively overemphasized, and their actual impact was given disproportionate weight in order to explain the survival of fascist ideologies over time.

These are, briefly, some of the theses developed over many years by Pierre-André Taguieff, who has shown that the denunciation of today's far-right political movements as 'fascist' has been a counterproductive strategy. In no way has evoking the past slowed down the progression of these movements, which cannot be understood merely as history repeating itself. The example of fascism invites us to reflect on the use of the past, not simply as an ideological weapon or as a 'lesson for the present', but as an antidote for the fear of the unknown, of what is new and unforeseen. The past – or a certain reading of the past – can mistakenly be seen in this context as a refuge, at a time when the present is not understood and the future not foreseen. A considerable number of current discourses on Vichy fall into this category.

French Antisemitism, an Exclusive Paradigm

One of the major effects of the 'Paxtonian revolution' – and one must include here Michael Marrus, with whom Paxton co-authored *Vichy and the Jews* (1981) – was rediscovering the importance of Vichy's antisemitism, and bringing to light Vichy's participation in the Final Solution. Of course, Paxton and Marrus were by no means the first. We must not forget the work of the Center for Contemporary Jewish Documentation, which remained semi-confidential for many years, or that of Serge Klarsfeld, which created a considerable stir. But Paxton and Marrus, as the first to integrate antisemitism with an overall interpretation of the regime and the period, made us more fully aware of the magnitude of the problem, which today is the principal issue at stake in the memory of the Occupation.

But once again, this re-evaluation crystallized an anachronistic view of the Vichy regime. Over the years, what began as an attempt to take a second look at French antisemitism has practically become an exclusive paradigm. Nearly all of today's polemics on the Vichy regime concern antisemitism and antisemitism alone – the so-called 'Jewish files' affair, the 'Jewish property' scandal, controversies surrounding François Mitterrand's past and his relations with René Bousquet, debates about the need to commemorate Vichy crimes (reduced to its crimes committed against Jews). And of course, antisemitism lies at the heart of the investigations and trials for crimes against humanity, which have probably constituted the most powerful, if not the most appropriate, vector of memory for the last twenty years.

The anachronism comes from confusing the moral attitudes of later generations with the truth of the past, and confusing what one might have wished for in retrospect with what actually happened. For those who witnessed the tragedy at the time, for the average French person in 1942, excluding of course the victims themselves, the persecution of Jews was not a major problem. In the hierarchy of concerns of contemporaries, this tragic dimension of the Occupation came far behind the shock of defeat, money problems, the status of prisoners of war, conscripted French labor, etc.

The centrality of antisemitism emerges from a perspective born long after the events themselves. It is entirely structured around the now generally accepted idea of the singularity of the Holocaust. Ironically, one of the defining features of the time was precisely the general indifference to the fate of the Jews, with some variation relative to time and place. This central role of memory, compensating for the absence of awareness at the time, is hardly unique to France. But in France, the significance of the memory of Vichy antisemitism can be linked to the particular situation of French Jews since the 1970s: mistrust of the classic model of assimilation, criticism of French foreign policy in the Middle East, and fear of a real resurgence of antisemitism.

Similarly, the idea that the Vichy regime can be viewed through the same lens as Nazi Germany, and that suggests that antisemitism was equally central and determining for both, is as widespread as it is false. Thanks in large measure to Robert Paxton and Michael Marrus, we know that Vichy made a clear leap from its policy in 1940–41 of legislated social exclusion of Jews (developed at home and not as the result of German pressure), to its participation in after 1942 in the Final Solution. That participation, part of Vichy's policy of 'State collaboration', was carried out under significant German pressure.

This does not relieve Vichy of its overwhelming degree of responsibility, nor of the need to recognize it, even a half-century later. But one consequence of placing antisemitism at the center of all public debate on Vichy is that, over the last twenty years, this debate has occasionally seemed more like a debate between French Jews and the rest of the nation than a debate between the nation and its own past. As soon as one removes from public debate those problems that were central at the time – the defeat, the choices made in the summer of 1940, the nature of the forms of collaboration or accommodation, the difficulty of resisting oppression – in order to concentrate exclusively on racial persecution, a gulf appears between the experiences of the wartime generations and those born after the war. Even the experiences of the victims themselves are thus fragmented. One need only think of the trials of Klaus Barbie and Paul Touvier, and of the fact that accusations of victims from the Resistance were deemed inadmissible. Or one may recall the Papon trial, in which Resistance leaders were attacked by the prosecution, because they affirmed that Papon had helped the Resistance at the end of the Occupation. And in the name of the singularity of the Holocaust, Jews once again are placed into a group strangely separated from the nation's memory. In one of the most emblematic examples of this paradoxical and frightening tendency, President Jacques Chirac decided to place the card files unearthed by Serge Klarsfeld, and later by the Rémond Commission, in the Memorial to the Unknown Jew rather than in the National Archives.[13]

The message that should have been sent was that Vichy's crimes concerned the entire nation, that the entire nation has to accept this legacy, that these crimes were not only crimes against Jews but crimes *against humanity.* Instead Chirac's gesture sent the opposite message; it was as if this part of history really concerned an affair of 'the community', rather than the whole French people.

A New Judicial Discourse on the Past

Robert Paxton has shown how he sought to differentiate himself from the judicial discourses that had so deeply influenced interpretations of Vichy through the 1960s. Historiographically, this departure had a liberating effect. It allowed historians gradually to move beyond an inquisitorial form of discourse. This may have been necessary from a moral perspective, but it proved to be cumbersome, not to say counter-productive, from a scholarly perspective. Above all, this departure allowed historians to seek out new areas of investigation that did not fit into the judicial logic of the post-war period. Analyses of such areas as the evolution of public opinion, the real impact of the regime on French society, and French antisemitic policies could be produced only after historians had thrown off the perspective of the early trials of Vichy leaders, precisely because those kinds of questions could not be raised during the trials of the post-war purge.

What a paradox now to see a different judicial discourse use these analyses, and even the historians who formulated them, in the context of belated prosecutions for crimes against humanity! During the Touvier and Papon trials, many historians, including Paxton, were called upon to testify as 'experts', raising a host of ethical and scholarly questions. It is indeed an irony of history that the 'Paxtonian' view of Vichy, born of a break from the judicial paradigm of the immediate post-war period, has played a decisive role in shaping the judicial paradigm of the past twenty years. Yet if historians are to re-adopt Paxton's strategy of twenty years ago, they should, it seems, move away from the new judicial paradigm, which greatly narrows the scope of historical vision. Today's paradigm focuses on racial persecution. It rests on a degree of forgetting the post-war repression of collaboration, and it highlights the responsibility of relatively minor officials, to the detriment of broader historical processes. Above all, it privileges a judicial logic inscribed in texts written after the fact, to the detriment of a historical vision of things.

The Image of the Foreigner

Robert Paxton has been lionized. But he has also, at least at the beginning, been strongly criticized. One criticism, expressed repeatedly over the past twenty-five years, is worth examining. In retrospect, this criticism is interesting not so much historiographically, but as an indicator of the position Robert Paxton, as a historian and as a foreigner, has occupied in the French imagination.

> After having studied collaboration, Paxton knew enough about French masochism to be sure that he would encounter commentators, in publications from the *Nouvel Observateur* to *Mademoiselle Age Tendre,* who were delighted to see their country dragged through the mud, even by an American.[14]
>
> Robert Paxton condemns Vichy as a choice, and especially the unchanging behavior of the regime. He does not, however, have corresponding praise for its adversaries. This is so much the case that a light scent of hostility toward France rises from this book, whose research and interpretation deserve so much praise.[15]

It is clear that for his detractors at the time, Robert Paxton's greatest fault was to have been a 'foreigner', and even worse, an 'American'. An unredeemable flaw in 1973, this characteristic has mutated over the years into a central virtue. 'Must one be American to write the history of Vichy France?' wrote Jacques Ozouf in 1973.[16] This leitmotif has been heard again and again since that time, even during the Papon trial. For the sake of anecdote, one can mention an example that caricatures this tendency to claim that enlightenment on the matter can come only from 'elsewhere'. It is a modest article, recently printed in an official publication of the *Centre National de la Recherche Scientifique* (CNRS – France's national scientific and research organization and parent of the *Institut d'histoire du temps présent*, which has been studying Vichy for twenty years). The article deals with the polemic on the alleged inaccessibility of the Vichy archives – another cliché that systematically invokes Robert Paxton and his experience early in the 1970's to describe a very different situation today: 'The first book to deal seriously with the 1940–1945 period in France was written by an American [Robert Paxton]; and one of the best-informed books on this same period was written by a Swiss historian [Philippe Burrin]. Could it be that there is more open access to foreign archives than to our own?'[17] In the deluge of criticisms aimed at French historians, their alleged failure to use Swiss archives is perhaps the most surprising. Do we need to remind ourselves that most of the documentation Philippe Burrin used in his book *La France à l'heure allemande* [*France Under the Germans*] came from French public archives?

One may certainly smile at such statements. But the cliché – that only 'foreigners', even today, can write the history of Vichy – deserves examination. For that cliché still matters in the ongoing debate over the ability of the French to confront their past. In this context, two questions can be asked: is this cliché justified? And, whether it is or not, what is its function, and to what use is it most often put?

We can easily answer the first question in the negative. First of all, one need only look at the abundant French scholarship on Vichy. Furthermore, history as a scholarly discipline is practiced in an environment that knows no boundaries, with all researchers belonging to the same community of scholars. In this regard, the idea of a 'foreign historian' simply makes no sense.

But these common-sense answers do not fully resolve the problem. First, the notion of a 'national historiography' always has a certain relevance, as shown above in the debate over French 'exceptionality'. Moreover, if one goes beyond generalities one can argue that historians of the Second World War face special difficulties depending on their position in relation to the subject-matter. Just like German historians of Nazism or Italian historians of fascism (to take but two examples), French historians of Vichy have been obliged to reflect not only on the traditional and intrinsic problems of sources or interpretations posed by the history of the 1930s and 1940s, but also (and perhaps more than some) on two much larger questions.

First they have been forced to think, often on the spot, about how to write their country's history – how best to present this history to the public, how to respond to society's need for memory. This public aspect has sometimes taken the form of pressure from the media or the judicial system. In France, this pressure has continued for twenty years. French scholars of Vichy have thus been more or less obliged to develop their own understanding of their professional responsibilities as historians. It is as if writing the history of Vichy, more than that of any other period, allows one to sense the limitations of the profession, as well as its profound necessity. Clearly, French historians of Vichy are far from alone in this respect. One does not need to be German to grasp what is at stake in the history of Nazism. Nor does one need to be a historian of the twentieth century to reflect on the profession of historian. But unlike their colleagues, historians of the recent and painful past become actors caught up in the controversies surrounding national memory, making the need to reflect on their professional role no longer a mere epistemological exercise, but a vital necessity. From the German *Historikerstreit* to French debates over Vichy, examples illustrating this particularity are plentiful. The emergence of historians as actors is especially striking in the positions historians have more or less willingly adopted, as 'official experts', judicial witnesses, and voices of moral conscience.

On the other hand, and just as importantly, interest has revived in contemporary history in most of the countries of Western Europe that experienced German occupation. This renewal has been accompanied by a reconsideration of the very possibility of writing the 'history of the present time'. Whole new scholarly institutions were created to that end. From Belgium to Italy, and including Holland, France and of course West Germany, the examples are numerous. In France, it is certainly not by chance that the 'history of the present time' emerged just a few years after the 'event' created by the publication of Paxton's *Vichy France*. Part of the mission of the *Institut d'histoire du temps présent* involved writing an alternative history of the Occupation, a period that had suffered from indifference on the part of university scholars. Yet the Occupation now came to be redefined, rightly or wrongly, as the womb from which was born the history of France in the second half of the twentieth century.

Seeing that the old cliché unintentionally reveals the role of 'foreignness' in writing the history of the Occupation, and that the situation of French historians has differed from that of others, what then is the significance of this cliché in public opinion? Why do some find it necessary even today to repeat endlessly that 'France is incapable of confronting its past', when it has been doing so almost daily for the past quarter-century? Why has the situation of the 1970s persisted as received wisdom in the 1990s, despite overwhelming evidence to the contrary? How have we gone from an amnesia or denial about the dark years to an obsession about them in collective memory? It is as hard today to *admit* that France is effectively confronting its Vichy past as it was twenty years ago!

It should be abundantly clear, however, that all aspects of the period do not present, or no longer present, the same moral and political difficulties for historical research that they did twenty years ago. It is much easier today to break the supposed 'taboos' about Vichy than those surrounding the history of the resistance, or anti-fascism, or communism. Recent examples are plentiful; the paths of inquiry in these areas will be just as long, difficult, and quarrelsome as they have been with French fascism and Vichy.

In effect, the real issue is not so much 'confronting' the past as coming to terms with and accepting it. That is, we need to live with the loss of de

Gaulle's 'certain idea of France' and instead live with the knowledge of the irreparable harm done by crimes the nation of the 'Rights of Man' committed. The problem is not so much facing up to this past with lucidity and courage. Younger generations surely can do this, all the more so because they did not live through the Occupation, with all its tragedies and dilemmas. Rather, the problem lies in integrating this past into the national narrative, and, even more, into the image we wish to fashion of our country's history. From this problem has come the recurrence of anachronisms, the tendency to excess, and the willed darkness of the reconstituted picture. Fundamentally, the phase of forgetting and the phase of obsession – if those characterizations can be considered accurate – describe one and the same reality. They speak to a past that will not become the past, a history we first tried to eliminate. But unable to do so, we created a past that we continually ruminate upon and chew over, in the Nietzschian sense. Our history of Vichy contains an 'overflow' of past and memory that demonstrates our difficulty in confronting the future, and no doubt a far deeper crisis of national identity than we care to admit.

It is in this sense that the figure of the 'foreigner' has been so important, as though only a stranger could have caused this salutary shock. But since, a half-century later, the difficulty persists, not in confronting the past but in accepting it, I find myself led to another difficulty, one that characterizes the task of the historian. How is one to restore the past to its proper place, how simultaneously to eliminate the distance created by the passage of time and to free oneself from the weight of this past in the present? How can one manage this dialectic of distancing and proximity – of 'the past as a foreign country' and the past that continues to live in our present?

In *The Sophist,* Plato begins with a brief exchange between Socrates and the mathematician Theodorus. The latter introduces him to one of the figures of pre-Socratic philosophy, a 'stranger from Elea'. Socrates replies:

> Are you bringing a visitor, Theodorus? Or are you bringing a god without realizing it instead, like the ones Homer mentions? He says gods accompany people who are respectful and just. He also says the god of visitors – who is at least as much a god as any other – is a companion who keeps an eye on people's actions, both the criminal and the lawful ones. So your visitor might be a greater power following along with you, a sort of god of refutation to keep watch on us and show how bad we are at speaking – and to refute us.[18]

Because historians confront the otherness of the past, because they do their best to distance themselves from the past and to bring back a critical image to their contemporaries, are they not, at least some of the time, like these strangers of classical philosophy?

In this sense, we are all 'foreign' historians, we are all 'American' historians.

Translated by David Lake and Leonard V. Smith

Notes

1. Pierre Nora, 'L'Ère de la commémoration', in Pierre Nora (ed.), *Les Lieux de mémoire,* volume III, *Les France,* vol. 3: 1004.
2. See Henry Rousso, *The Vichy Syndrome: History and Memory in France since 1944*, trans. Arthur Goldhammer (Cambridge, MA, 1991): 276. The concept of *nouvelle histoire* has been used in the media and the academic world since the early 1970s to emphasize the growing popularity of historians like Georges Duby, Jacques Le Goff, Emmanuel Le Roy Ladurie and many others, who drew in various ways from the tradition initiated by the *Annales*.
3. Information generously supplied by the Éditions du Seuil in November 1997.
4. See Stanley Hoffmann's account (in *Revue française de science politique,* XXIII, 3, June 1973) of the conference organized by René Rémond, and held in 1970 at the *Fondation nationale des sciences politiques*. The proceedings of the conference itself were published as: *Le gouvernement de Vichy. Institutions et politiques* (Paris, 1972).
5. See Eric Conan and Henry Rousso, *Vichy, An Ever-Present Past,* trans. Nathan Bracher (Hanover, NH, 1998): 91. This judgment was overturned, and Touvier finally faced trial in 1994.
6. Quoted by Ruth Zylberman, 'Robert Paxton. Un Américain tranquille à Vichy', *L'Histoire,* no. 203 (October 1996): 20.
7. According to Paxton himself, he was not explicitly 'denied' access to the French archives. Rather, he was implicitly 'dissuaded' from requesting from the National Archives the special authorizations needed to consult documents dated after 10 July 1940, the legislated limit date in effect at the time. Theoretically, no public documents after this date were available for consultation. The system of 'exemptions' (*dérogations*) did not exist until the law of 3 January 1979.

Special authorizations had been refused to Paxton for the most part, even though some years later the National Archives had the nerve to say that they had not been asked directly by him at the time.

8. A card file dating from the war years with information about Jews in the Seine Department resurfaced in 1991, raising a furor about where it came from, whether it issued from the census of Jews taken under the antisemitic Alibert laws in October 1940. Another furor arose over what to do with the card file, and a commission headed by the notable French historian René Rémond was appointed to decide where the card file would eventually reside. For more on this controversy, see Conan and Rousso, *Vichy, Un passé qui ne passe pas*, 1st ed., (Paris, 1994), 67-83.
9. Alain-Gérard Slama, 'Les yeux d'Abetz', *Contrepoint,* April 1973.
10. See Conan and Rousso, *Vichy, An Ever-Present Past.*
11. See *Le Monde,* 22 July 1997. Emphasis added.
12. Stanley Hoffmann, 'Chagrin et pitié?', *Contrepoint,* April 1973.
13. See Stanley Hoffmann, 'Battling Clichés', *French Historical Studies,* vol. 19, no. 2 (Fall 1995).
14. Alain-Gérard Slama, 'Les yeux d'Abetz', *Contrepoint* (April 1973): 20.
15. Henri Michel, *Revue d'histoire de la Deuxième Guerre mondiale,* no. 93 (January 1974): 117.
16. Jacques Ozouf, 'Maréchal, vous voilà!', *Le Nouvel Observateur,* 29 January 1973.
17. *CAES Info,* January 1997, 8. This is the newsletter of the community service branch of the CNRS.
18. Plato, *The Sophist,* trans. Nicholas P. White (Indianapolis, IN, 1993): 1.

Appendix

Table 1. Reviews or notices of Paxton's *La France de Vichy*, compiled by John Sweets

L'Agent de Liaison	February–March 1973	
Alfred Fabre-Luce vous parle	No. 5, 1 March 1973	A. Fabre-Luce
Amitié Judéo-Chrétienne	February–March 1974	Jean-Rémy Palanque
Annales, E.S.C.	Vol.28, #2, March–April 1973	'Les Choix des Annales'
Aspects de la France	17 May 1973	Pierre van Altena
L'Aurore	3 February 1973	Dominique Jamet
Biblio, Hebdo	No. 68, 1 March 1973	Jean-Pierre Rioux
Bulletin des lettres	15 May 1973	François Miaudet
Bulletin critique du livre	December 1973	
Les Cahiers Bourbonnais	July 1974	
Cahiers d'Histoire de l'Institut Maurice Thorez	No. 3, Nouvelle Série (31), April–May–June 1973	Roger Martelli
Centre Presse (Limoges)	14 June 1974	
Centre protestant d'études et de documentation	January 1974	
Combat Lettres	24 January 1973	Jean Texier
Contrepoint	Vol. 10, April 1973	Alain-Gérard Slama
Défense Nationale	July 1973	A.N.
La Dépêche la Liberté (St-Etienne) and ***Echo la Liberté (Lyon)***	4 April 1973	
Droit de Vivre	February 1973	Jean Pierre-Bloch
L'Education	22 March 1973	Gérard Fournier
Esprit	No.427, September 1973	Jean-Pierre Azéma

Table 1. *(continued)*

L'Express	#1127, 12–18 February 1973	Max Gallo
Le Figaro	10 February 1973	Jean-François Kahn
France Catholique-Ecclesia	No. 1379, 18 May 1973	Michel Denis
France Nouvelle	1974?	Roger Bourderon
Frontière	April 1973	
Historama	April 1973	
Information Juive	March 1973	Henry Bulawko
Les Informations	26 February 1973	A.-G. S.
Informations ouvrières	#607, 18–26 April 1973	
Journal de Dimanche	15 February 1973	René Maine
Journal de Genève	28 April 1973	
Magazine Littéraire	April 1973	Frantz-André Burguet
Le Maréchal	No. 90, April–May 1973	Amiral P. Auphan
Marie Claire		Pierre Serval
La Marseillaise	26 May 1976	Pierre Durand
Le Monde	1 February 1973	Paul Gillet
Le Monde	22 March 1973	P. Auphan and J. de Launay
Le Monde	12 April 1973	S. Hoffmann and P. Dhers
Le Monde	17 May 1973	J. Borotra, A. Fabre-Luce, P. Picon, and P. Auphan
Le Monde Juif	No. 70, April–June 1973	
La Nouvelle Critique	No. 63, April 1973	Jean Charles
Paris Normandie	15 March 1973	
Le Patriote Résistant	No. 402, April 1973	Gérard Bouaziz
Presse Nouvelle Hebdo	No. 257, 20 April 1973	Lucien Steinberg
Preuves	2nd Trimester 1973	Roger Massip

Table 1. *(continued)*

Le Progrès de Lyon	25 March 1973	Robert Buheau
La Quinzaine Littéraire	16–28 February 1973	Marc Ferro
Revue de la politique française	March 1973	
Revue française de science politique	Vol. 23,#3, June 1973	Janine Bourdin
Revue Générale	May 1973	
Revue d'Histoire de la deuxième guerre mondiale	No. 93, January 1974	Henri Michel
Revue Historique	#516, Oct.–December 1975	Georges Soutou
Techniques Nouvelles	May 1973	
Témoignage Chrétien	22 February 1973	F. Fonvieille Alguier (?)
La Tribune de Genève	14 May 1973	Henri Guillemin
La Tribune Socialiste	14 June 1973	Jean François Merle
Université des sciences juridiques politiques et sociales de Strasbourg	3rd Trimester 1974	
L'Unité	26 January 1973	Nicolas Bruno
La Vie Catholique Illustrée	20 June 1973	

Table 2. Reviews or notices of Paxton's *Vichy et les Juifs*, compiled by John Sweets

L'Alsace	18 October 1981	Michel Cornaert
L'Arche	June 1981	Arnold Mandel
Bulletin de ADBR	No. 154, November 1981	Jacques Goldstain
Cahiers Bernard Lazare	October 1981	Yehoshua Rash
Cahiers Bernard Lazare	February 1982	
Le Canard Enchainé	13 May 1981	Jean Clémentin
Centre Protestant d'Etudes et de Documentation	No. 365	M.C. Kok-Escalle
La Croix	17–18 May 1981	Jean-Pierre Rioux

Table 2. *(continued)*

Différences	October 1981	Pierre-André Taguieff
Le Droit de Vivre	June 1981	Paul Giniewski
Les Echos	2 June 1981	J. CH.
Etudes	July 1981	Jean Legrès
L'Express	No. 1556, 5–11 May 1981	Max Gallo
Le Figaro	22 May 1981	Gilles Lambert
Histoire	No. 38, October 1981	
Histoire Magazine		
Historiens et Geographes	February 1982	J.-M. d'Hoop
L'Humanité		Paul Dupont
Information Juive	1–6 June 1981	Claude Lévy
Le Matin	7 May 1981	Daniel Lindberg
Le Matin	8 July 1981	Philippe Serre
Le Monde des Livres	8 May 1981	Alain Guichard
Le Monde Juif	No. 103, July–September 1981	Georges Wellers
Nouvel Observateur	27 April–3 May 1981	François Furet
Les Nouvelles Littéraires	21 May 1981	P.E.
Les Nouvelles Littéraires	11 June 1981	Pierre Enckell
Les Nouvelles Littéraires	11 June 1981	Laurent S. Munnich
Nouvelle République du Centre Ouest	5 June 1981	O. Noyer
Panorama du Médecin		
Le Patriote Résistant	July 1981	Guy Morel
Le Point	No. 448, 18 April 1981	
Projet	1982	
La Quinzaine Littéraire	16 September 1981	Jean-Pierre Azéma
Le Quotidien de Paris	14 May 1981	Emile Malet
Réforme	27 June 1981	F. Lovsky

Table 2. *(continued)*

Revue d'histoire de la deuxième guerre mondiale et des conflits contemporains	No. 133, January 1984	Georges Wellers
Revue française de science politique	Vol. 33, no.4, August 1983	Nicole Racine-Furlaud
Revue Juive (Geneva)		Roland S. Sussmann
Rouge	No. 970, 22–28 May 1981	Jean-François Vilar
Sens	1982–83	Jacques Madaule
Témoignage Chrétien	6 July 1981	Annette Wieviorka
Tribune Juive	30 October–5 November 1981	Roger Berg
La Vie	21 May 1981	M.F.
VSD	25 June 1981	Pascal Lainé

Contributors and Editors

Jean-Pierre Azéma
Institut d'études politiques, Paris
From Munich to the Liberation 1938–1944; with François Bédarida, *Vichy et les Français* and *La France des années noires*

Philippe Burrin
Institut Universitaire de Hautes Etudes Internationales, Switzerland
La Dérive fasciste; Hitler and the Jews; France under the Germans: Collaboration and Compromise

Laura Lee Downs
Department of History
University of Michigan
Manufacturing Inequality: Gender Division in the French and British Metalworking Industries 1914–1939

Yves Durand
Université d'Orléans
Vichy, 1940–1944; La Captivité: Histoire des prisonniers de guerre français 1939–1945; Le Loiret dans la guerre; La France dans la 2e guerre mondiale 1939–1945

Sarah Farmer
Department of History
University of Iowa
Oradour: Arrêt sur mémoire; Martyred Village: Commemorating the 1944 Massacre at Oradour-sur-Glane

Sarah Fishman
Department of History
University of Houston
We Will Wait: Wives of French Prisoners of War, 1940–1945

Bertram Gordon
Mills College
Collaborationism in France during the Second World War; Editor, *Historical Dictionary of World War II France: The Occupation, Vichy, and the Resistance (1938–1946)*

W. D. Halls
formerly of St. Antony's College
University of Oxford
The Youth of Vichy France; Politics, Society and Christianity in Vichy France

John Hellman
Department of History
McGill University
The Knight Monks of Vichy France; Emmanuel Mounier and the New Catholic Left

Stanley Hoffmann
Center for European Studies
Harvard University
Decline or Renewal? France Since the 1930s; Editor, *In Search of France;* 'Collaborationism in France During World War II', *Journal of Modern History*, September 1968

H. R. Kedward
School of European Studies
University of Sussex
Resistance in Vichy France; In Search of the Maquis: Rural Resistance in Southern France 1942–1944

Pierre Laborie
Centre de Recherches Historiques
Ecole des Hautes-Etudes, Université de Toulouse-Le Mirail
Résistants, Vichysois et autres; L'Opinion française sous Vichy

Michael Marrus
School of Graduate Studies
University of Toronto
The Holocaust in History; The Unwanted: European Refugees in the 20th Century; The Politics of Assimilation: The French Jewish Community at the Time of the Dreyfus Affair; with Robert Paxton, *Vichy France and the Jews*

Pascal Ory
Contemporary History
University of Paris I, Sorbonne
Les Collaborateurs 1940–1945; La France allemande: paroles du collaborationisme français

Denis Peschanski
Institut d'histoire du temps present
Ecole Normale Superieure de Cachan
Vichy 1940–1944: Contrôle et exclusion; La France de Vichy: Archives inedites d'Angelo Tasca; with Laurent Gervereau, *La Progagande sous Vichy 1940–1944*

Miranda Pollard
Department of History
University of Georgia
Reign of Virtue: Mobilizing Gender in Vichy France

Jean-Pierre Rioux
Institut d'histoire du temps present
Ecole Normale Superieure de Cachan
La vie culturelle sous Vichy; Contributor to Azema and Bedarida, *Vichy et les français* and *La France des années noires*

Henry Rousso
Institut d'histoire du temps présent
Ecole Normale Superieure de Cachan
The Vichy Syndrome: History and Memory in France Since 1944; with Eric Conan, *Vichy: Un Passé qui ne passe pas*

Ioannis Sinanoglou
Executive Director, Council for European Studies
Columbia University
Articles in *French Politics and Society*, *International History Review*, *Cahiers du Monde russe et soviétique*

Leonard V. Smith
Department of History
Oberlin College
Between Mutiny and Obedience: The Case of the French Fifth Infantry Division during World War I

John Sweets
Department of History
University of Kansas
The Politics of Resistance in France, 1940–1944: A History of the Mouvements Unis de la Resistance; Choices in Vichy France

Dominique Veillon
Institut d'histoire du temps présent
Ecole Normale Superieure de Cachan
'*Le Franc-Tireur*', *un journal clandestin, un mouvement de résistance; La Collaboration; La Mode sous L'Occupation; Vivre et Survivre en France, 1939–1947*

Robert Zaretsky
Honors College and Department of Modern and Classical Languages
University of Houston
Nîmes at War: Religion, Politics, and Public Opinion in the Department of the Gard, 1938–1944

Select Bibliography

Added, Serge. (1992) *Le théâtre dans les années Vichy*, Paris: Ramsay.

Alary, Eric. (1996) *La ligne de démarcation*, Paris: Presses Universitaires de France.

Andrieu, Claire. (1990) *La Banque sous l'occupation*, Paris: Fondation Nationale des Sciences Politiques.

Aron, Robert. (1958) *The Vichy Regime, 1940–1944,* trans. Georgette Elgey. London: Putnam.

Atkin, Nicholas. (1998) *Pétain*, London: Longman.

Azéma, Jean-Pierre. (1975) *La collaboration*, Paris: Presses universitaires de France.

Azéma, Jean-Pierre. (1979) *De Munich à la Libération, 1938–1944*, Paris: Le Seuil.

Azéma, Jean-Pierre. (1990) *L'Année Terrible*, Paris: Seuil.

Azéma, Jean-Pierre and Bédarida, François (eds). (1992) *Le Régime de Vichy et les Français*, Paris: Fayard.

Azéma, Jean-Pierre and Bédarida, François (eds). (1993) *La France des Années Noires* (2 vols), Paris: Seuil.

Azéma, Jean-Pierre and Bédarida, François (eds). (1995) *Les années de tourmente, dictionnaire critique, 1938–1948*, Paris: Flammarion.

Azéma, Jean-Pierre, Prost, Antoine, and Rioux, Jean-Pierre (eds). (1986) *Le Parti communiste français des années sombres, 1938–1941*, Paris: Seuil.

Azéma, Jean-Pierre and Wieviorka, Olivier. (1997) *Vichy 1940–44*, Paris: Perrin.

Bailly, Jacques-Augustin. (1993) *La Libération confisquée, le Languedoc, 1944–45*, Paris: Albin Michel.

Barthélémy, Joseph. (1989) *Ministre de la Justice, Vichy 1941–1943. Mémoires*, Paris: Pygmalion.

Baruch, Marc-Olivier. (1996) *Le régime de Vichy*, Paris: La Découverte.

Baruch, Marc-Olivier. (1997) *Servir l'Etat français: l'administration en France de 1940 à 1944*, Paris: Fayard.

Bédarida, François. (1979) *La Stratégie secrète de la drôle de guerre*, Paris: Presses de la fondation nationale des sciences politiques.

Bédarida, Renée. (1977) *Les Armes de l'esprit: Témoignage chrétien, 1941–1944*, Paris: Editions ouvrières.

Benedite, Daniel. (1984) *La filière marseillaise*, Paris: Clancier Guénaud.

Bertin, Célia. (1993) *Femmes sous l'Occupation*, Paris: Stock.

Bertin-Maght, Jean-Pierre. (1989) *Le cinéma sous l'occupation*, Paris: Olivier Orban.

Bertrand-Dorléac, Laurence. (1993) *L'art de la défaite*, Paris: Seuil.

Bloch, Marc. (1990) *L'étrange défaite*, Paris: Gallimard.

Boegner, Philippe (ed.) (1992) *Carnets du pasteur Boegner, 1940–45*, Paris: Fayard.

Bordeaux, Michèle. (1987) 'Femmes hors d'Etat français, 1940–1944', in *Femmes et fascismes*, ed. Rita Thalmann, Paris: Tierce.

Boulanger, Gérard. (1994) *Maurice Papon, un technocrate dans la collaboration*, Paris: Seuil.

Bourderon, Roger and Avakoumovitch, Yvan. (1988) *Détruire le PCF: archives de l'Etat français et de l'occupant hitlérien, 1940–44*, Paris: Messidor.

Boussard, Isabelle. (1980) *Vichy et la Corporation Paysanne*, Paris: Fondation Nationale des Sciences Politiques.

Brossat, Alain. (1992) *Les Tondues: un carnaval moche*, Paris: Manya.

Burrin, Philippe. (1986) *La dérive fasciste, Doriot, Déat, Bergery*, Paris: Seuil.

Burrin, Philippe. (1995) *La France à l'heure allemande: 1940–1944*, Paris: Le Seuil.

Canaud, Jacques. (1981) *Les Maquis du Morvan 1943–1944: La vie dans les maquis*, Château-Chinon: Académie du Morvan.

Chauvière, Michel. (1980) *Enfance inadaptée, l'héritage de Vichy*, Paris: Les Editions ouvrières.

Chevance-Bertin, Maurice. (1990) *Vingt Mille Heures d'angoisse, 1940–45*, Paris: Laffont.

Cochet, François. (1992) *Les Exclus de la victoire. Histoire des PG, déportés et STO, 1945–1985*, Paris: Kronos.

Cohen, Asher. (1993) *Persécutions et sauvetages, Juifs et Français sous l'Occupation et sous Vichy*, Paris: Cerf.

Cohen-Grillet, Philippe. (1997) *Maurice Papon, de la collaboration aux assises*, Paris: Le Bord de l'Eau.

Cointet, Jean-Paul. (1993) *Pierre Laval*, Paris: Fayard.

Cointet, Jean-Paul. (1995) *Histoire de Vichy*, Paris: Plon.

Cointet, Jean-Paul. (1995) *La légion française des combattants*, Paris: Albin Michel.

Cointet-Labrousse, Michèle. (1987) *Vichy et le fascisme*, Brussels: Complexe.

Conan, Eric and Rousso, Henry. (1994) *Vichy, un passé qui ne passe pas*, Paris: Gallimard 'Folio'.

Cone, Michèle. (1992) *Artists under Vichy*, Princeton, NJ: Princeton University Press.

Courtois, Stéphane, Peschanski, Denis and Rayski, Adam. (1989), *Le sang de l'étranger*, Paris: Fayard.

Courtois, Stéphane and Rayski, Adam (eds). (1987) *Qui savait quoi? L'extermination des Juifs, 1941–1945*, Paris: La Découverte.

Couteau-Begarie, Hervé and Huan, Claude. (1989) *Darlan*, Paris: Fayard.

Craipeau, Yvan. (1978) *La Libération confisquée: 1944–1947*, Paris: Savelli Syros.

Delperrie de Bayac, Jacques. (1975) *Le royaume du maréchal: histoire de la zone libre*, Paris: Laffont.

Delperrie de Bayac, Jacques. (1994) *Histoire de la Milice, 1918–1945*, Paris: Fayard.

Dermenjian, Geneviève (ed.) (1991) *Femmes, Famille et Action ouvrière: pratiques et responsabilités dans les mouvements familiaux populaires (1935–1958)*, Villeneuve d'Ascq: Les Cahiers du Groupement pour la Recherche sur les Mouvements Familiaux.

Dompnier, N. (1996) *Vichy à travers chants: pour une analyse politique du sens et de l'usage des hymnes sous Vichy*, Paris: Nathan.

Douzou, Laurent. (1995) *La Désobéissance: histoire d'un mouvement et d'un journal clandestins: Libération Sud (1940–1943)*, Paris: Odile Jacob.

Douzou, Laurent, Frank, Robert, Peschanski, Denis and Veillon, Dominique (eds) (1995) *La Résistance et les Français: villes, centres et logiques de décision*, Cachan/Paris: Institut d'histoire du temps présent.

Douzou, Laurent, Frank, Robert, Peschanski, Denis and Veillon, Dominique (eds) (1997) *La Résistance et les Européens du sud: Pré-Actes*, Aix-en-Provence: UMR Telemme1997.

Duquesne, Jacques (1966) *Les catholiques français sous l'occupation*, Paris: Grasset.

Durand, Yves. (1973) *Vichy, 1940–1944*, Paris: Bordas.

Durand, Yves. (1987) *La Captivité: Histoire des prisonniers de guerre français 1939–1945*, Paris: FNCPG-CATM.

Durand, Yves. (1993) *La France dans la deuxième guerre mondiale*, Paris: Armand Colin 'Cursus'.

Duroselle, Jean-Baptiste. (1990) *Politique étrangère de la France, l'abîme, 1939–1944*, Paris: Seuil, 'Points'.

Farmer, Sarah. (1999) *Martyred Village: Commemorating the 1944 Massacre at Oradour-sur-Glane*, Berkeley, CA: University of California Press.

Faure, Christian. (1989) *Le Projet culturel de Vichy: folklore et révolution nationale*, Lyons: Presses universitaires de Lyon.
Ferro, Marc. (1990) *Pétain*, Paris: Hachette, 'Pluriel'.
Finger, Blanche and Karel, William. (1992) *Opération 'Vent printanier'. 16–17 juillet 1942: La rafle du Vel'd'Hiv*, Paris: La Découverte.
Fishman, Sarah. (1991) *We Will Wait: Wives of French Prisoners of War*, New Haven, CT: Yale University Press.
Fondation Charles de Gaulle. (1996) *Le rétablissement de la légalité républicaine*, Brussels: Complexe.
Footit, Hilary and Simmonds, John. (1988) *France 1943–45*, Leicester University Press.
Fourcade, Marie-Madeleine. (1989) *L'arche de Noé,* Paris: Plon.
Frenay, Henri. (1973) *La nuit finira*, Paris: R. Laffont.
Froment, Pascal. (1994) *René Bousquet*, Paris: Stock.
Fry, Varian. (1997) *Surrender on demand*, Boulder, CO: Johnson Books.
Gervereau, L. and Peschanski, D. (1990) *La Propagande sous Vichy, 1940–44*, Paris: BDIC.
Giolitto, Pierre. (1991) *Histoire de la jeunesse sous Vichy*, Paris: Perrin.
Giolitto, Pierre. (1997) *Histoire de la Milice*, Paris: Perrin.
Golsan, Richard J. (ed.) (1996) *Memory, the Holocaust, and French Justice: The Bousquet and Touvier Affairs,* Hanover, NH: University Press of New England.
Gordon, Bertram M. (1980) *Collaborationism in France during the Second World War*, Ithaca, NY: Cornell University Press.
Gordon, Bertram M. (1998) *Historical Dictionary of World War II France: The Occupation, Vichy and the Resistance, 1938–1946*, Westport, CT: Greenwood.
Le Gouvernement de Vichy (1972) Paris: Colin.
Grandjonc, Jacques and Grundtner, Theresia (eds). (1990) *Zone d'Ombres, 1933–1944*, Aix-en-Provence: Alinéa.
Greilsamer, L. and Schneiderman, D. (1994) *Un certain monsieur Paul*, Paris: Fayard.
Grynberg, Anne. (1991) *Les camps de la honte*, Paris: La découverte.
Guillon, Jean-Marie. (1994) *Le Var, la guerre, la résistance, 1939–45, Imprim*. Le Revest: Hemisud.
Guillon, Jean-Marie and Buton, Philippe (eds). (1994) *Les pouvoirs en France à la Libération*, Paris: Belin.
Guillon, Jean-Marie and Laborie, Pierre (eds). (1995) *Mémoire et Histoire: la Résistance*, Toulouse: Privat.
Halls, W. D. (1981) *The Youth of Vichy France*, Oxford: Oxford University Press.

Halls, W. D. (1995) *Politics, Society and Christianity in Vichy France*, Oxford and Providence: Berg.

Hawthorne, Melanie and Richard J. Golsan (eds). (1997) *Gender and Fascism in Modern Europe*, Hanover, NH: University Press of New England.

Hellman, John. (1993) *The Knight-Monks of Vichy France: Uriage, 1940–1944,* Montreal: McGill-Queen's University Press.

Hirschfield, Gerhard and Marsh, Patrick (eds). (1989) *Collaboration in France*, New York: Berg.

Hoffmann, Stanley. (1968) 'Collaborationism in Vichy France', *Journal of Modern History* 40, no. 3 (1968): 375–95.

Hoffmann, Stanley. (1974) *Decline or Renewal? France Since the 1930s*, New York: Viking.

Jaeckel, Eberhard. (1968) *La France dans l'Europe de Hitler*, trans. Denis Meunier, Paris: Fayard.

Jankowski, Paul. (1989) *Communism and Collaboration: Simon Sabiani and politics in Marseille, 1919–1944*, London: Yale University Press.

Joutard, Philippe, Jacques Poujol and Patrick Cabanel (eds). (1987) *Cévennes, terre de refuge 1940–1944*. Montpellier: Club Cévenol.

Kaspi, André. (1991) *Les Juifs pendant l'occupation*, Paris: Seuil.

Kedward, H. R. (1978) *Resistance in Vichy France*, Oxford: Oxford University Press.

Kedward, H. R. (1985) *Occupied France. Collaboration and Resistance*, Oxford: Basil Blackwell.

Kedward, H. R. (1993) *In Search of the Maquis: Rural Resistance in Southern France, 1942–1944*, Oxford: Oxford University Press.

Kedward, H. R. and Austin, R. (1995) *Vichy France and the Resistance: Culture and Ideology*, London: Croom Helm.

Kedward, H. R. and Wood, Nancy. (1995) *The Liberation of France. Image and Event*, Oxford: Berg.

Klarsfeld, Serge. (1983) *Vichy–Auschwitz. Le rôle de Vichy dans la solution finale de la question juive en France, 1942*, 2 vols, Paris: Fayard.

Klarsfeld, Serge. (1993) *Le calendrier de la persécution des Juifs en France, 1940–44*, Paris: Les Fils et Filles des déportés Juifs de France.

Kupferman, Fred. (1980) *1944–1945: le procès de Vichy: Pucheu, Pétain, Laval*, Brussels: Complexe.

Kupferman, Fred. (1983) *Laval, 1883–1945*, Paris: Flammarion.

Laborie, Pierre. (1980) *Résistants, vichyssois et autres. L'évolution de l'opinion et des comportements dans le Lot de 1939 à 1945*, Paris: CNRS.

Laborie, Pierre. (1990) *L'Opinion française sous Vichy*, Paris: Le Seuil.

Lambert, Raymond-Raoul. (1984) *Carnets d'un témoin, 1940–43*, Paris: Fayard.

Lazare, Lucien. (1996) *Rescue as Resistance, How Jewish Organizations Fought the Holocaust in France*, New York: Columbia University Press.

Le Crom, Jean-Pierre. (1994) *Syndicats nous voilà*, Paris: Editions de l'Atelier.

Levy, Paul. (1995) *Un camp de concentration français: Poitiers, 1939–1945*, Paris: Sedes.

Lottman, Herbert. (1985) *Pétain: Hero or Traitor*, New York: Morrow.

Madjarian, Grégoire. (1980) *Conflits, pouvoirs et société à la Libération*, Paris: Union Générale des Editions.

Marcot, François (ed.) (1996) *La Résistance et les Français: lutte armée et Maquis*, Besançon: Annales littéraires de l'Université de Franche-Compté.

Marrus, Michael and Paxton, Robert O. (1981) *Vichy France and the Jews*, New York, NY: Basic Books.

Michel, Henri. (1972) *Pétain, Laval, Darlan, Trois politiques?* Paris: Flammarion.

Michel, Henri. (1980) *La Deuxième guerre mondiale commence*, Brussels: Editions Complexe.

Michel, Henri. (1986) *Pétain et le régime de Vichy,* Paris: Presses universitaires de France.

Milza, Pierre and Berstein, Serge. (1992) *Dictionnaire historique des fascismes et du nazisme*, Brussels: Complexe.

Muel-Dreyfus, Francine. (1996) *Vichy et l'éternel féminin,* Paris: Seuil.

Novick, Peter. (1968) *The Resistance versus Vichy: The Purge of Collaborators in Liberated France*, London: Chatto & Windus.

Ophuls, Marcel. (1972) *The Sorrow and the Pity: A Film by Marcel Ophuls*, trans. Mireille Johnston, New York: Outerbridge and Lazard.

Oppetit, Christian (ed.) (1993) *Marseille, Vichy et les nazis. Le temps des rafles, la déportation des juifs*, Marseilles: Amicale des Déportés d'Auschwitz et des camps de Haute-Silésie.

Ory, Pascal. (1976) *Les Collaborateurs, 1940–1945*, Paris: Le Seuil.

Ory, Pascal. (1995) *La France Allemande*, Paris: Gallimard 'Folio-Histoire'.

Paxton, Robert O. (1966) *Parades and Politics at Vichy: The French Officer Corps under Marshal Pétain*, Princeton, NJ: Princeton University Press.

Paxton, Robert O. (1975 [1972]) *Vichy France. Old Guard and New Order, 1940–1944*, New York: Columbia University Press.

Peschanski, Denis (ed.). (1986) *Vichy 1940–44. Archives de guerre d'Angelo Tasca*, Paris: CNRS.

Peschanski, Denis. (1997) *Vichy 1940–1944. Contrôle et exclusion*, Brussels: Complexe.

Piteau, Michel (ed.). (1994) *La Provence et la France de Munich à la Libération (1938–1945)*, Aix-en-Provence: Diffusion Edisud.

Pollard, Miranda. (1998) *Reign of Virtue: Mobilizing Gender in Vichy France*, Chicago: University of Chicago Press.

Poznanski, Renée. (1994) *Etre Juif en France pendant la Seconde Guerre Mondiale*, Paris: Hachette.

Rayski, Adam. (1993) *Le Choix des Juifs sous Vichy*, Paris: La Découverte.

Rémond, René, Azéma, Jean-Pierre, and Bedarida, F. (1992) *Paul Touvier et l'Eglise*, Paris: Fayard.

Remy, Dominique (ed.). (1992) *Les lois de Vichy*, Paris: Romillat.

La Résistance et les Européens du Nord (1994), Brussels: Centre de Recherches et d'Etudes historiques de la Seconde Guerre Mondiale.

La Résistance et les Européens du Sud: Pré-Actes (1997), Aix-en-Provence: UMR Telemme.

Richer, Philippe. (1990) *La drôle de guerre des français, 2 septembre 1939–10 mai 1940*, Paris: Olivier Orban.

Rioux, Jean-Pierre (ed.). (1990) *La Vie culturelle sous Vichy*, Brussels: Complexe.

Rioux, Jean-Pierre, Prost, Antoine and Azéma, Jean-Pierre. (1987) *Les communistes français de Munich à Châteaubriant*, Paris: FNSP.

Rossignol, Dominique. (1981) *Vichy et les Francs-maçons. La liquidation des sociétés secrètes, 1940–1944*, Paris: J. C. Lattès.

Rossignol, Dominique. (1991) *Histoire de la propagande en France de 1940 à 1944. L'utopie Pétain*, Paris: Presses universitaires de France.

Rougeyron, A. (1996) *Agents for Escape. Inside the French Resistance, 1939–45*, Louisiana State University Press.

Rouquet, François. (1993) *L'épuration dans l'administration française*, Paris: CNRS.

Rousso, Henry. (1987) *La Collaboration*, Paris: Editions MA.

Rousso, Henry. (1990) *Le syndrome de Vichy de 1944 à nos jours*, 2nd edn, Paris: Le Seuil.

Rousso, Henry. (1992) *Les années noires: Vivre sous l'occupation*, Paris: Gallimard.

Ryan, Donna. (1996) *The Holocaust and the Jews of Marseilles: The Enforcement of Anti-semitic Policies in Vichy France*, Urbana, IL: University of Illinois Press.

Sadoun, Marc. (1982) *Les socialistes sous l'occupation*, Paris: FNSP.

Sainclivier, Jacqueline and Bougeard, Christian (eds). (1995) *La Résistance et les Français: enjeux stratégiques et environnement social*, Rennes: Presses Universitaires de Rennes.

Schor, Ralph. (1985) *L'opinion française et les étrangers, 1919–1939*, Paris: Publications de la Sorbonne.

Schor, Ralph. (1992) *L'anti-sémitisme en France pendant les années trente*, Brussels: Editions Complexe.

Schwartz, Paula. (1989) '*Partisanes* and Gender Politics in Vichy France'. *French Historical Studies* (Spring, 1989).

Schwartz, Paula. (1999) 'The Politics of Food and Gender in Occupied Paris', *Modern and Contemporary France* 7-1.

Semelin, Jacques. (1989) *Sans armes face à Hitler. La résistance civile en Europe (1939–1943)*, Paris: Payot.

Servent, P. (1992) *Le mythe Pétain–Verdun ou les tranchées de la mémoire*, Paris: Payot.

Shennan, Andrew. (1989) *Rethinking France: Plans for Renewal, 1940–46*, Oxford: Clarendon Press.

Short, K. R. M. (1983) *Film and Propaganda in World War Two*, London: Croom Helm.

Siclier, Jacques. (1990) *La France de Pétain et son cinéma*, Paris: Henri Veyrier.

Simonin, Anne. (1994) *Les éditions de minuit, 1942–1955: le devoir d'insoumission*, Paris: IMEC Editions.

Singer, Claude. (1996) *Vichy, l'université et les Juifs*, Paris: Hachette 'Pluriel'.

Slitinsky, Michel. (1997) *Procès Papon, le devoir de justice*, Paris: L'Aube.

Steinberg, Lucien. (1980) *Les Allemands en France 1940–1944*, Paris: Albin-Michel.

Sweets, John. (1976) *The Politics of Resistance in France, 1940–1944*, Chicago: Northern Illinois University Press.

Sweets, John. (1986) *Choices in Vichy France: The French under Nazi Occupation*, Oxford: Oxford University Press.

Szpiner, Francis. (1986) *Une affaire de femmes*, Paris: Balland.

Teissier du Cros, Janet. (1992) *Divided Loyalties: A Scotswoman in Occupied France*, Edinburgh: Canongate.

Thalmann, Rita. (1991) *La mise au pas. Idéologie et stratégie sécuritaire dans la France occupée*, Paris: Fayard.

Veillon, Dominique. (1977) *Le Franc-Tireur: Un journal clandestin, un mouvement de résistance 1940–1944*, Paris: Flammarion.

Veillon, Dominique. (1990), *La Mode sous l'occupation*, Paris: Payot.

Veillon, Dominique. (1995) *Vivre et survivre en France, 1939–1941*, Paris: Payot.

Vercors [Jean Bruller], (1951) *Le silence de la mer*, Paris: Albin Michel.

Verdés-Leroux, Jeannine. (1996) *Refus et violences, politique et littérature à l'extrême droite des années trente à la Libération*, Paris: Gallimard.

Vinen, Richard. (1991) *The Politics of French Business 1936–1945*, Cambridge: Cambridge University Press.

Violet, Bernard. (1997) *Le dossier Papon*, Paris: Flammarion.

Webster, Paul. (1990) *Pétain's Crime: The Full Story of French Collaboration in the Holocaust*, London: Macmillan.

Weisberg, Richard H. (1996) *Vichy Law and the Holocaust in France*, NY: New York University Press.

Wieviorka, Olivier. (1996) *Une Certaine Idée de la Résistance: Défense de la France, 1940–1949*, Paris: Seuil.

Zaretsky, Robert. (1995) *Nîmes at War: Religion, Politics and Public Opinion in the Department of the Gard, 1938–1944*, Pennsylvania: Penn State Press.

Zucotti, Susan. (1993) *The Holocaust, the French and the Jews*, New York: Basic Books.

Index

Abetz, Otto, 91, 92, 93, 94
L'Abîme (Duroselle), 17
abortion
  as threat to Vichy, 199–202
  policies on, 191–3, 203n4
  reasons for, 195–6
  stories of, 193–4, 196–9
  see also 300 Law
ACA (Assembly of Cardinals and Archbishops), 231, 236–7, 238
accommodation of culture, 222, 226–7, 228, 280
ACJF (Association Catholique de la Jeunesse Française), 241
Action Catholique, 239
Action Française, 17, 113, 122n4, 238, 278
Aktion Reinhard program, 42
Algiers, secret telegrams of, 16
Allies
  airmen shot down, 132–3
  as blamed for French starvation, 154
  knowledge of Holocaust, 43
Amitié Chrétienne, 234
anthropological research on rural resistance, 132–6
anti-Bolshevism, 67
anti-clericalism, 81, 130, 231
anti-Communism, 67, 96, 232, 239
anti-democratic movements, 91–100, 102n22, 155
anti-republicanism, 277–8
anti-Semitism
  as motive for collaboration, 68–70
  French responsibility for, 36–9, 45
  German vs. French, 39–40
  historical French, 30
  in other European countries, 63, 64, 68
  legislation of, 39
  propaganda of, 41
  research paradigm for, 110–12, 294–6
  see also Final Solution
Antonescu, General Ion (Conducator), 63, 65, 72
Aragon, Charles d', 188–9n9
archives, unavailability of, 53, 301–2n7
Arendt, Hannah, 269, 272–3n21
Ariége, 133, 135–6
Armistice agreement
  Article 3 of, 74n1
  French attitudes, 15, 51, 62–3, 109–10, 115
  organizational development, 116
  vs. surrender, 276
Aron, Robert
  Histoire de Vichy, 51–2
  on judicial paradigm, 288–9
  on *Ordre Nouveau,* 92, 100n5, 101n7
  on *Vichy France* (Paxton), 15, 27, 36
arrests of resisters, 165, 168, 176n23
Aryanization, 37, 39
Assembly of Cardinals and Archbishops (ACA), 231, 236–7, 238
Association Catholique de la Jeunesse Française (ACJF), 241
Astier, Emmanuel d', 168, 173
Attali, Jacques, 188
Au Nom du peuple (Todorov), 264
Auphan, Paul, 4, 23
Au Pilori, 43
L'Aurore, 24
authoritarianism
  crime, 206, 216
  non-conformist groups, 93, 95, 98
  Vichy regime's, 16, 108–9, 116, 153–4
Averyon, 128, 150
Azéma, Jean-Pierre, 21, 28, 30, 113

Bakhtin, Mikhail, 264
Bancal, Jean, 216

Bardeche, Maurice, 51
Bardet, Antoine, 255
Barthélemy, Joseph, 108, 216
Barthes, Roland, 261
Baruch, Marc-Olivier, 276, 281
Basch, Victor, 266
Basse-Normandie, 126–7
Bastiat, Frédéric, 150
Bauchau, Henri, 93, 95
Baudouin, Paul, 95, 113
Bazaine, Jean, 223
Beauvoir, Simone de, 187
Becker, Raymond de, 91, 93, 94, 95, 102nn
Belgium
  collaboration of, 61–2, 63, 70, 74–5n2
  deportations from, 64
  forced labor draft in, 66
  non-conformist movements of, 91, 92, 93, 102n22
  resistance in, 73, 277
  surrender of, 276
Belin, René, 25, 102–3n30, 113
Bell, David, 49
Benjamin, René, 97
Benoist-Méchin, Jacques, 71, 113
Berg, Roger, 31
Berge, François, 96
Bergery, Gaston, 92, 94, 95, 116
Bernanos, Georges, 187
Bertin, Célia, 191
Bettex, André, 134
Beuve-Méry, Hubert, 97, 99
Bidault, Georges, 238
Billes, Valerie, 256
Billig, Joseph, 17
Bingen, Jacques, 189–90n17
black market, 150, 154, 211
Blanchard, Daniel, 265, 266, 267
Blanchot, Maurice, 95
Bloch, Marc, 188, 284
Blom, J. C. H., 87n4
Bobkowski, Andrzej, 77, 89n27
Boeschoten, Riki van, 134
Bohemia-Moravia, 64, 65
Boivin, Michel, 126
Bolshevism, movement against, 67
Bougeard, Christian, 128, 130–1
Bourdet, Claude, 168
Bourdieu, Pierre, 134
Bourdin, Janine, 25
Bout de l'An, Francis, 265, 266, 267
Brasillach, Robert, 98
Breton, France, 131
Brévaire de haine (Poliakov), 36
Brinon, Fernand de, 67
Brittany, 131
Brooks, Peter, 262
Buckmaster, Maurice, 131
Bulgaria, 65, 67, 69
Burgundy, 128
Burrin, Philippe
  accommodation of culture theory, 222, 226–7, 228, 280
  as foreigner, 297–8
  Vichy France (Paxton), 28
Burzio, Giuseppe, 43

Cabanel, Patrick, 128, 130
Cagoule organization, 98, 170
Cahiers d'Histoire de l'Institut Maurice Thorez, 27
Cailliau, Michel, 173, 174
Canaud, Jacques, 125
Carette, Louis (Félicien Marceau), 95, 103n35
Carey, Henry Charles, 150
Cassou, Jean, 189n17
Catholic Church
  and resistance, 128, 241
  and unions, 240–1
  anti-Communism of, 232, 239
  authority, loss of, 232–3, 242
  Christian Democrat party, 238–9
  collaboration of, 231–3
  ethnic cleansing, support of, 64
  family movements, 241–2
  historical influence of, 279
  Holocaust silence, 43, 236–7
  inter-denominational relationships, 233–4
  non-conformist movement, 91–2, 93
  schools, 236
  theological issues caused by Vichy, 234–5
  youth movements and, 95, 96, 112–13, 241
Catrice, Abbé, 237

Caziot, Pierre, 149, 150, 151
Cévennes, terre de refuge 1940–1944 (Joutard, Poujol, Cabanel), 125, 126, 127
Cévenol, 126, 130
CFDT (Confédération Française Démocratique du Travail), 241
CFTC (Confédération Français des Travailleurs Chrétiens), 239, 240
CGPGR (Repatriated Prisoner-of-War Commission), 172, 173
CGT (Confédération Générale du Travail), 113, 240
Le Chagrin et la pitié see The Sorrow and the Pity (Ophuls)
Chaillaud, Georges, 266
La Chaîne, 173
Chambrun, René de, 52
Charles, Jean, 27, 28
children *see* youth
Chirac, Jacques, 283, 291, 295–6
choice and collaboration, 62–3
Chombart de Lauwe, Paul-Henri, 97
Christian Democrats, 164, 238–9
chronological approach to Vichy, 117
Churchill, Sir Winston Leonard Spencer, 43
CIMADE (Comité Inter-Mouvement auprès des Evacués), 234
civil disobedience, 166
civil resistance, 227
Clare, George, 68
Claudel, Paul, 97
Claudius-Petit, Eugéne, 173, 177n31
CLC (Commissariat á la lutte contre le chômage et le travail), 252
Cochet, Gabriel, 164–5, 167
codes of conduct, 83–4, 184
collaboration
  Armistice agreement and, 15
  as only choice, 62–3, 108
  definition of, 61–3
  economic, 66–7
  France vs. other European countries, 61–2, 63, 65, 70, 74–5n2, 276
  French attitude toward, 50, 51
  historical views of, 3–4
  Holocaust and, 40, 41–2, 64–5, 68–70
  motives for, 67–8
  National Revolution and, 14, 15, 109–10, 168, 288
  non-conformist movement and, 95
  of Catholic Church, 231–3
  of Fascists, 70–4
  resistance and, 165, 166
  under Darlan, 116
  urban vs. rural, 152–4
collective memory *see* memory of history
Combat
  Mitterrand and, 104–5n54
  New Order and, 94
  resistance of, 99, 168
  Vichy and, 98, 169
  vs. Free French, 170
Combattants voluntaires de la Résistance (CVR), 126
Comité Inter-Mouvement auprès des Evacués (CIMADE), 234
Commissariat á la lutte contre le chômage et le travail (CLC), 252
Communism
  and schools, 96
  as motive for collaboration, 67
  banning of party, 121
  Catholic Church's attitude, 232, 239
  legislation against, 110–11
  resistance by party, 116
  Vichy's view of, 50, 51
  within Vichy government, 113–15
communitarian non-conformist movements, 91–100, 102n22, 155
Comte, Bernard, 112
concentration camps, 42, 44, 264, 269
Confédération Français des Travailleurs Chrétiens (CFTC), 239, 240
Confédération Française Démocratique du Travail (CFDT), 241
Confédération Générale du Travail (CGT), 113, 240
"confronting the past," 55, 299–300
La Conquête de l'Amérique (Todorov), 262, 263
Conseil National de la Résistance, 238, 240
Contancin, Fernand, 216
Contrepoint, 23–4
Cordier, Daniel, 167
Corporation paysanne, 149–52

corporatism, 125, 148, 150, 156, 240
Corvignoles network, 170
Couteau-Begarie, Hervé, 17
crime, youth
as resistance, 207–8
authoritarianism and, 206, 216
economic hardship, 209–11
policing of, 208–9
rehabilitation of delinquents, 214–17
statistics on, 205–7, 212, *213*
types of, 208
crimes against humanity, 296
see also Final Solution
Croatia, 64, 70
La Croisade (Loustaunau-Lacau), 170
culture, French
accommodation of, 222, 226–7, 228, 280
codes of conduct, 83–4, 184
continuity of, 221–3, 280
fascism in, 292–3
of national unity, 279–82
Popular Front, policies of, 222–3
research consideration, 224–8
rigidity of, 282
role of, 49
Vichy contributions to, 223–4
WWI vs. WWII, 225–6, 228
CVR (Combattants voluntaires de la Résistance), 126

Dandieu, Arnaud, 100n5
Darlan, François
arrests under, 165, 176n23
collaboration of, 116
forced labor draft under, 253
impact of administration, 116–17
secret telegrams of Algiers, 19n8
Darnand, Joseph, 67, 71
Déat, Marcel
collaboration of, 71
Corporation paysanne, 150, 151
L'Oeuvre, 43
single party system, quest for, 116
Vichy peasant policies, 152–4
Debord, Guy, 187
Défense de la France, 165–6
Defense Nationale, 22
Défense paysanne, 129, 134
De Gaulle, Charles, 51–2, 168, 170–1, 173–4, 188n5
Degrelle, Léon, 94
Delalande, Bernard, 266, 268, 270, 273–4n31
Délégation française auprès de la Commission française d'armistice, 14
Denis, Michel, 23
Denmark, 63, 67, 70, 276
deportations
children, 64, 68–9, 76n12
complexity of, 42–3
Eichmann and Paris train cancellation, 35
family separation during, 255
forced laborers, 253, 254
from other European countries, 64, 65, 69
international awareness of, 43
internment camps, 68–9, 252, 259n5
to concentration camps, 42, 44, 264, 269
La Dernière Colonne, 163
Desourteaux, André, 256
The Destruction of the European Jews (Hilberg), 37, 46n6
discrimination, racial/ethnic *see* racism
Doncoeur, Paul, 113
Dorgères, Henry
and Déat, 152
Défense paysanne, 129
"greenshirts," 143n31, 145
political ideology of peasants, 146
Vichy and, 134–5
Doriot, Jacques, 92, 93, 113, 121
"double game," 4, 16, 21, 280
"double think," 186–7
Dower, John, 83
Drancy, 253
Dreyfus affair, 226, 283
"dual man," French as, 186, 189n13, 276–7
Dumora-Ratier, Hélène, 133, 135–6
Dunoyer de Segonzac, Pierre, 97, 99, 105n61, 171
Duroselle, Jean-Baptiste, 17, 50

Ecole Nationale d'Administration, 99
Ecole Nationale des cadres d'Uriage, 96–7, 99, 104n45, 171–2

Index

Ecole Nationale Supérieure des Cadres, 96
economic issues
  and abortion, 195–6, 199
  and collaboration, 66–7
  and crime, 209–11
  black market, 150, 154, 211
  under Vichy, 109–10, 117–18
Editions du Seuil, 99
education *see* schools
Education, 27
L'Effort, 114
Eichmann, Adolf, 35, 42–3
elitism, 116, 120–2, 171
Emmanuel, Pierre, 96
emotions of occupied peoples, 84, 89n27
Enckell, Pierre, 29
Esprit Movement
  and L'Esprit Nouveau, 103n33
  organization of, 91, 92–3, 94
  under Vichy, 96, 98, 99, 101n13, 222
L'Esprit Nouveau, 103n33
ethnic cleansing, 64
evil, 268–9, 272–3n21
exclusion, policy of, 110–12
executions, 193–4
exotopy, 264, 265, 272n16

Fabrégues, Jean de, 92, 94, 97, 98
Face à l'extreme (Todorov), 268
families
  abortion and, 196–8
  deportations, 255
  policies of Vichy, 148, 241–2
  see also youth
farms, Vichy support of, 149, 150–1
  see also peasantry
fascism
  and peasantry, 145, 146, 155–6
  collaboration role, 70–4
  historical French, 292–3
  in other European countries, 70–2
  of non-conformist movements, 93–4
"fascist constellation," 71–4, 75n3
Faure, Paul, 114
Ferro, Marc, 27, 28
Fessard, Pére Gaston, 235
FFI (Forces Françaises de l'intérieur), 265
Le Figaro, 27, 278
Final Solution
  Catholic Church's role, 43, 236–7
  ending of, 44–5
  French awareness of, 43–4
  French collaboration in, 40, 41–2, 64–5, 68–70
  French responsibility for, 35, 36–9
  Milice, role of, 111
  see also deportations
Flamand, Paul, 92, 94, 95, 101n8
La Flèche, 92, 94, 102n28
Fondation Nationale de Sciences Politiques, 14–15, 16, 53
Font, Christian, 128
food supply, 133, 148, 149, 152
forced labor draft
  as exclusionary measure, 252–3
  foreigners in, 249–50
  France vs. other European countries, 66–7
  Jews in, 253–7, 259n8
  organization of, 66, 251–2
  peasantry, 155
  resistance to, 129, 241
Forces Françaises de l'intérieur (FFI), 265
foreigners
  as forced laborers, 249–50
  as French historians, 4, 297–301
  Jewish, 36–7, 44, 65, 69, 256
  legislation against, 110–11
Forestier, Marcel-Denys, 113
Fouilloux, Etienne, 183
Fourcaud, Pierre, 170
Français si vous saviez (Harris and de Sedouy), 53
La France á l'heure allemande (Burrin), 28
La France dans l'Europe de Hitler (Jaeckel), 13
La France de Vichy 1940-1944 (Paxton) *see Vichy France: Old Guard and New Order* (Paxton)
France-Liberté, 163
La France Libre, 136–7
La France Nouvelle travaille, 136–7
La France sous l'occupation (Chambrun), 52
Francs-Tireurs et Partisans (FTP), 128, 131
  see also resistance

Free French, 163, 169, 170, 232
Freemasons, 110–11
Frenay, Henri, 99, 105n61, 167–71, 176n18
French military, 73, 166–7, 170
French National Archives, 17
French National Committee, 43
French people
  anti-Semitism of, 30, 36–40, 45, 294–6
  Armistice agreement views, 15, 51, 62–3, 109–10, 115
  as "dual man," 186, 189n13
  assistance to Jews, 68, 75–6n10, 254, 255–7
  on Germans, 84, 89n27
  on Paxton, 28–9, 31–2
  on Vichy, 184–7
  research considerations, 82–5, 184
  view of history, 49, 287
  violence of, 84–5
French Socialist Party (SFIO), 93, 114
French Tragedy: Scenes of Civil War, Summer 1944 (Todorov), 265
Friedländer, Saul, 40
Front Social, 92, 101n10
FTP (Francs-Tireurs et Partisans), 128, 131
see also resistance

Galey, Louis-Emile, 91, 92, 93, 98
Gaulle, Charles de, 51–2, 168, 170–1, 173–4, 188n5
Gaullists, 50, 51, 235
Gérard-Libois, J., 74–5n2
Gerlier, (Cardinal), 231
German Existentialism, 91
German government *see* Third Reich
German military, 81–2, 196
  see also occupations, military
"German trap," 14, 67
Gillouin, René, 97
Giolitto, Pierre, 220
Giono, Jean, 152
Giraud, Marie-Louise, 192, 193–4, 199
Giraudists, 166, 172, 173
Giraudoux, Jean, 115
Globocnik, Odilo, 42
Godin, Abbé, 233
Gombös, Gyula, 64
Gotovitch, José, 74–5n2
Grandhay, Jean-Claude, 128
Greece, 63
"greenshirts," 143n31, 145
Grenier, Jean, 96
Groupement de Travailleurs Etrangers (GTE), 250–8, 259n8
GTE (643rd Foreign Labor Battalion), 250–8, 259n8
Guillon, Jean-Marie, 126, 129, 132
Guitton, Jean, 98

Hague Convention, 61–2, 74–5n2
Halluin, Henri-Auguste d' *see* Dorgères, Henry
Harris, André, 53
Haute-Saône, 128
Henriot, Philippe, 67, 71
Hervieu, Bertrand, 156
Hilberg, Raul, 37, 38, 43, 44, 46n6
Himmler, Heinrich, 64
Histoire de Vichy (Aron), 36, 51–2
historical memory *see* memory of history
Hitler, Adolf, 14, 43, 72–4
Hobsbawn, Eric, 134
Hoffmann, Stanley
  and Michel, 26
  and Paxton, 4, 15–16, 17
  on Vichy debate, 22
  "state collaboration," 288
Holocaust, 43, 64–5, 236–7
  see also deportations; Final Solution
Horne, John, 81
hostages, 82, 266
Huan, Claude, 17
Huguenots, 130
humanitarian resistance, 127
human nature, 268–71
Hungary, 63, 67, 68, 71, 250

Idées, 113
identity, French, 49, 81–2, 283, 287
L'Idéologie française (Lévy), 293
ideology of Vichy regime
  complexity of, 55
  fascist, 292–4
  from National Revolution, 109
  in support of collaboration, 67–70
  Paxton's scholarship on, 292–4

resistance and, 166–71
rural, 129, 131, 149
vs. Nazi, 39–40
IHTP (Institut d'Histoire du Temps Present*),* 54
individualism, 235
Institut d'Histoire du Temps Present (IHTP), 54, 299
intellectual engagement, 272n11
international law, 61–2, 78–9
internment camps, 68–9, 252, 259n5
Izard, Georges, 91, 92, 93

Jaeckel, Eberhard, 13–14, 15–16, 17, 25
Jakubowicz, Jankiel, 254–5
Jamet, Dominique, 4, 24
Jardin, Jean, 99, 100n5
Je suis partout, 278
Jeune France, 95, 96
Jeunesse Ouvrière Chrétienne (JOC), 240
Jews
as scapegoats, 266–7
assistance to, 68, 75–6n10, 254, 255–7
forced labor of, 253–7, 259n8
French population vs. Eastern Europe, 41–2
influence on Vichy memory, 39–40, 111–12, 225, 294–6
legislation against, 110–11
native vs. foreign, 36–7, 44, 65, 69, 256
see also anti-Semitism; Final Solution
JOC (Jeunesse Ouvrière Chrétienne), 240
Joliot-Curie, Frédéric, 227
Jollivet, Marcel, 132
Journal de Genève, 28
journals *see* media; *specific journal names*
judicial paradigm, 288–9, 296
just war, 234

Kanzler, Joseph, 256–7
Kedward, H. R., 154–5
Klarsfeld, Serge, 295
Koshwitz, Edouard, 83
Krameisen, Charles, 266–7
Kramer, Alan, 81
Kristallnacht, 237
Kuisel, Richard, 239

Laborie, Pierre, 28, 116, 132, 133, 137
la Chapelle, Frédéric de, 113
la Laurencie, B. L. Fornet de, 163, 168
Lalonnier, Hubert, 265
Lambert, Gilles, 30
Lamirand, Georges, 95, 102n28, 171
La Porte du Theil, Joseph de, 113
La Rocque, Colonel François de, 92
Lavagne, André, 110, 122n4
Laval, Pierre
German relations, 15
history's view of, 52
Holocaust, support of, 36, 37, 69
on collaboration choice, 108
political elite, 120
prisoners of war, 66, 67
trial of, 51
Uriage Leadership school, 104n45
Lécussan, Joseph, 266
Lederberg, Marguerite, 255
legal issues, international, 61–2, 78–9
Légion des volontaires français contre le bolchévisme (LVF), 67
Légion française des combattants, 73, 170
Le Pen, Jean-Marie, 293
Le Roy Ladurie, Gabriel, 113
Le Roy Ladurie, Jacques, 129
Le Riou, 134
Lesage, Gilbert, 254
Lévy, Bernhard-Henri, 293
Lévy, Claude, 29–30
Lévy, Jean-Pierre, 163
Liberation, 2–3, 50–1, 121–2, 189–90n17
Libération-Nord, 163, 174–5n4
Libération-Sud, 163, 168
Liberté, 164, 168
Liebe, Max, 94
Liénart, (Cardinal), 231, 236, 237, 238, 240
Lieux de Memoire: l'Etat and la Nation (Nora), 49
Ligue Ouvrière Chétienne (LOC), 242
Limoges, 255
Lindberg, Daniel, 30–1
Lithuania, 250
LOC (Ligue Ouvrière Chétienne), 242
L'Oeuvre, 43
Loiret, France, 149
Lorenz, Chris, 87n4

Loustau, Robert, 92, 93, 95, 97, 101nn
Loustaunau-Lacau, Georges, 170–1, 176n23
Lovetch concentration camp, 264, 269
Lozère, 128
Lubac, Henri de, 97
LVF (Légion des volontaires français contre le bolchévisme), 67
Lyautey, Louis-Hubert, 112

Macquis du Morvan (Canaud), 125
Madaule, Jacques, 30
Man, Henri de, 94
maquis
  Catholics and, 241
  forest rights, 135
  peasants, 127, 128, 155
  research on, 125–6, 130–1
  Saint-Amand, 265–8
  Saint Victurnien, 255–6
  see also resistance
Marc, Alexandre (Otto Neumann), 91, 92, 94, 96, 100n3
Marceau, Félicien (Louis Carette), 95, 103n35
Marcel, Gabriel, 91, 96
Marcot, François, 126, 127, 140
Marcy, Jean-Philippe, 133
Margairaz, Michel, 110, 117–18
Marie, Angélique, 128
Marion, Paul, 92, 98, 99, 101n9, 113
Maritain, Jacques, 92
Marrou, Henri-Irénée, 96
Marrus, Michael R., 29–31, 237, 259n8, 294
massacres, 249–51, 257–8
Massis, Henri, 97
Mauduit, Antoine, 105n55
Maurras, Charles, 92, 131, 231
Maux, Henri, 254
Maze, Jean, 98
media
  civil resistance and, 227
  peasantry and, 147
  post-Liberation, 51
  radio, 95, 116
  reviews of Paxton's books, 22–6, 27–8, 303–7
  role in myths, 52–3
  "Vichy Syndrome," 278
  see also specific newspaper or journal
memory of history
  and Jewish question, 39–40, 111–12, 225, 294–6
  collective, 181–7, 183
  effects of "Vichy syndrome," 49
  of resistance, 128
  Paxton's impact on, 285–8
  research issues, 270
Menthon, François de, 164, 168, 169
Merdsche, Fritz, 266
Michel, Henri, 14, 16, 26–7
Milice
  Cagoule organization and, 98
  Final Solution role, 111
  organization of, 105n55
  schools and, 99
  uprising against, 265–8
  violence of, 85
military activities/organizations
  French, 73, 166–7, 170
  German, 81–2, 196
  occupations, 77–86, 90n30, 184–5
Milward, Alan, 14
Mission de France, 233
Mission de Paris, 233
Mitterrand, François, 98, 104–5n54, 105n62, 172–4, 188n5
MLN (Mouvement de Libération Nationale), 167–71, 175–6nn
MLP (Mouvement de Libération du Peuple), 242
MNPGD (Mouvement Nationale des prisonniers de guerre et déportés), 174
monarchy, 73, 75n3, 279
Le Monde, 22, 99, 114
Montaigne, Michel Eyquem de, 181
Montesquieu, Baron de La Brède et de, 263
moral issues
  conviction vs. responsibility, 265–8
  human nature, 268–71
  Paxton's approach, 269
  research dimension, 283–4
  universal truths, 262–5
Morandat, Yvon, 169
Moulin, Annie, 148
Moulin, Jean, 105n61, 169, 170

Mounier, Emmanuel
Alexandre Marc and, 100n3
Esprit and, 103n33
Jeune France and, 96
non-conformist movement, 91, 92
on Munich Accords, 188n7
Personalist Manifesto, 93
Mouvement de Libération du Peuple (MLP), 242
Mouvement de Libération Nationale (MLN), 167–71, 175–6nn
Mouvement de Résistance des prisonniers de guerre et des déportés (MRPGD), 173–4
Mouvement Nationale des prisonniers de guerre et déportés (MNPGD), 174
Mouvement Républican Populaire (MRP), 238–9
Mouvements Unis de Résistance (MUR), 174
Moysset, Henri, 114
MRPGD (Mouvement de Résistance des prisonniers de guerre et des déportés), 173–4
MRP (Mouvement Républican Populaire), 238–9
Munich Accords, 188n7
MUR (Mouvements Unis de Résistance), 174
myths
confronting of past, 55, 299–300
double game, 16, 21
media and, 52–3
nation of resisters, 4, 21, 292
of Pétain, 16, 78, 292
of rural France, 129–30, 148
Vichy as shield, 2, 18, 52, 55

National Front, 293
National Revolution
anti-Semitism of, 39, 40
as political mistake, 18
Catholic Church support of, 231
divisiveness of, 99
ideology of, 129, 149
non-conformist movements, 98, 99–100
resistance and, 163, 167, 172–3
support of collaboration, 14, 15, 109–10, 168, 288
Uriage Leadership School, 171–2
"nation of resisters," 4, 21, 292
Navarre, 170
Nazis *see* Third Reich
Netherlands, The
collaboration with Reich, 61–2, 63
fascism, 70, 72
governmental exile, 276
Holocaust, 64
single party system of, 73
Neumann, Otto (Alexandre Marc), 91, 92, 94, 96, 100n3
New European Order, 62, 63
New Order
and Aron, 100n5, 101n7
and non-conformist movement, 92, 94, 99
and youth revolutionaries, 91
The New Order and the French Economy (Milward), 14
newspapers *see* media; *specific newspaper names*
non-conformist movements, 91–100, 102n22, 155
Nora, Pierre, 285–6
Norway, 62, 70, 72, 276

occupations, military, 77–86, 90n30, 184–5
Offen, Karen, 29
Ophuls, Marcel *see The Sorrow and the Pity* (Ophuls)
Oradour-sur-Glane, 249–51, 256–8
ORA (Organisation de Résistance de l'Armée), 173
Ordre Nouveau *see* New Order
Organisation de Résistance de l'Armée (ORA), 173
Organisation de secours aux enfants (OSE), 75–6n10
Organisation Todt, 252, 255, 259n12
Ory, Pascal, 22
OSE (Organisation de secours aux enfants), 75–6n10
Ouest, 94
Ozouf, Jacques, 297

Papon, Maurice
radical origins, 278

trial of, 1–2, 55, 276–7, 286, 291
Parades and Politics at Vichy (Paxton), 21
Paris, and crime during Vichy, 209
Parti Populaire Français (PPF), 93, 113, 121, 238
Paxton, Robert O.
as "site of memory," 285–8
at Papon trial, 2
French attitude towards, 28–9, 31–2
Michel and, 26–7
moral issues, 269
on Cardinal Liénart, 237
on Jews under Vichy, 29–31, 38–9, 259n8, 305–7
on rural resistance, 134, 145, 148
on Vichy endurance, 45
Pétainists and, 23
see also Vichy France: Old Guard and New Order (Paxton)
peasantry
alienation of, 135
and allied airmen, 132–3
as resistance leaders, 135–6
attitudes toward Vichy, 146–7
dislike of Germans, 155–6
during Third Republic, 147–8
during World War I, 148, 155–6
fascism and, 145, 146, 155–6
food supply, 133, 153–4
forced labor draft, 155
ideology of Vichy, 129, 131, 149
media and, 147
modernization of, 145–6, 147
myths of, 129–30, 148
non-conformist movements, 155
research considerations, 125–9, 132–6
schools, 147
support of resistance, 127, 128, 130–2, 134, 154, 155
under Vichy, 149–52
vs. urban collaborationists, 152–4
xenophobia of, 130
Pelorson, Georges, 94
Perroux, François, 93
personalism, 91, 93, 94, 96, 104n45
Pétain, Marshal Philippe
anti-Semitism of, 39
Armistice agreement, 62–3
Final Solution, role in, 68
Hitler and, 72–3
myths of, 16, 52, 78, 292
National Revolution, 15
peasantry and, 149, 150, 152, 160n55
resistance and, 163, 167–71
role of army under, 166–7
secret telegrams of Algiers, 19n8
trial of, 45, 51
youth movements and, 241
Pétainists
as resisters, 164–6
kidnap of Maréchal's body, 22
Paxton and, 23
resisters and, 163
Uriage Leadership School, 171–2
view of Vichy, 52
Petit, Paul, 174n3
Philip, André, 236
Pineau, Christian, 174–5n4
Pinède, Robert, 256
Pinot, Maurice, 172–3
Piquet, Gabriel, 234
Pius XII, 232
Le Plateau Vivaris/Lignon: Accueil et Résistance, 127
Plato, 300
pluralist dictatorship, Vichy as, 17, 112
Poinso-Chapuis decree, 236
Poland, 79, 250, 254–5
Poliakov, Léon, 36, 38, 39, 43, 44
police, 116, 118–19, 208–9
Pompidou, Georges, 188n2, 290
Popular Front, 93, 215, 222–3
Pourrat, Henri, 151
POWs *see* prisoners of war (POWs)
Poznanski, Renée, 29, 44
PPF (Parti Populaire Français), 93, 113, 121, 238
prejudice *see* racism
prisoners of war (POWs)
collaboration and, 66–7
disruption caused by, 120, 149
juvenile crime and, 214
resistance of, 172–4
wives and abortion, 195, 196
propaganda, 41, 95
Prost, Antoine, 191
public opinion
about Germans, 84, 89n27

about Paxton, 28–9, 31–2
assessment of, 18, 28, 30–1
during military occupations, 77–8, 83–5, 90n30, 184–5
under Vichy, 117, 146–7, 184–7
Pucheu, Pierre, 97–8, 168, 241, 253, 280
purges, 50, 52, 288

Quellien, Jean, 126
Quercy, France, 132
Quisling, Vidkun, 62, 70, 72

Racine, Paul, 173
racism
ethnic cleansing, 64
exclusionary policies, 110–12
of occupied people, 83
of Third Reich, 39–40, 86
see also anti-Semitism
Rademacher, Franz, 41
radio *see* media
Radio Jeunesse, 95
rape, 82–3
Rassemblement National des prisonniers de guerre (RNPG), 173
Rassemblement National Populaire (RNP), 151
re-christianization, 233
redemptive anti-Semitism, 40
refugees, 249, 250, 251–2, 254–5
Le régime de Vichy et les Français (1990), 77
Reitlinger, Gerald, 36–7, 38, 43, 44
relève program, 66
religion and anti-clericalism, 81, 130, 231
see also Catholic Church
Remond, René, 14–15, 53, 238, 302
Renouvin, Jacques, 176n21
Renseignements généraux, 257
Repatriated Prisoner-of-War Commission (CGPGR), 172, 173
republicans and Resistance, 131, 166
research issues
absence of comparisons, 292
anti-Semitism paradigm, 110–12, 294–6
archive unavailability, 53, 301–2n7
assessing public opinion, 18, 28, 30–1
assimilationist ideology, 282–3
broadening of, 17–18, 78, 185
chronological, 117
comparative sociological approach, 78–80
conceptual interpretations, 279–82
contextual interpretations, 278–9
cultural aspects, 224–8
ethical codes, 262
foreign perspective, 4, 297–301
French people, 82–5, 184
German occupying forces, 81–2
impact of younger generation, 54
judicial paradigm, 288–9, 296
maquis, 125–6, 130–1
memory and, 270
moral issues, 283–4
peasantry, 125–9, 132–6
perspective of scholars, 181–2, 264, 297–301
"putting Germans back in," 8, 289, 291–2
resistance, 125–9, 132–6, 137, 140, 161–2
structural approach, 80–1
use of models, 269–70
resistance
arrests among, 165, 168, 176n23
Catholic Church's role, 128, 232
crime as, 207–8
forced labor draft and, 129, 241
ideological links with Vichy, 166–71
in Saint-Amand, 265–8
myths of, 4, 21, 128, 292
national continuity and, 280–1
National Revolution, 163, 167, 172–3
peasantry, 125–36, 154, 155
prisoners of war, 172–4
research considerations, 125–9, 132–6, 137, 140, 161–2
Saint Victurnien, 255–6
types of, 162–6
Uriage Leadership School, 171–2
violence and, 84–5
within Vichy government, 114–15, 171–4
"return to the land," 129, 149, 150
Revue Générale, 27
Revue Historique, 25
Richard, Raymond, 152
Richards, Brooks, 131, 133

Richter, Charles de, 129
The Right, 4, 17
Rioux, Jean-Pierre, 27, 30
RNPG (Rassemblement National des prisonniers de guerre), 173
RNP (Rassemblement National Populaire), 151
Rollin, (Ministry of Interior), 168
Roman Catholic Church *see* Catholic Church
Romania
  anti-Semitism in, 68
  collaboration with Reich, 63
  deportations, 65, 69
  fascism, 71, 72
  refugees in France, 250
Roosevelt, Franklin Delano, 176n18
Röthke, Heinz, 35
round-ups, 254, 266
Rousseau, Jean Jacques, 263
Rousso, Henry, 29, 181, 275
Rucard, Marc, 215
rural support networks, 127
  see also peasantry

Sadrin, René, 266, 273nn
Sahlins, Peter, 135
Sainclivier, Jacqueline, 129, 131, 133
Saint-Amand, 265–8
Saint-Goazec, 130–1
Saint Victurnien, 255–6
Saliège, (Archbishop), 238
Salleron, Louis, 148, 150–1
Sallust, 268
Sartre, Jean-Paul, 272n11
Sauckel, Gauleiter Fritz, 66
Scapini, Georges, 66
Scavenius, Eric, 67, 75n8
Schaeffer, Pierre, 95–6
schools
  anti-Communism and, 96
  Catholic, 236
  for juvenile reform, 215–16, 220n31
  Milice and, 99
  peasantry and, 147
  role of history, 49
  under Vichy, 95, 96–7, 99, 205–6
  Uriage Leadership School, 96–7, 99, 104n45, 171–2
scouting movement, 112–13
secret telegrams of Algiers, 16, 19n8
secularism, 279
Sedouy, Alain de, 53
Semelin, Jacques, 227
Sens, 30
Sept, 92, 93, 102n23
Service d'Ordre Légionnaire (SOL) *see* Milice
Service du Travail Obligatoire (STO) *see* forced labor draft
SFIO (French Socialist Party), 93, 114
Silence of the Sea (Vercors), 90n30
"site of memory," 285–8
643rd Foreign Labor Battalion (GTE), 250–8, 259n8
Skocpol, Theda, 8
Slama, Alain-Gérard, 23–4
Slovakia
  anti-Semitism in, 68
  collaboration with Reich, 63, 65
  fascism, 70–1
  forced labor draft, 67
  refugees in France, 250
Sochet, Fernand, 265
Socialism, 93, 99, 114
sociological approach to Vichy, 78–80
Sohlbergkreis, 92
SOL (Service d'Ordre Légionnaire) *see* Milice
The Sorrow and the Pity (Ophuls)
  and *Vichy France* (Paxton), 275, 282, 290
  attendance, 287
  impact of, 3, 28, 52–3
Soutou, Georges, 25
sovereignty
  and occupations, 80, 86
  as Vichy objective, 40, 62–3, 69, 109–10, 276–7
  Vichy France vs. Belgium, 62, 64
Soviet Union, 86, 250
Spaak, Paul-Henri, 93, 94
Spanish refugees, 249, 250, 251–2
"spirit of the thirties," 113
Spivak, Gayati, 200
Stauning, Thorwald, 75n8
Steinberg, Maxine, 64, 75n4
Stéphane, Roger, 169, 176n21

Index

Sternhell, Zeev, 292–3
STO (Service du Travail Obligatoire) *see* forced labor draft
structural approach to Vichy, 80–1
St Victurnien, 255–6
Suhard, (Cardinal), 231, 233, 238

Tacitus, 268
Taguieff, Pierre-André, 293
Tasca, Angelo, 108, 114
Teitgen, Pierre-Henri, 164
Témoignage Chrétien, 27, 232
Le Temps, 99, 278
Tessier, Gaston, 241
Third Force, 93
Third Reich
  appropriation of French food production, 149
  attitude toward Vichy government, 16
  distrust of single-party systems, 73
  establishment of political elite, 121
  ideology, 86
  peasantry and, 155–6
Third Republic
  abortion during, 193
  and peasantry, 147–8
  use of foreign labor, 251–2
300 Law, 192–3, 203n4
Todorov, Tzvetan, 261–71
Touvier, Paul, 111, 266, 286, 288, 290
traditionalists, 17, 63, 113
Trégor, 131
trials
  accounts of, 17
  Laval, 51
  Papon, 1–2, 55, 276–7, 289, 291
  Pétain, 45, 51
Trochu, Robert, 14

ULB (Université Libre de Bruxelles), 277
Union Nationale des Syndicats Agricoles (UNSA), 150
unions, 150, 240–1
United States
  and occupations, 86
  reaction to *Vichy France: Old Guard and New Order* (Paxton), 22
  view of history, 49
Université Libre de Bruxelles (ULB), 277
UNSA (Union Nationale des Syndicats Agricoles), 150
Uriage Leadership School, 96–7, 99, 104n45, 171–2

Vallat, Xavier, 37
Van Gaver, René, 265, 266, 267
Vatican, 232, 233
  see also Catholic Church
Vedrine, Jean, 173
Veil, Simone, 185
Veillon, Dominique, 226
Vercors, Jean Bruller, 90n30
Viannay, Philippe, 165
Vichy and the Jews (Paxton and Marrus), 29–31, 38–9, 259n8, 305–7
Vichy année 40 (Michel), 14
Vichy France: Old Guard and New Order (Paxton)
  impact of, 4, 28, 53–6, 77, 107, 275, 289–91
  new perspective, 288–9, 292, 294, 295, 296
  public opinion, 18, 28
  reactions to, 4, 22–4, 53–4
  reviews of, 22–6, 27–8, 303–5
  sales of, 29, 287
  scholarly influence of, 13–14
  scholarly reception, 25–7
  sources used, 16–17, 289
  themes of, 3–4, 15–16, 292–4
Vichy government
  as pluralist dictatorship, 112–17
  autonomy of, 77
  beginning of, 1
  duality of, 276–7
  historical views of, 77–8
  unifying ideology of, 107–12
"Vichy Syndrome"
  contemporary, 1–2, 181–2
  definition of, 49–50, 275–6
  De Gaulle era, 51–2, 188n5
  Liberation period, 2–3, 50–1, 189–90n17
  media and, 278
  memory of history and, 49
  national identity and, 186–7, 276–7, 283

obsession of scholars with, 181–3
Paxtonian Revolution, 53–5
pre-Paxton (1960s to 1970s), 52–3
reasons for, 277–8
view of Germans, 8, 291–2
Vico, Giambattista, 263
Villatte, François, 266, 267
Vincent, René, 98
violence
during occupations, 84–5
executions of abortionists, 193–4
massacres of civilians, 249–51, 257–8
of Milice, 85
rape, 82–3
Vivarais, France, 130

Waffen SS, 67
war crimes, 296
see also Final Solution
Weber, Eugen, 155
Weber, Max, 268
Wieviorka, Annette, 30
Wieviorka, Olivier, 165
Wilhelmstrasse, 14
women
and crime, 210, 211, 216
and Resistance, 127
as targets of Vichy policies, 191–2
Catholic voting, 239
during occupations, 84–5, 90n32
German soldiers and, 196
"in the home," 129
view of Pétain, 166
violence toward, 84–5
see also abortion
World War I, 148, 155–6, 226–7, 228
Wright, Gordon, 146

X-Crise, 101n7, 102n28
xenophobia of peasantry, 130, 293
see also foreigners; racism

youth
Catholic movements, 95, 96, 112–13, 241
deportations of, 64, 68–9, 76n12
non-conformist movements, 91, 92, 93
resistance of, 165–6
under Vichy, 95–6, 205–6
view of rural France, 152
see also crime, youth
Yugoslavia, 63, 276